ASIANS AND THE NEW MULTICULTURALISM IN AOTEAROA NEW ZEALAND

Asians and the New Multiculturalism in Aotearoa New Zealand

EDITED BY
Gautam Ghosh &
Jacqueline Leckie

OTAGO
UNIVERSITY PRESS

Published by Otago University Press
Level 1, 398 Cumberland Street
Dunedin, New Zealand
university.press@otago.ac.nz
www.otago.ac.nz/press

First published 2015
Copyright © the authors as named.
Volume copyright © Otago University Press

The moral rights of the authors have been asserted.
ISBN 978-1-877578-23-6

A catalogue record for this book is available from the National Library of New Zealand. This book is copyright. Except for the purpose of fair review, no part may be stored or transmitted in any form or by any means, electronic or mechanical, including recording or storage in any information retrieval system, without permission in writing from the publishers. No reproduction may be made, whether by photocopying or by any other means, unless a licence has been obtained from the publisher.

Publisher: Rachel Scott
Editor: Imogen Coxhead
Design/layout: Fiona Moffat
Index: Diane Lowther

Original cover art by Simon Kaan, Dunedin

Printed in New Zealand by Printstop Ltd, Wellington

Contents

1. INTRODUCTION: Multi-multiculturalisms in the new New Zealand
   Gautam Ghosh — 7

PART I: Biculturalism and Multiculturalism

2. 'I MADE A SPACE FOR YOU': Renegotiating national identity and citizenship in contemporary Aotearoa New Zealand *Paul Spoonley* — 39
3. NEGOTIATING MULTICULTURALISM AND THE TREATY OF WAITANGI *Camille Nakhid and Heather Devere* — 61

PART II: The Performance of Asian Multiculturalism

4. NATIVE ALIENZ *Hilary Chung* — 93
5. UNDER THE KIWI GAZE: Public Asian festivals and multicultural Aotearoa New Zealand *Henry Johnson* — 119

PART III: Multiculturalism and Religion

6. WHITHER CULTURAL ACCEPTANCE? Muslims and multiculturalism in New Zealand *Erich Kolig* — 159
7. THE NEW ASIAN FACES OF KIWI CHRISTIANITY *Andrew Butcher and George Wieland* — 193
8. (MIS)REPORTING ISLAM: New Zealand Muslim women viewing 'us' viewing 'them' *Stephanie Dobson* — 217

PART IV: Multicultural Economies

9. IMMIGRANT ECONOMIES IN ACTION: Chinese ethnic precincts in Auckland *Paul Spoonley, Carina Meares and Trudie Cain* — 237
10. VALUING MULTICULTURALISM: Business engagement with the challenge of multiculturalism *Tim Beal, Val Lindsay and Kala Retna* — 265

11. AFTERWORD: Multiculturalism, being Asian and belonging in Aotearoa New Zealand *Jacqueline Leckie* — 285

CONTRIBUTORS — 300
INDEX — 304

1. INTRODUCTION: MULTI-MULTICULTURALISMS IN THE NEW NEW ZEALAND

GAUTAM GHOSH

The Tiger has no need of Tigritude. In other words, Tigritude appears necessary only at the point where two uncertain beasts mirror themselves in each other's exiled eyes. – FRANTZ FANON[1]

In the twenty-first century multiculturalism is a key lens through which some persons and polities envision themselves and each other. Aotearoa New Zealand is now more culturally diverse than ever. Yet in both popular and academic circles multiculturalism has received comparatively less attention here than in other countries.

This book is based on a symposium entitled 'Interrogating Multiculturalism in Aotearoa New Zealand: An Asian Studies Perspective', convened by the University of Otago in Dunedin, New Zealand.[2] The aims of the symposium were first, to stimulate discussion about multiculturalism, and second, to do so with particular attention to the histories and circumstances of 'Asians' – that all-too-generic label for what is a diverse group in Kiwi society – given the roles Asians have played in the new immigration patterns since the late 1980s.

Debating multiculturalism in Aotearoa New Zealand is exigent precisely because here, as elsewhere, it is not a singular phenomenon, as the title of this chapter, and the chapters to follow, underscore. There are many ways terms such as multicultural and multiculturalism are debated, defined and deployed. Likewise here as elsewhere multiculturalism is a fraught and vexing issue. There are arenas of debate in multiculturalism where people see eye-to-eye, but many where they do not. The aim of this volume is to clarify how and where these confluences and contentions are visible in Aotearoa. Insofar as the tensions among the volume's chapters point to tensions in multiculturalism, each can shed light on the other.

Section One of this chapter offers my general observations on the initial aims of the symposium and the book and some broad reflections on the chapters. In Section Two I provide more detailed interpretations of the chapters and highlight myriad kinds of multiculturalism as these manifest themselves in, through and about Asians in Aotearoa, and in the scholars' different modes of analysing such phenomena. My aim throughout is to interpret the chapters and consider how they indicate avenues for further reflection and research. Finally, in Section Three, I point to some *leitmotifs* in the volume, closing with some particular reflections on the relation between multiculturalism and the nation, on the one hand, and the role of vision itself in framing multiculturalism on the other.

Section One: Diversity and its discontents

Discourses of multiculturalism have emerged in the last decades as a way of speaking about, more often than not, cultural and ethnic[3] differences within a nation-state. One reason there are multiple multiculturalisms in the world today is because multiculturalism's expressions will vary depending on, among other factors, the nation-state that putatively contains – some would say generates – these differences. Relations between nation-states and cultural and ethnic diversity have surfaced repeatedly as a point of discussion and contention since the close of the Cold War at the end of the 1980s, around the same time that new immigration policies were implemented in Aotearoa.[4]

If different multiculturalisms vary depending on the character of the nation and, especially, the nationalism to which they are related, what is the character of New Zealand? Is the country, as some of our authors hold, a European (in other words Western) nation? Is this Europe resurgent or in decline? Is Aotearoa an Asian country, as declared by former Prime Minister Jim Bolger in 1993? And, if so, is it part of what some have called 'the Asian Century'? Perhaps the nation is at once, and uniquely, both Oceanic and OECD. How 'character' is defined and discerned will change with the commitments – political, ethical, economic, aesthetic and so on – of those doing the characterising.

Insofar as the country has seen itself as European it must be noted that key European leaders have been highly critical of multiculturalism in the recent past. Multicultural projects have been rebuked by the German Chancellor Angela Merkel, by Nicholas Sarkozy, ex-President of France and, perhaps most significantly for a Commonwealth member country like Aotearoa New Zealand, by David Cameron, Prime Minister of Britain. In a 2011 speech he stated, 'We have encouraged different cultures to live separate lives, apart from each other and the mainstream ... We have even tolerated these segregated communities behaving in ways that run counter to our values.' Cameron went on to link multiculturalism to terrorism.[5] The backlash against multiculturalism in the UK is also evinced in the 2014 'Trojan Horse' controversy, in which it was claimed that in the English city of Birmingham, which has a substantial Muslim population, there was a conspiracy by Islamic extremists to take over schools, oust non-Muslim staff and implement an extremist curriculum for the children.[6] A key member of Cameron's cabinet eventually apologised for comments that seemed to support the conspiracy theory. Although Aotearoa New Zealand has not witnessed controversies of this scale and (dis)repute, multiculturalism is not without its contentions, as the chapters here make abundantly clear.

The chapters also show that different groups in New Zealand have different understandings of multiculturalism. Whether multiculturalism is an 'ism' – like, say, nationalism or capitalism – or an institutional arrangement, a form of subjectivity, a demographic description, a threat or an opportunity, will differ depending on how particular polities and their segments articulate their investments and interests. It is also important to consider that communities overlap: communities of commerce can also be, in significant and specific ways, communities of religion, of urban proximity, of electoral inclination. From my socio-cultural anthropological perspective, attending to these contexts and contingencies is crucial in order to avoid de-contextualisation and reification.

The Dunedin symposium sought to address multiculturalism from an Asian Studies perspective; the papers submitted focused on forms of multiculturalism within New Zealand.[7] It also proposed to 'interrogate' multiculturalism. 'Interrogation' proliferated in the titles of academic conferences and literature in the 1980s and 1990s and is now perhaps a term that has undergone 'conceptual inflation'.[8] Still, the idea of interrogation is also an index of something specific and important: the notion, for me, is set in contradistinction to the positivist notion of testing, as in generating hypotheses and testing them – a model of inquiry valorised most in the natural sciences. The idea of testing is linked with propositional logic, whereas that of interrogating is affiliated with the logic of question and answer – a form of dialectics, if dialectics is broadly construed to include, at the least, dialogics.[9]

The idiom of interrogation as a mode of inquiry suggests a different sort of relationship between the knower and what is known and, indeed, what it means to know. It suggests relations between subjects, or agents, and foregrounds the dialectical and dialogical relations among them. Interrogation also suggests that the dynamics of power in generating knowledge must also be considered, and vigilantly so, as the forms of this power are protean and, though the deleterious dimensions of power can be mitigated, they cannot be eliminated altogether; the latter would be a utopian ideal. The knower is in the privileged position of interrogating, of presenting and deciding on questions to pose to the witness (or suspect?) and, thereby, to elicit certain sorts of answers. This is also to concede, in a sense, that a different interrogation (or cross-examination) could produce different answers and different accounts, even if the same facts are at hand and the same questions are posed. The notion of interrogation is thus in tension with one that takes the world as composed of objects and objective facts that, ultimately, through unilateral analysis, become instances of general principles, as the falling apple instantiates gravity. Interrogation is a process, with a significant hermeneutic component, that emerges as uncertain subjects mirror themselves in each others' exiled understandings and agendas.

The reason I interrogate the notion of interrogation is because it raises questions that are not unrelated to the culture-specific – especially national – forms of multiculturalism this volume aims at understanding. In Aotearoa New Zealand the backdrop for recent multicultural-related debates has been, in the main, the relationships among nationalism, biculturalism and the new immigration from Asia in the last quarter century.[10] The number of Asian communities has trebled since the late 1980s, representing the fastest growing demographic in Aotearoa. These are comprised mainly of Chinese and Indian immigrants, albeit not solely from China or India (such as Chinese from Malaysia, Indians from Fiji). If current trends continue, in the next two decades those who identify or are identified as Asian will become the largest minority group, superseding Māori, the tangata whenua. Part One of this book focuses on the pivotal relationship between biculturalism and multiculturalism, a relationship that is certainly one of the unique features of Kiwi multiculturalism.

Section Two: The routes of Kiwi multiculturalism

Part One comprises two chapters that have as their central concern how to negotiate between biculturalism and multiculturalism – a theme that is found throughout the volume. Paul Spoonley's chapter, '"We made a space for you": Renegotiating national identity and citizenship in contemporary

Aotearoa New Zealand', was one of two invited keynote addresses at the symposium. The other was by Hilary Chung, and is discussed later.

Spoonley's chapter provides an incisive overview of histories and relations within Aotearoa New Zealand, between Māori, Pākehā, people from other parts of the Pacific and Asians.[11] He establishes that the nature of contemporary Asian migration, combined with changes in how the relationship between the New Zealand state and Māori – whether in the form of concessions to Māori or in (neo-liberal inspired) cuts to welfare policies – has altered the way the nation-state is constructed in New Zealand.

Spoonley gives attention to debates about nation, state and rights, drawing attention to moments particularly salient for this volume. For example, he notes that full New Zealand citizenship (not tied to being a British subject) was established comparatively recently, in 1977; and only in the 1980s was the Treaty of Waitangi truly elevated to the status of a founding national document that described relations between Māori and Pākehā as a partnership, suggesting that Māori, as tangata whenua, were entitled to special recognition from the state. In this way, Māori challenged the simple equation of nation with state long before what some have tendentiously called the 'Asian invasion', that is, the new migration mentioned above. Spoonley also addresses broad processes such as globalisation, de-territorialisation and international migration that have also contested the equation of nation with state. He notes, as do others in the volume, that migration has long been central to New Zealand's nation-building project.

In-migration of both tangata Pasifika (from various islands in the Pacific) and, more recently, Asians, has significantly altered the demographic profile of the nation. This new demographic reality has contributed to questioning whether and how biculturalism could – or for some, should – accommodate multiculturalism. Noting that immigration has generated moral panics within 'host' societies, Spoonley invokes Stephen Vertovec's neologism 'superdiversity' to argue that the idea of the New Zealand state representing the interests and activities of a relatively homogenous nation is all the more unsustainable. Given Māori and Pākehā reactions to Asian migration, Spoonley asks how a new notion of national citizenship is to be generated. Like other authors in the volume, he draws the distinction between those who are 'New Zealand born' and those who are not – an issue, I believe, that points to an important part of the nationalist imaginary.[12]

Like Spoonley, Camille Nakhid and Heather Devere's chapter, 'Negotiating multiculturalism and the Treaty of Waitangi: An immigration policy to enable social unity', provides a useful historical perspective. They are concerned with bringing multiculturalism and the Treaty of Waitangi into colloquy, with the specific hope of making immigration a complement to unity. They examine actions by the New Zealand government, pointing to migration policies, the Waitangi Tribunal and, in particular, the government's aim to make European culture paramount through discriminatory immigration policies, and suggest that 'Immigration policy has [not incorporated] the contributions of new arrivals in building social cohesion.' Dominant parties, including New Zealand government regimes, have promulgated policies in ways that exhibit deliberate attempts to stir contention between less-powerful minority groups.

Nakhid and Devere investigate, specifically, whether the Treaty of Waitangi can serve as the basis for cohesion between the new arrivals and longer-standing communities of Māori, Pākehā and Pasifika. They describe the Treaty as 'the country's first official immigration agreement' and suggest that since the arrival of non-indigenous people on the shores of New Zealand, the country has been 'multicultural' – here using the term as a demographic description, if not as an attitude or policy or even a debate: multiculturalism as an 'ism' is certainly a more recent development.

Nakhid and Devere analyse concerns that the new immigrants have generated among many, including Māori groups apprehensive that a burgeoning Asian population would eclipse their standing in the country. The promulgation of policy changes allowing new immigration was seen by some as evidence of this: it was held that the Treaty guaranteed the right of Māori to participate in policy formation, and some felt there was inadequate consultation over this migration policy. Not only was the population changing in ways that could potentially dilute the position of Māori, but Māori standing in relation to the Treaty was being undermined as well. At the same time Asian communities, including those foreign-born, have expressed concerns about being marginalised in debates about biculturalism and the Treaty. The authors conclude that 'The lack of a planned, considered and consultative multicultural approach can lead to the isolation of ethnic communities …'

Ultimately, Nakhid and Devere categorise the Treaty as the country's 'founding document'. They write, drawing on Durie, that its preamble speaks to 'the arrival of many settlers and the need for peace and *good order*

... *founded not on legalism*[13] but on a philosophy of good faith'. In spite of the distancing from 'legalism', the two authors do speak of the Treaty in legal and juridical terms insofar as they speak of 'good order' and the Treaty as a 'contract' – though this does not, in itself, counter an interpretation of the Treaty as expressing a philosophy of good faith. Indeed, in Aotearoa New Zealand diverse groups share key experiences, from being subject to discrimination to the importance placed on family and kinship, which in my view, are not themselves inherently or entirely about contractual relations. The authors state that the Treaty's democratic principles of promoting 'self-determination, empowerment and cultural pluralism' can bring diverse people together and promote the 'social cohesiveness of [the] nation'. Let the Treaty inform multiculturalism in Aotearoa New Zealand, and set an example for other nations, particularly those with indigenous populations, to follow.[14]

The two chapters in Part Two examine what might be called the performance of Asian multiculturalism. Hilary Chung's 'Native Alienz' demonstrates that the study of Asian Theatre in Aotearoa New Zealand offers unique insights into Kiwi culture, and into contemporary debates about multiculturalism in international academia. The focus of her chapter is a 2009 Auckland theatre performance, the first production to be funded by the Oryza Foundation, established to support Asia-related performances. Entitled *Asian Tales: Native Alienz, stories from the lips of Asia*, it consists of seven short plays that, in Chung's analyses, raise questions about national identity and its links with race, multiculturalism and biculturalism, among other issues.

With suggestive subtlety Chung describes and analyses how racial embodiment is presented in *Native Alienz*, in other words how the bodies performing on stage appear to the audience as racially marked. She draws on and expands Lo and Gilbert's typology[15] according to which multicultural theatre may (i) reflect the melting pot notion of cultural pluralism or, alternatively, fetishise difference, or (ii) be truly 'counterdiscursive'.

An example of the problematic melting-pot approach is blind casting,[16] an approach that erases difference and often tacitly endorses the status quo. In fetishisation, difference is celebrated but often presented in thin, stereotypical and most problematically, immutable fashion. Following Lo and Gilbert,[17] Chung argues that counter-discursive theatre does not seek to hide racial differences (along with the cultures, histories and experiences that such differences catalogue) nor to fetishise them. Rather it brings such differences to the fore and challenges the audience to interrogate what such differences mean: for example for national identities and narratives. Counter-discursive theatre offers an opportunity for transcending differences that are discriminatory while embracing those that are salutary. It allows for the pursuit of greater participation in the nation. For Chung, *Native Alienz* is an example of counter-discursive theatre. She notes, for example, '[w]hereas diasporic narratives tend to be posited as marginal to the national narrative, these explorations [in *Native Alienz*] present themselves insistently as being part of it'.

In Aotearoa New Zealand the official doctrine of biculturalism is central to the way the state manages ethnic and cultural difference. Chung sees biculturalism as somewhat overshadowing alternative ways of envisioning national belonging. This is because biculturalism, like many other 'isms', can serve to promote discriminatory thinking, in this case racial thinking: it is the 'insufficiently acknowledged discourse of race that limits access to national belonging'. *Native Alienz* challenges the audience to recognise 'the invisibility and exclusion of Asian-ness ... from the New Zealand paradigm of national identity'. Although Chung is critical of the way the state manages ethnic and cultural difference, she identifies a 'pressing' need for 'official intervention' with regard to the 'paradigm' of national identity.

Perhaps the most important word in the title of Henry Johnson's chapter, 'Under the Kiwi gaze: Public Asian festivals and multicultural Aotearoa New Zealand', is the word 'and'. By using 'and' instead of 'in' he signals that he will not take anything for granted about what multiculturalism in the country is today. Rather, through three case studies, he shows how particular practices can come to be represented as part of the multicultural topography of the nation.

Johnson looks at the 'transplantation' of Chinese, Indian and Southeast Asian communities, and in particular the celebrations they have brought to this country. This transplantation is a crucial effect of the flows that have impacted New Zealand in the last two decades of globalisation. Johnson's argument pivots on how such celebrations as the Lantern Festival, Diwali and the Southeast Asian Market, which 'index ethnicity and migration', are transformed when brought under the purview of the Kiwi gaze 'in a media spectacle' in the form of large-scale public events, through politically-motivated 'top-down' 'intervention'.[18]

Johnson is concerned about the ways these celebrations are transformed or recontextualised from diasporic Asian community contexts to sites of mass consumption. He suggests that Diwali, for example, when organised top-down, is 'moulded' into a public spectacle with performance 'at its core'. In this process it loses its religious and cultural meanings, which are better retained when Diwali is celebrated by families or smaller community groups. He discusses how this intervention, also described as a form of top-down 'festivalisation', has an impact on multiculturalism in New Zealand, even in the absence of any official policy regarding multiculturalism. Though local cultural groups participate in Diwali, the top-down intervention 'homogenise[s] Diwali into a form that is the vision of the organisers, rather than of the participants'. On the other hand, he proposes that these events 'may help Asian migrants ... engage with their new cultural context'. Johnson pointedly asks why some Asian cultures are celebrated in 'public' while others are not.

Johnson leaves open for interpretation in what specific sense he is using the term 'gaze' – whether in a sociological sense of, say, institutional oversight and hierarchy, or in a post-structuralist or psychoanalytical sense of subject-formation. The term 'multicultural gaze' certainly includes 'official' power – that of the government, city councils and, in particular, the Asia New Zealand Foundation (ANZF).[19] But he also implicates multiple and cross-cutting gazes in Aotearoa New Zealand, the intersections of which generate multicultural practices, ethos and attitudes. Johnson is wary of simplifying the complex dynamics between formal, informal and other social practices.

Likewise Johnson avoids framing his analysis in simplistic black and white terms. He is cautious about ANZF's 'collaboration' with city councils and the like, suggesting this may lead to the commodification (mass consumption) and de-contextualisation of culture. Johnson concludes, however, that intervention also has positive effects: it makes the nation more open to multiculturalism, and encourages New Zealanders not only to see that their society is multicultural, but also to endorse this. Like Chung, Johnson also acknowledges the influence of international multicultural practices on developments in Aotearoa.

Part Three explores the relation between multiculturalism and religion. The first of the three chapters in this section, Erich Kolig's 'Whither cultural acceptance? Muslims and multiculturalism in New Zealand' speaks of how the West is seen, in various ways, as 'modern', 'enlightened', 'progressive', 'liberal', 'tolerant', 'secular', where 'religious and cultural freedom' and 'human rights' are respected. To what extent can and should the West accommodate Islam's inclination towards a 'theocentric world view' that can make it incompatible with liberal democracy? Kolig suggests that '[i]n terms of multiculturalism in a Western liberal democracy, Muslims pose possibly the greatest challenge.'

He asks why there have not been problems between Muslims and the 'host society' in New Zealand as there have been in Europe, and offers a broad discussion of this. One factor, Kolig says, could be a matter of numbers: in New Zealand, Muslims are a small minority of only 1 per cent. An important difference between Europe and New Zealand is that the latter 'is fortunate to have one of the most peaceful and complacent Muslim minorities in the Western world'. In New Zealand 'Muslims en bloc have not come to the public's attention by making concerted, vociferous demands to have aspects of their culture officially recognised, or through their antagonistic, violent behaviour'. Kolig adds that in New Zealand Muslims have been 'discrete' rather than demanding, and have not resorted to 'undemocratic political pressure, public spectacle or violence' and 'have done nothing to earn the nation's distrust'. 'Muslims have had nothing to fear.'

In the 1980s and 1990s New Zealand moved away from assimilation as a goal, becoming oriented more towards multiculturalism – the recognition and celebration of diversity. Kolig asks if such shifts could damage the social 'fabric' of the encapsulating 'host society', undermine national social cohesiveness and increase the risk of conflict. As he notes, some would avoid speaking in such broad terms about a group (Muslims); Kolig calls such caveats 'mantras' which, in his view, are of little help in a global perspective. In matters of policy, he says, '[c]elebrating diversity and avoiding moral judgment is very New Age and post-modernist, but lacks in practical reason.'

Kolig identifies concerns about 'social disintegration' and 'parallel societies'. However, he is certain that globalisation will change the nature of the nation-state and engender new notions of national citizenship, and thinks this might generate possibilities for new forms of integration of Muslims – including an acceptance in society that persons may have multiple loyalties. He cautions that 'even a very liberal democracy such as New Zealand will have to insist on the adherence to certain principles ... in order to preserve a functioning society'. He notes that some societies are tightening their immigration policies: 'Some spectacular cases of maladjustment of Muslims have encouraged a revision of rules relating to immigration and asylum seekers.'

Andrew Butcher and George Wieland's chapter 'The new Asian faces of Kiwi Christianity' notes that '[r]eligion generally and Christianity specifically' have been more significant to New Zealand's history and culture than current scholarship would suggest. 'The contribution of this Christian world view, traditions and practice, along with that of religion generally, has not received the attention it merits in accounts of the making of New Zealand and its national identity.' They subsequently iterate that religion has played and continues to play 'a more significant role than is often acknowledged in the making of New Zealand'.

Still, the number of local-born Kiwis who say they are not religious is increasing, both as a proportion of the population and in absolute terms. Overall the number of those who identify as Christian is declining in New Zealand; at the same time, the most marked recent growth of Christianity – more precisely, in the number of Christians – in New Zealand is among its migrant populations, particularly those from Asia. Taken together these two facts raise questions about how Christianity may be changing in New Zealand, and about the lived experience of Asian immigrant Christian communities and their place in transnational Christian networks – most certainly in relation to multiculturalism, but also with regard to secularisation and modernity.

Butcher and Wieland discuss the reception these immigrants have found in New Zealand. For them, the diverse sorts of Christianity that are being practised become highly relevant to the constitution of multiculturalism.[20] They note that while New Zealanders are warming to Asian peoples, there is substantial evidence that discrimination against them is wide and deep. There is 'a significant disquiet' about New Zealand's immigrant Asian populations. These matters are complicated further by an increase in the number of New Zealanders who identify with more than one ethnicity.

The authors suggest that, in New Zealand, religion has been in the private sphere but is now increasingly public. This is certainly true in the way that religion has become more visible. Butcher and Wieland show that other religions such as Hinduism and Buddhism have grown alongside the new migrations. This seems to have sparked a concern, in some quarters, that immigration is hazardous for Christianity in New Zealand. The authors specify further that 'much of this disquiet relates to the threat to New Zealand's perceived Christian heritage and values'. These views are expressed most stridently by 'majority' Anglo-Celtic Christians. Although Asian immigrants are bolstering the numbers of Christians, they practice 'rather different forms of Christian faith and tradition' provoking the 'host' population to criticise and resist Asians as a threat to the dominant New Zealand expression of Christianity (indicating, yet again, the ways in which Kiwi national identity and Christianity are entwined).

Butcher and Wieland point to a number of tendentious statements: new immigration increases the risk of 'communal violence ... like [in] Kosovo, Sri Lanka or Northern Ireland'; 'Because it is my home I am entitled to be choosy'; it is 'their [immigrants'] responsibility to respect our nation's Christian founding values'. Along the lines of such statements the authors also quote an Archbishop, former head of the Church of England, saying 'migration threatens the DNA of our nation', and further, 'immigrants should respect the Christian nature and history of our nation'. It is worth noting the resonance between this invocation of DNA (and threats to it) and ideologies that equate nation with race.

Stephanie Dobson's chapter '(Mis)reporting Islam: New Zealand Muslim women viewing "us" viewing "them"', seems less content with the status of multiculturalism in Aotearoa New Zealand than Kolig. Like Butcher and Wieland, Dobson highlights the importance of attending to background and context in relation to religion. 'When watching media reports the public can be left with an overall impression of conflict being solely the fault of religious motivations or ideology ... The emphasis on Islam can sometimes be misleading.'

Dobson examines New Zealand media representations of Muslim women, including Asian women, and about Muslim groups. She finds that Muslims are subject to 'significant "othering" and essentialism' within New Zealand mass media, 'in the form of a type of discursive orientalism ...' Through interviews with Muslim women she shows how popular media portrayals cause anxiety and insecurity, undermine esteem, and hamper these women's sense of belonging to New Zealand.[21] The women see racism and prejudice as 'just products of ignorance'. However, they consider the media culpable of creating this ignorance through the propagation of stereotypes and prejudiced language in what is nevertheless presented as 'objective reporting'.

Dobson describes the ways such discourses affect Muslim women in their 'everyday lives'.[22] Significantly, the links between ethnic and religious prejudice have, according to the interviewees, changed over time. While in the 1970s religion was less of an issue than skin colour, since 9/11 being Muslim has become the main marker. There was unanimous agreement among the interviewees that coverage of terrorism since 9/11 has had tangible effects on the women's lives. But religion becomes the new racism; 'Paki', the derogatory term for people with kinship ties to the country of Pakistan, has come to mean 'Muslim', deployed also in a derogatory sense.[23] Some of the interviewees noted that Muslims are represented in a 'universalising' manner, despite differences of ethnicity, culture and other factors. Islam is presented as brewing violence. It is an unhappy irony, to say the least, that a 19-year-old Muslim woman reported she 'lived in fear of retaliation for terrorist actions elsewhere'. The interviewees also noted that violence, including that against women, happens in every culture and nation in the world. It is hardly exclusive to Islam.

The media's preoccupation with gender inequality was also considered a way in which the media misrepresent Islam. The *Dominion Post*, a leading newspaper based in the nation's capital, declared in an editorial that in Saudi Arabia women 'are treated as the personal property of their menfolk'. The broader society's focus on the hijab (head covering) was also noted: the association of the hijab with the image of oppressed women contributed to the sense that these women did not belong in New Zealand.

Dobson's chapter raises perennial and pivotal questions about objective vs. subjective accounts in the human sciences. She uses the notion of 'subjective' in two ways, mostly in relation to a theory of subjectivity, but at times also as the counterpart to objective, as in 'media reporting is far from objective' and in advocating for reporting that is 'balanced' and based on 'accurate knowledge'.

In 2014 an Asian nation, China, became for the first time New Zealand's largest export partner. The two chapters in Part Four focus on what might be called the business of belonging. Both look at how multiculturalism does or can contribute to New Zealand's economic relations with Asia.

The chapter 'Immigrant economies in action: Chinese ethnic precincts in Auckland', by Spoonley, Meares and Cain, describes how the 1980s and 1990s were a pivotal period for multiculturalism in Aotearoa New Zealand.[24] These were also the years in which immigration from Asia to Aotearoa increased markedly, provoking, as the chapter observes, a 'vigorous and very negative political and public response'.

An ethnic precinct is defined in this chapter as an area with a 'co-location of businesses owned by ... minority ethnic communities'.[25] Although ethnic precincts have existed in, and been endorsed by, destination cities for immigrants – Vancouver has had something comparable for a quarter of a century – it is a rather new phenomenon in Aotearoa New Zealand. It is in fact so new that the authors caution against drawing quick conclusions from the available data. The chapter examines the economics of precincts and some of the policy issues these economies raise. The authors suggest that government agencies could have worked more effectively with ethnic precinct economies, and vice versa, to mutual advantage, and that there has been a 'general lack of government recognition at both local and national level of ethnic-specific dynamics and outcomes'. This in turn generated unwillingness on the part of some Asian business owners to turn to government support because they perceived 'a lack of understanding or responsiveness to their particular (ethnic) practices or beliefs'. Among the barriers to cooperative action was the adoption of neo-liberal imperatives by the government. These imperatives include a reliance on what, in the US, is at times called the 'bootstraps' ideology: capable and deserving people should be able to pull themselves up by their own bootstraps, without assistance and even against the odds. In the Auckland precincts the government emphasised 'immigrant agency' and *laissez faire* economics, offering little support for settlement or entrepreneurship.

The chapter provides two compelling case-studies of the emergence of ethnic precincts that are commercial in nature and primarily part of the retail sector. Both studies demonstrate how 'monocultural' Auckland has become, or at least has the potential to become, a 'superdiver-city'.[26] The first case-study shows how an area with poor housing, low incomes and gang activity was transformed into a thriving 'multicultural centre ... [with] a strong identity and a unique community', and a palpable Asian presence. The second case study considers precincts that were 'purpose built' by an entrepreneurial immigrant from Hong Kong to serve the growing – and, especially, newly arrived – Chinese population.

Neither of these case-studies of urban makeover settle the long-standing debates about whether ethnic precincts – which some call 'enclaves', albeit with different connotations – ultimately facilitate or fetter immigrants' economic mobility. The precinct can allow immigrants to enter the labour market without confronting the language and cultural barriers – not to mention the discrimination – they could face in the mainstream market. It can also provide support for the establishment of businesses, for example by facilitating access to capital,[27] labour, supplies or customers, thereby creating upward mobility within the community. But does the nature of that mobility help or hinder mobility beyond the precinct? On the whole, the authors are inclined to see the emergence of ethnic precincts in positive terms. Those they discuss do not seem to lead to isolation. Rather, they are sites where the Asian inhabitants create vital 'new forms of consumption and economic activity' that contribute to the wider city. The authors encourage the governing bodies of cities and the country to see ethnic precincts as opportunities for productive, competitive and strategic growth.

In their chapter, 'Valuing multiculturalism: Business engagement with the challenge of multiculturalism', Beal, Lindsay and Retna discuss the economic costs and benefits of multiculturalism. They speak of multiculturalism at the socio-cultural (as distinguished from economic) level, and endorse an approach that reconciles cultural diversity with social cohesion. Still, their central concern in this chapter is less about whether multiculturalism is valuable in itself, and more about the ways it can be utilised by businesses and the government to improve international trade. They state that multiculturalism in business is 'a major contributor to a country's economic improvement', and explore how multiculturalism operates in a range of organisational contexts, with a focus on Asian immigrants and entrepreneurs from China and India.

The authors note and rebuff the idea that immigrants have a negative impact on a country's economy – for example, in relation to state benefits, housing prices and the ownership of farmland[28] – and demonstrate the economic benefits to cultural diversity at both macro-economic and organisational levels. Immigrants from Asia can and do provide 'human capital' to improve trade and other relations with Asia. According to the authors the full potential of this capital will only be realised if a set of strategies is put in place, such as the government's 'Seriously Asia' initiatives that support 'proactive engagement with multiculturalism in New Zealand'. The authors distinguish between 'passive multiculturalism' – for instance the sorts of festivals that Johnson's chapter describes, which they find 'superficial'[29] – and 'proactive multiculturalism', of which they approve.

Migrants from Asia can add to the business sector's cultural awareness, productivity, creativity and flexibility. The category 'migrant from Asia' of course contains a diverse range of people. In relation to their economistic concerns, the authors subscribe to a typology of migrants based on 'the extent of [their] social embeddedness' in the 'host' country. 'Immigrant employees', for example, have a high degree of embeddedness, while 'returnee migrants', who may also be referred to as 'contemporary diasporic entrepreneurs', are resettled in their home country but retain ties with their erstwhile 'host' country. They are less socially embedded than immigrant employees. 'Transnational entrepreneurs' reside in the host country and pursue business that links host with home.

The authors elaborate on these distinctions – and imply, in the process, that benefits that accrue in relation to 'social embeddedness' are not only a matter of degree ('extent') but also of kind: there are different sorts of embeddedness at issue. The authors conclude that New Zealand is and will be multicultural; the more New Zealand promotes its Asian immigrants as human capital, 'the better we will engage in the complex, demanding, but profitable markets that lie offshore'.[30]

Section Three: Multiculturalism inside out

Tim Ingold has famously declared that, in academia, 'the intensity of debate concerning its theoretical and intellectual foundations is a good measure of its current vitality'.[31] Inspired by Ingold, and drawing on my own interests in the intersections between cultural anthropology and political and social theory, I now point to some *leitmotifs* in the book: urbanisation, historical trajectory, social cohesion and national identity.

I note, at the outset, that I define multiculturalism as an attitude that endorses, celebrates or promotes cultural and ethnic diversity. Such an attitude can be accompanied by new demographic realities (or the recognition of older ones), accommodations in a society's institutions (including policy implementation), changes in the way subjectivities (or agents) are formed and the changing relation each of these has to the society's imaginary.

Urbanisation

Through the chapters one gets a sense of how central the urban or urbanisation (as a process) is to matters multicultural in New Zealand. The chapters point to multicultural demographics, economics, governments and events, all in urban centres. When the rural is mentioned, it is most significantly so in the context of migration to cities. Auckland, in particular, draws attention. For example, Auckland is shown to be more culturally diverse than any other part of Aotearoa. It is also less hostile to multiculturalism and migration than many other parts of the country. That increased diversity is correlated with increased tolerance has been noted for some time. But whether this correlation is indicative of causation – that is, whether diversity causes an increase in tolerance – could be a topic for further research.

Also for further research are the ways urbanisation, as a process, plays a constitutive role in the myriad forms of multiculturalism. There is a vast and rapidly increasing literature on urbanisation, spurred in part by the projection that soon most of the population of the planet will live in urban settings. A productive line of inquiry for future studies may be to bring this literature – including that which speaks, in a theoretical register, to how urbanisation impacts agency – into conversation with investigations of multiculturalism in Aotearoa New Zealand. Literature on the 'global city' and the 'migrant metropolis'[32] could be of particular relevance.

An aspect of the investigation of the urban could be to probe the idea of mass, also an important concept in some of the chapters – for example, 'mass media' and 'mass consumption'. Mass and urban may be intertwined in unique ways, particularly in relation to the idea of the nation. Mass and nation both imply a circumscribed group: mass is not used to refer to everyone in the world. Mass implies both horizontal differences (there are other masses) just as nations do (there are other nations). Mass and nation also imply that there are vertical differences as well as horizontal ones: they both seem to imply a separate elite or, in the plural, separate elites. A group of people, when conceived as a mass, implies there are experts and specialists: those who will govern the group, or those who will generate objective knowledge in different fields, or those who will be leaders in various ways. When we think of the mass, do we imagine prime ministers, plutocrats, or professors?

Similar points could be made with regard to the issue of citizenship, so central to debates about multiculturalism, namely that it is another way of distinguishing one people from another; it is perhaps worth keeping in mind that the idea of the citizen is rooted in city-zen, an inhabitant of a city. Theorists such as R.G. Collingwood and Giorgio Agamben[33] have, importantly, seen the city less as a location or place and more as a model of political participation (agency). Understanding the urban from this perspective may offer fresh insights into the complex and dynamic inter-relationships between citizenship and multiculturalism. Here again, debates regarding myriad sorts of migration (irregular, forced, economic, diasporic) and sorts of 'dwellers' (denizen, sojourner, netizen) could also be relevant.

Historical trajectory

Some chapters seem to suggest that Aotearoa New Zealand has, as a nation, a historical directionality. This is implied when New Zealand and/or New Zealand multiculturalism are described as 'not yet mature', 'adolescent', 'evolving', or 'incomplete' – when reference is made, explicitly or otherwise, to an unfinished project. Complementary terms are also encountered, such as arguments about transcending or moving beyond the present.

These ideas bring to mind both Jürgen Habermas's argument about modernity being an unfinished project and Francis Fukuyama's argument that we have already reached the end of history.[34] There are very profound differences between Habermas and Fukuyama, but one potential similarity (that must be confirmed carefully) may be that human society or societies can be completed, can arrive, can have a destiny and fulfil it. Such ideas seem to be a backdrop of some of the chapters – backdrop in the sense of social imaginary or of Collingwood's similar but more processual notion 'absolute presuppositions'.[35] One expression of this is the sense, in the volume, that New Zealand can and should find a way to engage in the interests of its own advancement with an historical epoch, the so-called Asian Century conceived as part of the global trajectory of history. This is not to criticise such an agenda: in key regards I agree with it. Here I just raise the possibility that such an imaginary or absolute presupposition is present and warrants attention as such.

Social cohesion

Recently the Royal Society of New Zealand contacted the New Zealand Asian Studies Association:

> *The Royal Society of New Zealand is undertaking a **major** review of **the rapidly changing New Zealand population**, and the implications of this for the economy, **social cohesion**, education, and health ... We welcome input ... from members of the NZ Asia [sic] Studies society on ... how we should understand Asian cultural influences on New Zealand, trends in Asian immigration, language diversity, **social cohesion**, NZ–Asia relations, identity, or other pertinent areas.*[36]

That the issue of 'social cohesion', in particular, is raised twice is indicative of its status as a concern for Kiwis.

Discussions about multiculturalism, wherever they take place, seem preoccupied with the challenge or risk it putatively poses for social cohesion or the social fabric. Concerns about cohesion arise when it is feared it might go missing. This fear recursively generates the idea that cohesion existed in the first place, which could then be diminished or displaced by multiculturalist policies. Socio-cultural differences such as ethnicity are seen as dangerously divisive and, again recursively, if viewed in this way there is a greater chance that divisiveness will actually eventuate. Often, in this register, the erroneous idea that people are defined through some objective essence is deployed in order to salvage what is seen as at risk, as Fanon's eloquent epigraph at the opening of this chapter suggests.

What is the ideal idiom of unity, the best conception of cohesion? How should we define 'we'? It is not always clear what terms such as cohesion and fabric, drawn from the world of material objects, mean, especially when it comes to human relations.[37] I propose to see, and promote, cohesion in the sense of collective cooperative action. Accordingly the collective is not an entity but an arena of activities defined in the first instance by the collectivity's goals. The collectivity, the 'we', is partially created in using the pronoun 'we' in the first instance. The Constitution of the US begins with the words 'We the People of the United States, in Order to form a more perfect Union ...' The three words, 'We the People' are for me the most important: they posit a collectivity that is anterior to the document itself.[38]

Following the philosophy of Collingwood – both his political philosophy and his philosophy of history – I suggest that cohesion can and should be pursued if it is understood as the ability of persons and peoples to build consensus regarding desirable goals and to make decisions about how to pursue these. From this perspective, social cohesion would be a process located in how consensus is achieved with regard to goals and strategies, and the willingness of parties to compromise, if necessary, in the process. When such processes encourage, rather than suppress, dissent, cohesion will be that much stronger: the odds increase that the goals articulated will be broader, nuanced, seen as legitimate and would garner the dissenters' endorsement.

Conceived in this way, a lack of social cohesion would be gauged by an inhibited ability to act in concert. In addition, cohesion is not something that can ever be completed. Attempts to finalise or close it would be utopian (thus unachievable) and, in that regard, perhaps even undesirable. The nature of the collectivity will change according to a number of factors, including the goals pursued and the resources for pursuing it – one resource being the capacity for cooperative action itself. In this approach, moreover, any person or people would always be part of multiple, overlapping collectivities. To the extent that a collectivity is connected to culture, seeing society as overlapping agents would mean seeing society as already, always, multicultural.

If the Treaty of Waitangi is a part of what is referred to as Aotearoa New Zealand's unwritten constitution, it could be worth scouring it for such invocations of 'we'. I am not a student of the Treaty so must just ask: does the Treaty contain this broad sense of 'we'? The Church of England missionary Henry Williams who, along with his son, played a significant role in translating the Treaty into te reo Māori, wrote in his recollections of the events leading to the signing that the British authorities gave the Māori chiefs a clause-by-clause explanation 'showing the advantage to them of being taken under the fostering care of the British Government, by which act they would become one people with the English, in the suppression of wars, and every lawless act; under one Sovereign, and one Law, human and divine'.[39] Similarly, Governor Hobson is reported to have said, as each chief actually signed, 'He iwi tahi tātou' ('We are now one people').[40] These quotations could support those who seek to interpret the Treaty in order to see it as expansive enough to accommodate multiculturalism; they are also ambiguous enough to support arguments to the contrary. In any case I believe that any definition of a Kiwi 'we' must make significant reference to the Treaty. Moreover, as suggested above, there could be multiple sources and resources, in addition to the Treaty, that New Zealand, like other polities, can find for evoking the 'we', especially if it is borne in mind that there will be different, overlapping 'we's', with possibly different values and agendas.

Escaping national identity

The sovereign idea of our time is, arguably, the idea of popular sovereignty: rule by the people, of the people and for the people. For better or worse it has then been presumed that popular sovereignty will manifest in the particular form of a nation-state. The idea of collective and consensual action, as articulated above, has come to be incorporated within that of the nation-state, particularly in postcolonial polities, including Aotearoa. Nations and identities are presumed to be the premise of collective action, rather than its products.

Advocates of nations seem to share, or claim to share, with proponents of multiculturalism the desire to make representation and participation in a polity more inclusive and empowering. In our present time, and given our present focus on multiculturalism, we should engage primarily with the nation – a polity comprising diverse and overlapping forms and genres of collective agency.

Most discussions of multiculturalism seem to adopt a default vision, one which takes as given that the world is organised as nations, each with some unique attributes and expressions that help to give it an identity, promote its prosperity and so on. Indeed, it is difficult to argue that the world is not organised in this way.[41] Thus conversations about multiculturalism are inclined towards expanding and modifying the nation-state, rather than replacing it. The goal of those who support multiculturalism is often, it seems, a multiculturalism that fits with the nation-state. This is the goal of establishing a multicultural nationalism, one that leaves the nation as the privileged term since it is a multiculturalism that is contained by the nation. If and how multiculturalism fits with nationalism is an explicit concern for many. That this concern assumes that multiculturalism must fit *within* a nationalism is often implicit.

There are states that officially promote multicultural nationalism, including Australia, Canada and many countries in the European Union. Again, to point to this is not to criticise it. The pursuit of a multicultural nation-state may be a most appropriate goal. Even those who might want to change the 'national order of things'[42] might find more success through gradual modification, rather than the utopian idea of total, revolutionary transformation to what might be called a 'multicultural order of things'. Could the goal of expanding and modifying the nation to make it more multicultural benefit from a rigorous theoretical consideration of what is involved in the on-going processes through which a polity affirms itself as a nation? Is the formation of national identity, as the epigraph by Fanon suggests, a consequence of uncertainty that, in turn, provokes assertions of an 'essence' in the form of a national identity?[43] The answer to these questions would surely vary according to the model of the nation, nationalism and nation-state that one adopts.[44]

Regardless of the model adopted, in discussions of multiculturalism Arjun Appadurai's idea of the 'ethnoscape'[45] is often invoked, both explicitly and implicitly, the latter for example when speaking of 'cityscapes' or 'festivalscapes'. I ask, to what extent is the idea of ethnoscape compatible with an agenda of pursuing a multicultural nation? For now, I will adumbrate some ways in which the two ideas, nation and ethnoscape, are in tension.

A nation is generally seen as something that has boundaries of various sorts, such as territorial, linguistic, juridical and aesthetic. These boundaries define the 'inside' of the nation against the 'outside' of the nation. Such boundaries may be seen by academics as constructed and imagined rather than natural and objective, but speaking of a nation (and especially a nation-state) invokes these boundaries. This often implicitly posits, as noted, that there are other comparable and in some regards similar polities – other nations and nation-states. It helps to picture a commonplace globe, and the ways that different nations are located, adjacent to one another. The synecdoche for this vision of knowledge is the telescope or the microscope.

To me, Appadurai's notion of ethnoscape is an alternative to this picture. The synecdoche here would be the kaleidoscope. The idea of the ethnoscape can be understood, I suggest, through considering the mathematical idea of fractals. Fractals provide a way to discern patterns in what would generally seem outside the grasp of analysis. Imagine a landscape with myriad plateaus, dips, curves, points and valleys. One cannot define when the landscape begins or ends. The picture will also change with the observer's perspective. It will look different depending on whether one is seeing it from the mountaintop, the valley, or from outer space. It is patterned, not chaotic: there are, after all, plateaus and dips and curves, albeit of different scales. If one pictures nations in this way one would have a rather different sort of picture of the globe, too.[46] Not only would boundaries no longer be crisp and clear, boundaries themselves would be 'fractalian' – with similarities but of different size and shape, some thin, some thick and, most importantly, overlapping, depending on the perspective one adopts. In such a vision, distinctions such as host versus diaspora would fade, and categories such as citizen and immigrant would be undermined. In such a world one would not be asked to picture a Kiwi or Korean or Kenyan citizen because one could not. Most importantly, one would speak less of nations, or envision multicultural ones.

Finally, I focus on the issue of vision, because both the national model and the above-mentioned 'ethno-scapes' model – in other words, both the telescope and the kaleidoscope – are, ultimately, visual. The issue of visibility and invisibility appear in the chapters in senses that are literal, metaphorical and theoretical. One sees this in the authors' allusions to race, dress, faces, dignity, location, public celebrations and the built environment. The chapters are replete with references to and metaphors of vision. This suggests that a theoretical exploration of vision could be worthwhile, for it is central to how power works. In Western contexts vision has arguably been the privileged sense in understanding the world, as my use of 'focus', 'appear' and 'sees' above, exemplifies.[47] It is not insignificant that the adage 'seeing is believing' emerged in Western culture. What might emerge if, in the study of multiculturalism, the primacy of vision was displaced? One step would be to notice other senses such as sounds or smells, as some chapters suggest. A further step would be to moderate the role vision has in Western epistemology as an edifice of what Charles Taylor has called 'the imaginary' and Collingwood 'absolute presuppositions', as mentioned above. If it is true that the approach we have brought to the study of multiculturalism is essentially and significantly visual, what might be summoned by aural, olfactory or tactile orientations?[48] Could the dynamics of power be understood differently, and perhaps changed, if invoked in this way?

Throughout we should keep in mind what Fanon cautions: that the encounter between agents can lead to uncertainty and then essentialism – from being a tiger to the need to define and assert tiger-ness – in exclusivist terms. Should we seek to shatter the mirror of which he speaks into shards? Would such shards be the fragments of postmodernity or of late capitalism? Perhaps. But in their multitude they may suggest unique patterns of association and sensation, and opportunities for articulating new forms of collective agency.

Endnotes

1. In Benedict Anderson, *The Spectre of Comparisons: Nationalism, Southeast Asia, and the world*, London: Verso, 1998, 44.
2. The symposium was held on 19–20 February 2011. It was organised under the auspices of the University of Otago's Asia-New Zealand Research Cluster, with generous co-sponsorship by the Asian Studies Group at Victoria University of Wellington (Associate Professor Stephen Epstein, in particular) and support from the Dunedin Public Art Gallery (Lynda Cullen in particular). For their help in supporting the symposium, I thank especially Paola Voci and Erica Baffelli. I also thank Les O'Neil, Vanessa Ward, Tushar Robins, Tui Clery, Catherine Waite and Brian Moloughney, who opened the symposium. For their help with my chapter I thank Greg Dawes, Cecilia Novero, University of Otago Press, Peter Rothblatt and especially, again, Paola Voci. For her help with, well, everything I thank the brilliant Bell Murphy. I dedicate my contribution to my own wee Kiwi, a veritable handful of diversity, Emilio Kumar Ghosh-Novero. All errors in the final product are his alone.
3. For incisive analyses of ethnicity see Borneman, John, 'Race, ethnicity, species, breed: Totemism and horse breed classification in America', *Comparative Studies in Society and History* 30, 1, 25–51, 1988; and 'Postscript: Reflections on totemism tomorrow: Horse breeds and breeding in the United States and France', in Aram

Yengoyan (ed.), *Modes of Comparison: Theory and Practice*, Ann Arbor: University of Michigan Press, 2008, 351–65; and John L. Comaroff and Jean Comaroff, *Ethnicity Inc.*, Chicago: University of Chicago Press, 2009.
4 The relation between these two – the end of the Cold war and new immigration regimes – remains under-explored with regard to the New Zealand context.
5 Speech to Munich Security Conference February, 2011. See also Steven Vertovec and Susanne Wesselsdorf (eds), *The Multiculturalism Backlash: European discourses, policies and practices*, London, New York: Routledge, 2010.
6 www.birminghammail.co.uk/all-about/trojan_horse
7 In my view, an Asian Studies perspective on multiculturalism would be one that would excavate how Asian Studies illuminates or influences multiculturalism in Aotearoa. Such a perspective would also situate movements of different communities, ideas and objects as these interrelate within both sending and receiving countries or regions. Ultimately the symposium focused more on issues of multiculturalism in New Zealand than the Asian Studies challenge, which thus remains for another occasion.
8 Robert Miles, *Conceptual Inflation*, London, New York: Routledge, 1989.
9 On dialogics see Mikhail Mikhaïlovich Bakhtin, *The Dialogic Imagination: Four essays*, Austin: University of Texas Press, 1982. On dialogics and post-Hegelian dialectics see R.G. Collingwood, *The New Leviathan: Or man, society, civilization and barbarism*, New York: Oxford University Press, 1993; and *An Essay on Philosophical Method*, New York: Oxford University Press, 2005.
10 For example Bandyopadhyay, Sekhar (ed.), *India in New Zealand: Local identities, global relations*, Dunedin: Otago University Press, 2010. By comparison, in the US multiculturalism was given impetus by the civil rights and women's movements. These social movements reverberated into the academy where the canon came under question: e.g., what is a classic of the country's literature, and why? What is more, the answers to such questions were increasingly sought in European intellectual currents, especially French currents of semiotic, post-structuralist and postcolonial thought and, more recently, in debates about sovereignty and political theology.
11 Less attention is given – in this chapter and throughout the volume – to tauiwi, those persons and things that are non-Māori but are not necessarily only Pākehā. For example, the Treaty was certainly intended as a template for Māori–Pākehā relations. But how would or should it apply to groups that are neither indigenous nor Pākehā? Tauiwi could be an important notion when considering the possibilities of multiculturalism in New Zealand.
12 The ideas of *jus solis* – membership established by being born in the country or 'of the land' – and *jus sanguinis* – membership by 'bloodline', are often taken for granted in debates about diversity. In this sense these ideas can be seen as part of the social imaginary that underpins discussions of multiculturalism in New Zealand. On social imaginaries see Charles Taylor, *Modern Social Imaginaries*, North Carolina: Duke University Press, 2004; and Amy Gutmann (ed.), *Multiculturalism*, Princeton, New Jersey: Princeton University Press, 1994.
13 Emphasis added.

14 Insofar as these concerns, debates and tensions have focused on the relation between the tangata whenua and Asian arrivals, I wonder if demands that Pākehā share more power might merit more attention. Non-Pākehā constituencies could be empowered not by taking it away from each other, but by claiming a share of Pākehā power. It may also be worth keeping in mind that both Asian and Māori include diverse groups – though that does not de-legitimise using these umbrella terms in a strategic way: Spivak's 'strategic essentialism' that Hilary Chung alludes to in her chapter.

15 Chung enhances the typology in noting: 'It might illuminate Lo and Gilbert's categories to construe them in terms of the multi-generational experience of migration and assimilation.'

16 For example, actors who are phenotypically of Asian origin may appear in the role of parents, with one daughter played by a person of African descent and her sibling from South America, but the whole family presented as 'white'. This illustration of blind casting is my own.

17 Jacqueline Lo and Helen Gilbert, 'Toward a topography of cross-cultural theatre praxis', *The Drama Review* 46.3, 2002, 31–53.

18 Whereas Chung calls for more intervention – albeit of a different sort than is currently in place – Johnson criticises intervention, suggesting both a general critique of what might be called 'interventionism' and of the specific interventions he discusses.

19 Given Chung's discussion of the Oryza Foundation and Johnson's of the Asia New Zealand Foundation, one can conclude that the role of foundations – in these cases apparently both privately and publically funded – is significant in the formation of Kiwi multiculturalism.

20 The converse is also likely to be found, namely, practices of multiculturalism may have an impact on the constitution of Kiwi Christianities. Particularly relevant for this volume is the implicit argument, here, that religion cannot be equated with culture, or vice versa. An even broader implication is that one arena of practice (religion) cannot be reduced to another (multiculturalism).

21 The full caption for the image reproduced in Dobson's chapter includes: 'Connecting to NZ: Despite experiencing verbal and physical harassment in their adopted city, *these members of WOWMA happily regard Hamilton as home.*' (Emphasis added.)

22 For an approach to the idea of 'everyday life' that engages issues of agency, see Gautam Ghosh, 'Outsiders at home? The South Asian diaspora in South Asia', in Diane Mines and Sarah Lamb (eds), *Everyday Life in South Asia*, Bloomington: Indiana University Press, 2002, 326–36.

23 In 2014 I asked a (white male) Copenhagen taxi-driver about reports of the rise of racism in Denmark. His reply was a rant about Muslims in the country. Race was seamlessly and unselfconsciously equated with religion – Islam in particular.

24 Melvin Westlake argues that the dissolution of the three worlds paradigm (the first, second and third worlds) also undermined the ability of key countries to engage in concerted action. 'Third World', after the label was appropriated by the countries it

putatively classified, became a platform for shared interests in promoting alternative models for the flows of, especially, money and media. Westlake, Melvin, 'The Third World (1950–1990) RIP', *Marxism Today*, August 1991, 14–17. I would add that this dissolution, which began in 1989–90 with the end of the Cold War, was followed by the widespread implementation of market-friendly policies that generated assemblages of cultures and economies which came to be codified, in some quarters, under the rubric 'globalisation'.

25 The authors emphasise that the owners of businesses in an ethnic precinct need not be of the same minority – but the definition suggests that the other owners must be from other minority groups.

26 The latter is a clever pun on Vertovec's idea of 'superdiversity' transposed, here, to a particularly urban setting. It is also a reference to how, in 2010, the Auckland City Council was re-organised to combine a number of subsidiary councils to create a so-called 'super-city'.

27 It would be important to explore what sorts of intangible social and cultural capital immigrants are able to convert in the context of the precinct, which they would not be able to do in other contexts, and the consequences of these processes – which may not always be salutary and empowering. I suspect this is part of the process of how ethnic precincts come to be established in the first instance.

28 There is such a preponderance of evidence that immigrants improve 'host' economies one wonders why such erroneous beliefs are so pervasive and persistent.

29 It is unlikely that Johnson would describe the festivals as superficial. For him they are significant, albeit in both negative and positive ways.

30 One caveat: in relation to a number of violent events – including the 2011 massacre in Norway by Anders Breivik of 78 people, mostly teenagers – the authors state that '[m]any critics [of multiculturalism] question whether these events are in part the result of too much tolerance of cultural diversity'. Whoever these critics may be, it must be clear that this editor does not believe that atrocities are caused by too much tolerance. That Breivik claimed he was at war against multiculturalism, and in defence of Europe, is another matter.

31 Tim Ingold: www.allegralaboratory.net/interview-tim-ingold-on-the-future-of-academic-publishing/

32 On the migrant metropolis see Nicholas de Genova: www.podcasts.ox.ac.uk/citizenship-and-migrant-metropolis-life-within-and-against-spaces-law

33 Collingwood 1993, 1994; Giorgio Agamben, *State of Exception*, Chicago: University of Chicago Press, 2005.

34 Habermas, Jürgen, 'Modernity: An unfinished project', in M.P. d'Entreves and Seyla Benhabib (eds), *Habermas and the Unfinished Project of Modernity: Critical essays on the philosophical discourse of modernity*, Boston: MIT Press, 1997; Fukuyama, Francis, *The End of History and the Last Man*, Free Press, 2006. See also Malkki, Liisa, 'Things to come: Internationalism and global solidarities in the late 1990s: A response to Jürgen Habermas', *Public Culture*, vol. 10, 2, 1998, 431–42.

35 Taylor, 2004 and 1994. See also Collingwood, 1994 and 2002. In most liberal nationalisms the imaginary includes the presuppositions 'social contract' and

'sacrifice'. How these ideas coincide or contend with each other as well as the idea of a multicultural nation could be explored, though lack of space will not allow for it here. The classical paradigm of contract, for example, does not include a sense of 'belonging', which is a key theme in the chapters. The idea of 'sacrifice' resonates more easily with the ideology of 'belonging'.
36 Emphases added. Circulated on the list-serve of New Zealand Asian Studies Association, 12 September 2013.
37 It is difficult to think about human relations without invoking metaphors of material relations – and vice versa.
38 The utterance of 'we', its very necessity, also suggests a collectivity that is thus always in the making.
39 www.waitangi.com/politics/sign.html
40 I thank Greg Dawes for bringing these statements regarding the Treaty to my attention.
41 I have attempted this in Ghosh, 'The (un)braiding of time in the 1947 partition of British India', in Anthony Grafton and Marc Rodriquez (eds), *Migration in History*, University of Rochester Press on behalf of the Davis Center of Princeton University, 2007.
42 Malkki, Liisa, *Purity and Exile: Violence, memory, and national cosmology among Hutu refugees in Tanzania*, Chicago: University of Chicago Press, 1995a; and 'Refugees and exile: From "refugee studies" to the national order of things', *Annual Review of Anthropology* 24, 1995b.
43 A non-essentialising approach to identity is as follows: if, when something is praised, you feel proud, it is part of your identity. Likewise, if something is denigrated and you feel embarrassed or angry, it is part of your identity. This would be an 'occasional' approach to identity: identity would be evinced in those occasions, or events, where the processes described above occur; one could utilise 'identity' as an analytical category without essentialising it.
44 In understanding the nation, I incline towards an unwise admixture of Benedict Anderson on seriality (*Imagined Communities: Reflections on the origin and spread of nationalism*, London: Verso, 1991), John Kelly and Martha Kaplan on glory and destiny (*Represented Communities: Fiji and world decolonization*, Chicago: University of Chicago Press, 2001) and Anthony Giddens on agency and the significance of a polity's 'external' relations (*The Nation-State and Violence: Volume two of a contemporary critique of historical materialism*, The University of California Press, 1986). Each of these accounts raises questions of whether nationalism and multiculturalism emerge as an internal or external dynamic of certain polities. One could argue that multiculturalism emerges from an internal dialectical/dialogic process that occurs within nationalism; nationalism is, after all, also a discourse of diversity where different nation-states represent different peoples. Alternatively, multiculturalism can be a sort of external imposition on nations provoked, for example, by broader dynamics of immigration or globalisation. A different approach is in Ernesto Laclau's elaboration of Derrida's 'constitutive outside'. See Laclau, *New Reflections on the Revolution of Our Time*, London: Verso, 1990 and *On*

Populist Reason, London: Verso, 2007, 17–26.

45 Appadurai identifies four other 'scapes' (mediascapes, technoscapes, financescapes and ideoscapes) though it is the ethnoscape idea that has gained the most currency – why so is worth an investigation in itself. See Appadurai, *Modernity at large: Cultural dimensions of globalization*, Minneapolis: University of Minnesota Press, 1996.

46 Here I proffer a Collingwoodian reading of Appadurai. See Collingwood 1993 and 2005.

47 Also relevant is Michel Foucault's discussion of surveillance in *Discipline and Punish: The birth of the prison*, translated by Alan Sheridan, New York: Vintage, 1995.

48 Insofar as Kiwi multiculturalism has been described as 'pragmatic' it is interesting to note that pragmatism has been associated with the sensation of touch more than that of vision. See Posner, Richard A., 'What has pragmatism to offer law?', 63 *Southern California Law Review* 1653 (1990), available at www.Chicago Unbound.

Bibliography

Agamben, Giorgio, *State of Exception*, translated by Kevin Attell, Chicago: University of Chicago Press, 2005.

Anderson, Benedict, *Imagined Communities: Reflections on the origin and spread of Nationalism*, London: Verso, 1991.

Anderson, Benedict, *The Spectre of Comparisons: Nationalism, Southeast Asia, and the world*, New York: Verso, 1998.

Appadurai, Arjun, *Modernity at Large: Cultural dimensions of globalization*, Minneapolis: University of Minnesota Press, 1996.

Bakhtin, Mikhail Mikhaïlovich, *The Dialogic Imagination: Four essays*, Austin: University of Texas Press, 1982.

Bandyopadhyay, Sekhar (ed.), *India in New Zealand: Local identities, global relations*, Dunedin: Otago University Press, 2010.

Borneman, John, 'Race, ethnicity, species, breed: Totemism and horse breed classification in America', *Comparative Studies in Society and History* 30 (1), 1988, 25–51.

Borneman, John, 'Postscript: Reflections on totemism tomorrow: Horse breeds and breeding in the United States and France', in Aram Yengoyan (ed.), *Modes of Comparison: Theory and practice*, Ann Arbor: University of Michigan Press, 2008, 351–65.

Collingwood, Robin George, *The New Leviathan: Or man, society, civilization and barbarism*, New York: Oxford University Press, 1993.

Collingwood, R.G., *The Idea of History*, New York: Oxford University Press, 1994.

Collingwood, R.G., *An Essay on Metaphysics* (revised edition), Oxford: Clarendon Press, 2002.

Collingwood, R.G., *An Essay on Philosophical Method*, New York: Oxford University Press, 2005.

Comaroff, John L. and Jean Comaroff, *Ethnicity Inc.*, Chicago: University of Chicago Press, 2009.
De Genova, Nicholas: www.podcasts.ox.ac.uk/citizenship-and-migrant-metropolis-life-within-and-against-spaces-law
Foucault, Michel, *Discipline and Punish: The birth of the prison*, translated by Alan Sheridan, New York: Vintage, 1995.
Fukuyama, Francis, *The End of History and the Last Man*, New York: Free Press, 2006.
Ghosh, Gautam (ed.), 'Civilization, vulnerability and translation: Reflections in the aftermath of September 11', *Anthropological Quarterly* 75, 1, Winter 2001, 92–203.
Ghosh, Gautam, 'Outsiders at home? The South Asian diaspora in South Asia', in Diane Mines and Sarah Lamb (eds), *Everyday Life in South Asia*, Bloomington: Indiana University Press, 2002, 326–36.
Ghosh, Gautam, 'The (un)braiding of time in the 1947 partition of British India', in Anthony Grafton and Marc Rodriquez (eds), *Migration in History*, New York: University of Rochester Press on behalf of the Davis Center of Princeton University, 2007.
Giddens, Anthony, *The Nation-State and Violence: Volume two of a contemporary critique of historical materialism*, Oakland: University of California Press, 1986.
Gutmann, Amy (ed.), *Multiculturalism*, Princeton, New Jersey: Princeton University Press, 1994.
Habermas, Jürgen, 'Modernity: An unfinished project', in M. Passerin d'Entrèves and Seyla Benhabib (eds), *Habermas and the Unfinished Project of Modernity: Critical essays on the philosophical discourse of modernity*, Boston: MIT Press, 1997.
Kelly, John D. and Martha Kaplan, *Represented Communities: Fiji and world decolonization*, Chicago: University of Chicago Press, 2001.
Laclau, Ernesto, *New Reflections on the Revolution of Our Time*, London: Verso, 1990.
Laclau, Ernesto, *On Populist Reason*, London: Verso, 2007.
Lo, Jacqueline and Gilbert, Helen, 'Toward a topography of cross-cultural theatre praxis', *The Drama Review* 46.3, 2002, 31–53.
Malkki, Liisa, *Purity and Exile: Violence, memory, and national cosmology among Hutu refugees in Tanzania*, Chicago: University of Chicago Press, 1995a.
Malkki, Liisa, 'Refugees and exile: From "refugee studies" to the national order of things', *Annual Review of Anthropology* 24, 1995b.
Malkki, Liisa, 'Things to come: Internationalism and global solidarities in the late 1990s: A response to Jürgen Habermas', *Public Culture*, vol. 10, no. 2, 1998, 431–42.
Miles, Robert, *Conceptual Inflation*, London: Routledge, 1989.
Mines, Diane and Sarah Lamb (eds), *Everyday Life in South Asia*, Bloomington: Indiana University Press, 2002.
Passerin d'Entrèves, Maurizio and Seyla Benhabib (eds), *Habermas and the Unfinished Project of Modernity: Critical essays on the philosophical discourse of modernity*, Boston: MIT Press, 1997.
Posner, Richard A., 'What has pragmatism to offer law?', 63 *Southern California Law Review* 1653 (1990), available at www.Chicago Unbound.
Taylor, Charles, *Multiculturalism*, Princeton, New Jersey: Princeton University Press, 1994.

Taylor, Charles, *Modern Social Imaginaries*, North Carolina: Duke University Press, 2004.
Vertovec, Steven and Susanne Wesselsdorf (eds), *The Multiculturalism Backlash: European discourses, policies and practices*, London, New York: Routledge, 2010.
Westlake, Melvin, 'The Third World (1950–1990) RIP', *Marxism Today*, August 1991, 14–17.

Part I: Biculturalism and Multiculturalism

2. 'I MADE A SPACE FOR YOU'[1]
Renegotiating national identity and citizenship in contemporary Aotearoa New Zealand

PAUL SPOONLEY

The project of 'imagining the nation' and the hyphenation of the state remains incomplete[2] in the territory that is labelled New Zealand. This is because such projects are inevitably complex and contested, and because of the particularities of settler colonialism. If the nation is defined as 'territorialized cultural belonging while the state formalises and controls legal membership',[3] then elements of national identity can be said to have emerged in New Zealand by the early and mid-twentieth century; but even at this point, there were other aspects that challenged this association between territory and belonging. Developments since the 1970s have made the tenuous assumption – that the state represents the interests and activities of a relatively homogenous nation – even more contested.

As Roche[4] has commented, nationhood and citizenship are based on myths which 'oversimplified the complex roots and forms of social membership and identity'. The presence of a demographically and politically significant indigenous population has, historically, created an interesting challenge for conceptions of nationhood. Policies and notions which assumed a national unity as the basis of an entity called 'New Zealand' came under more sustained challenge by the 1970s. The presence of an assertive Māori politics which posits its own Māori sovereignty (tino rangatiratanga) confronted any notion that an undifferentiated nation existed. The issues raised by the historical and contemporary experiences of Māori provided a direct challenge to traditional conceptions of a unitary citizenship. Communal rights, defined by historical agreements and yet denied by historical process, have become the basis for new (often partial) settlements in the post-welfare state. While the state's functions and citizenship rights have been renegotiated, there are other substantial pressures. Castles (1996) identifies three issues: the first is that 'globalisation breaks the territorial principle, the nexus between power and place' (Castles, 1996:3; see also

Morris, 1997); the second is the undermining of the ideology of the nation-state being based on 'relatively autonomous national cultures'; and the third is the impact of immigration (Castles, 1996:4). In New Zealand, the internal challenge of a rejuvenated Māori politics has been underscored by new immigration flows – first from elsewhere in the Pacific and then from Asia – and more extensive trans-border activities and alliances.

If biculturalism reflects the recognition of indigenous rights, there is still little to indicate what adjustments – if any – will be made to recognise multicultural diversity and citizenship. These developments highlight the unfinished business of colonisation and migration. The issues are becoming clearer, but the resolution of them is not. If the issues of the citizenship rights deriving from the Treaty of Waitangi are being addressed – at least to a degree – they do not presuppose the national or local structures that may be required to mediate and govern in the future, especially given the superdiversity (Vertovec, 2007) that immigration has produced. This raises questions of how new notions of citizenship are to be debated and agreed upon in a postcolonial Aotearoa. This essay is about what Amin (2013, 2–3) refers to as the use of the 'armoury of the state' to mediate strangeness/strangers/otherness in the construction of public spaces and cultures. It does not explore the diverse realities and identities that emerge from the 'everyday negotiations of, and attachments with, spaces, objects, cultural domains, projects and interests shared with others …' (Amin, 2013, 3).

Constructing a nation: Understanding nationality

It is important to problematise notions such as 'nation', 'nationality' and 'nationhood', as well as the hyphenating of a nation with a state (see Appadurai, 1997). The construction of nations and the assumptions about the coincidence of states with nationality have had a problematic history, especially in those cases where an exclusive nationalism has produced pogroms and genocide as a way of 'purifying' a nation. New Zealand provides a variant on this theme, as European settlers sought to impose a particular set of institutions, values and practices on a colonised people (cf. Belich, 1996). Those that contributed to such narrow and exploitative narratives about the 'civilising' of Aotearoa, including academic interpretations, have come under scrutiny through the twentieth century as a more critical reading of colonisation and its impacts has developed.

In the latest edition of *The New Oxford History of New Zealand*, there is a questioning of histories that articulate a 'colony-to-nation' narrative (Byrnes, 2009, 7). Peter Gibbons is credited (see the *New Zealand Journal of History*, 45(1), 2011) with an important role in querying the colonial project of constructing a nation in the Antipodes:

> *From a local perspective ... the idea of the nation with regard to New Zealand history is problematic. Peter Gibbons argues that the construction by Pākehā[5] of a New Zealand national identity was not a sign that the colonisation phase of history had ended in some way but was instead an important part of the ongoing (and still incomplete) process of colonisation. He suggests that we interrogate the seemingly innocent terms 'New Zealand' and 'New Zealand national identity'... But perhaps the greatest weakness of 'the nation' is that it assumes a singular shared identity within it and denies difference within its borders* (Byrnes, 2011, 4).

Byrnes (2011:4–5) goes on to note that '... the nation may be defined as an historical category and a matrix through which to view past actions, decisions and events; at worst, it is seen to be complicit in continuing, rather than addressing, the excesses of the colonial project.'

Postcolonialism is a broad approach that encompasses those who seek to critically engage with the political processes of nation-building that were at the core of the settlement of Aotearoa.[6] It operates as an alternative to those who continue to deploy notions such as 'nation' and 'nationalism' uncritically. Such contra-positions encompass many who are politically engaged in emancipatory projects such as anti-racism, feminism or Māori sovereignty, as well as the critiques offered by disciplines such as literary criticism, anthropology, sociology and history[7]. As Byrnes[8] notes, '... postcolonial interventions aim to destabilize, deconstruct and even undermine this [colonial] project'.[9] It is important to see such endeavours as including a range of forms of engagement and experience, with different voices and orientations. This chapter seeks to reflect these post-colonial ambitions. The role of colonial settlement policies will be briefly discussed.

The role of Māori resistance and struggle provides an important contribution to the de-hyphenating of the nation and the state. However, relatively little attention has been paid to tensions that emerged in the late twentieth century, as new immigration policies have provided complicating and problematic layers to questions of identity and place in twenty-first century New Zealand. Globalisation, transnationalism, superdiversity and multiple identities – within and between minority and majority ethnic communities – have produced a complicated political terrain of identity. Moreover, New Zealand, somewhat reluctantly and without a lot of political or policy understanding of exactly what was being unleashed,[10] has become a particularly interesting site in terms of identity politics and recognition. It is that new stage and its complicating characteristics that provide the endpoint of this chapter – but hardly the endpoint of a New Zealand journey.

New Zealand exceptionalism? Settlement politics and policy

The colonial project of settling Aotearoa and constructing New Zealand echoed the 'framing assumptions of the British state' that privileged 'whiteness' and equated 'Christian' with 'civilised'.[11] Compared to the mix of arrivals in the other classic immigrant-receiving societies of the period, such as the US, Canada and Australia, the Eurocentric approach to the 'civilising' of New Zealand was the almost exclusive focus of British (and to a lesser extent Irish) settlement, and the creation of a 'Britain in the south seas'. As Pool points out,[12] this resulted in extremely high levels of homogeneity in terms of the origin, ethnicity, religion and occupation of those arriving. This was further reinforced by marriage patterns, the maintenance of customs, standardised education, internal mobility and shared pro-British jingoism.[13] In the European colonisation projects of the eighteenth and nineteenth centuries, such hyper-homogeneity of immigrant flows (98 per cent were from the UK and Ireland for much of this history) was unusual, as were some of the resulting consequences for the construction of community (including nationality), institutions and values.

The historical settlement of New Zealand reflects deliberate patterns of immigrant recruitment and exclusion. The first can be seen in the various phases: the significance of the New Zealand Company in the 1840–52 period (14,000 of the 18,000 settlers who arrived in this period were recruited by the New Zealand Company); and the next stage of recruitment, in which 82 per cent of arrivals in Wellington, Whanganui, Nelson and New Plymouth came from England and another 15 per cent from Scotland.[14]

The significant increase in the number of settlers arriving from 1853 reflected the discovery of gold, the expropriation of land from Māori, and the development of infrastructure and settlements. The Irish potato famine, the drop in cattle prices in Scotland (from 1848), growing rural unemployment, the contraction of opportunities in rural areas of Britain and the hardship of rapid industrialisation and urbanisation, all constituted significant push factors. The availability of land and the offer of free passage to New Zealand saw a steady flow of predominantly British immigrant arrivals through the nineteenth century. Later, as Belich observes,[15] the womb became more important than the ship in providing residents. This influx, combined with population growth from births in New Zealand, was to continue unabated through the first half of the twentieth century, a period also punctuated by wars and depression:

> *During the inter-war years, so-called 'British stock' was considered the unquestioned 'race' with which to populate the dominions and create a vaster and more successful British Empire. A social imperialist doctrine of the time saw the dominions as an opportunity for economic development and a means of renewal for a 'British race' polluted by industrial urbanism.*[16]

From 1840 until after World War II, these imperial ambitions and the almost total dominance of immigrants from the UK were reinforced by the racialisation of particular 'others'. Following the discovery of gold, the arrival of Chinese sojourners provided the starting point for a legislative framework that sought to racialise the 'yellow peril'[17] and exclude them as a threat to the 'purity' of the colony of New Zealand. Murphy[18] argues that between 1890 and 1907, notions of 'racial purity' grew in importance; the perception of Asians (mostly Chinese, but increasingly extended to Indian arrivals) as a 'particularly dangerous moral and physical threat to New Zealand' became established. '[C]oncepts of whiteness and empire were … used to bind a disparate community and create a national identity for New Zealand [that] was to be white, British and imperial.'[19] This extended to liberal and left-wing politicians such a William Pember Reeves.[20] From the early legislation in 1879 through to the Immigration Restriction Amendment Act 1920, populist racial sentiments became embedded in 33 Acts that sought to restrict or exclude specific immigrants, dictated the conditions under which they might live and work in New Zealand, and, until 1951, ensured that they did not become citizens. The homogeneity of immigrant arrivals was reinforced by an elaborate and widely supported exclusionary framework that evoked and embedded explicit beliefs about 'race' and 'nation'. This project and the assumptions underpinning it were to be challenged and largely discarded in the second half of the twentieth century.

Destabilising homogeneity, de-hyphenating the nation-state

Polynesian migration (both internally and from elsewhere in the Pacific) in the decades after World War II dramatically altered the character of the nation-building project. The first element was provided by the rural–urban migration of Māori in a very significant displacement of the spatial and cultural centres of Māori existence. Between 1945 and the 1970s, the bulk of Māori moved from their traditional rohe (the territory or boundaries of tribal/iwi groups) to the main urban centres of New Zealand. This was partly as a result of push factors – the changing nature of primary production, the liberating experiences of being involved in the war effort, and the sense that these communities could no longer provide the economic and social foundations for a Māori future – and the pull of cities and the employment they offered as a period of industrial and urban expansion took place. The nature of this displacement and the consequences for tikanga (customs and protocol) and te reo Māori (Māori language) have been widely rehearsed (see Walker, 1990). It effectively marks a turning point in terms of the colonial marginalisation of Māori in several senses: it highlighted the extent and impacts of the cultural and economic losses resulting from colonisation; and it encouraged a new set of resistance or anti-colonial politics. It meant that Māori went from the periphery of New Zealand – culturally, economically and geographically – to the centre, if not in terms of full participation and acceptance, at least in terms of residence and a new involvement in national institutions and political debates.

By the 1970s, Māori resistance politics were confronting the 'Britishness' of colonialism and the hegemonic disregard for the rights and resources of Māori. The adoption of the decolonisation politics of writers such as Franz Fanon, by groups such as Ngā Tamatoa at the University of Auckland, combined with the protest strategies of the US civil rights movement, saw the development of new conceptions of what it meant to be tangata whenua (see also Greenland, 1984; Harris, 2004). This produced new challenges to the state and to the complacency of Pākehā (and some Māori) New

Zealanders, and new proposals for the notion of 'national identity'. A key moment came when Donna Awatere (1984) referred to 'Māori sovereignty'. The possibility that there might be a sovereignty other than that associated with the state and a 'homogeneous' nation, and that Māori might be able to claim that sovereignty, were revolutionary ideas that challenged even liberal and left-wing Pākehā, and the institutions and ethos of a modern, liberal state.

The 1980s proved to be the important transition decade in terms of the renegotiation of tangata whenua status and therefore the nature of rights and citizenship in New Zealand. A new understanding of what constituted the nation-state emerged, especially as the constitution of the 'nation' was problematised while the notion of citizenship was recalibrated – although not without opposition from those who sought to retain a relatively narrow and exclusionary view. The Treaty of Waitangi was reinscribed into quasi-constitutional and legislative statements, and a new language – which included terms such as 'Treaty partners' and 'Treaty obligations' – appeared. For some, this constituted a rather problematic contribution to postcolonialism:

> ... *in terms of understanding 'the nation', the Treaty might be seen as a sort of a limiting instrument, and a tool of control and submission rather than promising possibilities* (Byrnes, 2009:127).

In some instances this might have been true, especially as certain iwi (tribes) and a number of Māori were co-opted as part of the state or corporate capitalism. But this rather denies the substantive changes that have occurred as adjustments were made, specifically in relation to acknowledging the impacts of colonialism on Māori (underpinned by a revisionist history), the substantial (but still inadequate) reparations as resources and control have been shifted from the state to iwi, and the implications that Māori-specific rights have had on conceptions of the 'nation' or contemporary citizenship. There was an enhanced sense of 'cultural autonomy of a non-territorial kind' as a form of accommodation to Māori as a 'national minority' (Bauböck, 2000:16), especially compared to colonial New Zealand. A new form of differentiation and recognition had emerged, thus fragmenting the unitary state-based citizenship which had putatively operated previously (Bauböck, 2000:17).

New immigrants, a new multiculturalism

The presumed homogeneity of settler colonialism was further disrupted by immigration in two distinct periods, and Labour governments played a key role in both. The first was the labour migration from the Polynesian Pacific from the 1960s. This was employer-driven and, for the first decade, the legality of many of the immigrants and their status in New Zealand was overlooked as employers' need for a workforce held sway. But this was to change with the Labour government of 1972–75. At the time when Prime Minister Norman Kirk, in an inspiring Waitangi Day speech, was beginning to suggest that New Zealand had started on a new and exciting journey of national understanding, the Labour government was responding to a reversal in New Zealand's economic fortunes. Part of that response was the racialisation of these new New Zealand residents from elsewhere in the Pacific. Kirk's speech largely focused on the significance of the Treaty of Waitangi and the need to reconsider the status of tangata whenua in Aotearoa, to question the links with a colonial 'homeland', and to more consciously reflect the country's South Pacific location. But the economic difficulties apparent in 1973 – the oil shock, a growing disparity in the balance of payments and growing unemployment – prompted a state-sponsored racism in the form of a moral panic about 'overstayers'. The demonising of Pacific immigrants – represented as a threat to the security of 'New Zealanders' in terms of employment, public safety and their association with deteriorating areas of major cities – was underpinned by the actions of various government departments, notably the police and the Immigration Department. The contradictions of the reversal – the involvement of the state in the racialisation of 'Pacific Islanders' once employer demand had diminished; the involvement of a left-of-centre government in initiating this racialisation; the fact that many of the arrivals were New Zealand citizens; the discrimination towards near neighbours and the privileging of colonial connections – were apparent to a relatively small group of Māori and Pākehā activists.

This racialisation had populist support. The subsequent Muldoon-led government continued the demonisation, and the government's reaction to the Privy Council decision concerning Falemai Lesa (the case involved the rights to residency in New Zealand for overstayers) and the rights of Samoans to New Zealand citizenship, had a negative impact on relations with key Pacific countries for most of the next decade (Macdonald, 1986). More positive assessments of the arrival and contribution of Pacific peoples[21] would not emerge until the 1990s, by which time the majority of Pacific peoples in Aotearoa were New Zealand-born, their communities had established institutions and practices in New Zealand, and their contribution to areas of public life was more visible.

The arrival from the 1960s of these immigrants from elsewhere in the Pacific added another element to the discourse of de-hyphenating of the nation-state, underscoring the growing importance of issues concerning (in this case) minority ethnicity for a modern, liberal state. The presence of Pacific peoples reinforced whanaungatanga connections (connections through ancestry) between Māori and other Polynesian communities, especially given their proximity in residential areas and institutions such as schools. As tangata whenua, Māori were able to gain the attention of the state in a way that these communities could not, but the latter were also part of New Zealand's colonial control of the Pacific – they, too, were victims of European/New Zealand colonisation. The state's racialisation of them soon attracted Māori opposition and reinforced alliances. Moreover, Pacific peoples were economically marginalised. This cultural and economic alienation of Pacific communities became a growing political concern which the state and governments were increasingly forced to recognise – and all the more so, given that the neo-liberal reforms of the 1980s contributed to the deindustrialisation of New Zealand and the disappearance of the Fordist jobs that were the reason for the migration of Pacific communities in the first place.

As immigrants from the Pacific were replaced by the New Zealand-born, especially after 1990, issues of the maintenance of language and culture became increasingly important. Kōhanga reo (Māori language preschools) were now paralleled by a'oga amata (Samoan early childhood education). But if these issues were more obvious, the state and politicians did not feel especially compelled to act by way of response, particularly given that public opinion polling continued (and indeed continues) to show that many other New Zealanders did not see Pacific peoples as desirable immigrants,[22] and the racialisation of them continued to inflect public discourse. While they were important in shifting the cultural diversity of New Zealand and reinforcing the country's connection with the rest of the South Pacific, there were few political concessions and only limited resourcing of matters of concern. And although they were a distinctive and important part of the new multiculturalism of the country, this did not result in any significant shifts towards a substantive multiculturalism in state policies and activities.

The second phase of this new cultural diversity was a product of the neo-liberalism of the fourth Labour government (1984–89). A selective and highly discriminatory immigration policy did not make sense for a government intent on opening up New Zealand to international influences and ownership, and seeking to extend its reach into growing Pacific rim economies. A review in 1986 followed by policy and legislative change in 1987 radically changed New Zealand's immigration framework.[23] The 'points system', implemented over the next decade, gave permanent residence to 'economic migrants', those who would bring capital and 'entrepreneurialism' to New Zealand or contribute valuable skills.

The most visible and culturally or linguistically different immigrants came from Asia, although this rather oversimplifies the nature of immigration flows after 1990. While arrivals from Asia now joined those from Britain as the most important sources of immigrants, another factor was the growing diversity of immigrant flows. There were a large number of smaller groups arriving from many parts of the world including Africa, the Middle East, North and South America and Europe. Immigration policy was an important dimension of contemporary neo-liberalism.[24] Table 1 indicates the extent of the shift from what Bedford[25] refers to as 'traditional' to 'non-traditional' immigrants.

Table 1: Traditional and non-traditional immigration flows to New Zealand, 1982–86 and 1997–2001

Permanent and long-term immigrants (excluding returning NZers) Bedford, 2004		
	1982–86 %	1997–2001 %
Traditional source countries	83.2	41.5
Non-traditional source countries (Asia)	16.2	58.5
Total Number (Net Migration)	91,723 (+2,960)	215,020 (+32,860)

Source: Bedford[26] (2004)

Perhaps it was inevitable that the moral panic directed at Pacific peoples in the 1970s would be repeated with the significant increase in immigration from Asia in the 1990s. Barely had these new immigrants arrived (in quite modest numbers it should be noted) when a second period of intense racialisation took place, directed at Asians. Elements were both the same as and different to the first moral panic 20 years earlier. Particular immigrants were demonised and seen as a threat to New Zealand and 'New Zealanders'. These new arrivals were accused, most famously by Winston Peters (leader of the conservative New Zealand First party), of diluting the British heritage of 'New Zealanders' and undermining core institutions. But these immigrants were different: they were skilled and relatively wealthy, and the negative characterisations of them focused on their purchase of expensive real estate in Auckland's eastern suburbs, the nature of their driving (in expensive cars), and their presence in elite state schools.[27]

The drop in arrivals from Asia in the late 1990s (due to several factors, including an economic crisis in Asia), and the growing realisation that such immigrants were economically significant to New Zealand, prompted a public re-evaluation of immigration in general, and of Asian immigrants in particular. Spoonley and Butcher[28] have identified media coverage as both influential in and representative of the nature of this change; after 2000, more positive and nuanced discussion characterised the importance of Asian migration to New Zealand, and various media presented a more obvious critique of anti-immigrant sentiments and politics. There were important exceptions, such as Coddington's 2006 article in *North and South* entitled 'Asian angst', and there are examples of vigorous and often extreme rejections of diversity and indigenous/minority ethnic rights on various blog sites.[29] But there was also growing acceptance, reflected in public opinion polling, that Asian immigration was important to New Zealand in various ways. Some indication of the public's ideas of positive outcomes is provided in Table 2; however, a number of concerns lingered, some of which are apparent in Table 3. There is also the issue of Māori concerns, which is discussed further below. What these and other polls demonstrate is that public attitudes towards Asian immigrants were highly negative at the height of the moral panic (essentially 1993–96) but, after a short lull, began to improve fairly rapidly after 2000.[30] This is in contrast to public opinion polling concerning Pacific peoples, which is characterised by ongoing negative attitudes.

Table 2: New settler attitudes survey 2003–06: Positives

Positives	Agreement	
	2003 %	2006 %
Immigrants make New Zealanders more open to new ideas and cultures	59.8	71.3
Improved standard of food and cuisine	73.7	74.6
Attracting new immigrants is vital to New Zealand economically	51.0	47.5
Immigrants provide skills that are in short supply	39.0	45.8

Source: Spoonley and Gendall, 2010

Table 3: New settler attitudes survey 2003–06: Concerns

Concerns/Negatives	Agreement	
	2003 %	2006 %
Many immigrants stick to their own and do not mix	76.7	75.4
Level of racist comment (often, very often)[31]	41.0	46.5
There should be more consultation with the general public about New Zealand's immigration policy	78.5	77.7

Source: Spoonley and Gendall, 2010

Colonial immigration patterns were disrupted in the late twentieth century first by arrivals from the Pacific, followed by much more diverse immigration flows, especially those involving Asians after 1990. These two stages of immigration change meant that New Zealand went from being a destination for one of the most homogeneous immigration flows of any settler society, to a recipient of one of the most diverse.[32] By the end of the first decade of the twenty-first century, in addition to a significant indigenous population, New Zealand had more immigrants (as a proportion of the resident population) than Canada, and was on a par with Australia.

Auckland, as the gateway city and major destination for immigrants, was now home to proportionately more immigrants than any Australian city and most US or Canadian cities, with the exception of Toronto and Vancouver.[33] Further complexity was added as the 1.5 generation (those born in another country but brought up in New Zealand) and the New Zealand-born began to explore new hybrid identities. (By 2013, 40 percent of Auckland's population had been born in another country – and the figure increased to 56 percent if the children of these were included). In a demographic sense, a new multiculturalism was now apparent. But this was yet to be reflected in policy. With one or two exceptions, New Zealand did not have anything approaching the multicultural policy frameworks of Canada or Australia (even though the latter's acceptance of cultural diversity began to change significantly under the John Howard government and has continued to be compromised since). When a more extensive 'rights' package was suggested for minority ethnic and immigrant groups, as part of the Office for Ethnic Affairs' 'Briefing to the incoming minister' (in early 2012) – specifically that 'civil, political, social and language rights of ethnic people' should be part of a New Zealand constitution – the reaction from both the minister, Judith Collins, and the media was immediate and dismissive.[34] Nevertheless, the presence of significant diversity has challenged the state in terms of what it might do by way of a political or policy response.

What would or should a locally relevant multiculturalism entail? Spoonley, Peace, Butcher and O'Neill[35] have suggested elsewhere (using a Canadian policy approach) that there are five core elements: belonging, participation, inclusion, recognition and legitimacy. These elements apply (in slightly different ways) to both immigrant and/or ethnic minorities and host communities. For the moment, New Zealand offers limited recognition of minority ethnic status, especially in relation to language maintenance policies, political participation and representation, and educational autonomy. But the more problematic issues relate to the recognition of minority ethnic rights alongside the rights of tangata whenua. As the next section indicates, there are tensions between what a local version of ethnic rights recognition might look like alongside a prior investment in biculturalism. Unfortunately, the development of a new immigration policy framework from 1986, and its consequences, has not involved the Crown's Treaty partners: Māori. This has had several effects, including a dampening of public debate or policy development on what a locally and biculturally sensitive multiculturalism might look like.

Tangata whenua and the new multiculturalism

A major impediment to the development of a New Zealand-specific multiculturalism is the privileging of biculturalism in the cultural politics of New Zealand. For the moment, biculturalism represents one of the state's concessions towards Māori (in relation to the activities of state agencies in particular) and a limited recognition of the rights associated with indigeneity. The outcome is a disjuncture between this biculturalism and how the state might recognise the enhanced diversity that is a product of the immigration flows of recent decades. This has resulted in quite specific tensions, and a number of concerns articulated by Māori.

The first and early concern was that multiculturalism was a means of yet again marginalising Māori and biculturalism. This has been voiced by Ranginui Walker, the Māori educator and author of *Ka Whawhai Tonu Mātou: Struggle without end*.[36] In 1993, after the then Prime Minister Jim Bolger had announced that New Zealand was now an Asian nation, Walker wrote in his *Metro* column:

> *I was the one who started using the term biculturalism in the 1970s to counter the ideology of monoculturalism, and it's worked: biculturalism is now thoroughly accepted as part of the discourse around who we are as a nation. The opponents of the ideology of biculturalism were always saying 'we're multicultural'. And, of course, the counter to this is that the Chinese who come here have no right to have their language taught here in the country, because their language is safe in China – similarly with all other immigrants. The only place that the Māori language and culture belongs is right here, so serve the indigenous cultures first. Now, that doesn't mean to deny the fact, the reality, that we are increasingly becoming multicultural, but the base cultures are Māori and Pākehā, the two mutually define each other.*[37]

The second concern is one of economic competition, largely involving (but not confined to) the labour market. The composition of post-1986 immigration flows resulted in immigrant labour being an important source of skill supply. But the nature of immigrants' skills, and their relative wealth, were seen to reinforce the post-1980s economic marginalisation of Māori households, whānau (family) and individuals. By the turn of the century – and emphasised by ongoing reforms to universal welfare provisions – the disproportionate number of Māori (and Pacific peoples) in lower socioeconomic housing and schools, and in negative health, justice statistics and poverty (benefit dependent, low individual or household income) provided a sharp contrast with the status/location of most immigrants. By the time of the Global Financial Crisis (GFC) in 2008, however, both Māori and recent (less than 10 years since arrival) visible immigrants had significantly lower labour market participation rates and higher unemployment rates than the rest of the New Zealand population – which were then further impacted by a soft labour market during the GFC.

The third element concerns the state's recognition and resourcing of cultural and linguistic programmes that underpinned minority ethnic or indigenous rights. If language maintenance was an issue, then did the resourcing of community (i.e. non-English or non-Māori) languages mean that there would be less resourcing of te reo? For a number of reasons, the recognition of other language communities was regarded as a zero-sum exercise by some Māori, thereby curtailing discussion of what was possible and/or desirable. The concerns of Māori are reflected in public opinion polling (Table 4), with an obvious difference in attitudes apparent between Māori and non-Māori.

Table 4: New settler attitudes survey, 2006

	Māori	Non-Māori
Recent arrival of Asian immigrants is changing NZ in undesirable ways	75	50
Attracting new immigrants is vital if NZ is to prosper economically	34	52
Māori should be consulted about NZ's immigration policy	53	17

Source: Spoonley and Gendall, 2010

The role of Māori in relation to immigration policy, or to the subsequent consequences associated with enhanced diversity, remains unclear and a key issue in relation to progressing either policy or public debate about the 'new' multiculturalism. As Byrnes notes,[38] what might be termed the 'bicultural project' has resulted in an 'insistence on binary difference, contestability and, for some, exclusivity'.

A new nation-building project?

New Zealand provides a unique example in the way it has approached the issues of nationality and national identity. Some of this arises from the exclusivity of the colonial settler project of populating New Zealand as a British outpost, which set New Zealand apart from other settler societies such as the US, Canada or Australia. That strong umbilical cord meant that connections with the UK were significant until well into the late twentieth century. And while the notion of New Zealand citizenship first emerged in legislation in 1948, it was not until further legislation in 1977 that a full New Zealand citizenship (i.e. not tied to being a 'British subject') emerged. One decade later, New Zealand finally changed its immigration policy, an act that not only disconnected New Zealand from the UK but also changed the diversity of New Zealand in new and fundamental ways. In many respects, the country has moved from a colonial nation-building project to a new phase (postcolonial?) relatively slowly, especially compared with Canada and Australia, both of which recognised the cultural diversity associated with immigration in the 1970s and have since moved, in the last 10 to 15 years, to a new phase of nationality construction. Australia, especially, has developed a much 'harder' regime of immigration control and expectations[39] concerning immigrant loyalty, with the administration of refugees and asylum seekers a notable aspect of this harsher approach. This is associated with an assertive nationalism, growing expectations about Australia's role in the world and its association with the US in particular (which has also adopted a much harder line towards immigrant acceptance and loyalty).

New Zealand, in contrast, privileges biculturalism and an historic treaty with Māori, and has a much softer regime towards immigrant rights and settlement. The latter is represented in assumptions about immigrant loyalty: in the 1960s, immigrants were not expected to become citizens, and even when New Zealand opened up to more diverse immigration flows this assumption remained. As a result, permanent residence provides nearly all the benefits of full citizenship, unlike other countries. Furthermore, there are relaxed attitudes about dual loyalties: New Zealand has many more dual citizenship and visa waiver arrangements than most countries. There appears to be an acceptance, at least in New Zealand policy and practice, that immigrants will continue to maintain split or multiple loyalties, and that circular migration is a reality in modern migration systems. The state asserts relatively few of the compliance requirements demanded by most other immigrant-receiving countries, such as exclusive citizenship, the demonstration of knowledge (a civics test), loyalty (citizenship as a preferred and a desirable outcome of migration), and regular demonstrations of that loyalty (such as the oath of allegiance, a singular and publically obvious act of support for the flag or constitution). Sports teams are one exception, in that there are significant nationalistic sentiments surrounding a team like the All Blacks: although the composition of the team and its pre-match haka do recognise Māori and Pacific peoples, they do nothing to acknowledge more recent diversity.

This discussion has largely focused on the public domain and official policy in relation to the complexities of rights and civic recognition. Another layer of complexity is provided by the 'everyday negotiations of, and attachments with, spaces, objects, cultural domains, projects and interests'. [40] The reaction to recognising the status/rights of tangata whenua or the increased diversity of New Zealand communities provoke a range of reactions including extremely negative responses. There is still a constituency for the concept of a New Zealand based on a single loyalty and status, and a narrow, exclusive sense of nationality. New Zealand First, the Conservative Party and ACT have been torch-bearers for this notion, and have been joined by extreme anti-diversity organisations such as 1Law4All (the self-styled 'anti-racism party'). Forays into this territory in a 2004 speech by then leader of the National Party, Don Brash, reflect an ongoing discomfort with the concessions that have been made towards Māori, along with an insistence that there should be a singular 'New Zealandness' that does not allow space for indigenous or minority ethnic loyalties and belonging. There remains a dissonance between public policy and the political understanding and positioning of some in New Zealand.

The major concession by the state with regard to ethnic/immigrant rights has been to maintain a relatively 'soft' approach. The challenge remains: how to characterise this new stage of rights recognition and growing cultural diversity, especially given the contrast between indigenous rights recognition and the reluctance to formally recognise ethnic/immigrant rights?

Conclusion

New Zealand's approach to cultural diversity and a nation-building project could be viewed as immature: because it has been so dominated by historical connections with the UK, the country and its people have yet to work out what the main elements ought to be. A much more charitable view would be to suggest that New Zealand represents an approach to migration that reflects the realities of contemporary migration – especially of skilled, cosmopolitan migrants with split or multiple loyalties and activities – combined with the fact that migration is often circular, and the new geopolitical realities of globalisation.

Byrnes[41] is right to argue that the 'nation' is:

> ... [a] *discursive construct; a rhetorical artefact translated into actuality* **usually** *by the rites/rights of citizenship;* **frequently** *by geography (land/ whenua/place) and* **increasingly** *by legal and constitutional jurisdictions.*

It remains all of these things, but this chapter argues that both the nature of contemporary migration, combined with concessions by the New Zealand state towards Māori, have altered how the state is conceived and constructed in contemporary Aotearoa. As always, however, it is a journey, and while some elements have changed significantly since the 1980s – the recognition of tangata whenua, new immigration flows and diversity – other elements, such as the economic marginalisation of Māori in terms of the labour market, and banal and substantive racism, remain much as they always have. There are unresolved tensions and possibilities as a result of immigration and the clash between an evolving biculturalism and the recognition of ethnic minority rights. The resolution of this tension – if there is one – is far from clear.

Endnotes

1 This phrase comes from Dave Dobbyn's song 'Welcome Home' (Dobbyn, *Welcome Home*, CD, 2006). For me, it highlights the tension between a deliberate and participative democracy in which the state recognises minority rights – perhaps inadequately – and the fact that any such recognition reinforces the state's power to decide such matters.

2 cf. Nina Glick Schiller, 'The situation of transnational studies', *Identities*, 4(2), 1997, 155–66; Arjun Appadurai, *Modernity at Large: Cultural dimensions of globalisation*, Delhi: Oxford University Press, 1997.

3   Lydia Morris, 'Globalisation, migration and the nation-state: The path to a post-national Europe?', *British Journal of Sociology*, 48(2), 1997b, 194.
4   Maurice Roche, *Rethinking Citizenship: Welfare, ideology and change in modern society*, Cambridge: Polity Press, 1992, 228.
5   I am not sure why this does not extend to those Māori who were complicit in the act of colonisation.
6   As Byrnes and Coleborne (2011, 3) note: '... the nation has been a central metaphor in the "knowing" and writing of New Zealand history for well over a century'.
7   See Spoonley, 1995 and more recent contributions to the *New Zealand Journal of History*, 45(1), 2011.
8   Giselle Byrnes, 'National and migration: Postcolonial perspectives', *New Zealand Journal of History*, 43(2), 2009, 123.
9   See also Giselle Byrnes and Catharine Colebourne, 'Editorial introduction: The utility and futility of "The Nation" in histories of Aotearoa New Zealand', *New Zealand Journal of History*, 45(1), 2011, 1–14.
10 The hollowing-out of the state as part of neo-liberal reforms of the 1980s and 1990s coincided with greater recognition by the state of Māori claims and identities and the restructuring of immigration policy.
11 Ali Rattansi, 'The uses of racialization: The time-spaces and subject-object of the raced body', in K. Murji and J. Solomos (eds), *Racialization: Studies in theory and practice*, Oxford: Oxford University Press, 2005, 282.
12 Ian Pool, 'British immigration 1800–1945 and New Zealand's morphology', *New Zealand Sociology*, 25(1), 2010, 156.
13 Ibid.
14 Jock Phillips, *Te Ara Encyclopedia of New Zealand*, Auckland: David Bateman, 2006, 26.
15 James Belich, *Making Peoples: A history of New Zealand*, Auckland: Allen Lane, 1996, 278.
16 Katie Pickles, 'Colonisation, empire and gender', in G. Byrnes (ed.), *The New Oxford History of New Zealand*, Melbourne: Oxford University Press, 2009, 255.
17 Nigel Murphy, '"Maoriland" and "Yellow Peril": Discourses of Maori and Chinese in the formation of New Zealand's national identity', in M. Ip (ed.), *The Dragon and the Taniwha: Maori and Chinese in New Zealand*. Auckland: Auckland University Press, 2009.
18 Ibid., 74.
19 Ibid., 62.
20 See his comments about the preferability of baboons compared to Chinese immigrants: Spoonley and Bedford, 2012, 37.
21 The descriptor 'Pacific peoples' was widely adopted after the Pacific Vision conference, in part to avoid the derogatory connotations of the label 'Pacific Islander'.
22 They remain the least-favoured immigrant groups: Paul Spoonley and Philip Gendall, 'Welcome to our world: Attitudes to immigrants and immigration', in A.

Trlin, P. Spoonley and R. Bedford (eds), *New Zealand and International Migration: A digest and bibliography, No.5*, Auckland: Integration of Immigrants Programme, Massey University, 2010.
23 It had been changing but largely in relation to the rights of access of traditional British immigrants with only small concessions to long-standing Asian communities already in New Zealand.
24 These immigrants, as economic recruits, were – and are – constructed as '… competitive, responsibilised and entrepreneurial selves' (Lewis et al, 2009, 167) who act as agents in their own interests in a much more 'open' and internationalised New Zealand. This neo-liberalism is also apparent in the involvement of immigrants, especially those from Asia, in the small business sector, business start-ups and ethnic precincts.
25 See Paul Spoonley and Richard Bedford, *Welcome to Our World? Immigration and the remaking of New Zealand*, Auckland: Dunmore Publishing, 2012, ch. 3.
26 Richard Bedford, Charlotte Bedford, Elsie Ho and Jacqueline Lidgard, 'The globalisation of international migration in New Zealand: Contribution to a debate', *New Zealand Population Review* 28(1), 2002, 69–97.
27 See Pat Booth and Yvonne Martin's material in Auckland community newspapers in 1993.
28 Paul Spoonley and Andrew Butcher, 'Reporting superdiversity: The mass media and immigration in New Zealand', *Journal of Intercultural Studies* 30(4), 2009, 355–72.
29 Spoonley and Bedford, *Welcome to Our World?* See also www.johnansell.wordpress.com or www.kiwiblog.co.nz
30 It is a useful test to compare the results of public opinion polling in New Zealand with those in other countries. There is an obvious contrast with the results from various European countries. As Amin (2013, 2) comments, in relation to these European polls: 'In Europe, the xenophobic turn finds its defence in liberal beliefs, shrouded in Orwellian doublespeak of stranger intolerance to safeguard the tolerant society … permitting opinion makers, publics and politicians to speak without guilt or reservation of asylum seekers, the Roma, Muslims and disadvantaged migrants and minorities as an encumbrance, out of place, a threat to historic community…'
31 This concerns the level of racist comment that the respondents have encountered in New Zealand (i.e. how often have you heard racist comments?).
32 Superdiverse; see Steven Vertovec, 'Super-diversity and its implications', *Ethnic and Racial Studies*, 30(6), 2007, 1024–54.
33 Spoonley and Bedford, *Welcome to Our World?*
34 See 'Half-baked ideas not what public needs', Editorial, *Dominion Post*, 14 February 2012.
35 Paul Spoonley, Robin Peace, Andrew Butcher and Damian O'Neill, 'Social cohesion: A policy and indicator framework for assessing immigrant and host outcomes', *Social Policy Journal of New Zealand*, 24, 2005, 85–110.
36 Ranginui Walker, *Ka Whawahi Tonu Motou: Struggle without end*, Auckland: Penguin, 1990.

37 Quoted in Paul Spoonley and Andrew Butcher, 'Reporting superdiversity', 355–72.
38 Giselle Byrnes, 'National and migration: Postcolonial perspectives', *New Zealand Journal of History*, 43(2), 2009, 123–32.
39 Tavan Gwenda, 'Long, slow death of white Australia', *The Sydney Papers*, 17 (3/4), 2005.
40 Ash Amin, 'Land of strangers', *Identities: Global studies in culture and power*, 20(1), 2013, 1–8.
41 Byrnes, 'National and migration', 124.

Bibliography

Amin, Ash, 'Land of strangers', *Identities: Global studies in culture and power*, 20(1), 2013, 1–8.
Andrews, John, *No Other Home Than This. A history of European New Zealanders*, Nelson: Craig Potton Publishing, 2009.
Appadurai, Arjun, *Modernity at Large: Cultural dimensions of globalisation*, Delhi: Oxford University Press, 1997.
Awatere, Donna, *Maori Sovereignty*, Auckland: Broadsheet Publications, 1984.
Bauböck, Rainer, book review of D. Jacobson, *Rights Across Borders: Immigration and the decline of citizenship, ethnic and racial studies*, 20(4), 1997, 849–50.
Bedford, Richard, Bedford, Charlotte, Ho, Elsie and Lidgard, Jacqueline, 'The globalisation of international migration in New Zealand: Contribution to a debate', *New Zealand Population Review* 28(1), 2002, 69–97.
Belich, James, *Making Peoples: A history of New Zealand*, Auckland: Allen Lane, 1996.
Byrnes, Giselle, 'National and migration: Postcolonial perspectives', *New Zealand Journal of History*, 43(2), 2009, 123–32.
Byrnes, Giselle and Colebourne, Catharine, 'Editorial introduction: The utility and futility of "The Nation" in histories of Aotearoa New Zealand', *New Zealand Journal of History*, 45(1), 2011, 1–14.
Castles, Stephen, 'Immigration and multiculturalism in Australia', in K.J. Bade (ed.) *Migration – Ethnizitäl – Konflikt : Systemfragen und Fallstudien*, Osnabrück: Universitätsverlag Rasch, 1996, 251–71.
Greenland, H., 'Ethnicity as ideolog', in P. Spoonley, C. Macpherson, D. Pearson and C. Sedgwich (eds), *Tauiwi: Racism and ethnicity in New Zealand*, Palmerston North: Dunmore Press, 1984.
Gwenda, Tavan, 'Long, slow death of white Australia', *The Sydney Papers*, 17 (3/4), 2005.
Harris, Aroha, *Hikoi: Forty years of Maori protest*. Wellington: Huia Publishers, 2004.
Lewis, Nick, Lewis, Owen and Underhill-Sem, Yvonne, 'Filling hollowed out spaces with localised meanings, practices and hope: Progressive neo-liberal spaces in Te Rarawa', *Asia Pacific Viewpoint*, 50(2), 2009.
Macdonald, Barrie, 'The Lesa case and the Citizenship (Western Samoa) Act, 1982', in A.D. Trlin and P. Spoonley (eds), *New Zealand and International Migration: A digest and bibliography, No. 1*, Palmerston North: Department of Sociology, Massey University, 1986.

Morris, Lydia, 'A cluster of contradictions: The politics of migration in the European Union', *Sociology*, 31(2), 1997a, 241–59.

Morris, Lydia, 'Globalisation, migration and the nation-state: The path to a post-national Europe?', *British Journal of Sociology*, 48(2), 1997b, 192–209.

Murphy, Nigel, '"Maoriland" and "Yellow Peril": Discourses of Maori and Chinese in the formation of New Zealand's national identity', in M. Ip (ed.), *The Dragon and the Taniwha: Maori and Chinese in New Zealand*, Auckland: Auckland University Press, 2009.

Phillips, Jock, *Te Ara Encyclopedia of New Zealand*, Auckland: David Bateman, 2006.

Pickles, Katie, 'Colonisation, empire and gender', in G. Byrnes (ed.), *The New Oxford History of New Zealand*, Melbourne: Oxford University Press, 2009.

Pool, Ian, 'British immigration 1800–1945 and New Zealand's morphology', *New Zealand Sociology*, 25(1), 2010, 150–65.

Rattansi, Ali, 'The uses of racialization: The time-spaces and subject-object of the raced body', in K. Murji, and J. Solomos (eds), *Racialization. Studies in theory and practice*, Oxford: Oxford University Press, 2005.

Roche, Maurice, *Rethinking Citizenship: Welfare, ideology and change in modern society*, Cambridge: Polity Press, 1992.

Schiller, Nina Glick, 'The situation of transnational studies', *Identities*, 4(2), 1997, 155–66.

Spoonley, Paul, Peace, Robin, Butcher, Andrew and O'Neill, Damian, 'Social cohesion: A policy and indicator framework for assessing immigrant and host outcomes', *Social Policy Journal of New Zealand*, 24, 2005, 85–110.

Spoonley, Paul and Butcher, Andrew, 'Reporting superdiversity: The mass media and immigration in New Zealand', *Journal of Intercultural Studies* 30(4), 2009, 355–72.

Spoonley, Paul and Gendall, Philip, 'Welcome to our world: Attitudes to immigrants and immigration', in A. Trlin, P. Spoonley and R. Bedford (eds), *New Zealand and International Migration: A digest and bibliography, No.5*, Auckland: Integration of Immigrants Programme, Massey University, 2010.

Spoonley, Paul and Bedford, Richard, *Welcome to Our World? Immigration and the remaking of New Zealand*, Auckland: Dunmore Publishing, 2012.

Vertovec, Steven, 'Super-diversity and its implications', *Ethnic and Racial Studies*, 30(6), 2007, 1024–54.

Walker, Ranginui, 'Immigration industry', *Metro*, June 1997, 117–18.

Walker, Ranginui. *Ka Whawahi Tonu Motou: Struggle without end*, Auckland: Penguin, 1990.

3. Negotiating multiculturalism and the Treaty of Waitangi

CAMILLE NAKHID AND HEATHER DEVERE

This chapter considers whether the Treaty of Waitangi can serve as the basis for New Zealand's immigration policy when determining the place of new arrivals to Aotearoa New Zealand and how to embrace their settlement in this country. It is argued that the Treaty contains provisions conducive to ensuring that the indigenous population remains the significant, if not major minority, and for the presence of the diverse range of ethnic peoples to tend towards social cohesion. If Aotearoa New Zealand is to mature from simple tolerance to acceptance, appreciation and celebration of its many cultural communities, the country's social wellbeing can be strengthened by this founding document that has robustly endured, despite being subject to debate.

The presence of multicultural communities in Aotearoa New Zealand has been a feature ever since groups of people from outside the country began arriving here. In 1840 the country's first official immigration agreement, the Treaty of Waitangi, established a basis for British citizens to settle in Aotearoa New Zealand. Initially this was set up to accommodate British settlers, to secure indigenous rights, resources and interests, and to recognise the tangata whenua (indigenous people of the land). Immigration policies since then have been designed, in the first instance, to keep the country white, and later to accommodate its economic goals. Immigration policy has been inconsistent and often discriminatory, without incorporating the contributions of new arrivals in building social cohesion. We are suggesting that the Treaty of Waitangi, as the founding document, should be incorporated more explicitly into the development of an immigration policy that acknowledges both the indigenous population and the various immigrant groups to Aotearoa New Zealand.

As Aotearoa New Zealand's economic relationships with Asian nations increased in the 1990s, changes to the country's racially motivated immigration policies were made. This resulted in increasing numbers of migrants from countries such as China, Korea, Taiwan, India and Japan.

The ensuing cultural diversity did not segue into social unity, and tensions between communities of these new migrants, the dominant European population, Pasifika peoples[1] and Māori as tangata whenua were obvious, particularly around national elections. By 2026, 'Asian' as a population entity is projected to displace Māori to become the major minority group, thus likely affecting the status of Māori and of Asian peoples' relationship with the Treaty of Waitangi.

Aotearoa New Zealand is often spoken of as a 'multicultural society' and, as Kate McMillan points out, many of New Zealand's settlement and ethnic policies 'might elsewhere be called "multiculturalism."'[2] However, Aotearoa New Zealand has 'never had a formal policy of multiculturalism'.[3] The dominant migration narrative of Aotearoa New Zealand refers to the colonisation of the country by British settlers from 1830 onwards, followed by the arrival of Pacific Islanders after World War II. The continued arrival of those from the UK and Ireland was supported in order to maintain Aotearoa New Zealand's 'whites only' immigration policy. In the 1980s, large numbers of migrants from Asia, particularly South Asia, began to arrive.[4] This dominant narrative overshadows an often-ignored period of migration of Asians, predominantly Chinese and Indians, from the mid-nineteenth century. These communities were marginalised by a Eurocentric political and cultural system that had been imposed in Aotearoa by the early British settlers.

A noticeable feature of Aotearoa New Zealand is the attempt to acknowledge the indigenous peoples, as well as the many different ethnic, settler and migrant groups in Aotearoa New Zealand. There are many areas, such as language and education, where principles of the Treaty of Waitangi are incorporated in the country's official policies and practices. In order for Aotearoa New Zealand to progress as a society, Māori need also to be involved as equal partners in the design and construction of any immigration policy, to ensure that both early and more recent settlers are included in this bicultural approach.

Treaty of Waitangi: The first immigration agreement

While written constitutions both found and define modern nations, Britain, Israel and Aotearoa New Zealand are regarded as three exceptions to this rule. Although the Treaty of Waitangi is considered to be Aotearoa New Zealand's written foundational document, the New Zealand constitution is conventionally described as 'unwritten'.[5] The country's current constitutional arrangements locate sovereignty not in 'the people', but rather in parliament, albeit one which is nominally representative of 'popular sovereignty'.[6] The Treaty, signed between the British Crown and Māori chiefs in 1840, is regarded as a written expression of consent by Māori to be governed by Britain. The British Crown had formally acknowledged the independent sovereignty of Māori tribes in 1836 and thus the Treaty of Waitangi has status as an international agreement based on the position of the parties as independent sovereignties.[7]

The Treaty was prepared in English and then translated into Māori by the missionary Henry Williams and his son Edward. The terms of the Treaty are brief. The preamble to the English version predicts 'the arrival of many settlers and the need for peace and good order ... in the context of an epilogue which serves to remind that ... it is founded not on legalism but on a philosophy of good faith'.[8] There are three short articles that 'secured governorship for the Crown, autonomy for Māori, and citizenship for all'. Article 1 concerns the relationship between Māori and the Queen of England; Article 2 guarantees certain rights to Māori, including rights in relationship to the land; Article 3 covers citizenship rights. The Treaty is currently regarded as a partnership between Māori and Pākehā.

Conflict surrounding the Treaty

Since the signing of the Treaty, Māori and Pākehā have established divergent histories of the document and there have been disagreements and conflicting tensions surrounding different understandings of it. Much of the debate centres on the actual wording of the Treaty. Eddie Durie[9] has argued that as most Māori chiefs signed the Māori language version just as Pākehā signed the English version, the Treaty 'must especially be seen through Māori eyes'.[10]

In the English version, the first article stated that the chiefs 'ceded the rights and powers of sovereignty' to the Queen of England. The Māori version held that 'kāwanatanga' or governorship, and not sovereignty, was ceded. The second article of the English translation guaranteed Māori 'the full, exclusive, and undisturbed possession of their Lands and Estates, Forests, Fisheries, and other properties ... so long as it is their wish and desire to retain the same in their possession'.[11] However, Māori lost many resources through the government purchase of large amounts of Māori land at low value, and through the confiscation of land following the

New Zealand wars and the actions of the Native Land Court. By the late nineteenth century, there had been a devastating reduction in the Māori population as well as the loss of most of their land and resources. Māori, however, continued to assert their rangatiratanga (autonomy) under the Māori version of the Treaty of Waitangi. The third article gave Māori the 'rights and privileges' of British subjects.[12]

In the late nineteenth and early twentieth centuries, Pākehā attempted to consign the Treaty to the past, while Māori battled to have their rights to self-determination recognised under the Treaty. Māori believe that the Treaty has been consistently breached by Pākehā and government, and that legal processes have largely ignored the Treaty. From the Privy Council's 1941 decision that the Treaty was only enforceable to the extent that it is incorporated in legislation, to the 1986 State Owned Enterprises Act that gave statutory force to the principles of the Treaty,[13] the Treaty is recognised in law, though the texts themselves are not binding legal documents. As historian Alan Ward notes, '[f]or the terms and principles of the Treaty to have any legal effect, they would need to be explicitly recognised in statutes of Parliament.'[14] In 1986, after two decades of a politically vocal Māori renaissance and cultural resurgence, the Labour government established a new Treaty policy in order to address this central argument. A key injunction of this policy was to 'regard the Treaty as always speaking'.[15]

The principles of the Treaty of Waitangi

The Treaty still governs the relationship between the Crown and Māori and, despite the debates surrounding its legal status, the rights proclaimed by the Treaty are enforceable by the courts in certain circumstances.[16] Although there have been various references to the Treaty as the 'Māori Magna Carta',[17] a 'sacred covenant',[18] a 'simple nullity',[19] a 'travesty'[20] and a 'fraud',[21] the Treaty has been perceived as central to the self-definition of the nation of Aotearoa New Zealand. The Treaty is seen as establishing a partnership between Māori and the Crown, or the government of Aotearoa New Zealand. It is a contract that is a commitment on the part of the government to uphold certain rights due to Māori as the people who occupied the land that the settlers and other newcomers to New Zealand wanted to share.

Around 60 separate Acts of parliament now make reference to the 'principles of the Treaty', although these have not been specified by parliament. An explanation of these principles has been attempted by

Te Puni Kōkiri, the Ministry of Māori Development.[22] In this, the key differences between the two Treaty texts – the ceding of sovereignty to the British Crown as stated in the English version, and the retention of tino rangatiratanga as read in the Māori version – are reconciled and unified as the two core principles of 'partnership' and 'active protection'. The principles of the Treaty are positively defined by the courts and the Waitangi Tribunal, and take place within the law, established and retrospectively legitimised by the Treaty. The principles are based on the idea that the Treaty is a 'living document to be interpreted in a contemporary setting'.[23] This means that principles can be modified or may evolve. The principles have established a means for making this a legal commitment in Aotearoa New Zealand's domestic law.[24]

On 11 December 2004 the New Zealand House of Representatives commissioned a parliamentary committee to review the country's existing constitutional arrangements. This inquiry was tasked with reviewing, among other issues, the place of the Treaty and its principles, the broader issue of historic claims, the idea of a written constitution, and Māori representation in Parliament.[25] The committee's report, published in August 2005, located the sources of the constitution and produced a time-line of its development, with 1840 – the year the Treaty was signed – marked as the origination point. In the report's overview, Aotearoa New Zealand is positioned, with Britain, in the group of countries with an 'unwritten' constitution, in which constitutional rules 'are contained in a mixture of statutes, court decisions and practices'.[26] Although the report affirmed that 'New Zealand's constitution is not in crisis',[27] it raised some areas of concern. Chief among these was the constitutional and legal position of the Treaty. The Treaty Tribes Coalition, established in 1994 to represent iwi in fisheries settlements, for example, considered that:

> *The greatest shortcoming of New Zealand's current constitutional arrangements is their failure to fully recognise the fundamental significance of the Treaty of Waitangi ... The review should consider* **how** *– not* **whether** *– the guarantees enshrined in the Treaty can be given greater legal and constitutional protection (emphasis in original).*[28]

Giving greater protection to the Treaty does not solve the issue of a partnership between Māori and Pākehā, which leaves out other migrant groups and provokes questions about their presence in Aotearoa New Zealand and their relationship to the Treaty of Waitangi.

Aotearoa New Zealand's immigration policy

Aotearoa New Zealand's history of immigration demonstrates an underlying racism. The British held a strong belief in their own superiority as people, accompanied by a fear of miscegenation. Encouraging the arrival and presence of the different ethnic groups into Aotearoa New Zealand was motivated, if not carefully developed, by the desire to maintain, sustain and develop the country's economy, while ensuring that European culture remained dominant through language, religion and allegiance to the British monarchy.

In the nineteenth century the colonial government in New Zealand actively sought the right to control immigration into the country. The 1881 Chinese Immigrants Act, designed to deter Chinese immigrants, was the first to restrict the entry of a specific group of people. It introduced a poll tax of £10, increased to £100 in 1896. In 1908 new measures were introduced: Chinese who wished to leave the country temporarily needed re-entry permits, which were thumb-printed. This procedure remained until 1920 when restrictions against all Asian immigration were tightened.[29] Although the Minister of Customs had waived the Chinese poll tax in 1934, it was not repealed until 1944; and only in 2002 did the government officially apologise to the Chinese for the suffering caused by the tax.

Unlike the Chinese, most Indians were British subjects and free to enter New Zealand, until the Immigration Restriction Act 1899 was introduced. This was not aimed overtly at Asians but prohibited the entry of immigrants who were not of British or Irish parentage and who could not fill out an application form 'in any European language' – which, in effect, limited immigration to whites. The Chinese Immigrants Amendment Act 1907 and the Immigration Restriction Amendment Act 1908 were prompted by the fear that immigrating Chinese, Indians and other 'race aliens'[30] would create competition for jobs.

German and Austrian nationals were targeted by the Undesirable Immigrants Exclusion Act of 1919, aimed at excluding those who might be disloyal to the British Empire. In the following year, Prime Minister William Massey proclaimed the Immigration Restriction Amendment Act to be 'the result of a deep-seated sentiment on the part of a huge majority of the people of this country that this Dominion shall be what is often called a "white" New Zealand'.[31] The Act was passed primarily to limit possible Asian immigration by further restricting the category of 'British' to those of British birth and parentage, thus excluding migrants from Britain's dominions, colonies and protectorates. It was also used to curb the entry of other non-British people, particularly southern Europeans such as Croatians (formerly Dalmatians) and Italians.

During the 1960s tentative steps were taken towards a non-discriminatory immigration policy through the Immigration Amendment Act 1961. Until then, most migration to New Zealand had involved European, and mainly British, migrants. From the 1960s, a substantial number of migrants from Pacific Island countries began to arrive on temporary work visas, seeking employment in primary and secondary industries and in occupations requiring manual or unskilled labour.

In 1970 the New Zealand Department of Labour stated that 'the great question of assimilation and integration' was second only to economic considerations in policy formulation and restrictions on entry. The concern was that 'the greater and more obvious the differences between the immigrant and the average New Zealander, the longer and more difficult the period of assimilation and [the] greater the tendency of immigrants to hive off into little colonies which become self sufficient and resistant to the process of assimilation.'[32] The immigration of certain groups was accordingly limited to numbers which posed little threat to the nation's racial balance and its seemingly harmonious intergroup relations. When Norman Kirk became prime minister in 1972, however, he argued that Aotearoa New Zealand's future lay with Asia and the Pacific and suggested that the country needed an immigration policy that ignored prospective migrants' race, colour and religion.

The Immigration Policy Review of 1986 was the culmination of a gradual shift that began in the 1960s. Immigrant selection would be 'based on criteria of personal merit without discrimination on grounds of race, national or ethnic origin'; and 'new settlers' would be encouraged to participate in Aotearoa New Zealand's multicultural society while maintaining 'valued elements in their own heritage'.[33] Assimilation was no longer the desired outcome, and social diversity facilitated by cultural maintenance was perceived to have a positive value. Any person who met specified educational, business, professional, age or asset requirements was to be admitted, regardless of race or nationality. This marked a clear break from the earlier emphasis on nationality and ethnic origin as the basis for admission.

In 1987 Aotearoa New Zealand's immigration policy changed again to eliminate 'preferred country' options, and the Immigration Amendment

Act 1991 replaced the occupational priority list with a points system giving precedence to migrants with education, business skills, capital and youthfulness. Applicants were awarded points for employability, age, educational qualifications and settlement funds, and the 'doors were opened to large numbers of skilled immigrants including those from non-English speaking backgrounds'.[34]

Between 1986 and 1990, for the first time, business immigrants from countries in Asia – primarily Hong Kong, Singapore, and Taiwan –became an explicit focus of Aotearoa New Zealand's immigration policy. During the early 1990s, following the 1991introduction of a points-based selection system, immigration into New Zealand from Asia – particularly from Hong Kong, Taiwan and the Republic of Korea – increased sharply. In 1995, immigration policy was amended to resolve problems in its operation, outputs and outcomes, and partly because of the realisation that economic objectives could not be pursued indefinitely without reference to the maintenance of social cohesion. The regulations were reviewed to ensure that Aotearoa New Zealand continued to attract migrants who would most benefit the country. One of the main reasons for the review was concern about the increasing number of Asians living in Aotearoa New Zealand, and the introduction of an English language proficiency requirement of at least a 'modest' level of English curbed the immigration of certain groups.[35] It was this immigration policy that gave the New Zealand First party its 'Asian invasion' slogan for the 1996 national elections.[36] Although immigration from Asia fell significantly after the Asian economic crisis in 1997, and later because of slow economic growth in Aotearoa New Zealand, it picked up significantly in 2001 as immigration policy again focused on skilled and business migrants.

In 2002 and 2003, the drive to attract immigrants in areas of skill shortages, and perhaps as a response to growing public concern about the levels of immigration from Asia, led to further changes. There was still encouragement for business immigrants, but those from 'non-comparable labour markets' could struggle to reach the points threshold.[37] In 2004 the country's immigration regulations remained 'blind' to race or nationality but there was some evidence that the focus on skills and an increased level of English language requirements had resulted in a reduction in the number of immigrants from Asia. The 2009 Immigration Act was driven by a perceived need to protect Aotearoa New Zealand from terrorism, and from increasing numbers of refugees and asylum seekers. It can be noted that there were few European countries or European peoples that were adversely affected by this legislation. As expressed by Peter Skilling,[38] although the official narrative of Aotearoa New Zealand's society since 1996 was 'openness, diversity and tolerance', its detailed construction focused 'around a narrower set of attitudes and behaviours: those, such as creativity, flexibility and innovation, deemed necessary for economic competitiveness' within a global system.

From the mid-1980s the immigration policies of successive New Zealand governments have sought, on the surface, to maintain high levels of social cohesion in a society that has become increasingly diverse in terms of its ethnic composition. However, while Aotearoa New Zealand's immigrant selection process is non-discriminatory on the basis of source country, it remains biased in favour of immigrants with English language skills who possess educational and professional qualifications that are recognised by the New Zealand Qualifications Authority and professional associations, and who might be perceived as able to integrate more easily into society.

It can be claimed that Aotearoa New Zealand's immigration practices differed from the international image it sought to cultivate. Monocultural culture and practices, which sought to preserve the European face of Aotearoa New Zealand, co-existed with an immigration policy that oversaw the segmentation of the labour market in which a brown and subservient working- and manual-class of labourers from the Pacific Islands would develop. This latter group's political, social and economic status at that time made it difficult for them to create a sufficiently powerful political or social profile to challenge New Zealand's white image.

Between 1991 and 2006 New Zealand's population increased by almost 18 per cent; residents claiming Asian or Pacific Island (Pasifika)[39] ethnicity increased by 358 per cent and 58 per cent, respectively. At the time of the 2001 census, 70 per cent of the Asian ethnic population resident in Aotearoa New Zealand had been born in countries in Asia. A total of 237,000 people identified with Asian ethnicities – the equivalent of just over six per cent of the total Aotearoa New Zealand population. Much of this change occurred in the country's main metropolitan and reception centre for new settlers, the greater Auckland urban area. In 2006 Auckland contained roughly two-thirds of those claiming both Asian and Pasifika ethnicity, so it is not surprising that this population component had become an increasingly visible target for anti-immigration political and public comment in Aotearoa New Zealand's largest city.[40] By 2013 the United Kingdom, traditionally the country of origin for most migrants to New Zealand, was replaced by China and India.[41] The Middle Eastern/Latin American/African and Asian ethnic groups increased by more than 30 per cent between the 2006 and the 2013 censuses. Of the major ethnic groups, those with the largest percentage increases were Middle Eastern/Latin American/African (up 35 per cent); Asian (up 33 per cent); European (up 13.8 per cent); Pacific peoples (up 11.3 per cent) and Māori (up 5.9 per cent).[42]

With the Asian population predicted to 'inevitably' exceed the Māori population, the implications of this for Māori need to be addressed in the immigration debate. As Paul Spoonley and Richard Bedford point out, 'The presence of a treaty settlement and the ongoing politics of Māori marginalisation and resistance, and the belated recognition of Māori treaty rights ... [have] implications for immigration and settlement.'[43]

The Treaty of Waitangi, biculturalism and immigration policy

It can be argued that with the arrival of the early British settlers New Zealand society was bicultural, as Māori and the settlers were living their own cultures alongside each other.[44] After the signing of the Treaty, and as the non-Māori population grew to outnumber Māori, British traditions and culture dominated and New Zealand became monoculturally British. By the second half of the twentieth century, New Zealand could be said to have evolved from a 'bicultural country with monocultural practices to a multicultural nation that increasingly recognised its bicultural constitution'.[45]

The preamble to the Treaty of Waitangi, which explicitly refers to the immigration of settlers from Great Britain and its colonies, can be considered as New Zealand's founding immigration policy document, allowing for the migration and settlement of British subjects. New Zealand is distinct from Canada, the United States and Australia in the emphasis that is given to biculturalism within a context of increasing ethnic and cultural diversity. From the 1990s, however, there has been increasing concern among some Māori that there are no official channels for addressing their interests in the broad area of population policy, including immigration.

Tony O'Connor[46] claims that the New Zealand origin of the term 'biculturalism' can be 'traced to the 1930s scholarship of one of the most influential Māori leaders of the twentieth century, Sir Apirana Ngata, who used the term to counter the assimilationist policies of the government'. Biculturalism is a contested concept which many writers believe has developed since the early 1970s as a Māori renaissance aimed to replace the aspiration, first expressed by Captain William Hobson at Waitangi in 1840, that 'we are all one people now', with a new slogan of 'two people in one country'.[47] The interpretation of the Treaty of Waitangi as a contract between two peoples has been key to the development of the concept of biculturalism and is a prominent feature in New Zealand political debate and the public policy arena. Ian Stuart[48] claims that the view that there are two cultures in New Zealand – Māori/indigenous and Pākehā/settler – is a political rather than a descriptive statement. According to Stuart, biculturalism means power-sharing, allowing these two power structures to function side by side, whereas multiculturalism is a descriptive or social anthropological statement about the nature of a society.

The concept of biculturalism facilitates the retention of Māori culture, making it familiar and legitimate within Aotearoa New Zealand. Alastair Campbell argues that biculturalism must '(in theory) be the hall mark of all social and political arrangements'.[49] Richard Hill[50] supports this by pointing out that biculturalism entrenches Māori culture as 'fundamental and of equal value to that of Pākehā culture and polity'. The Treaty of Waitangi is recognised by many Pākehā as well as Māori[51] as the basis for biculturalism and, as stated, the principles of the Treaty have appeared in legislation and have been used in setting policy agenda.

For Māori, the government's unilateral development and implementation of immigration policy was perceived as negating the concept of partnership, usurping their rights, and breaching the terms of the Treaty. Ranginui Walker interpreted the Treaty's preamble as an agreement for immigration from only Europe, Australia and the United Kingdom.[52] Any variation on what was agreed upon, he argued, required genuine consultation with the descendants of the Crown's Treaty partners, a view shared by other Māori.[53] Walker claims the lack of consultation is intended 'to suppress the counter-hegemonic struggle of Māori by swamping them with outsiders who are not obliged to them by the Treaty'.[54] If new immigrants are not bound by the Treaty then New Zealand's official policy of biculturalism is negated.

On the other hand, bicultural policies have been seen by some to overly privilege Māori. In 2004, the newly appointed leader of the National Party and New Zealand Opposition, Don Brash, in a highly publicised speech 'castigated the fifth Labour government's record on issues of biculturalism and made an argument for "one New Zealand"', claiming that 'we are a country of many peoples, not simply a society of Māori and Pākehā where the minority has a birth-right to the upper hand.'[55] The claim has also been made that biculturalism has produced 'aggressive alliances in New Zealand formed by Māori and Pākehā against the perceived threat of Asian immigrants'.[56]

Not all new migrants consider a bicultural Treaty tradition to be detrimental to them. Mervin Singham, former director of the Office of Ethnic Affairs, suggests that the rigorous debate about the Treaty and the reconciliation processes between the Crown and Māori have given Aotearoa New Zealand 'experience in dealing with complex issues about relations between the Crown and community and relationships between diverse communities', and that 'Māori have paved the way for new minority communities' as a journey that 'illuminates the way for others'.[57]

Migration and attitudes towards migrants

In Aotearoa New Zealand the boundaries between social groups are increasingly diffuse due to a range of factors including immigration, intermarriage, social mobility, education and political capital. The implication for multiculturalism is that it is more difficult to demarcate ethnic groups, as the boundary between these and the majority culture is not always clearly defined. On the other hand, multiculturalism can be viewed as a form of cultural separation that exacerbates the problem of reconciling group differences.

Immigration has been a significant driver of population change in Aotearoa New Zealand since the mid-nineteenth century. The country's immigration rate of just under 20 per cent is one of the highest proportions of overseas-born individuals in the population of any country in the Organisation for Economic Co-operation and Development (OECD) – behind Australia's 24 per cent but ahead of Canada's 17 per cent and the 10 per cent in the US. The ethnic diversification of New Zealand immigration has occurred extremely rapidly and the anti-immigrant politics of the 1990s indicate the strains on local communities as they adjusted to these altered circumstances. Perhaps it is surprising that there have not been more strongly expressed anti-immigrant sentiments or conflict. Nevertheless, there are still unresolved issues.

Underlying these public attitudes toward Asians, especially in the mid-1990s, were mixed or negative feelings about the value of Asian immigration and investment in Aotearoa New Zealand. The reasons for such feelings primarily concerned perceived threats to the country's distinctive social and cultural characteristics (for example, the perceived lack of integration by Asians); Aotearoa New Zealand's identity (such as being taken over by large numbers of arrivals who purchased land, businesses and other valued resources); and the New Zealand economy, in terms of foreign ownership and possible job losses.[58]

In a 1995 nationwide public opinion poll, a majority of New Zealanders believed that there were 'too many' immigrants from Asia (51 per cent) and the Pacific Islands (57 per cent). In comparison, only 24 and 21 per cent were of the same opinion about the numbers from South Africa and the United Kingdom, respectively.[59] Over the next five years, public opinion softened with regard to each of these origins.[60] By October 2002, however, the percentage that said there were 'too many' immigrants from Asia had increased from 29 per cent in 2000 to 45 per cent, compared with a continued softening of opinion on the number of immigrants from the Pacific Islands (35 per cent), South Africa (12 per cent) and the United Kingdom (9 per cent).[61]

Since June 2002 the debates around race and the composition of migration flows have intensified in New Zealand's media, in parallel with similar recent debates in Australia, Europe and North America.[62] In July 2002 immigration became a significant issue in the national elections, largely because the government's annual quota for immigrant approvals (a maximum of 53,000 in all categories, equivalent of 1.4 per cent of the population) was seen by some politicians to be much too high. The fact that the majority of immigrants approved for residence in Aotearoa New Zealand in recent years have come from countries in Asia (especially China and India) has added to the concerns of anti-immigration groups and a number of political parties.

The role of contact as a possible influence on attitudes to immigration in Aotearoa New Zealand has been inferred in opinion polls and was investigated by Colleen Ward and Anne-Marie Masgoret in 2005.[63] Aucklanders were reported to be less likely to object to Asian immigration than those participants least affected by it, for example in provincial North Island areas and the South Island. Ward and Masgoret's modelling suggests that those who experience inter-group contact in their workplaces, social lives and neighbourhoods are more likely to be positively inclined towards multiculturalism and to perceive fewer threats from immigrants. Consequently, they are more likely to be positively inclined towards immigrants and to endorse the country's immigration policy. Despite this, the overall impression from the respondents in Ward and Masgoret's study was the belief that there were too many immigrants in the country.

Biculturalism and Māori–Asian relations

According to census data, the percentage of people living in New Zealand who were born overseas is rising: 25.2 per cent in 2013; 22.9 per cent in 2006 and 19.5 per cent in 2001, with people from the Asian continent forming an increasingly visible component.[64] Relations between Māori and migrants, particularly Asians, are likely to be an important part of the country's ethnic relations. Survey research suggests that Māori view a growing migrant presence, especially Asian, with suspicion.[65] The concerns centre on the possibility of Asians displacing Māori as the country's ethnic major minority, and that 'the perceived preference of migrants for multiculturalism over biculturalism will diminish Māori rights and the status of the Treaty of Waitangi.'[66] Conversely, Asian national communities, both local and foreign-born, have expressed concerns about being sidelined in debates about biculturalism and the Treaty.[67] Challenges have arisen about whether the Treaty is an appropriate vehicle for framing intergroup relations in a nation that is becoming ever more ethnically diverse. Much will depend on how relations unfold between Māori and the children of new Asian migrants. The increase in dual- and multi-ethnic-identified people and the apparent decline of European demographic dominance will impact on Māori–migrant relations, because dealings between ethnic minorities are unavoidably influenced by their relationships with the majority group. Historical interactions between Māori and Chinese, for example, have been strongly shaped by their power relations with Europeans.[68] Tahu Kutukai[69] sees a cooperative rather than adversarial relationship between Māori and Asian populations. Kukutai suggests that 'because relations between minorities are inextricably shaped by their relations with the dominant group, there is potential for Māori and Asian peoples, as racialised minorities with historical experiences of discrimination, to find a common structural basis for co-operation and collaboration, rather than adversarial or ambivalent relations.'

Māori are at present the largest minority group in New Zealand. However, as Māori population growth is primarily driven by natural increase (compared to Asian population growth, which is likely to be primarily through migration supplemented by natural increase), it is predicted that they will be outnumbered by people of Asian heritage within the next 30 years. Māori are concerned about what that will mean for their status as first nation people. Furthermore, the relationship between the different ethnic groups and Māori will depend on how old identities evolve in new settings, and how groups define themselves and are defined by others. Chinese and South Koreans have different identities, cultural legacies and migration histories, yet they are ascribed a generic 'Asian' label by the average New Zealander and treated accordingly. Though pan-ethnic labels may have originated as imposed categories informed by racist ideologies and dominant group interests, in some cases such labels have also been successfully reinterpreted in ways that support group goals. 'If the pan-ethnic Asian label becomes a widely accepted descriptor of a political community (if not a meaningful social identity) and intergroup comparisons on that basis are seen as legitimate, the prospect of an Asian majority minority has various implications for Māori and the Treaty.'[70]

Māori claims have traditionally advanced on the basis of indigeneity, and the weight given to those claims has been greatly aided because Māori have historically been the nation's largest ethnic minority. However, demographic changes and shifts in the political economy mean this will not always be the case.[71] Like other indigenous peoples in wealthy settler states, Māori are diverse with respect to culture and socio-economic attainment. At the group level, they remain overrepresented among the country's poor, undereducated, sick and incarcerated;[72] and despite state efforts to incorporate positive Māori images into the national polity, negative stereotypes of Māori people and culture persist in the workplace and in media representations.[73] To the extent that Māori are presented as a problem, both statistically and substantively, Asians have often faced the opposite dilemma: of being seen as a solution. Chinese New Zealanders have been positioned as the country's model minority in contrast with the portrayal of Māori as indolent.[74] Future relations between these two groups may be shaped by these contrasting descriptions providing the potential for antagonism.

The main issue for those migrants who do not identify as Pākehā is where they fit into society and the political partnership in Aotearoa New

Zealand. Can biculturalism be reconciled with multiculturalism? It is argued that there will be affinities between Māori and immigrant groups as both have been subjected to racism and discrimination. There is also the view that the values of biculturalism – self-determination, empowerment and cultural pluralism as well as an understanding of individual and institutional racism – are of benefit to democracy, and therefore to society generally.[75] Dominic O'Sullivan[76] argues that biculturalism is good for democracy as it is 'emancipatory, helps to mediate rather than mask differences, and to manage not dismiss conflicting ideas'. Hill[77] believes that Māori and Pasifika people have established what he calls a 'de-facto' alliance on the basis of their shared socioeconomic marginalisation, their ancestral ties, and 'shared attitudes and values on fundamental issues such as the relationship between indigeneity and the land, for example, or on the spiritual dimensions to life', and their 'close spatial proximities' in the poorer suburbs, most notably in Auckland.

Conclusion

Signed in 1840, the Treaty of Waitangi is considered to be the founding document between the indigenous people and the British Crown, and established the basis for immigration to Aotearoa New Zealand. Immigration policy since then, except for brief periods, has been tainted with racial overtones. If New Zealand is to be a society in which there is an active, participatory and harmonious integration of the different ethnic groups and the indigenous population, there must be a similar approach to setting an immigration agenda and policy. We believe that the Treaty of Waitangi, an enduring document in the history of Aotearoa New Zealand, may be a place to start. In the absence of a written constitution, it stands as the founding document for the country, and has been a constant vehicle for debate, viewed with both derision and reverence. Yet even as more New Zealanders come to recognise the Treaty as a vital part of the nation and its history, it remains a contentious reminder of the country's first attempt at population control and immigration policy.

However, the principles of the Treaty, as stated earlier, can arguably sustain the wellbeing and social cohesiveness of a nation. If, as some contend, the Treaty does not account for immigrants other than those of British origin, there is a danger that non-British migrants would disavow any loyalty or adherence to it. If such migrants are allowed for under the Treaty, however, there are two significant outcomes. First, New Zealand's biculturalism, which allows for Māori sovereignty and significant partnership in decision-making, would not be contested and the status of Māori as tangata whenua would be recognised and acknowledged, even if they were no longer the second largest ethnic population in Aotearoa New Zealand. Second, New Zealand could lay claim to having developed an innovative, robust immigration policy that incorporates multiculturalism along with a mechanism for respecting and acknowledging the indigenous or first nation peoples, a policy that would gain credibility among indigenous groups internationally.

High Court judge and former chairperson of the Waitangi Tribunal, Joe Williams,[78] envisages a Treaty relationship 'after grievance', when settlements have made recompense for historical discrimination and deceit, and where conflict is no longer an expected outcome. He believes that, in partnership, Māori and the Crown (in its role as representing the interests of the non-Māori Treaty partners) can begin realising the 'audacious vision' for an ambitious yet realistic project of a relationship of mutual advantage. The importance of relationships, especially kinship or whanaungatanga, is the basis of Māori philosophy. Kinship relationships are also recognised as especially important by many of the newer migrant groups.

There are a number of other concerns discussed which New Zealand must contend with if these relationships between Māori, settlers and migrant populations are to develop, and if we are to consider how an immigration policy based on the Treaty of Waitangi and its inherent principles may be interpreted and received. There has been a consistent resistance to non-British or non-Western migrants in New Zealand as evidenced in the controversies over the *Tampa* refugees, the 'Asian invasion' of the mid- to late 1990s and the Pacific Island 'over-stayers' in the 1970s and 1980s.[79] All have been the subject of racist comments and attacks, both in the media and in the community. In contrast, the migration of significant numbers of white South Africans to New Zealand after 1994, following the election of Nelson Mandela, barely drew a response from the New Zealand public. Racism towards other groups is usually initiated by members of the dominant society who wield the power both in popular discourse and in the political arena, and this can have lasting effects both on the dominated group and on society at large.

In New Zealand's majoritarian democracy with 'the fastest law-making in the West',[80] policy-making is often temporary and ad hoc. When developed in response to the economic situation or public sentiment, immigration policies can arouse emotion as their emphases and foci are usually based on one or more particular ethnic groups. Further, capture of the debate by self-interested groups in order to present their own interpretations to the public can be damaging to race relations generally. Policies developed as a result of open and public consultation are more likely to engender meaningful engagement, understanding and support.

The tensions that surround discussions on the preparation and planning of New Zealand's future populations mean that such debate is often neglected. Given the percentage composition of both the ageing and youth populations of the country's ethnic and indigenous groups, however, population and growth planning – including the development of immigration strategies which have a major impact on these populations – are necessary, as they relate directly to the multicultural wellbeing of New Zealand.

Citizens often take their cue from the government. If the government's immigration policies imply a racist or exclusionary position, these are likely to influence the behaviour and attitudes of the country's peoples. It can be argued that New Zealand governments have taken steps to strengthen Aotearoa New Zealand's position and identity as a Pacific nation and to extend relationships to the governments and people of this region. This has served to warm relationships between descendants of the early migrants of British ancestry and those of Pacific Island heritage. In addition, the New Zealand government's apology to the country's Chinese communities for the poll tax imposed on early Chinese migrants was also favourably accepted, and highlighted the long history of Chinese in New Zealand.[81] In contrast, the government's reluctance to release asylum seeker Ahmed Zaoui from prison, after initially granting him refugee status, provoked both negative reactions from the New Zealand public towards Muslims and those perceived to be of Middle Eastern heritage, and positive support for Zaoui, mainly from religious groups.[82]

The lack of a constitution makes it difficult for Aotearoa New Zealand to determine who its citizens are and how they should be treated. Indeed, the 2005 Citizenship Amendment Act disallowing citizenship to certain individuals born in Aotearoa New Zealand may not have been allowed to proceed in the presence of a constitution. Such a significant attack on entitlement to citizenship should have been subject to much greater debate and engagement. The failure to do so highlighted the apathy that the New

Zealand public displayed towards the ideal of citizenship, and in their attitude towards the reasons for calling for such an act in the first place.

The lack of a planned, considered and consultative multicultural approach can lead to the isolation of ethnic communities if they are uncertain of their status in society. In the face of concerns about racism and racist acts of violence towards them, these communities may separate themselves as a form of protection. However, isolation prevents communities accessing information, services and opportunities that could assist them to settle in a new country. In Aotearoa New Zealand, an immigration policy that is not considered robust and enduring may portray the country as an easy target for those who wish to take control of the multicultural agenda and direction. If the approach is not seen as sustainable, such a policy may worsen the situation for Aotearoa New Zealand in the face of current or predicted crises, either globally or nationally. And while a flexible approach to multiculturalism can be considered a strength, in that the state is not bound to a fixed policy and is able to act accordingly to safeguard its citizens and those seeking to make their home there, a set of principles that can be agreed upon provides a guide and a reference for a country's ideals and actions towards old and new migrants.

This chapter has provided a brief history of immigration since the signing of the Treaty, focusing in particular on Asian migrants. An approach to multiculturalism that recognises all groups equally could reduce Māori status as one of the two party signatories to Aotearoa New Zealand's founding document, the Treaty of Waitangi. Conversely, immigrants who are not British or white Pākehā may feel excluded from the partnership agreement with Māori.

In a hostile environment, positive attitudes toward immigrants fostered by intergroup contact may wither in the face of economic adversity and politically engendered issues of national identity and nationalism. Ward and Masgoret[83] suggest the need to foster 'contact under favourable circumstances' as a deterrent to new immigrants becoming 'ghettoised' and isolated from the rest of society.[84] Social cohesion among the indigenous and ethnic populations in Aotearoa New Zealand, with their different behaviours and traditions, will benefit from an immigration policy with agreed-upon principles that honour the status of all populations.

We argue that there is scope within the Treaty of Waitangi to be the basis of an immigration policy agreement that allows for multiculturalism. Rather than aiming for Captain Hobson's vision of being 'all one people', the concept of biculturalism as a key feature of immigration policy and the role of the Treaty as a unifying document should be further explored.

ENDNOTES

1. Pasifika is a collective term used to refer to people of Pacific heritage or ancestry who have migrated to or been born in Aotearoa New Zealand. Not all people of Pacific Islands descent identify with or use this term.
2. Kate McMillan, 'The politics of immigration and multiculturalism in New Zealand', *Social Europe Journal*, 1 December 2010: www.social-europe.eu/2010/12/the-politics-of-immigration-and-multiculturalism-in-new-zealand
3. Wendy Larner, 'Brokering citizenship claims: Neo-liberalism, biculturalism and multiculturalism in Aotearoa New Zealand', in Evangelia Tastsoglou and Alexandra Dobrowolsky (eds), *Women, Migration and Citizenship: Making local, national and transnational connections*, Aldershot/Burlington: Ashgate, 2006, 139.
4. Jock Phillips, 'The New Zealanders – multiculturalism', Te Ara – The Encyclopedia of New Zealand: www.TeAra.govt.nz/en/the-new-zealanders/
5. Judith Pryor, *Constitutions: Writing nations, reading difference*, Abington/New York: Routledge, Birkbeck Law Press, 2008, 87.
6. See Paul McHugh, *The Māori Magna Carta: New Zealand law and the Treaty*, Auckland: Oxford University Press, 1991, 12–16, 31–34; F.M. Brookfield, *Waitangi and Indigenous Rights: Revolution, law and legitimacy*, Auckland: Auckland University Press, 1998, 5.
7. E.T.J. Durie, 'The Treaty in Māori history', in William L. Renwick (ed.), *Sovereign Indigenous Rights: The Treaty of Waitangi in international contexts*, Wellington: Victoria University Press, 1991, 156.
8. Ibid.
9. Eddie Durie is regarded as a leading legal expert on the Treaty of Waitangi.
10. Durie, 'The Treaty in Māori history', 156.
11. Richard S. Hill, 'Ngā whakataunga tiriti – Treaty of Waitangi settlement process – Origins of the settlement process', Te Ara – the Encyclopedia of New Zealand: www.TeAra.govt.nz/en/nga-whakataunga-tiriti-treaty-of-waitangi-settlement-process/page-1
12. John Wilson, 'Nation and government – the origins of nationhood', Te Ara – the Encyclopedia of New Zealand: www.TeAra.govt.nz/en/nation-and-government/page-1
13. *Inquiry to Review New Zealand's Existing Constitutional Arrangements*, Report of the Constitutional Arrangements Committee, August, Wellington, 2005, 70–71.
14. Alan Ward, *An Unsettled History: Treaty claims in New Zealand today*, Wellington: Bridget Williams Books, 1999, 20.
15. Cabinet Treaty Policy, Cited in Jane Kelsey, *A Question of Honour? Labour and the Treaty, 1984–1989*, Wellington: Allen and Unwin, 1990, 66.
16. Wilson, 'Nation and government'.

17 See Paul McHugh, *The Māori Magna Carta*.
18 See Claudia Orange, *The Treaty of Waitangi*, Wellington: Bridget Williams Books, 1987, 90; Jane Kelsey, *A Question of Honour? Labour and the Treaty, 1984-1989*, Wellington: Allen and Unwin, 1990, 9.
19 See Paul McHugh, 'A history of Crown sovereignty in New Zealand', in Andrew Sharp and Paul McHugh (eds), *Histories, Power and Loss: Uses of the past – a New Zealand commentary*, Wellington: Bridget Williams Books, 2001, 193.
20 Stuart C. Scott, *The Travesty of Waitangi: Towards anarchy*, Dunedin: Campbell Press, 1995.
21 See Joanna Consedine and Robert Consedine, *Healing our History: The challenge of the Treaty of Waitangi*, Auckland: Penguin Books, 2001, 105.
22 Te Puni Kōkiri, *A Guide to the Principles of the Treaty of Waitangi as expressed by the Courts and the Waitangi Tribunal*, Wellington: Te Puni Kōkiri, 2001.
23 Janine Hayward, 'The principles of the Treaty of Waitangi, appendix to Alan Ward', *National Overview Rangahaua Whanui Report*, vol II, Waitangi Tribunal, 1997, 475-94, 475.
24 The five principles announced by the Labour government in 1989 for dealing with issues arising from the Treaty of Waitangi are: 1. *The principle of government or the kāwanatanga principle* that gives the government the right to govern and make laws as long as Māori interests are given appropriate priority. 2. *The principle of self-management or the rangatiratanga principle* guarantees to iwi Māori the control and enjoyment of the resources and taonga that they wish to retain. 3. *The principle of equality* gives Māori the same legal equality as other New Zealand citizens. 4. *The principle of reasonable cooperation* implies a partnership that respects both duality and unity. 5. *The principle of redress* is the responsibility of the Crown to provide a process to resolve grievances arising from the Treaty. Hayward, 'The principles of the Treaty of Waitangi', 493-94.
25 Steven Young, 'Human rights and the Treaty of Waitangi: A view from the Asian community', paper presented to the Human Rights Commission, 2004: www.stevenyoung.co.nz/The-Chinese-in-New-Zealand/Biculturalism-Multiculturalism/Human-Rights-Commission-Treaty.html
26 *Inquiry to Review New Zealand's Existing Constitutional Arrangements*, Report of the Constitutional Arrangements Committee, August, Wellington, 2005, 70-71.
27 Ibid.
28 *Inquiry to Review New Zealand's Existing Constitutional Arrangements*, 8, cited in Judith Pryor, 'Unwritten constitutions? British exceptionalism and New Zealand equivocation', *European Journal of English Studies* 11, 1. 2007, 79-92.
29 Manying Ip, 'Chinese – Later settlement', Te Ara – the Encyclopedia of New Zealand: www.TeAra.govt.nz/en/chinese/page-3; Manying Ip and David Pang, 'New Zealand Chinese identity: Sojourners, model minority and multiple identities', in James Ho-fu Liu, Tim McCreanor, Tracey McIntosh and Teresia Teaiwa (eds), *New Zealand Identities: Departures and destinations*, Wellington: Victoria University Press, 2005, 174-190; Jacqueline Leckie 'South Asian: Old and new migrations', in Stuart Greif (ed.), *Immigration and National Identity in New*

Zealand: One people; two peoples, many peoples?, Palmerston North: Dunmore Press, 1995, 23–49.

30 Keith Banting and Will Kymlicka, 'Canadian multiculturalism: Global anxieties and local debates', *British Journal of Canadian Studies* 23:1, 2010, 43–72; Manying Ip, 'Māori–Chinese encounters: Indigene–immigrant interaction in New Zealand', *Asian Studies Review* 27:2, 2003, 227–52; Patrick Ongley and David Pearson, 'Post-1945 international migration: New Zealand, Australia and Canada compared', *International Migration Review* 29:3, 1995, 766–93; Ann Beaglehole, 'Immigration regulation – 1881–1914: Restrictions on Chinese and others' Te Ara – the Encyclopedia of New Zealand: www.TeAra.govt.nz/en/immigration-regulation/page-2

31 Tom Brooking and Roberto Rabel, 'Neither British nor Polynesian: A brief history of New Zealand's other immigrants', in Stuart Greif (ed.), *Immigration and National Identity in New Zealand*, Palmerston North: Dunmore Press, 1995, 23–49.

32 New Zealand Department of Labour, *A Look at New Zealand's Immigration Policy*, Wellington: Immigration Division, Department of Labour, 1970, 3.

33 Kerry Burke, 'Review of immigration policy', *Appendices to the Journal of the House of Representatives G.42*, New Zealand Parliament, Wellington, 1986, 11.

34 Anne Henderson, Andrew Trlin and Noel Watts, 'English language proficiency and the recruitment and employment of professional immigrants in New Zealand', Palmerston North: Occasional Publication No.11. New Settlers Programme, Massey University, 2006, 2.

35 Ibid.

36 Richard Bedford and Elsie Ho, 'Asians in New Zealand: Implications of a changing demography', Wellington: Asia NZ Foundation, 2008, 1.

37 Extra points could be claimed by applicants with no job offer but who had work experience in comparable labour markets.

38 Peter Skilling, 'The construction and use of national identity in contemporary New Zealand political discourse', *Australian Journal of Political Science* 45: 2, 2010, 175–89.

39 The New Zealand government's definition refers to people who come from or have ancestry from one or more of the Pacific Islands.

40 Richard Bedford, 'New Zealand: The politicisation of immigration', paper presented at the Migration Research Group, University of Waikato, Hamilton, January 2003.

41 OECD (2013) Recent developments in international migration movements and policies, in International Migration Outlook 2013, OECD Publishing: www.keepeek.com/Digital-Asset-Management/oecd/social-issues-migration-health/international-migration-outlook-2013/recent-developments-in-international-migration-movements-and-policies_migr_outlook-2013-4-en#page12

42 Statistics New Zealand, '2013 Census QuickStats about culture and identity', 2014: www.stats.govt.nz/Census/2013-census/profile-and-summary-reports/quickstats-culture-identity.aspx

43 Paul Spoonley and Richard Bedford, *Welcome to our World? Immigration and the reshaping of New Zealand*, Auckland: Dunmore Publishing, 2012, 10.

44 See for example, Richard S. Hill, 'Fitting multiculturalism into biculturalism: Māori–Pasifika relations in New Zealand from the 1960s', *Ethnohistory* 57:2, 2010, 291–319; Colleen Ward and Anne-Marie Masgoret, 'Attitudes toward immigrants, immigration, and multiculturalism in New Zealand: A social psychological analysis', *International Migration Review* 42:1, 2008, 227–48; James H. Liu and Chris G. Sibley, 'Attitudes towards biculturalism in New Zealand: Social dominance and Pākehā attitudes towards the general principles and resource-specific aspects of bicultural policy', *New Zealand Journal of Psychology* 33:2, 2004, 88–99; Janine Hayward, 'Biculturalism – biculturalism in the state sector', Te Ara – the Encyclopedia of New Zealand: www.TeAra.govt.nz/en/biculturalism/page-2; David R. Thomas and Linda Waimarie Nikora, 'From assimilation to biculturalism: Changing patterns in Māori–Pākehā relationships', in D.R. Thomas and A. Veno (eds), *Psychology and Social Change: Creating an international agenda*, Palmerston North: Dunmore Press, 1992, 231–56.

45 Wardlow Friesen, 'Planning for cultural diversity', in Michelle Thompson-Fawcett and Claire Freeman (eds), *Living Together: Towards inclusive communities in New Zealand*, Dunedin: Otago University Press, 2006, 59.

46 Tony O'Connor, 'New Zealand's biculturalism and the development of publicly funded rongoā (traditional Māori healing) services', *Sites: A Journal of Social Anthropology and Cultural Studies* 4:1, 2007, 70–94, 71.

47 See Hill, 'Fitting multiculturalism into biculturalism', 291–319, 294.

48 Ian Stuart, 'Māori and the mainstream: Towards bicultural reporting', *Pacific Journalism Review* 8, 2002, 42–58, 43–44.

49 Alastair V. Campbell, 'A report from New Zealand: Ethics in a bicultural context', *Bioethics.* 9:2, 1995, 149–54.

50 Hill, 'Fitting multiculturalism into biculturalism', 296.

51 See Thomas and Nikora, 'From assimilation to biculturalism'.

52 Ranginui Walker, 'Māori sovereignty: The Māori perspective', in Hineani (ed.), *Māori Sovereignty: The Māori perspective*, Melbourne Auckland: Hodder Moa Beckett, 1995, 284–85.

53 Cluny MacPherson, 'Reinventing the nation: Building a bicultural future from a monocultural past in Aotearoa New Zealand', in Paul R. Spickard (ed.), *Race and Nation: Ethnic systems in the modern world*, New York: Routledge, 2005, 215–38; Paul Spoonley and Cluny MacPherson, 'Immigrants and cross-border connections and activities', in Paul Spoonley, Cluny MacPherson and David George Pearson, (eds), *Tangata Tangata: The changing ethnic contours of New Zealand*, Southbank, Victoria: Thomson, 2004, 175–94; Wilson, 'Nation and government'.

54 Ranginui Walker, *Nga Pepa a Ranginui: The Walker Papers*, Auckland: Penguin Books, 1996, 192.

55 Wendy Larner, 'Brokering citizenship claims: Neo-liberalism, biculturalism and multiculturalism in Aotearoa New Zealand', in Evangelia Tastsoglou and Alexandra Dobrowolsky (eds), *Women: Migration and Citizenship: Making local, national and transnational connections*, Aldershot/Burlington: Ashgate, 2006, 131–48, 139.

56 John M. Lowe, 'Late-modernity and the theorisation of race in New Zealand', *British Review of New Zealand Studies*, 2008/09, 25.

57 Mervin Singham, 'Multiculturalism in New Zealand – the need for a new paradigm', *Aotearoa Ethnic Network Journal* 1:1, 2006, 34.
58 Manying Ip, 'Māori–Chinese encounters', 227–52.
59 Johnston, Ron, Phillip Gendall, Andrew Trlin and Paul Spoonley, 'Immigration, multiculturalism and geography: Inter-group contact and attitudes to immigrants and cultural diversity in New Zealand', *Asian and Pacific Migration Journal* 13:3, 2010, 343–69.
60 Ibid.
61 Ibid.
62 See for example, Ilham Boumankhar, 'Immigrant communities, cultural institutions and political space: The success of the immigration museum in Melbourne, Australia', *Human Architecture* 9:4, 2011, 61–92; E. Bleich, 'Immigration and integration studies in Western Europe and the United States: The road less traveled and a path ahead', *World Politics* 60:3, 2008, 509–38.
63 See Colleen Ward, Anne Margaret Masgoret and C.H. Leong, 'Immigration, acculturation and intergroup relations in New Zealand', paper presented at the 18th International Congress of the International Association for Cross-cultural Psychology, Spetses: Greece, 2006; Colleen Ward and Anne Margaret Masgoret, 'Attitudes toward immigrants, immigration, and multiculturalism in New Zealand: A social psychological analysis', *International Migration Review* 42:1, 2008, 227–48.
64 Statistics New Zealand, 2013: www.search.stats.govt.nz/
65 See James Chang, 'Māori views on immigration: Implications for Māori–Chinese interactions', in Manying Ip (ed.), *The Dragon and the Taniwha: Māori and Chinese in New Zealand*, Auckland: Auckland University Press, 2009, 185–208.
66 Tahu H. Kukutai, 'The structure of Māori–Asian relations: An ambivalent future?', *New Zealand Population Review* 33/34, 2007, 129–51, 130.
67 See Steven Young, 'Human rights and the Treaty of Waitangi: A view from the Asian community', paper presented to the Human Rights Commission, 2004: www.stevenyoung.co.nz/The-Chinese-in-New-Zealand/Biculturalism-Multiculturalism/Human-Rights-Commission-Treaty.html; Manying Ip, 'Māori–Chinese encounters', 227–52.
68 Ip, 'Māori–Chinese encounters', 249.
69 Kukutai, 'The structure of Māori-Asian relations', 147.
70 Ibid., 141.
71 Ibid., 129–51.
72 Te Puni Kōkiri, *Progress Towards Closing Social and Economic Gaps between Māori and Non-Māori: A report to the Minister of Māori Affairs*, Wellington: Te Puni Kōkiri, 2000.
73 Kelly Holmes, Tamar Murachver and Donn Bayard, 'Accent, appearances and ethnic stereotypes in New Zealand', *New Zealand Journal of Psychology* 30, 2001, 79–86.
74 Ip, 'Māori–Chinese encounters', 241.
75 Thomas and Nikora, 'From assimilation to biculturalism'.
76 Dominic O'Sullivan, 'Māori have a right to super city seats as first occupants', *New*

Zealand Herald, 23 November 2009: www.nzherald.co.nz/nz/news/article.cfm?c_id=1&objectid=10565554
77 Hill, 'Fitting multiculturalism into biculturalism', 297.
78 Joe Williams, 'Wai 262 Claim of the Waitangi Tribunal', Treaty Debate Series at Te Papa, Wellington: Radio New Zealand, 29 January 2012.
79 A. Quazi, 2009, 'Quota refugees in New Zealand: Approvals and movements (1999–2008)', Wellington: Department of Labour: www.dol.govt.nz/publications/research/refugee-sector-perspectives-developments/perspectives-and-developments_04.asp, page 8; Teresia Teaiwa and Sean Mallon, 'Ambivalent kinships: Pacific peoples in New Zealand', in James H. Liu, Tim McCreanor, Tracey Mcintosh, and Teresia Teaiwa (eds), *New Zealand Identities: Departures and destinations*, Wellington: Victoria University Press, 2005, 207–29; Melenaite Taumoefolau, 'Tongans – Migrations', Te Ara – the Encyclopedia of New Zealand: www.TeAra.govt.nz/en/tongans/page-1
80 Geoffrey Palmer, 'The fastest law-makers in the west', *New Zealand Listener*, 25 May 1977, 13.
81 Lincoln Tan, 'New Zealand Chinese support Australian racism apology', *New Zealand Herald*, 30 April 2011: www.nzherald.co.nz/nz/news/article.cfm?c_id=1&objectid=10738017
82 'September 11: New Zealand's decade-long reaction', *New Zealand Herald*, 7 September 2011: www.nzherald.co.nz
83 Ward and Masgoret, 'Attitudes toward immigrants, immigration, and multiculturalism in New Zealand', 242–43.
84 Ron Johnston, Phillip Gendall, Andrew Trlin and Paul Spoonley, 'Immigration, multiculturalism and geography: Inter-group contact and attitudes to immigrants and cultural diversity in New Zealand', *Asian and Pacific Migration Journal* 13:3, 2010, 343–69.

BIBLIOGRAPHY

Banting , K. and Kymlicka, W., 'Canadian multiculturalism: Global anxieties and local debates', *British Journal of Canadian Studies* 23:1, 2010, 43–72.
Beaglehole, Ann, 'Immigration regulation – 1881–1914: Restrictions on Chinese and others', Te Ara – the Encyclopedia of New Zealand: www.TeAra.govt.nz/en/immigration-regulation/page-2
Bedford, Richard, 'New Zealand: The politicisation of immigration', paper presented at the Migration Research Group, University of Waikato, Hamilton, January 2003.
Bedford, Richard and Elsie Ho, *Asians in New Zealand: Implications of a changing demography*, Wellington: Asia–NZ Foundation, 2008.
Bleich, E., 'Immigration and integration studies in Western Europe and the United States: The road less traveled and a path ahead', *World Politics* 60:3, 2008, 509–38.
Boumankhar, I., 'Immigrant communities, cultural institutions and political space: The success of the immigration museum in Melbourne, Australia', *Human Architecture* 9:4, 2011, 61–92.

Brookfield, F.M., *Waitangi and Indigenous Rights: Revolution, law and legitimacy*, Auckland: Auckland University Press, 1998, 5.

Brooking, T. and Rabel, R., 'Neither British nor Polynesian: A brief history of New Zealand's other immigrants', in Stuart Greif (ed.), *Immigration and National Identity in New Zealand*, Palmerston North: Dunmore Press, 1995, 23–49.

Burke, K., 'Review of immigration policy', *Appendices to the Journal of the House of Representatives G.42*, New Zealand Parliament, Wellington, 1986, 11.

Campbell, Alastair V., 'A report from New Zealand: Ethics in a bicultural context', *Bioethics*. 9:2, 1995, 149–54.

Chang, James, 'Māori views on immigration: Implications for Māori–Chinese interactions', in Manying Ip (ed.), *The Dragon and the Taniwha: Māori and Chinese in New Zealand*, Auckland: Auckland University Press, 2009, 185–208.

Consedine, Joanna and Robert Consedine, *Healing our History: The challenge of the Treaty of Waitangi*, Auckland: Penguin Books, 2001.

Durie, E.T.J., 'The Treaty in Māori history', in William L. Renwick (ed.), *Sovereign Indigenous Rights: The Treaty of Waitangi in international contexts*, Wellington: Victoria University Press, 1991, 156.

Friesen, W., 'Planning for cultural diversity', in Michelle Thompson-Fawcett and Claire Freeman (eds), *Living Together: Towards inclusive communities in New Zealand*, Dunedin: Otago University Press, 2006, 59.

Hayward, Janine, 'The principles of the Treaty of Waitangi, appendix to Alan Ward', *National Overview Rangahaua Whanui Report*, vol. II, Waitangi Tribunal, 1997, 475–94, 475.

Hayward, Janine, 'Biculturalism – biculturalism in the state sector', Te Ara – the Encyclopedia of New Zealand: www.TeAra.govt.nz/en/biculturalism/page-1

Henderson, Anne, Andrew Trlin and Noel Watts, *English Language Proficiency and the Recruitment and Employment of Professional Immigrants in New Zealand*, Palmerston North: Occasional Publication No.11, New Settlers Programme, Massey University, 2006.

Hill, Richard S. 'Fitting multiculturalism into biculturalism: Māori-Pasifika relations in New Zealand from the 1960s', *Ethnohistory* 57(2), 2010, 291–319.

Hill, Richard S., 'Ngā whakataunga tiriti – Treaty of Waitangi settlement process – Origins of the settlement process', Te Ara – the Encyclopedia of New Zealand: www.TeAra.govt.nz/en/nga-whakataunga-tiriti-treaty-of-waitangi-settlement-process/page-1

Holmes, Kelly, Tamar Murachver and Donn Bayard, 'Accent, appearances and ethnic stereotypes in New Zealand', *New Zealand Journal of Psychology* 30, 2001, 79–86.

Inquiry to Review New Zealand's Existing Constitutional Arrangements, report of the Constitutional Arrangements Committee, August, Wellington, 2005.

Ip, Manying, 'Māori–Chinese encounters: Indigene–immigrant interaction in New Zealand', *Asian Studies Review* 27:2, 2003, 227–52.

Manying Ip, 'Chinese – later settlement', Te Ara – the Encyclopedia of New Zealand: www.TeAra.govt.nz/en/chinese/page-3

Johnston, Ron, Phillip Gendall, Andrew Trlin and Paul Spoonley, 'Immigration, multiculturalism and geography: Inter-group contact and attitudes to immigrants

and cultural diversity in New Zealand', *Asian and Pacific Migration Journal* 13:3, 2010, 343–69.
Kawharu, Hugh, [nd], English Translation of Treaty of Waitangi: www.waitangi-tribunal.govt.nz/treaty/kawharutranslation.asp
Kelsey, Jane, *A Question of Honour? Labour and the Treaty, 1984–1989*, Wellington: Allen and Unwin, 1990, 66.
Kukutai, Tahu H., 'The structure of Māori–Asian relations: An ambivalent future?', *New Zealand Population Review* 33/34, 2007, 129–51, 130.
Larner, Wendy, 'Brokering citizenship claims: Neo-liberalism, biculturalism and multiculturalism in Aotearoa New Zealand', in Evangelia Tastsoglou and Alexandra Dobrowolsky (eds), *Women, Migration and Citizenship: Making local, national and transnational connections*, Aldershot/Burlington: Ashgate, 2006, 139.
Leckie, Jacqueline, 'South Asian: Old and new migrations', in Stuart Greif (ed.), *Immigration and National Identity in New Zealand: One people; two peoples, many peoples?*, Palmerston North: Dunmore Press, 1995, 23–49.
Lowe, John M., 'Late-modernity and the theorisation of race in New Zealand', *British Review of New Zealand Studies*, 2008/09, 25.
MacPherson, Cluny, 'Reinventing the nation: Building a bicultural future from a monocultural past in Aotearoa New Zealand', in Paul R. Spickard (ed.), *Race and Nation: Ethnic systems in the modern world*, New York: Routledge, 2005, 215–38.
McHugh, Paul, *The Māori Magna Carta: New Zealand law and the Treaty*, Auckland: Oxford University Press, 1991, 12–16, 31–34.
McHugh, Paul, 'A history of Crown sovereignty in New Zealand', in Andrew Sharp and Paul McHugh (eds), *Histories, Power and Loss: Uses of the past – a New Zealand commentary*, Wellington: Bridget Williams Books, 2001, 193.
McMillan, Kate, 'The politics of immigration and multiculturalism in New Zealand', *Social Europe Journal*, 1 December 2010: www.social-europe.eu/2010/12/the-politics-of-immigration-and-multiculturalism-in-new-zealand
New Zealand Department of Labour, *A Look at New Zealand's Immigration Policy*, Wellington: Immigration Division, Department of Labour, 1970, 3.
New Zealand Herald, 'September 11: New Zealand's decade-long reaction', 7 September 2011: www.nzherald.co.nz/nz/news/article.cfm?c_id=1&objectid=10750128
O'Connor, Tony, 'New Zealand's biculturalism and the development of publicly funded rongoā (traditional Māori healing) services', *Sites: A Journal of Social Anthropology and Cultural Studies* 4:1, 2007, 70–94, 71.
Ongley, Patrick and David Pearson, 'Post-1945 international migration: New Zealand, Australia and Canada compared', *International Migration Review* 29:3, 1995, 766–93.
Orange, Claudia, *The Treaty of Waitangi*, Wellington: Bridget Williams Books, 1987, 90.
O'Sullivan, Dominic, 'Māori have a right to super city seats as first occupants', *New Zealand Herald*, 23 November 2009: www.nzherald.co.nz
Palmer, Geoffrey, 'The fastest law-makers in the west', *New Zealand Listener*, 25 May 1977, 13.

Pang, David, 'New Zealand Chinese identity: Sojourners, model minority and multiple identities', in James Ho-fu Liu, Tim McCreanor, Tracey McIntosh and Teresia Teaiwa (eds), *New Zealand Identities: Departures and destinations*, Wellington: Victoria University Press, 2005, 174–90.

Jock Phillips, 'The New Zealanders – multiculturalism', Te Ara – The Encyclopedia of New Zealand: www.TeAra.govt.nz/en/the-new-zealanders/

Pryor, Judith, *Constitutions: Writing nations, reading difference*, Abington/New York: Routledge, Birkbeck Law Press, 2008, 87.

Pryor, Judith, 'Unwritten constitutions? British exceptionalism and New Zealand equivocation', *European Journal of English Studies* 11, 1, 2007, 79–92.

Scott, Stuart C., *The Travesty of Waitangi: Towards anarchy*, Dunedin: Campbell Press, 1995.

Sibley, Chris G. and James H. Liu, 'Attitudes towards biculturalism in New Zealand: Social dominance and Pākehā attitudes towards the general principles and resource-specific aspects of bicultural policy', *New Zealand Journal of Psychology* 33:2, 2004, 88–99.

Singham, Mervin, 'Multiculturalism in New Zealand – the need for a new paradigm', *Aotearoa Ethnic Network Journal* 1:1, 2006, 34.

Skilling, Peter, 'The construction and use of national identity in contemporary New Zealand political discourse', *Australian Journal of Political Science* 45: 2, 2010, 175–89.

Spoonley Paul and Richard Bedford, *Welcome to our World? Immigration and the reshaping of New Zealand*, Auckland: Dunmore Publishing, 2012, 10.

Spoonley, Paul and Cluny MacPherson, 'Immigrants and cross-border connections and activities', in Paul Spoonley, Cluny MacPherson and David George Pearson, (eds), *Tangata Tangata: The changing ethnic contours of New Zealand*, Southbank, Victoria: Thomson, 2004, 175–94.

Statistics New Zealand, 2006: www.search.stats.govt.nz/

Statistics New Zealand, '2013 Census QuickStats about culture and identity', 2014: www.stats.govt.nz/Census/2013-census/profile-and-summary-reports/quickstats-culture-identity.aspx

Stuart, Ian, 'Māori and the mainstream: Towards bicultural reporting', *Pacific Journalism Review* 8, 2002, 42–58, 43–44.

Tan, Lincoln, 'New Zealand Chinese support Australian racism apology', *New Zealand Herald*, 30 April 2011: www.nzherald.co.nz/nz/news/article.cfm?c_id=1&objectid=10738017

Taumoefolau, Melenaite, 'Tongans – Migrations', Te Ara – the Encyclopedia of New Zealand: www.TeAra.govt.nz/en/tongans/page-1

Teaiwa, T. and Sean Mallon, 'Ambivalent kinships: Pacific peoples in New Zealand', in James H Liu, Tim McCreanor, Tracey Mcintosh, and Teresia Teaiwa (eds), *New Zealand Identities: Departures and destinations*, Wellington: Victoria University Press, 2005, 207–29

Te Puni Kokiri, *Progress Towards Closing Social and Economic Gaps between Māori and Non-Māori: A report to the Minister of Māori Affairs*, Wellington: Te Puni Kokiri, 2000.

Te Puni Kokiri, *A Guide to the Principles of the Treaty of Waitangi as Expressed by the Courts and the Waitangi Tribunal*, Wellington: Te Puni Kokiri, 2001.

Thomas, D.R. and Linda Waimarie Nikora, 'From assimilation to biculturalism: Changing patterns in Māori–Pākehā relationships', in D.R. Thomas and A. Veno (eds), *Psychology and Social Change: Creating an international agenda*, Palmerston North: Dunmore Press, 1992, 231–56.

Walker, Ranginui, 'Māori sovereignty: The Māori perspective', in Hineani (ed.), *Māori Sovereignty: The Māori perspective*, Melbourne Auckland: Hodder Moa Beckett, 1995, 284–85.

Walker, Ranginui, *Nga Pepa a Ranginui: The Walker Papers*, Auckland: Penguin Books, 1996.

Ward, Alan, *An Unsettled History: Treaty claims in New Zealand today*, Wellington: Bridget Williams Books, 1999, 20.

Ward, Colleen, Anne Margaret Masgoret and C.H. Leong, 'Immigration, acculturation and intergroup relations in New Zealand', paper presented at the 18th International Congress of the International Association for Cross-cultural Psychology, Spetses: Greece, 2006.

Ward, Colleen and Anne Margaret Masgoret, 'Attitudes toward immigrants, immigration, and multiculturalism in New Zealand: A social psychological analysis', *International Migration Review* 42:1, 2008, 227–48.

Williams, Joe, 'Wai 262 Claim of the Waitangi Tribunal', Treaty Debate Series at Te Papa. Wellington: Radio New Zealand, 29 January 2012.

Young, Steven, 'Human rights and the Treaty of Waitangi: A view from the Asian community', paper presented to the Human Rights Commission, 2004: www.stevenyoung.co.nz/The-Chinese-in-New-Zealand/Biculturalism-Multiculturalism/Human-Rights-Commission-Treaty.html

Part II: The Performance of Asian Multiculturalism

4. Native Alienz

HILARY CHUNG

In recent years there has been considerable academic discussion on ways in which theorisations of multiculturalism can be applied to the New Zealand context.[1] Such discussion necessarily explores multiple intersections: between the nature of specific national discourse and culture, and the balance between rights and expectations of both established society and in-comers; and between recognition, accommodation, assimilation and integration[2] on the one hand, and New Zealand's unique cultural paradigm of biculturalism, deriving from the Treaty of Waitangi on the other, especially as this is interrogated by the multicultural realities of New Zealand's urban centres. Despite such discussion, New Zealand has not engaged the paradigm shift that might become possible through the enactment of policy. This paper examines such intersections from the perspective of Asian New Zealand theatre and argues that performative culture itself can embody possibilities of multicultural social practice.

Questions of assimilation or integration by in-comers[3] presuppose that there is some kind of common cultural framework in a society. Even though it has not officially been adopted as such,[4] and there exists a spectrum of continually evolving interpretations,[5] biculturalism became de facto government policy only in 1986.[6] Nevertheless, this myth of national identity informs the dominant contemporary conceptualisation of New Zealand nationhood and its retrospective projection. At the same time, as numerous studies have indicated, no recognition is afforded within the myth to the multiple ethno-cultural identities within New Zealand. To varying degrees, these are excluded from the British-configured version of European civilisation[7] which dominates the bicultural relationship. In this context the definition of the term 'Pākehā' is crucial. First used to designate the fair-skinned in-comers from Britain, more recently it has come to denote, in popular parlance, whites born in New Zealand and their descendants. Key in the development of Pākehā identity was (and is) the need for a category that functions primarily to distinguish itself from Māori, rather than articulating internal differences. By 1985 historian Michael King was able to reframe the term Pākehā to denote 'non-Māori New Zealanders'.[8] While, in practice, this reframing perpetuated earlier racial implications and reflects the exclusion of minorities of colour from the paradigm, at the same time it enables a consideration of multiculturalism whereby such minorities might be placed within it. The focus here on the term Pākehā in preference to alternatives such as tauiwi[9] reflects the way in which this term, while it originally referenced a particular historical relationship, necessarily incorporated implicit notions of racial empowerment which, as they have become increasing explicit, have literally 'coloured' the discourses of multiculturalism in New Zealand.

The desire to authenticate the location of minorities of colour within the bicultural framework is one force that has fuelled the energies behind the creation of The Oryza Foundation for Asian Performing Arts. The performances discussed below participate in the bicultural dialogue with Māori and thereby offer reflections on questions at the heart of the theoretical debates on multiculturalism, that is, the dominance of a monoculturalist agenda behind the screen of pluralist rhetoric;[10] the danger of the permanent marginalisation via ethnicisation of the migrant; and the extent of the exclusionary nature of the bicultural framework.

What is indisputable is that the national politics of multiculturalism shape both the material practice of multicultural theatre and its critical reception. Equally indisputable is the way the deployment of the ethnically or racially marked body is key to such theatre praxis.[11] But as soon as we deploy descriptors such as 'multicultural' or 'cross-cultural' we enter into a multiplicity of intersecting discourses which have been deployed in other cultural contexts long before they began to be used in New Zealand. Although New Zealand's cultural paradigm has a unique delineation, it is through understanding the critical discourses surrounding 'multicultural theatre' elsewhere that we may more insightfully examine what is happening at home. This is particularly important because of the very adolescence of New Zealand's own multicultural theatre practice, because that practice does not exist in a vacuum, and since much of the dominant critical scholarship in this area arises from cultural contexts that differ from that of New Zealand.

In general terms multiculturalism refers to the ways in which a nation engages with diversity, and relates directly to the ways in which national identity is constructed. In countries such as Australia and Canada, multiculturalism is official federal policy, which provides a structure for recognising difference and incorporating it into the mosaic of national polity and culture, while maintaining a commitment to equality, social stability and justice.[12] 'Migrants are encouraged – and, to a certain extent, forced by the logic of the discourse – to preserve their cultural heritage, and the government provides support and facilities for them to do so.'[13]

By comparison, the national identity of the United States has an ideological rather than a cultural basis, as encapsulated in the Declaration of Independence, whereby cultural and ethnic specificity are transcended by a 'secular political universalism'.[14] The specifically American metaphor of the 'melting pot' envisaged the incorporation of a diverse range of ethnic and racial groups, thereby 'liberating' them from past allegiances and blending them into a unified whole.[15] A central critique of this assimilationism, from the perspective of a specific ethnicity or race, is precisely its hegemonic nature, which privileges white bourgeois patriarchal culture.[16] This 'ideal of assimilation-as-amalgamation'[17] was superseded by the salad-bowl metaphor, where each colourful salad component maintains its separate integrity while contributing to the dish as a whole. This conception privileged cultural recognition over recognition of the 'systematic, economic, political and social conditions that contribute to the domination of many subordinate groups'.[18] Post-September 11 2001, however, the pendulum has swung back to a preoccupation with shared American values.

Australian multiculturalism derives in greater part from its Canadian counterpart, but differs in its marginalisation of indigenous cultures.[19] Whereas all three domains are both products of British colonialism and settler societies, postcolonial Britain itself, especially since the publication in 2000 of the *Report of the Runnymede Trust Commission on the Future of Multi-Ethnic Britain*, is yet to find ways to transcend an historic association of British-ness with white-ness or to reconcile the rights and protections of the individual with the collective rights of ethnic communities, in consideration of a more multi-ethnic understanding of national identity.[20]

These differences in approach to national identity inflect the way multicultural theatre is understood, funded and practised, whether as enactments of official cultural policy or as racially and/or ethnically defined interest groups with distinct agendas. In their 'Topography of Cross-Cultural Theatre Praxis', Jacqueline Lo and Helen Gilbert identify two major types of multicultural theatre: what they call small 'm' multicultural theatre and big 'M' multicultural theatre.[21] They also divide each of these into a number of sub-categories – which, although, necessarily unstable and contestable, do provide interesting reference points for an analysis of New Zealand practice. The following discussion draws on Lo and Gilbert's typology.

Small 'm' multicultural theatre refers to theatre practice that reflects the 'melting pot' notion of cultural pluralism. It tends to assume an audience from the dominant culture and appears to neutralise the racial and cultural differences of performers. Typical of such theatre is the use of non-traditional or 'blind casting' in the deployment of a deliberately racially mixed cast, although it often does not address the potential incongruities that might thereby be created between the text and the performance. This is most often seen in productions of canonical plays staged for a mainstream audience. For example, Pao describes the controversy that arose over JoAnne Akalaitis's 1989 production of Shakespeare's *Cymbeline* for the New York Shakespeare Festival, in which she cast a white actor as the Queen and a black actor as her son Cloten.[22] While such interventions challenge assumptions that 'the neutral space is implicitly white'[23] they can only be meaningful in the representation of national identity on stage if they are understood in terms of the tension between verisimilitude (what is enacted on stage should replicate or reflect the audience's experience of everyday life) and illusionism (the performance on stage transcends real life) implicit in the realist aesthetic.[24] Such casting practice provides opportunities for actors of colour in roles which transcend racial stereotyping, but it embodies the central problematic of the melting pot, namely that it gives the appearance of diversity without addressing the privileged position of the dominant culture. This approach has been rigorously critiqued as 'assimilationism' – the 'white-washing' of racial and cultural specificities.[25]

An extreme enactment of non-traditional casting is practised by companies such as the National Asian American Theatre Company in the US, which has an ethnically specific agenda to 'promote and support Asian American actors, directors, designers and technicians'. In their production of *Othello*, the actor playing Othello appeared to be white but the company's website described him as being of British, Filipino, Spanish, Russian and Turkish descent. Indeed that small fraction of Asian descent was needed for the company to adhere to its mission.[26]

A second theatrical form included in the small 'm' multicultural category is what Lo and Gilbert describe as 'folkloric display'. This type of practice promotes performance that is seen as encapsulating the history and tradition of a specifically categorised minority group. While it might appear to enable recognition for the traditional cultural practice of that group, Lo and Gilbert argue that such theatre fetishises cultural difference by overdetermining the ways through which a minority group and its identity can be represented and articulated.[27] By locating a notion of authenticity of cultural practice in the past and as static, and associating it with the place of origin, articulations of hybridised identity that negotiate with dominant cultural values are rendered impossible. Further, assuming audience values that represent the dominant culture, it can be argued that this form does not enable a mode of interaction – only one of performance and observation.[28]

By contrast, big 'M' multicultural theatre is generally what Lo and Gilbert call 'a counterdiscursive practice that aims to promote cultural diversity, access to cultural expression, and participation in the symbolic space of the national narrative'.[29] Unlike their small 'm' counterparts, these types of theatre practice engage directly with contemporary cultural politics and may also seek to envisage future multicultural possibilities. They may also be enabled by government funding at either a local or national level. Lo and Gilbert name three types of theatre practice under the broad category of big 'M' multicultural theatre: *ghetto theatre*, *migrant theatre*, and *community theatre*, which could be construed in terms of the multi-generational experience of migration and assimilation. *Ghetto theatre* refers to a form of monocultural practice located within a specific community, which is likely to be performed in the language/s of that community for an audience drawn from that community. It suggests a greater sense of connection to the place of origin and a nostalgia for a real or imagined homeland. *Migrant theatre*, on the other hand, foregrounds narratives of migration and cultural adaptation into the society of settlement and thus suggests a second-generation perspective. As such it has broader audience appeal than the former, although both these types of practice are primarily directed at audiences from migrant communities. *Community theatre* is characterised by a more active engagement with the society in which it is located. Indeed, it seeks to bring about attitudinal change and draws on a range of cultural resources from the community to which it performs. Such theatre may be associated with a particular interest group or a specific location, but central to its ethos is its engagement with audiences drawn both from minority groups and from the cultural mainstream.

Multicultural theatre then, whether with a small or large 'm', is most likely to be associated, either directly or indirectly, with state-determined cultural policy. Its practice is necessarily shaped by both conceptualisations of citizenship and the ways in which cultural and ethnic difference is managed by the state. At the same time it also responds to the realities of life in a culturally plural society. In the New Zealand case discussed below, both elements are apparent: the bicultural paradigm has a distinct inflection, and the multicultural realities of life – particularly in Auckland – are explored.

The Oryza Foundation for Asian Performing Arts was incorporated in July 2007. Its mission statement is expressed on the Oryza website as follows: 'We strive to facilitate, produce, promote and advocate for Asian performing arts.'[30] This is expanded in a vision statement:

> *We aspire to raise the bar of Asian performing arts by:*
> - *being a sustainable arts body,*
> - *nurturing performing arts creatives and producers in developing and creating Asian content,*
> - *supporting the capacity building of Asian performing arts societies, groups and organisations,*
> - *developing audiences both within and beyond the Asian community,*
> - *fostering cross-cultural and multi-sector buy-in,*
> - *challenging stereotypes,*
> - *encourage authentic representation of Asian culture, and*
> - *providing funding advice and support and creating business and networking opportunities.*[31]

This vision statement is a construct, the existence of which was originally enabled by policy-driven support. In an earlier iteration of the Oryza website, Creative New Zealand and Asia New Zealand Foundation were prominently featured as sponsors. In the vision statement the counterdiscursive drive is explicitly articulated in the desire to challenge stereotypes, and to provide the advice and opportunities to do so. There is also a clear promotion of cultural diversity and access to cultural expression, both in terms of audience development and opportunities for Asian artists. This is an agenda that seeks to enable participation in the symbolic space of the national narrative. At the same time the claim is made to authenticity in the representation of what is termed 'Asian culture'. While this represents an attempt to claim agency, such a claim runs the risk of fetishising the racially marked performance. The category of 'folkloric display' described above problematises notions of authenticity by locking them into a backward-looking enactment of tradition. If the aspirations of Oryza do not suggest that the authenticity of a performance should be designated by the ethnicity of the performer, they perpetuate an ethnic essentialism in the broader context of theatre production. This is best understood as a strategic essentialism in Spivakian terms, 'a *strategic* use of positivist essentialism in a scrupulously visible political interest',[32] which engages with the hegemony of Pākehā culture. These two statements evidence strong affinities to the community theatre category. In this case, the notion of community is pluralised via the widest possible application of the category of 'Asian-ness' – which is a recalibration of normative usage in New Zealand.[33] This is given articulation in the explanation of the name of the organisation:

> *Naming ourselves was not an easy affair. We sought to reflect as wide a representation of Asia as possible and decided very early on that we needed to identify an element that binds Asia together. It is testament to the diversity of Asia and Asians, in terms of ethnicity, culture, heritage and of course, performing arts, that it took us a rather long time to find an appropriate name for the Trust – 'Oryza'.*
>
> *Oryza is a genus of 15–20 species of grasses in the subfamily Oryzoideae, native to tropical and subtropical regions of Asia and Africa. They are tall wetland grasses, growing 1–2 metres tall; the genus includes both annual and perennial species. One species, Asian Rice (Oryza sativa) – and its close cousin African Rice (Oryza glaberrima) – are food crops of major global importance.*
>
> *Asia is bound together by this humble but important plant, which sustains and supports people and communities in over half the world. Almost all Asian cultures have a unique rice-based dish; and while the Western world also has rice-based dishes, it is undeniable that rice has more importance on an Asian table.*
>
> *Therefore, Oryza was chosen as the symbol of The Oryza Foundation™, a charitable organisation set up to nourish and support a wide range of Asian arts communities, be it South East Asian, South Asian, Central Asian, Middle or Far Eastern, here in this corner of the world.*[34]

The recalibration of 'Asian-ness' beyond its standard New Zealand usage is naturalised by the covert iconisation of what is dangerously close to a cliché: the use of rice to represent all things 'Asian'.

This articulation of community gives insight into the publicity design for the event 'Asian Tales: Native Alienz', the first production of the Oryza

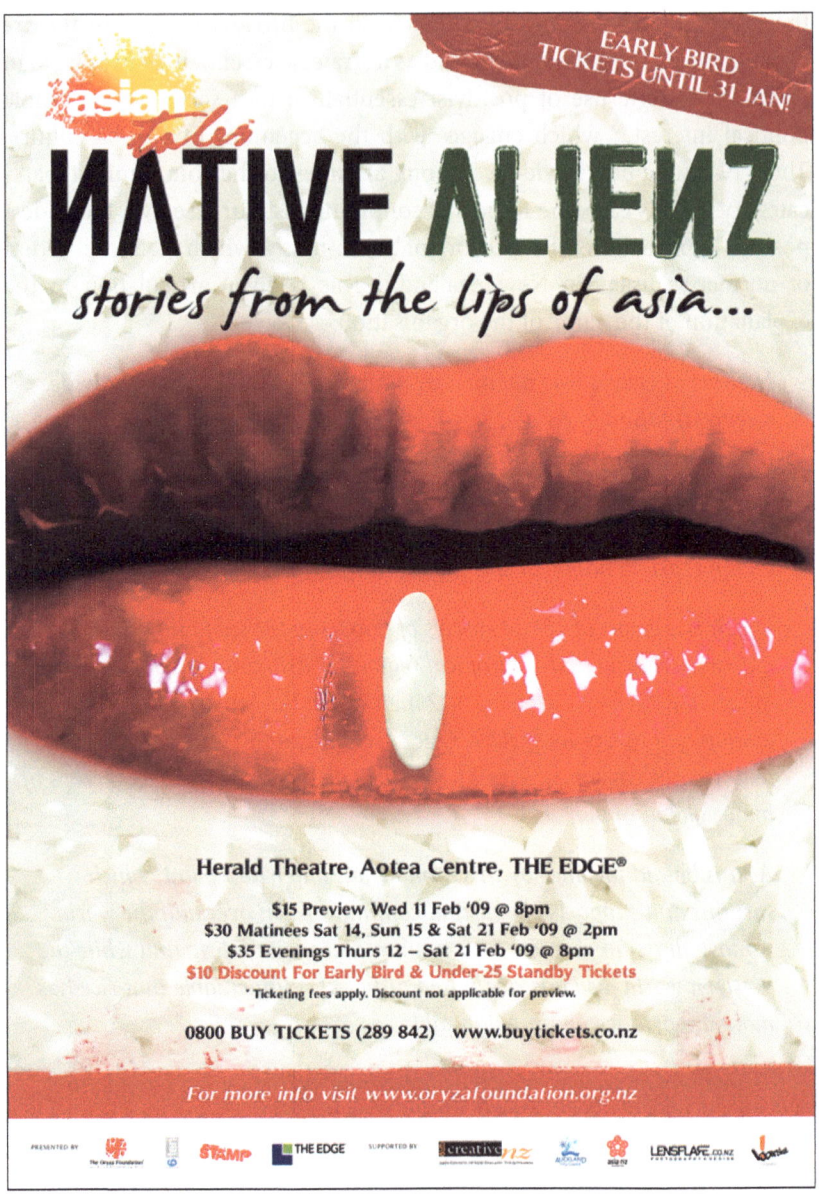

Figure 1. The poster for Native Alienz. Courtesy of the Oryza Foundation

Foundation, a suite of seven short plays which were staged at the Herald Theatre in the Aotea Centre, Auckland, in February 2009.

As can be seen in Figure 1, this is literally rice speaking, privileging articulations of New Zealand Asian identity which are necessarily able to defy stereotyping by dint of a clear ethnically marked affiliation. Importantly, the production offered creative opportunities for artists of Asian descent. This was intended to be the inaugural event of a recurring series. The aesthetics of the poster offer multiple constructions of the envisaged audience. The diasporic paradigm is clearly evoked in the main title with its vague filmic reference, suggesting that the alien is within us and raising questions about how the alien might emerge and what consequences might ensue in the process. It challenges the viewer to ask from whose perspective these 'natives' are considered alien. There are nuances of both alienation and objectification, but regardless of perspective, the alien is literally inscribed within 'NZ'. This problematisation of perspective broadens the envisaged audience beyond the immediate community, but does not preclude Asian insiders from extrapolating their own alienation also. The reversed and incomplete lettering also both evokes and explodes stereotypes, simultaneously suggesting both a less than full 'Asian' grasp of English text and a deliberate appropriation of how NZ is to be re/written. Care was taken to avoid obvious stereotyping: in an earlier draft the words 'Asian Tales' were depicted on a fan, but this design was rejected as being too clichéd.[35] At the same time the sensual feminine lips self-reflexively evoke the archetypal cliché of exoticised orientalism and simultaneously subvert it. The anticipated kiss is confounded by the suspended grain of rice, which incorporates in its tiny form the agenda of Oryza and by extension the wider discourses of multicultural engagement.[36] By locating the alien firmly within New Zealand and appealing both to a community audience and a wider New Zealand one, such theatre explicitly enters the symbolic space of the national narrative. At the same time it disrupts the diasporic identity paradigm by failing to triangulate with a clearly articulated place of origin.[37] Place of settlement is privileged to the extent that the catch-all Kiwi signifier 'Asian' is the singular referent of identity.[38] Whereas diasporic narratives tend to be posited as marginal to the national narrative, these explorations present themselves insistently as being part of it.

Meaning in a performance text is embodied and contingent. It is a transaction negotiated between the bodies on stage and those in the audience. It is contingent upon which bodies are deployed in which space and at which moment, and upon the infinite assumptions, discourses and stereotypes that are brought to bear. Thus the performance of this set of one-act plays enabled multiple re-articulations of the national narrative via the deployment of variously marked bodies on the stage, the meanings of their embodiment of the various texts made possible in transactions with each audience member.

The Plays

Mount Head

A tragi-comedy on the absurdity of human existence.

Written and performed by Hiroshi Nakatsuji.
Directed by Tony Forster.

A stingy man greedily munches on cherries and their seeds. One seed germinates within him and grows into a cherry tree...on his head! This surreal story showcases Rakugo - a traditional Japanese form of storytelling.

The Loyal Customer

An opportunity presents itself at a Vietnamese food stall.

Written and directed by Ying Ly.

In the contemporary world of Auckland's food hall culture, a pregnant girl who dreams of fashion school becomes a regular customer at a Vietnamese stall. An opportunistic action inadvertently changes the course of the chef's life.

Vang	Gary Young
Emma	Ema Barton
Young	Katlyn Wong
Chris	Hiroshi Nakatsuji

Intrusions

A story of invasion, double standards, and love.

Written by Misa Tupou. Directed by Gerald Urquhart.

Despised and condemned for the colour of his skin, a Lone Figure holds on to his golden dream of being with his lover. When the pressure invades his soul, he snaps into action to fight for his rights.

Lone Figure/ Politician	Leand Macadaan
Chorus	John Giang
	Ally Xue
	Gary Young

Midnight, State Highway 01

A young man and woman form a connection after a midnight car accident.

Written by Mukilan Thangamani.

A young Indian man and an East-Asian woman meet after a late-night accident on a deserted highway. As they wait for a tow truck, they find things to share...

Lisa	May Lee Allen
Ray	Alvin Maharaj

The Mooncake & The Kumara

A non-romantic romance about relationships and belonging.

1927: In a market garden in Manawatu just before the mid-autumn Moon Festival, a relationship grows between Chao, a Chinese man, and Alice, a Maori girl. But in the shadow is Chao's wife back in China.

Written by Mei-Lin Te-Puea Hansen & Kiel McNaughton. Directed by Alex Lee & Tony Forster.

Chao	Ezra Low
Wife	Mei Chen
Alice	Amber Curreen

Mask

A father and daughter's quest for identity.

A Chinese girl growing up in New Zealand tries to come to terms with her split identity, while her father tries to respond to his daughter's changing ideas. Masks both hide and reveal... including bravery in the face of change.

Written by Renee Liang. Directed by Gerald Urquhart.

Father	Ezra Low
Daughter	May Lee Allen

Citizen 3

An exploration into sense of identity.

Sean is a young Malaysian-Chinese man having trouble living up to the expectations of both his nationality and ethnicity. A sudden turn of events exposes the effects of Sean's upbringing.

Written by Davina Goh. Directed by Yee Yang 'Square' Lee.

Sean	Leand Macadaan
Penelope	Andrea Bates
Ping	John Giang
Interviewer/ Taxi Driver/ Waiter	Alvin Maharaj

End

Figure 2.

The first performance opens with the appearance on stage of Hiroshi Nakatsuji wearing a *haori* jacket. This traditionally clothed, ethnically Japanese male actor welcomes the audience with a mihi (greeting) in perfectly articulated te reo (Māori language). By so doing, he steps adroitly into the symbolic space of the New Zealand narrative, mirroring the classic Pākehā gesture of incorporating Māori into formal oratory.[39] This gesture of familiarity predisposes the audience towards the performer and enables him to lead them into his performance, which derives from the traditional Japanese story-telling form *rakugo*.[40] This surrealist piece entitled *Mount Head*, written by Nakatsuji and directed by Tony Forster, tells the story of an avid cherry-eater whose body is taken over by a cherry tree that grows through his head. Nakatsuji kneels on bamboo mats, which remain on stage, and tells his tale with the aid of the traditional *rakugo* props of handkerchief and fan. Both the programme notes and the local reviews that refer to them[41] emphasise the traditional flavour of the performance – the irony being that this performance, as the programme notes elsewhere reveal, while being inspired by a *rakugo* story, is part of Nakatsuji's stand-up comedic routine and is far from 'authentic' in a Japanese sense, not least since it is delivered in English and te reo. Key to the way this opening act both sets the scene for the whole sequence of performances and engages with multiculturalist discourse, is the double embodiment of perceived 'authenticity' by this Japanese performer. His use of te reo lends a sense of authenticity in New Zealand terms by locating the performance within the bicultural superstructure; at the same time, a performance derived from *rakugo*, and authenticated by Nakatsuji's embodied 'Japanese-ness', is able to claim a place there also. The opening introduces the way in which all the performances that follow are squarely located in the New Zealand context, while at the same bringing aspects of 'Asian' cultures or values into that space. It also raises the central question of the relationship between the body's appearance and its performance, which is sustained throughout the sequence of playlets.

At the outset of Ying Ly's *The Loyal Customer*, ethnically marked bodies follow stereotyped modes of behaviour. In an Auckland food hall, a scene quintessentially familiar to most Aucklanders,[42] a friendship develops between Vang, the proprietor of a Vietnamese food stall, and his customer, Emma, a pregnant white arts student. Emma is friendly and provides humour by being somewhat loud and uncouth. Her unborn child, it is revealed, has no acknowledged father, and the audience is encouraged to share Vang's initial disapproval. He is hardworking and laconic but is eventually won over by her engaging loquaciousness. She partially fills the empty space left by his own absent daughter who, following expectations, has studied hard (in apparent contrast to Emma) and become a successful professional overseas. Vang wishes his own daughter was pregnant and providing him with a longed-for grandchild. He is attentive towards the young woman even when he learns that she is a surrogate mother, a fact that offends his sense of the context in which babies should be born and the implications about descent and race that derive therefrom. The audience again is encouraged to sympathise with Vang's views. In an ironic twist, Emma's departure heralds the arrival of Vang's own daughter with her Asian husband and a baby: having experienced difficulty conceiving, the couple has arranged a surrogate birth.

This playlet disrupts multiple stereotypes – those that might be sustained by mainstream cultural values, and those sustained by the 'Asian community' – and negotiates meaning with the range of views that might be held by the mixed audience. In her apparent lack of concern for her unborn child's father, Pākehā Emma gives the impression of sexual promiscuity and appears irresponsible in 'Asian' eyes, but is revealed to be both generous-hearted and single-minded, using the surrogacy fee to pay for her studies. The poignant human feelings displayed by the middle-aged Vang are foregrounded. As a father he cares deeply for his daughter, even if he does not make his feelings known. Speaking to the archetypal stereotype of Asian parenthood, Ying Ly reminds her audience that a parent's expectations for their children can have unexpected consequences, and that paradigms of 'happy families' need not be set in stone. At the same time the issue of surrogacy offers the potential for reconfiguring notions of lineage and citizenship.

The explicit agenda of the Oryza Foundation is to deploy the racially marked body in order to foreground issues of racial exclusion, and thus racial intrusion, into the exclusive bi-racial parameters of New Zealand's national identity construction. *Intrusions* by Misa Tupou (directed by Gerald Urqhart) enacts racial exclusion in all its extreme physicality. The programme notes read: 'Despised and condemned for the colour of his skin, a Lone Figure holds on to his golden dream of being with his lover. When the pressure invades his soul, he snaps into action to fight for his rights.' Inspired by the experience of Chinese gold miners in Otago, this piece presents a stylised and hallucinatory yet extraordinarily physical portrayal of the anguish of exclusion. The central figure is surrounded and tormented by a malevolent chorus, foregrounding the significance of individual relationships in the perpetuation of exclusionary practice. While there are possibilities for transcendence through the universal appeal of the love theme, these are eclipsed by the unremitting suffering of the protagonist.

In other playlets, bodies visibily identifiable in ethnic terms are deployed in ways that enable this specific ethnic framing to be transcended. *Midnight, State Highway 1*, by Mukilan Thangamani, is played on an empty stage with very low lighting. A man, Ray, is contemplating suicide in his parked unlit car at night. A second driver, Lisa, collides with his car. Neither are hurt. During the long wait for the tow truck they share their hopes and fears and reach an understanding. Ray is played by Alvin Maharaj, an actor with ethnic origins in the Indian subcontinent, but in the reduced lighting this is not overtly apparent. Lisa is played by May Lee Allen who appears to be white. Ray has been driven to despair by the expectations of others, particularly family, which he is unable to fulfil. Lisa is running away from a difficult relationship. There is no overt cultural framing for these pressures, however: they may be interpreted variously according to the multiple perspectives of the audience. The programme notes present a racially delineated encounter and an intention to explore commonalities of experience between different Asian communities: '[a] young Indian man and an East-Asian woman meet after a late night accident on a deserted highway.' Yet the deployment of ambiguously coded bodies allows for the possibility of appeal across the audience spectrum to commonalities of experience not marked by race or ethnicity. The potential paradigm shift is literally embodied by May Lee Allen who is of mixed race, although this was not readily apparent on the night. The lighting employed can be taken to be a reflection on vision itself, insofar as vision is, among the senses, privileged in Western modernity as a means for apprehending reality.

The performance of *Mask* by Renee Liang (directed by Gerald Urqhart) highlights how textual meaning can be multiplied or problematised by embodiment. A Chinese father and a second-generation daughter each wear stylised opera masks. As the daughter grows up she increasingly wishes to separate the role of Chinese daughter from her identity as an individual. The generational and cultural gap between them widens until, in the penultimate scene, the daughter faces the audience, pulls off her mask and declares: 'I don't want to be Chinese any more.' The implications of this dramatic moment depend on the body that is revealed. The audience expects a Chinese face, but it is May Lee Allen's face that is revealed. If the actor's appearance is construed as white, cultural identity is decoupled from race. Further, the performance is removed from the specificity of the Chinese cultural context and made applicable to other New Zealand contexts – are we not all bounded to a greater or lesser extent by the roles we are expected to play? If the actor's appearance is construed as Chinese, the moment encapsulates the dilemma of an ethnic minority but also interrogates the meaning of New Zealand-ness and demands inclusion.

The disconnectedness of race from identity, whether cultural, ethnic or national is taken further in *Citizen 3* by Davina Goh (directed by Yee Yang 'Square' Lee) through the character Sean. While this play is also disconnected from a specifically New Zealand context, Sean is stranded by the conflicting expectations that arise from an identity that is defined in multiple ways. Born in the Philippines, brought up and educated in Dubai and now negotiating the racially charged identity politics of Malaysia, his sense of belonging and affiliation is rather determined by his relationships with those close to him, including his white girlfriend, Penelope. This playlet is the final performance of the suite and leaves the audience to ponder the intractability of the racially defined identity paradigm, which they necessarily inhabit as New Zealanders.

The practice of blind casting simultaneously foregrounds and downplays the deployment of the ethnically or racially marked body. In the off-stage decision-making the body is foregrounded, as it is in the politics that frame the production. On stage the audience is expected to see and yet not see the marked body. While the deployment of racial difference on stage is a gesture towards equality and inclusion in the national narrative, the expectation that the audience both sees and yet does not see it in the context of the performance itself means that the normative cultural assumptions of an audience from the dominant culture remain 'white-washed'. By contrast, and in the context of the mission statement of the Oryza Foundation, the deployment of the racially marked body in 'Asian Tales' seeks to be perpetually foregrounded. The audience is expected to read and interpret the body at all times; even when its racial delineation is ambiguous or confounds expectations it still must be read within the discursive parameters of the production, with some iteration of 'Asian' identity or culture as a consistent point of reference. The performance of the playlet *Midnight, State Highway 1* is of particular interest in this respect because, apart from the programme notes that specify racially defined characters for the two roles, there are no specific cultural reference points in the script, only those brought to the transaction by individual audience members in the way they interpret the bodies that perform. In this way the playlet is able to look beyond the racial specificity of the body in the embodiment of New Zealand discourses of identity.

This insistence on making racial difference visible returns us to the central problematic of New Zealand's national identity paradigm, namely that what is termed b*iculturalism* has long since become predicated on white-ness rather than British affiliation in the relationship with Māori.[43] While the process of evolution over time from specifically British-derived cultural practice to what Gunew has described as 'notions of European cosmopolitanism'[44] was far from smooth, it denotes the slippage from race to culture to race in discourses of biculturalism. While a range of cultural practices inflected by different waves of immigration can be subsumed within the bicultural framework on the basis of white-ness, when the divergence of cultural practice is accompanied by racial difference, or even when there is no obvious cultural divergence, the framework cannot contain it.[45] It is this insufficiently acknowledged discourse of race that limits access to national belonging.[46] This can be understood as an important driver of the agenda of the Oryza Foundation, as *embodied* in this production. The short play which most explicitly places the Asian body into the bicultural framework is *The Mooncake and the Kumara* by Mei-Lin Te-Puea Hansen and Kiel McNaughton (directed by Alex Lee and Tony Forster.) Whereas Hiroshi Nakatsuji incorporates a facility with the Māori language into a performance that derives from the Japanese comic storytelling form *rakugo* which is likely to be unfamiliar to many, this play returns to the more familiar ground of the historical encounter with Māori, upon which the discourse of New Zealand nationhood is founded, but gives it a different racial colouring.

In the programme notes the two co-authors, who are also cousins, present this piece as a romantic reimagining of their shared Chinese and Māori ethnic roots, but it can also be understood as an encapsulation of the bicultural encounter between Māori and in-comers in microcosm. The importance of the small scale of the encounter is that it brings the problematics of national discourse down to the personal level. The action downstage presents the growing relationship between Chao, a Chinese market gardener in 1920s Manawatu (played by Ezra Low) and Alice, a Māori girl (played by Amber Curreen) who also tends her vegetable plot; yet it also encompasses the presence of Chao's wife (played by Mei Chen) who remains in China. Chao is beset by his inability to belong in this new land. In particular he despairs at his invisibility, when the Māori girl he watches appears at first not to notice him. 'She does not seem to see me, no one sees me.' Not only is he invisible, despite his race, but he has no voice: 'My words have no meaning so I don't speak. I am a voiceless numb shadow'. He remains connected to the wife he left behind, who is located upstage, by the letters he writes to her which travel between the two by means of a laundry line that both actors manipulate. Chao's mute invisibility is sustained as long as this connection remains intact. The romantic connections between Chao and the two women are framed by his attempts to celebrate the Chinese moon festival, which is, poignantly, a time not only to celebrate the harvest but also family unity and togetherness, which is symbolised by the full moon at its roundest and brightest. Incorporated into traditional lunar symbolism is the Chinese poetic conceit that, even when separated by distance, lovers can be symbolically conjoined by both viewing the moon in their separate locations. Chao begins by remembering past moon festivals spent with his wife in China but the memories are indistinct and unreliable. In a sense memory itself becomes the moon-that-connects, but insufficiently and precariously. The play closes with Alice and Chao viewing the moon together, sharing mooncake and kumara while the wife remains aloof and softly lit upstage.

This is the only play in the suite that features a Māori character. Alice speaks (and sings) Māori for the most part, incorporating just enough English for those in the audience without Māori to follow.[47] She is self-confident and generous, coming to Chao's aid when he injures his hand harvesting vegetables. While the script is predominantly a monologue in English by Chao, he speaks Chinese to Alice. As the letters between Chao and his wife travel across the stage Chao's reading in English is taken up by the wife's reading in Chinese. This acknowledgement of language and culture both offers respect and empowerment to the Māori side of the bicultural partnership and suggests the potential to dislocate 'English-ness' as the dominant delineation of those who form the other side of the partnership. While *The Mooncake and the Kumara* evokes the invisibility, voicelessness and powerlessness of the non-white other when marginalised from the bicultural framework, it also envisages how, by incorporation within it, agency and visibility can be attained. The setting in the past reminds the audience of the presence of non-British settlers, particularly the Chinese, since the earliest days. It not only offers an alternative frame for encounters with Māori by in-comers, but it speaks to a legacy of exclusion which continues to problematise New Zealand's sense of itself.

This examination of one performance of a series of short plays exemplifies how creative texts can be a powerful means of representing and meditating upon major and complex political and social issues. Their power, and particularly that of live theatre performance, lies in the ways in which these issues are enacted in intimate and personal terms, and thereby made meaningful and accessible. One of the primary preoccupations of this suite of plays is the invisibility and exclusion of Asian-ness, specifically as racially delineated, from the New Zealand paradigm of national identity. This is strategically addressed by the deliberate foregrounding of racial difference on stage, thereby embodying the agenda of the Oryza Foundation. Specifically, what is being addressed is the delineation of who is envisaged in the national consciousness as being represented by the Crown under the bi-cultural framework. Not only do the plays reflect the multicultural realities of New Zealand urban life, for example, the way that an Asian food stall is a ubiquitous and instantly recognisable feature of everyday life, but they equally present experiences which are enacted by Asian bodies who are part of the everyday New Zealand experience, a fact which is affirmed by the audience. This points to the need, first, for recognition of the underlying race-based delineation of national identity, and second, for intervention such that other ethnicities can be envisaged in the popular consciousness as being represented under the Crown. These plays make a claim to a share of the space occupied by Pākehā in the New Zealand paradigm of identity; but while they seek to envisage that space as transcending the discourse of race, at the same time they reaffirm the necessary recognition of Māori as treaty partner. Nakatsuji's performance of a mihi at the opening of the show mirrors the 'ritual incantations'[48] routinely performed by Pākehā at such occasions in evocation of the partnership. It deliberately highlights the way an Asian body performing a mihi is conceived as strange; it does not engage with – and perhaps cannot, by dint of Asian or tauiwi exclusion from it – nor explore the problematic of inequality embedded in Treaty relations per se. (As suggested above, the only play that in any way approaches such territory is *The Mooncake and the Kumara*.)

Such an interpretation of these plays suggests a resolution of the fundamental antagonism between multicultural and bicultural discourses, the latter privileging the two founding treaty partners to the exclusion of later arrivals, particularly those of colour, and the former threatening to conflate Māori collective rights and their status as indigenous people with the individual rights of more recent immigrants.[49] Rather, on the one hand, the insistence by scholars such as Kymlicka – that national culture should accommodate both immigrants and cultural, ethnic and religious diversity[50] – should apply to those represented under the Crown; while, on the other hand, cultural adaption by immigrants should recognise the implications of the partnership with Māori in which they should be officially included. To a considerable extent this is suggestive of Fleras and Spoonley's proposition of multiculturalism within a bi-national framework:

> *Multiculturalism addresses the concerns of voluntary immigrants who are seeking symbolic legitimation of their status within and contribution to society. The focus is on discouraging the mainstream from prejudiced attitudes and discriminatory practices at individual and institutional levels. Bi-nationalism, by contrast, acknowledges the primacy of indigeneity and original occupancy in establishing agendas and setting priorities. The sharing of power in a spirit of partnership between equals is pivotal in giving practical effect to bi-nationality.*[51]

The common critique of Kymlicka is that he overprivileges the dominant culture. This has also been leveled at Fleras and Spoonley's sense of multiculturalism as 'grafting bits of diversity onto a mainstream core'.[52] These plays suggest the mutual cultural accommodations that are already occurring in everyday life in New Zealand. They also stress the inevitable assimilation to Pākehā norms by long-established minority communities, which both enables recognition of common experiences by a mixed audience, and emphasises the way this is problematised by the discourse of race embedded in the national identity paradigm. If intervention to shape the way in which national identity is popularly envisaged is by way of the institution of policy, 'Native Alienz' is resistant to the commonly critiqued[53] problematic of official multiculturalism, namely that by recognizing a fixed cultural mosaic through which it redefines national identity, it tends to 'freeze the fluidity of identity' and to permanently 'ethnicise' minorities in a marginalising discourse of migration.[54] 'Native Alienz' eschews the fetishisation of cultural difference by deliberately disaggregating race, culture and identity. At the same time the international success of theatre and other performing arts that represent the 'multicultural voice of Aotearoa',[55] including the Indian Ink Theatre Company,[56] has led to discussions of ethnicity as a form of cultural capital[57] for the nation. This returns us to the question of the ways New Zealand is envisaged in the national imaginary and its relationship with the way it is culturally represented overseas. The need for official intervention, which engages in a meaningful way with the problematics of the national identity paradigm, would appear to be all the more pressing.

'Native Alienz' responds to the hesitancy to move beyond the fetishisation of 'ethnic' difference that is reflected in the continued preoccupation with the racial/ethnic origin of performers and playwrights in the discourses of New Zealand theatre.[58] The imperative to write and perform the racially marked body in multiple ways has the potential to occupy and reconfigure the symbolic space of the national narrative, and reflects a desire to revivify the national debate. In so doing New Zealand 'ethnic theatre' practice necessarily engages with the more established ethnic theatre practices overseas, in the US and elsewhere, and therefore with other discourses of multiculturalism. Thus an understanding of those discourses and practices can enable more nuanced readings of performances such as the 'Native Alienz' suite. For example, while the Asian American Theatre Company effects a strategic deployment of the racially marked body in order to engage a discourse of national identity that transcends cultural and ethnic specificity yet implicitly privileges white hegemony, the Oryza Foundation does so to envisage a transcendence of race-based exclusion within the national imaginary. In an interview in the anthology of plays entitled *Tokens? The NYC Asian American experience on stage*, edited by Alvin Eng, director Diana Son expresses her relief that a new generation of Asian American playwrights are no longer under so much pressure to explicitly portray Asian American experience.[59] In its adolescence, Asian New Zealand theatre, reflecting perhaps the adolescence of New Zealand multiculturalism, remains under a certain pressure to represent New Zealand experience as inflected with racial or ethnic specificity, particularly as the enactment of policy lags far behind New Zealand's demographic and cultural realities.

Endnotes

1. See for example David Bromell, *Ethnicity, Identity and Public Policy: Critical perspectives on multiculturalism*, Wellington: Institute of Policy Studies, Victoria University of Wellington, 2008; or the summary provided in Henk Huijser, *The Multicultural Nation in New Zealand Cinema: Production–Text–Reception*, Saarbrücken: VDM Verlag, 2009, ch.5.
2. Sune Laegaard, 'Introduction', in Nils Holtug et al (eds), *Nationalism and Multiculturalism in a World of Immigration*, Basingstoke: Palgrave Macmillan, 2009, ix–xxiii.
3. For a nation founded on immigration, where even the native peoples arrived from elsewhere, the choice of nomenclature which is not freighted with prejudicial baggage is a challenge. I have chosen to use the term 'in-comers' in an attempt to avoid the negative connotations associated with terms such as 'immigrant'. In-comers can also include both historical settlers and more recent immigrants.
4. Bromell, *Ethnicity, Identity and Public Policy*, 38.
5. Augie Fleras and Paul Spoonley, *Recalling Aotearoa: Indigenous politics and ethnic relations in New Zealand*, Auckland: Oxford University Press, 1999, 238.
6. Ibid., 232.
7. Mark Williams, 'Crippled by Geography? New Zealand Nationalisms', in Stuart Murray (ed.) *Not on Any Map: Essays on postcoloniality and cultural nationalism*, Exeter: University of Exeter Press, 1997, 20.
8. Michael King, *Being Pakeha*, Auckland: Hodder and Stoughton, 1985, 12.
9. Tauiwi is a less politically charged Māori word of which the original meaning of stranger (i.e. non-Māori) potentially incorporates all non-Māori equally. Its dictionary definition also includes the exclusive meaning of (white) European (see www.maoridictionary.co.nz). Its contemporary usage, however, has come to mean non-Māori people of colour (see for example www.mellowyellow-aotearoa.blogspot.co.nz/2013/08/tau-iwi-people-of-colour-supporting.html) although this distinction reflects usage that dates back to the 1830s. See Manuka Henare, 'The Māori Leaders' Assembly, Kororipo Pā, 1831', in Judith Binney (ed.), *Te Kerikeri 1770–1850: The meeting pool*, Wellington: Bridget Williams Books, 2007, 114–16.
10. See for example Anne Maxwell, 'Ethnicity and education: Biculturalism in New Zealand', in David Bennett (ed.), *Multicultural States: Rethinking difference and identity*, London and New York: Routledge, 1998, 205.
11. As Helen Gilbert and Joanne Tompkins make clear: 'As *visual* markers of "identity", race and gender are particularly significant in theatrical contexts ... such markers are inscribed on the body through discourse – visual, verbal or otherwise – rather than simply being unmediated or objectively given' (*Post-colonial Drama: Theory, practice and politics*, London & New York: Routledge, 1996, 205, emphasis in original).
12. Fleras and Spoonley, *Recalling Aotearoa*, 225.
13. Jon Stratton and Ien Ang, 'Multicultural imagined communities: Cultural difference and national identity in the USA and Canada', in *Multicultural States*, 138.
14. Ibid., 143.
15. Ibid., 144.

16 See for example Yongsuk Chae, *Politicising Asian American Literature: Towards a critical multiculturalism*, New York and London: Routledge, 2008, 2.
17 See Peter Kivisto, *Multiculturalism in a Global Society*, Oxford: Blackwell, 2002, 188.
18 Henry Giroux, 'The politics of insurgent multiculturalism in the era of the Los Angeles uprising', in Barry Kanpol and Peter McLaren (eds), *Critical Multiculturalism*, London and Westport: Bergin & Garvey, 1995, 117.
19 Australian multicultural policy developed in the 1970s in response to concerns that 'Anglo-conformist' assimilationism was ineffective in ensuring the successful absorption of immigrants. However, in contrast to the Canadian model, indigenous Australians were not recognised by this policy. See Katharine Smits, 'Justifying multiculturalism: Social justice, diversity and national identity in Australia and New Zealand', *Australian Journal of Political Science*, 46.1, 2011, 91.
20 See Kivisto, *Multiculturalism in a Global Society*, 154. There is an interesting parallel with the problematic that emerged after the 2006 New Zealand census as to whether and how the category of 'New Zealander' could and/or should be decoupled from the category 'New Zealand European'. See 'Profile of New Zealander Responses, Ethnicity Question: 2006 Census', www.stats.govt.nz/Census/about-2006-census/profile-of-nzer-responses-ethnicity-question-2006-census.aspx
21 Jacqueline Lo and Helen Gilbert, 'Toward a topography of cross-cultural theatre praxis', *The Drama Review* 46, no. 3, 2002: 33–35.
22 Angela C. Pao, 'Changing faces: Recasting national identity in all-Asian (-) American dramas', *Theatre Journal* 53, no. 3, 2001, 396–97.
23 Alan Nadel, 'August Wilson and the (color-blind) whiteness of public space', in 'Beyond the Wilson-Brustein debate', *Theater* 27, no. 2-3, 1997, 39. Quoted in Pao, 'Changing faces', 403.
24 Stanton B. Garner, Jr., *Bodied Spaces: Phenomenology and performance in contemporary drama*, Ithaca: Cornell University Press, 1994, 101. Quoted in Pao, 'Changing faces', 399.
25 See for example Benny Sato Ambush, 'Pluralism to the bone', *American Theatre* 61.5, 1989,. Quoted by Lo and Gilbert, 'Toward a topography of cross-cultural theatre praxis', 33.
26 See Pao, 'Changing faces', 393.
27 Lo and Gilbert, 'Toward a topography of cross-cultural theatre praxis', 34.
28 David Carter, 'The natives are getting restless: Nationalism, multiculturalism and migrant writing', *Island Magazine* 25/26, 1986, 5. Quoted by Lo and Gilbert, 'Toward a topography of cross-cultural theatre praxis', 34.
29 Ibid.
30 'Our mission': www.oryzafoundation.org.nz/our-mission
31 Ibid. Emphasis in original.
32 Gayatri Chakravorty Spivak, 'Subaltern studies: Deconstructing historiography', in *In Other Worlds: Essays in cultural politics*, New York: Methuen, 1987, 25.
33 For the 'average person on the New Zealand street' the designation 'Asian' is associated with the 'Far East'; for their UK counterpart the same designation is associated with the Indian subcontinent.

34 'What does 'oryza' mean?': www.oryzafoundation.org.nz/what-does-oryza-mean
35 Personal conversation with playwright Renee Liang, July 2010.
36 Renee Liang recalls the popularity of the poster, which was routinely appropriated by passers-by.
37 See for example Ien Ang, 'Can one say no to Chineseness? Pushing the limits of the diasporic paradigm', in Rey Chow (ed.), *Modern Chinese Literary and Cultural Studies in the Age of Theory: Reimagining a field*, Durham: Duke University Press, 2000, 28–300.
38 There are more specific references in the programme notes on some individual actors and writers.
39 Of course such articulations can also be understood as appropriation. Yet, in terms of the problematic national paradigm, such a speech act is both commonplace and frequently understood as a gesture towards an acknowledgement of the bicultural framework, however perfunctory.
40 *Rakugo*: a traditional Japanese comic story-telling performance art where a lone storyteller sits on stage and tells a complicated but comical tale using only a paper fan and a small cloth as props.
41 See for example Jessie Kollen, 'Life is simply very complicated', 13 February 2009: www.theatreview.org.nz/reviews/review.php?id=1894
42 One reviewer notes the food-stall's 'authentically flickering fluorescent light'! See Janet McAllister, 'Review: Asian Tales: Native Alienz at Herald Theatre', 16 February 2009: www.nzherald.co.nz/theatre/news/article.cfm?c_id=343&objectid=10556881
43 Radhika Mohanram, '(In)visible bodies? Immigrant bodies and constructions of nationhood in Aotearoa New Zealand', in Rosemary Duplessis and Lynne Alice (eds), *Feminist Thought in Aotearoa New Zealand: Connections and differences*, Auckland: Oxford University Press, 1998, 27.
44 Sneja Gunew, 'Denaturalising cultural nationalisms: Multicultural readings of "Australia"', in Homi K. Bhaba (ed.), *Narrating the Nation*, London: Routledge, 1990, 99–120. Quoted in Huijser, *The Multicultural Nation*, 69.
45 The deployment of the term 'ethnicity', such as in the Office of Ethnic Affairs, suggests a mechanism of denial of the discourse of race that problematises notions of a unified imagined community of the nation. Statements on the home page of this office are interestingly coy: 'The Office of Ethnic Affairs is focused on people whose culture and traditions distinguish them from the majority in New Zealand' and '[t]his website celebrates New Zealand and its ethnic communities. Ethnic people and their families are part of New Zealand's national identity and support our nation's economic transformation' (www.ethnicaffairs.govt.nz/). This language shows unreflexive multiculturalism starkly. The dominant culture is able to incorporate 'other' ethnicities without ceding its centrality.
46 See Stratton and Ang, 'Multicultural imagined communities', 159, for a discussion of the role of race in the problematics of national identity construction in Australia and the US.
47 In this production Amber Curreen is not obviously Māori, which undermines somewhat the strategic foregrounding of race on this particular stage. However the

following year this play went on to success in the Auckland Short and Sweet Festival of Ten Minute Theatre in 2010, winning Best Drama Script for Kiel McNaughton and Mei-Lin Hansen as well as the Best Actor Runner-Up for Gary Young, who played Chao. See 'Gala final winners': www.shortandsweet.org/shortsweet-theatre/auckland/gala-final-winners. In this iteration Alice is played very successfully by Kura Forrester. A video of the 2010 performance in two parts is viewable on YouTube: www.youtube.com/watch?NR=1&v=zQaAJW1dgBY&feature=endscreen and www.youtube.com/watch?v=qOHt7rYUy6Q&feature=relmfu

48 Jane Kelsey, 'Tino rangatiratanga in the 1990s: Potential for alliances', *Race Gender Class* 11-12, 1991, 45. Quoted by Fleras and Spoonley, *Recalling Aotearoa*, 219.
49 See for example Fleras and Spoonley, *Recalling Aotearoa*, 240.
50 Kymlicka, *Politics in the Vernacular*, 40. We note the way in which perceptions of the racially marked body as other combine with the effects of changes to patterns of immigration to construct all those differentiated by their race as being recent arrivals.
51 Fleras and Spoonley, *Recalling Aotearoa*, 248.
52 Ibid., 246. See also Huijser, *The Multicultural Nation*, 151-66.
53 See for example Stratton and Ang, 'Multicultural imagined communities', 157; or Huijser, *The Multicultural Nation*, 149, among others.
54 Huijser, *The Multicultural Nation*, 157-58.
55 See programme page of Radio New Zealand's *The Arts on Sunday*, 13 May 2012: www.radionz.co.nz/national/programmes/artsonsunday/20120513
56 See www.indianink.co.nz/index.php
57 See the agendas of the three EthnicA conferences organised by the Office of Ethnic Affairs in 2012: www.ethnicaffairs.govt.nz/oeawebsite.nsf/wpg_URL/Resources-EthnicA-Conferences-Index. Note, this page is now defunct having been replaced by the following which, unfortunately, does not have the agenda I refer to: www.ethnicaffairs.govt.nz/story/ethnica-conferences-2012
58 See for example Lisa Warrington, 'A place to tell our stories: Asian voices in the theatre of Aotearoa', in Marc Maufort and David O'Donnell (eds), *Performing Aotearoa: New Zealand theatre in an age of transition*, Brussels: Peter Lang, 2007, 349-68. Warrington at one point refers to 'work of Asian origin in Aotearoa', 365.
59 'The earlier generation [...] felt the responsibility to first present images of Asian Americans and say "We are here." And I think it is my generation who's going to say, "We are weird."' Alvin Eng (ed.), *Tokens? The NYC Asian American experience on stage*, New York: Asian American Writers' Workshop, [Philadelphia], distributed by Temple University Press, c. 1999, 415.

Bibliography

Ambush, Benny Sato, 'Pluralism to the bone', *American Theatre* 61:5, 1989.
Ang, Ien, 'Can one say no to Chineseness? Pushing the limits of the diasporic paradigm', in Rey Chow (ed.), *Modern Chinese Literary and Cultural Studies in the Age of Theory: Reimagining a field*, Durham: Duke University Press, 2000, 281-300.

Auckland Short and Sweet Festival of Ten Minute Theatre, 'Gala final winners': www.shortandsweet.org/shortsweet-theatre/auckland/gala-final-winners

Bromell, David, *Ethnicity, Identity and Public Policy: Critical perspectives on multiculturalism*, Wellington: Institute of Policy Studies, Victoria University, 2008.

Carter, David, 'The natives are getting restless: nationalism, multiculturalism and migrant writing', *Island Magazine*, 25–26:5, 1986.

Chae, Yongsuk, *Politicising Asian American Literature: Towards a critical multiculturalism*, New York and London: Routledge, 2008.

Eng, Alvin (ed.), *Tokens? The NYC Asian American experience on stage*, New York: Asian American Writers' Workshop [Philadelphia], distributed by Temple University Press, c. 1999.

Fleras, Augie and Spoonley, Paul, *Recalling Aotearoa: Indigenous politics and ethnic relations in New Zealand*, Auckland: Oxford University Press, 1999.

Garner, Stanton B. Jr., *Bodied Spaces: Phenomenology and performance in contemporary drama*, Ithaca: Cornell University Press, 1994.

Gilbert, Helen and Tompkins, Joanne, *Post-colonial Drama: Theory, practice, politics*, London & New York: Routledge, 1996.

Gunew, Sneja. 'Denaturalising cultural nationalisms: Multicultural readings of "Australia"', in Homi K. Bhaba (ed.), *Narrating the Nation*, London: Routledge, 1990, 99–120.

Giroux, Henry, 'The politics of insurgent multiculturalism in the era of the Los Angeles uprising', in Barry Kanpol and Peter McLaren (eds), *Critical Multiculturalism*, London and Westport: Bergin & Garvey, 1995.

Henare, Manuka, 'The Māori Leaders' Assembly, Kororipo Pā, 1831', in Judith Binney (ed.), *Te Kerikeri 1770–1850: The meeting pool*, Wellington: Bridget Williams Books, 2007.

Huijser, Henk, *The Multicultural Nation in New Zealand Cinema: Production–Text–Reception*, Saarbrücken: VDM Verlag, 2009.

Indian Ink Theatre Company: www.indianink.co.nz/index.php

Kelsey, Jane, 'Tino rangatiratanga in the 1990s: potential for alliances', *Race Gender Class* 11–12, 1991, 42–47. Quoted by Fleras and Spoonley, *Recalling Aotearoa*, 219.

King, Michael, *Being Pakeha*, Auckland: Hodder and Stoughton, 1985.

Kivisto, Peter, *Multiculturalism in a Global Society*, Oxford: Blackwell, 2002.

Kollen, Jessie, 'Life is simply very complicated', 13 February 2009: www.theatreview.org.nz/reviews/review.php?id=1894

Kymlicka, Will, *Politics in the Vernacular: Nationalism, multiculturalism and citizenship*, Oxford: Oxford University Press, 2001.

Laegaard, Sune, 'Introduction', in Nils Holtug, Kasper Lippert-Rasmussen and Sune Laegaard (eds), *Nationalism and Multiculturalism in a World of Immigration*, Basingstoke: Palgrave Macmillan, 2009, ix–xxiii.

Lo, Jacqueline and Gilbert, Helen, 'Toward a topography of cross-cultural theatre praxis', *The Drama Review*, 46.3, 2002, 31–53.

Maxwell, Anne, 'Ethnicity and education: Biculturalism in New Zealand', in David Bennett (ed.), *Multicultural States: Rethinking difference and identity*, London and New York: Routledge, 1998, 197–207.

McAllister, Janet, 'Review: Asian tales: Native Alienz at Herald Theatre', *New Zealand Herald*, 16 February 2009: www.nzherald.co.nz/theatre/news/article.cfm?c_id=343&objectid=10556881

Mohanram, Radhika. '(In)visible bodies? Immigrant bodies and constructions of nationhood in Aotearoa New Zealand', in Rosemary Duplessis and Lynne Alice, *Feminist Thought in Aotearoa New Zealand: Connections and differences*, Auckland: Oxford University Press, 1998.

Nadel, Alan. 'August Wilson and the (color-blind) whiteness of public space', in 'Beyond the Wilson-Brustein debate', *Theater*, 27.2–27.3, 1997. Quoted in Pao, 'Changing faces', 403.

Office of Ethnic Affairs, Te Tari Matawaka: www.ethnicaffairs.govt.nz/

Office of Ethnic Affairs, Te Tari Matawaka. 'EthnicA Conferences': www.ethnicaffairs.govt.nz/oeawebsite.nsf/wpg_URL/Resources-EthnicA-Conferences-Index

Oryza Foundation, 'Asian Tales: Native Alienz. Stories from the lips of Asia …' [February 2009] Programme Notes.

Oryza Foundation, 'Our mission': www.oryzafoundation-about.tumblr.com/

Oryza Foundation, 'What does 'Oryza' mean?': www.oryzafoundation-about.tumblr.com/post/1190217940/what-does-oryza-mean

Pao, Angela C., 'Changing faces: Recasting national identity in all-Asian (-)American dramas', *Theatre Journal*, 53.3, 2001, 389–409.

'Profile of New Zealander responses, ethnicity question: 2006 Census': www.stats.govt.nz/Census/about-2006-census/profile-of-nzer-responses-ethnicity-question-2006-census.aspx

Radio New Zealand, *Arts on Sunday*, 13 May 2012: www.radionz.co.nz/national/programmes/artsonsunday/20120513

Smits, Katharine, 'Justifying multiculturalism: Social justice, diversity and national identity in Australia and New Zealand', *Australian Journal of Political Science*, 46.1, 87–103.

Spivak, Gayatri Chakravorty, 'Subaltern studies: Deconstructing historiography', in *In Other Worlds: Essays in cultural politics*, New York: Methuen, 1987.

Stratton, Jon and Ang, Ien, 'Multicultural imagined communities: Cultural difference and national identity in the USA and Canada'. in David Bennett (ed.), *Multicultural States: Rethinking difference and identity*, London and New York: Routledge, 1998, 135–62.

Warrington, Lisa, 'A place to tell our stories: Asian voices in the theatre of Aotearoa', in Marc Maufort and David O'Donnell (eds), *Performing Aotearoa: New Zealand theatre in an age of transition*, Brussels: Peter Lang, 2007, 349–68.

Williams, Mark, 'Crippled by geography? New Zealand nationalisms', in Stuart Murray (ed.), *Not on Any Map: Essays on postcoloniality and cultural nationalism*, Exeter: University of Exeter Press, 1997, 19–42.

5. Under the Kiwi Gaze
Public Asian festivals and multicultural Aotearoa New Zealand

HENRY JOHNSON

Introduction

The aim of this chapter is threefold: (1) to document the changing soundscape of New Zealand as influenced by Asian migration over the past few decades; (2) to explore the notion of multiculturalism in this context and the extent to which Asian communities perform culture from their homeland; and (3) to offer case-studies that show specific theoretical and/or ethnographic examples of three representative Asian performance practices in New Zealand. The case-studies offer a discussion of aspects of cultural performance that fit within the paradigm of multicultural New Zealand. In comparing the cultures, the discussion draws on ideas offered by Nancy Green[1] in connection with 'comparison of national [immigrant] groups within one country'.[2] While each of the festivals has its own mix of musics and performance, several of these styles are foregrounded with the aim of showing the cultural dynamics at work within any one particular group. The discussion cannot cover every Asian-related festival; rather, examples are provided and discussed through a critical lens in the context of discourse on multiculturalism, and in terms of how some members of particular Asian communities have responded, through performance, to their New Zealand social setting. As a Western nation on the rim of Asia and the Pacific, and with its indigenous population and close Pacific ties, New Zealand has relaxed its immigration policy in a way that has witnessed increased immigration from various Asian nations. This chapter presents contexts that show the influence of globalisation on New Zealand over the past few decades and contributes to a re-centring of Asia – a relocation of the study of Asia to other contexts.[3]

As a nation with a distinct identity based on recent and not-so-recent migrations,[4] Aotearoa New Zealand has developed its own version of biculturalism dating from colonial times and the Treaty of Waitangi, and especially from the 1970s with a Māori renaissance. New Zealand's biculturalism is an engagement, or partnership, between the indigenous Māori and the Crown (i.e. non-Māori peoples), albeit within a context of cultural diversity.[5] In the contemporary context of global cultural flows and migration,[6] and in comparison to other nations that have a long history of inward migration and multiculturalism such as Australia and Canada,[7] New Zealand still has few signs of formally embracing a notion of multiculturalism more broadly, even though the concept is increasingly on the political agenda. Even centre-right New Zealand Prime Minister John Key (National Party) mentioned notions of biculturalism and multiculturalism in a 2011 interview, which raise questions about state, or other publically funded, intervention: 'I think for the most part people are proud of the bicultural foundation New Zealand is built on and the fact that we are a multicultural society ... New Zealand is a much stronger country for being a multicultural society.'[8] Also in the political realm, one leader of a small party has publically noted his political agenda for New Zealand to officially develop multiculturalism:

> *United Future leader Peter Dunne has reiterated the urgent need for New Zealand to formally establish itself as a multicultural nation to stamp out the blatant racism of groups such as the National Front:*
>
> 'United Future wants to see Parliament pass a Multiculturalism Act, similar to Canada's, formally recognising New Zealand's growing multicultural flavour, and further protecting immigrant communities from racism,' Mr Dunne said in the wake of a recent anti-Asian pamphlet campaign in Christchurch. 'Official statistics already show that almost one in three New Zealanders today are of non-European origin – within the next 15 years that is likely to increase to over 40 per cent.' By 2021, for example, a quarter of our population will be of either Asian or Pacific origin. 'A Multiculturalism Act should ensure everyone enjoys equal treatment and protection under the law, while formally acknowledging the freedom of all members of New Zealand society to preserve, enhance and share their cultural heritage without fear of persecution.'[9]

While the cultural make-up of New Zealand has been diverse for many years among Māori and non-Māori peoples, it is perhaps since immigration laws in 1987,[10] which introduced a system of immigration based on skills rather than ethnicity or country of origin, that New Zealand has witnessed an increase in migration from Asia. There has been nearly a century and a half of Asian migration to New Zealand,[11] but since the revision of the Immigration Act in 1987 the number of Asians migrating to New Zealand increased dramatically in the predominantly European New Zealand ethnoscape.[12] Along with the visibly growing Asian population, as seen in the past four censuses (Table 1), this new era of migration featured the influence of an international policy of multiculturalism as practised in some other Western countries and setting the scene for an increase of multicultural practices in New Zealand, whether top-down (i.e. by the state) or bottom-up (i.e. by the people).[13] In 2006, for example, New Zealand's Asian population represented about 9.2 per cent of the population, or over 354,000 people of a total population at the time of just over four million.[14] In connection with the Asian community, Statistics New Zealand's broad classification of diverse peoples included various countries of origin or cultural identity, with Chinese, Indian, Korean and Filipino cultures representing the four largest ethnicities respectively.[15] This new Asia–New Zealand cultural and political milieu has helped to increase multicultural awareness, as well as social, cultural and political activism. Subsequent questions about the place of such new New Zealanders in their adopted bicultural home were brought into scholarly and everyday discourse. It seems that the rapidly changed and continually changing nature of New Zealand's cultural diversity, and especially that from Asia, is embraced by politicians, academics and the general public, yet little has been done to ensure that the nation's new and old communities can live in a contemporary society that celebrates the notion of multiculturalism. As Ip and Pang[16] have summarised, 'the problem of the bicultural discussion at present is that it does not seem to acknowledge and engage with the multicultural reality as part and parcel of a larger demographic shift in New Zealand.'

In this changing New Zealand cultural context, public performance in the Asia–New Zealand ethnoscape takes many manifestations. Focusing on large-scale festivals in this discussion, events include Chinese New Year festivities and Diwali, as organised by the Asia New Zealand Foundation (hereafter ANZF),[17] with the city councils of Auckland, Wellington and Christchurch supporting one or both of these events. By 'public', I refer to performance contexts that are beyond the ethnic community and are oriented toward a mass audience as the target consumer, rather than 'private' settings that are intended for a small, select or specific community audience.[18] These festivals are media spectacles designed to attract widespread public interest and show an inherent top-down approach to promoting multiculturalism through cultural performance based on the new New Zealand Asian ethnoscape.[19] As noted by ANZF: 'In New Zealand, the Foundation plays a crucial role in bridging cultural gaps by bringing thousands of New Zealanders into contact with Asian cultures through festivals, exhibitions and performances.'[20] While considerable integration between cultures has already occurred, especially in the performing arts where, for example, much Western music is practised in Asian countries, what occurs in such New Zealand festivals is often a re-discovery of a traditional past that comes to act as an identity marker for recent immigrants, or a show-casing of contemporary styles that have hybridity at their core. In summary, there is an essentialising process on the one hand, and hybrid styles on the other. This cultural setting shows a dramatic increase in the public performance of culture as expressed by recent immigrants from Asia to New Zealand:

> *The importance of cultural events and festivals has increased markedly in the past decade. In a 2008 survey for Auckland City Council and Creative New Zealand, Diwali and the Lantern Festival were listed in the top five events that made Aucklanders feel most proud. Diwali did not receive a mention in the earlier 2005 results.*[21]

Before 1987 there was less Asian performance portrayed in the public domain, possibly because there were fewer Asian migrants – although when performances by Asians in New Zealand, or Asian–New Zealanders, did take place, their ethnicity was often foregrounded in discourse as a way of showing its place in New Zealand.[22] In other words, performances with an underpinning raison d'être that indexed ethnicity and migration (which might be described as a 'synthetic sonic experience of surface impacts'),[23] and especially where culture was exoticised[24] were increasingly placed under the Kiwi gaze in media and performative spectacles.[25]

This chapter is based on several research methods. I undertook fieldwork at several of the festivals discussed, using ethnographic methods and interviewing several key informants, but also calling on my experience as an audience member. On a theoretical level, the discussion builds on ideas offered by Heywood,[26] who defines multiculturalism in two main ways: descriptive and normative. The former definition implies a society where cultural diversity is seen as a usual part of the community, and the latter implies:

> ... *a positive endorsement of communal diversity, based upon the right of different cultural groups to recognition and respect. In this sense, it acknowledges the importance of beliefs, values and ways of life in establishing a sense of self-worth for individuals and groups alike.*[27]

In New Zealand, multiculturalism has both descriptive and normative characteristics, although it has no official place in state policy, and discussion of this concept is largely in bottom-up discourse by community groups, especially those representing New Zealand's Asian peoples. The dualism or political axis of multiculturalism vs. monoculturalism is, like many other binaries, an over-simplification of some of the complexities of cultural identity.

This chapter contributes to the re-thinking of multiculturalism in New Zealand.[28] Debates about multiculturalism are found in many spheres of academic scholarship.[29] From scholars to politicians, and including a wide range of everyday New Zealanders, over the past few decades there has been an increase in multicultural awareness.[30] The work of Steven Young on Chinese New Zealanders shows a growing engagement with multicultural ideas, and puts forward ideas that advocate engagement in a multicultural debate.[31] Even as recently as 2008, the New Zealand Federation of Ethnic Councils (NZFEC) 'unanimously endorsed the request to Government to enact a Multicultural Act in New Zealand that is inclusive of all New Zealanders'.[32] At this meeting, the NZFEC represented 20 Ethnic Councils from around the country, which include an estimated total of 600,000 New Zealanders. Comparisons were made with Australian and Canadian acts, and the aim of achieving multiculturalism was to 'ensure that every individual in New Zealand is equal, their heritage and history is nurtured and protected equally'.[33] The NZFEC was established in 1989 in an era of cultural change and increased immigration to New Zealand; 20 years later in 2009 it was renamed The New Zealand Federation of Multicultural Councils, a move that perhaps reflected the politics of multiculturalism at the time. Even in the branding of New Zealand by such companies as New Zealand Tourism Guide, there are very clear references to the country being multicultural: 'a unique and vibrant multicultural society'.[34]

Another face of multiculturalism in New Zealand is a framework where minorities who are not European, Māori or Pacific Islanders are grouped to form a political voice. For example, the Multicultural Services Centre (MSC) in Wellington notes that it is a 'one-stop-shop providing support to refugee and migrant communities'.[35] Government, too, has various ministries and offices that attempt to recognise New Zealand's cultural diversity, including the Office of Ethnic Affairs, Te Puni Kōkiri (Ministry of Māori Development), the Ministry of Pacific Island Affairs, and the Human Rights Commission. The idea of multiculturalism has many contested forms; New Zealand, as with the US and UK, has been described as having a 'modest' form of multiculturalism, compared to the 'strong' forms in Australia and Canada.[36]

In this cultural context, Asian festivals offer a 'spectacle' context to study people and processes, and are increasingly the focus of diverse scholarly studies.[37] As argued by Duffy,[38] 'festivals are sites for on-going dialogues and negotiations within communities as individuals and groups attempt to define meaningful concepts of identity and belonging'. The study of festivals in New Zealand as markers of cultural identity has received growing interest in music research in recent years.[39] While drawing on such literatures and interests, this chapter also contributes to the study of festivals in New Zealand, and especially those that have emerged as a result of recent Asian migrations to the country's main urban centres.

Case-studies

Lantern Festival. Public performance among Chinese New Zealanders is represented widely under the Kiwi gaze in the sphere of entertainment during the Chinese New Year (the 15th day of the first lunar month, falling in either January or February). There are various ways that this important and symbolic annual event is expressed publically, including large-scale events such as the Lantern Festival organised by ANZF, and celebrations run by community groups often with local council support. The Lantern Festival is traditionally held on the last day of Chinese New Year celebrations; lanterns are included as a symbolic way of helping people to see celestial spirits as they fly around during the first full moon. The festival involves many forms of entertainment including dragon dancing, lion dancing, celebratory foods and lantern viewing. While celebrations for the Chinese New Year might range from small to large events[40] and be promoted under a variety of names, such as the Chinese New Year or the Asian New Year, the Lantern Festival as sponsored by ANZF offers a large-scale public spectacle in two main urban centres, celebrating a unique aspect of contemporary multicultural New Zealand.

Spectators at the final night of the Auckland Lantern Festival in Albert Park, Auckland, March 2007. Martin Sykes/*New Zealand Herald*

ANZF has been organising the Auckland event since 2000, and the one in Christchurch since 2005 (Appendix 1 shows a programme from the 2012 Auckland event). There are also various other celebrations in many other cities and towns around the country, although these are usually small-scale community-oriented events. The two ANZF events, staged for the largest urban populations in the North and South islands, are organised as top-down celebrations. That is, ANZF, as a partly government-funded organisation, has provided institutional and fiscal support as a way of contributing to its role in helping to raise awareness of Asia among New Zealanders. Jennifer King of ANZF notes some of the traditional aspects of the festival that were part of her vision for the event, although in practice the performances usually include contemporary offerings too:

> *My input into the lantern festival has been that I wanted it to be quite a nostalgic event – so that Chinese might remember what it was like back in China in the old days, maybe when they were children. The lantern festivals in China have become quite commercial these days, with a lot of corporate sponsors and Hello Kitty and cartoon lanterns. I wanted our [belonging to ANZF] lanterns to say something about the lovely old traditions of the spring festival (Chinese New Year) in China.*[41]

From its modest beginnings in 2000, ANZF now sponsors not only the physical lanterns themselves, which these days fill 20 shipping containers, but also brings to New Zealand significant Chinese entertainers to contribute to the celebrations. In 2012, for example, the event included such contrasting international acts as 'Sanlin Dragon and Lion Dance Team' from Shanghai, and 'Long Shen Dao' (Way of the Dragon Spirit), a Chinese reggae band from Beijing that incorporates traditional Chinese musical instruments into its performance. It is estimated that in 2012 more than 100,000 people attended the three-day event in Auckland[42] and over 40,000 in Christchurch.[43]

The Lantern Festival is, thus, eclectic. Even though the festival might be viewed as a traditional part of Chinese culture, the event promoted by ANZF mixes traditional and contemporary entertainment. As shown in Appendix 1, the three-day (late afternoon to late evening) performance held at the main stage in Auckland's Albert Park in 2012 was a spectacle with a variety of entertainers, including such contrasting styles as popular music, Chinese opera, folk dancing and classical music. The musical highlight of this part of the Lantern Festival was the Long Shen Dao Reggae Band, which closed each evening, followed on the last day by a fireworks display. In connection with this hybrid act several questions might be asked. What is the place of a contemporary reggae band from China at the Auckland Chinese Lantern Festival? Why is contemporary music included in this traditional festival? The simple answer to such questions is that the group was included to provide a modern face to Chinese culture at an event that is mostly seen in terms of a perceived 'traditional' culture (e.g. lanterns), at least from an imagined perspective. While the display of lanterns was one visual aspect, the evening stage events offered a variety of entertainment oriented towards a younger generation. Indeed, from the very first ANZF-sponsored event, which in 2000 included two professional popular singers from Hong Kong, there has been a wide range of popular entertainment at the Lantern Festival. As noted by Ng,[44] who has undertaken extensive research on Chinese music in New Zealand, the first event attracted very few non-Chinese to the free festival, and seemed to be targeted primarily to the Chinese community (an estimated 40,000 people from a variety of backgrounds attended the first event).[45]

In terms of the Lantern Festival's place in multicultural New Zealand, there are several themes that stand out, as discussed below. These themes include top-down event management by ANZF; diversity of performance events, including traditional and contemporary Chinese culture; and large-scale public spectacle in two large urban centres.

Diwali. The largest public celebrations of South Asian culture (especially Indian) in New Zealand are the two public Diwali events held in Auckland and Wellington respectively, organised in part by ANZF. As with the Lantern Festival, there are various other Diwali celebrations around the country, small and large, some public and some intended for only the South Asian or Indian community, but the events in the largest city (Auckland) and capital city (Wellington) help show the extent to which globalisation and top-down intervention are inherent in the events' raison d'être. There are other Diwali events in both cities, but in terms of event management, publicity, sponsorship and media hype, ANZF does much in collaboration with the respective city councils to promote both events, and has been partly responsible for organising these Diwali celebrations since 2002.[46] (Appendix 2 shows a programme from the 2011 Auckland event.)

As already shown with the Lantern Festivals, the Diwali events are essentially part of a top-down process of intervention where multiculturalism is celebrated and displayed as a festival event for mass consumption in the broader public domain. The very fact that Diwali is observed and promoted

Then Prime Minister Helen Clark opened the 2005 Diwali Festival of Lights at Auckland's Aotea Centre, October 2005. Kenny Rodger/*New Zealand Herald*

Diwali Festival, Wellington, October 2007. Pixeload

in a public and mass media context in New Zealand is a consequence of the rapid Asian cultural flows into the country, especially since 1987.[47] This human form of globalisation, or the changing immigration trends that show the widespread movement of people from one part of the world to another, is inherent in Diwali. While a South Asian presence existed in New Zealand for many years before 1987, the changing immigration demographics since that time show an exceptional increase in new Asian flows to the country, and have had an impact on cultural performance in two main ways.

The first of these was a bottom-up, immigrant-led expression of cultural identity from the immigrants themselves. Movement from one country to another often includes the transferral of culture in such forms as language, belief systems and the performing arts. One of the ways many new immigrants respond to their lives in a new country is to form or join cultural associations, and New Zealand has a plethora of such associations based on the country or culture of both established and more recent immigrants.[48] Sometimes using nomenclature such as 'organisation', 'association', 'society' or 'club', these groups do much to maintain their cultural heritage in their new home, while at the same time providing a centre of community and social, cultural or religious solidarity. Such organisations are not for everyone, of course, but their sheer number and public presence is evidence of their established place in the contemporary New Zealand ethnoscape,[49] and there is a long history of such organisations holding private and public celebrations around the country.[50]

Another side of Diwali is when it is organised from the top-down (i.e. by a state-funded organisations). It is here that intervention by non-South Asian organisations is evidence of a desire to contribute in one way or another to the celebrations of new New Zealanders. In terms of the Auckland and Wellington Diwali events, intervention by ANZF and the respective city councils has done much to mould a traditional festival into something quite different to those held by families or smaller community groups. Diwali in New Zealand is perhaps best known by most non-South Asian New Zealanders as a public spectacle,[51] rather than anything to do with its religious or cultural meaning. That is, ANZF's Diwali events are large-scale public extravaganzas that mostly have performance at their core, and involve the display of South Asian culture in New Zealand. While similar events to those held in Auckland and Wellington occur the world over, New Zealand has responded to South Asian immigration in a way that celebrates multiculturalism through top-down intervention. Both events include an array of local cultural groups from many spheres of the local South Asian diaspora, as well as invited performers from India, but they are also festivals that do much to homogenise Diwali into a form that is the vision of the organisers, rather than of the participants.

Southeast Asian Night Market. The Southeast Asian Night Market, a festival held in Wellington, is a more recent event that is also co-organised by ANZF and Wellington City Council.[52] First held in 2008, the festival is based on celebrating the diverse cultures of the ten member countries of the Association of Southeast Asian Nations (ASEAN): Brunei Darussalam, Cambodia, Indonesia, Lao PDR, Malaysia, Myanmar, Philippines, Singapore, Thailand and Viet Nam. There are far fewer Southeast Asians in New Zealand than Chinese or Indians, however (see Tables 2 and 3). As a consequence, unlike the Lantern and Diwali festivals, the Southeast Asian Night Market is held on only one day and only in the capital city, Wellington. (Appendix 3 shows a programme from the 2011 event).

In its first year the event included contributions from six ASEAN members: Indonesia, Malaysia, Philippines, Singapore, Thailand and Viet Nam, with a smaller contribution from members of the Cambodian and Myanmar communities. The event was free and held from 2 pm to 10 pm at the TSB Bank Arena, Queens Wharf, which has a capacity of 3000 people. As well as food stalls scattered around the setting (as with the other main festivals discussed above), the event included a number of performances by resident New Zealanders, including Thai kick boxing, martial arts from the Philippines and Vietnam, Indonesian *gamelan* and *wayang kulit* (shadow puppetry), traditional Asian games and demonstrations of batik printmaking.[53] About 20,000 people are estimated to have attended the first event.[54]

Speaking at the opening ceremony on behalf of the Prime Minister, Statistics Minister Darren Hughes' address included many references to New Zealand's changing demographics. He noted that New Zealanders in 2006 at the last census self-identified with over 200 ethnicities, and that New Zealand is:

> *... becoming more ethnically and culturally diverse than ever before. This presents New Zealanders with the opportunities to connect with the dynamic cultures of the world, here in New Zealand ... We need to find ways to ensure that the benefits of our newfound diversity are experienced by all people, and that the cultural richness of our society is protected, valued and respected.*[55]

The next event was held in 2010 from 4 pm to 10 pm on Saturday 20 March at Frank Kitts Park, Jervois Quay, Wellington's waterfront.[56] On this occasion the night market included Indonesian, Malaysian, Filipino, Singaporean, Vietnamese, Cambodian, Thai and Myanmar communities and, like the previous event, had many performances and cultural displays at its core. AZNF declared:

> *A highlight will be the four-member Cynthia Alexander Group who will be playing a mix of standard instruments as well as ethnic Filipino instruments including* tungkaling, bungkaka *and* Maguindanaon *brass gongs to produce an East-West hybrid sonic landscape. Band leader Cynthia Alexander comes from a family of artists and musicians – daughter of poet-painter Tita Lacambra-Ayala and fictionist-painter Jose V. Ayala Jr and sister of famed Philippine ethnic folk-rocker Joey Ayala. Cynthia is known for being one of the first who began the wave of independent music in the Philippines. She is a formidable producer, arranger, and songwriter with myriad side projects and collaborations. Other highlights of the Night Market include open-air Indonesian*

South East Asian night market, Wellington, March 2010. Pixeload

> *puppetry with gamelan orchestra, local performers, delicious Southeast Asian food stalls and colourful souvenirs.*[57]

In 2011 the night market ran from 4 pm to 10 pm on Saturday 16 April on the Wellington waterfront, in and around Frank Kitts promenade, park and Shed 6. As before, performance was at the core of the 2011 event and included Malaysian children, Thai peacock dance, Aceh (Indonesian) dancers, Indonesian shadow puppetry, Javanese gamelan, Filinartizts Ati-atihan group from the Philippines, Chinese Lion dancing, Filipino drumming, and Indonesian, Malaysian, Philippines, Vietnamese, Burmese, Singaporean and Thai dancing from local communities, as well as live bands. Unlike the Lantern and Diwali festivals, however, which are aimed at the Chinese and Indian communities respectively (although celebrated by many others), the Southeast Asian Night Markets are intended for a far broader range of people. They are smaller than the other ANZF festivals, yet function as a catalyst for celebrating New Zealand's diaspora cultures from a diverse range of Southeast Asian countries.

Discussion

The three case-studies outlined above help foreground some of the ways that New Zealand in the twenty-first century is embracing cultural celebrations of some of its more recent migrants from Asia. These three festivals are distinct in that they are organised by ANZF as a way of helping New Zealand in terms of its external (international) and internal (within New Zealand) links with Asia. While there are indeed numerous Asian cultural festivals celebrating specific countries or cultures throughout New Zealand, the vast majority are usually locally focused within specific cultural groups or associations. And while some events may receive support from local funding bodies such as city councils, very rarely do they have the same organisational framework, sponsorship and public visibility as the Lantern Festival, Diwali or the Southeast Asian Night Market. Considering the intervention by ANZF, this warrants elaboration by that organisation:

Asia:NZ's [ANZF] commitment to building awareness of Asia through its Diwali and Lantern Festivals continued in 2010/11. This year we tied this in with the Business Education Partnership by hosting a networking event for members to preview the Lantern Festival.

During the year the foundation's culture programme continued to inspire, entertain and enthral. The 12th annual Auckland Lantern Festival was a particular highlight, attracting record crowds, with more than 250,000 people in attendance to welcome the Year of the Rabbit. The three-day festival brought to New Zealand a dazzling array of international performers, including Beijing-based rock band Askar Grey Wolf.

Sadly the Christchurch Lantern Festival 2011, scheduled for a week later, had to be cancelled in the wake of the devastating earthquake.

India's best-loved festival, Diwali, was once again held in Wellington and Auckland, organised in partnership with Wellington and Auckland City Councils. Auckland's 10th Diwali Festival was held at its new home in Aotea Square. Highlights included stalls of delicious food, traditional and contemporary dance and music, the hotly contested Bollywood dance competition and a grand finale fireworks display.

Despite the rain, our third Southeast Asian Night Market on Wellington's waterfront, held in partnership with Wellington City Council in April, was well attended. Ten member nations of the Association of Southeast Asian Nations (ASEAN) brought delicious food, colourful crafts and non-stop entertainment.[58]

Public festivals are prevalent in many spheres of New Zealand culture. Whether Pasifika, the Santa Parade, a heritage festival or an arts festival, to name only a few, the festivalisation of culture in an emerging multicultural paradigm has become part of a broader way of celebrating culture in more recent years, and a phenomenon that produces a type of touristic and thematic engagement that often has as much to do with fiscal success as it does with cultural production and consumption. With the three festivals outlined above, and especially in terms of Asian cultures as part of New Zealand's multicultural ethnoscape, select Asian regional themes have been elevated as a way of attempting not only to celebrate distinct cultures, but also to extend those cultures to the wider New Zealand public.

In any multicultural setting, funders and organisers often confront a paradox inherent in multiculturalism when making decisions on what to support and how to support it: why should one culture receive more support than any other? For example, as shown in Tables 1–3, Koreans represent the third-largest Asian community in New Zealand, yet one seldom sees Korean events under the public gaze. Likewise, some of the smaller Asian communities are rarely represented in large-scale public festivals, although Japan has been the focus of various Japanese festivals over the past few decades, many of which have been sponsored by ANZF. In the New Zealand context, therefore, one might ask several questions about the extent of the public celebration of Asian festivals. Which Asian cultures should be celebrated, and why? What about others? What about other non-Asian cultures? While such questions are the topic for a much longer piece of research, in the framework of the three festivals discussed in this chapter there are both national reasons for their inclusion on the contemporary festivalscape, and questions about their place in a multicultural setting.

With regard to the Chinese Lantern Festival, New Zealand has a long and celebrated engagement with peoples from China. In terms of the Chinese diaspora in New Zealand, the Chinese (broadly speaking) represent the largest number of Asian migrants currently self-identified in census data.[59] Indeed, 'New Zealand's ethnic Chinese population jumped more than seven-fold in 20 years between 1996 and 2006, from 19,600 to 147,600. In Auckland it rose almost tenfold, from 10,500 to 97,400. Parts of Botany, Epsom and New Lynn are now more than 30 per cent Chinese.'[60]

Chinese people do, of course, celebrate many Chinese festivals throughout the annual cycle, including Spring Festival (New Year), Lantern Festival (as part of the Spring Festival), Double Seventh Festival, Winter Solstice and many others. While celebrating the Lantern Festival in New Zealand helps close the Chinese New Year festivities – a particularly important time for Chinese people – the event, as it is held in Auckland and Christchurch, is a mixture of traditional and contemporary culture. As well as highly visible, colourful and decorative Chinese traditional lanterns, the two ANZF events offer Chinese New Zealanders and others attending the celebrations a taste of aspects of contemporary Chinese culture too. For example, the inclusion of Long Shen Dao (as noted above) at the 2012 events helped make the festival one that embraced different aspects of Chinese culture and therefore potentially more interesting to both Chinese and non-Chinese people. More broadly, the band's inclusion shows that global culture is transformed and recontextualised through music and cultural celebration. A Jamaican music genre is popularised globally, and has influenced many New Zealand musicians (e.g. Fat Freddy's Drop, Herbs and Katchafire); Chinese musicians travel to New Zealand and their music is listened to by Chinese and non-Chinese enthusiasts alike.

Diwali, too, as it is produced as a festival in Auckland and Wellington, has many similar characteristics. South Asians, and Indians in particular, are New Zealand's second largest Asian ethnicity, and it seems fitting that nationally there are two very highly visible public events sponsored by ANZF as part of a celebration of the country's emerging multicultural political milieu. Many of the points raised in connection with the Chinese Lantern Festival might also be related to Diwali. That is, Indians and other South Asians celebrate many festivals; India itself is a multicultural nation; and the inclusion of contemporary culture in the New Zealand manifestation of this traditionally religious celebration contributes to its popularisation in its diaspora setting.

Diwali is one festival of South Asia and its diasporas. There are many other times of celebration, and the diverse peoples of this vast geographic region have their own unique cultures and sub-cultures. One of the contradictions of multiculturalism is that to be successful it must have representation from all of the contributing cultures. However, when funding is directed towards one culture, perhaps as a result of its sheer size in terms of numbers of people, and proportional funding is not awarded to a smaller culture, there are clearly issues to be addressed – in scholarly circles as well as elsewhere.

By grouping many South Asian cultures together to offer a large-scale festival such as Diwali, there is a paradox of belonging. Diwali might be a part of someone's culture so they want to participate in such a public celebration, but by participating they are a product of a newly created and homogenous event that does little to acknowledge cultural diversity among South Asians in New Zealand.

The Southeast Asian Night Market is slightly different to the other two festivals discussed above. While the theme recalls a typical night market found in many Southeast Asian cultures, the overarching event brings together many of the Southeast Asian cultures who are represented in New Zealand. Rather than being a celebration of a single cultural festival, this is a thematic event that brings cultures together – inter-Asian and non-Asian. As an attempt to represent multicultural New Zealand in terms of its Asian peoples, the Southeast Asian Night Market is ideally placed; it inherently encompasses as many of these culturally diverse countries as possible and is inclusive within its broad geographic and cultural spheres.

Overall, the three festivals offer some similarities and differences. While the Lantern Festival and Diwali offer a similar mix of traditional and contemporary themes, the Southeast Asian Night Market represents diverse Asian cultures in a celebration of geographic region. In this discussion, several distinct themes emerge from these three events; these are outlined below as a way of attempting to understand the relevance and significance of these festivals for multicultural New Zealand today.

Intervention is at the core of each of these events. The type of 'multicultural' festivals that ANZF has developed are what Parekh[61] might define as 'equal intercultural interaction with judicious government help and intervention . . . [which] interpenetrate and permeate all areas of life'. As noted earlier, there are numerous bottom-up cultural organisations throughout New Zealand that do much to represent the nation's established and new Asian migrants, and within these contexts there are often cultural celebrations that help sustain traditional beliefs and cultural practices. However, with ANZF's events, there is a distinct top-down state intervention in terms of organisation. ANZF brings people together with the aim of celebrating Asian cultures in New Zealand; it collaborates with city councils, local community groups and individuals to stage the events; and it offers a means of raising cultural awareness of Asia in the wider public at a time when the nation is looking increasingly towards Asia in its geopolitical and economic goals. As noted by ANZF in connection with

Diwali and the Lantern Festivals: 'Popular events like the Chinese Lantern and Indian Diwali festivals ... build awareness of these cultures in New Zealand ... [and illustrate] the success of Asia:NZ's domestic agenda to make New Zealanders more aware of the countries of Asia and to integrate Asian culture into mainstream New Zealand society'.[62] Such a process is also important to long-term global economic relations, especially in terms of strengthening trading partnerships with Asian countries.

Intervention has positive and negative effects on the festivals. While Chinese and Indian celebrations in New Zealand such as the Lantern Festival and Diwali would undoubtedly be held without the support of ANZF, and indeed are in many cities and towns around the country, with ANZF's influence the events take on a new meaning. ANZF's events are large-scale and put a media spotlight on Asians in New Zealand and their cultural celebrations. While the two largest Asian communities (Chinese and Indian) are represented by the intervention of ANZF and the respective city councils of Auckland and Wellington, many smaller Asian communities receive little or no representation of a similar nature. While multiculturalism might aspire to represent all cultures equally, when some cultures are elevated above others through mass spectacle it is hard not to ask questions about cultural representation and the reasons behind it. Furthermore, if multiculturalism were practised throughout the nation, then there would be many other public cultural celebrations of all ethnicities that nowadays make up the country's diverse population.

In this context, the notion of cultural representation vis-à-vis cultural homogenisation is evident. On the one hand, multiculturalism asserts that all cultures should be represented, although on the other hand it is difficult to represent every community. Moreover, the criteria for representation in the case of the three festivals discussed in this chapter shows that cultures are merged: the Lantern Festival is intended to represent many Chinese in New Zealand from diverse backgrounds and histories; Diwali stands for Indian culture, yet it is traditionally a religious festival with Hinduism at its core; and the Southeast Asian Night Market merges a range of countries with the aim of standing for a broad geographically, culturally and politically diverse part of the world.

Each of the events discussed is a public spectacle. They are staged with a public dimension that is portrayed through the media as a celebration or festival open to all and not solely to the cultures they inherently represent. It is here that the theme of intervention is also evident in that these specific events are supported from the top down; one might wonder if such festivals would ever have achieved such a public presence in contemporary New Zealand without the support of ANZF. Nevertheless, the events are now part of the cultural fabric of the main urban centres in which they are held, and are part of an emerging cultural tradition that is seeing the nation become more openly multicultural despite the absence of an official state policy on multiculturalism.

The urban settings that form the main location for each of these events help show migratory trends in New Zealand. Auckland is the country's largest city, Wellington is the capital, and Christchurch is the South Island's largest city. Each of these centres has a large and diverse Asian population, with Auckland being by far the preferred place for many recent Asian migrants (Table 4). Nevertheless, New Zealand has many other centres and a geographically distinct rural population, which raises the question of how Asians might be represented in these other contexts. For example, should Diwali be celebrated only in main centres, or should every centre actively celebrate this festival (and others) on an annual basis? The locations of the festivals reflect the size of the communities, but also point towards an 'ethnoscape as spectacle'[63] where the events are given purpose in an 'exoticised urban landscape'. They also help brand the respective cities as contemporary cosmopolitan multicultural urban settings.[64]

The last theme that links the events discussed is that of their traditional and contemporary components. It is here that the events help showcase traditional culture as it is perceived by many Asians and non-Asians alike, and also more contemporary culture such as Bollywood dancing, Chinese reggae and Indonesian jazz.

Conclusion

The three case-studies presented in this chapter help in understanding the developing dynamics of the multicultural New Zealand festivalscape in the twenty-first century in relation to the nation's rapidly growing Asian population. In particular, the public and mediatised festivals included in the current discussion have been constructed under the Kiwi gaze through the organisation of ANZF in what is primarily a top-down process of intervention. In this cultural sphere, the festivals may help Asian migrants in New Zealand to engage with their new cultural context, and for all New Zealanders to become more aware of Asia and to experience performed culture in this context. This type of ethno-festival has become part of the cosmopolitan urban landscape for New Zealand's three largest cities – Auckland, Wellington and Christchurch – where the resident Asian populations are well positioned to participate through performance, as stall holders or as members of the audience, and the non-Asian population is able to share the multicultural experience.

Each of the festivals shows distinct themes, including: intervention by ANZF and the respective city councils that help organise the events; cultural representation/homogenisation where the diversity of Asia is represented in a type of multicultural extravaganza, yet grouped in a way that does little to truly reflect that diversity; public spectacle with traditional and contemporary components that are often situated in the events and juxtaposed against 'authentic' elements; and urban settings that represent New Zealand's Asian communities in recent migratory patterns.

In terms of contributing to multiculturalism in New Zealand, these three large-scale public festivals do much to offer a celebration of contemporary and diverse New Zealand cultures through media spectacle. They help Asians bring aspects of their culture into mainstream New Zealand life in select urban centres; they help raise awareness of Asian New Zealanders and their cultures to the broader public, whether through audience/public participation or through media publicity and reports; and they contribute to an ongoing discourse on how and when the nation will embrace multiculturalism as a way of life for all New Zealanders.

Table 1. Ethnic group (grouped total responses)[1, 2, 3] by sex[4]
1991–2006 censuses

	1991 Census Total	1996 Census Total	2001 Census Total	2006 Census Total
European	2,783,028	2,879,085	2,871,432	2,609,589
Māori	434,847	523,374	526,281	565,329
Pacific Peoples	167,070	202,233	231,798	265,974
Asian	99,759	173,502	238,176	354,549
Middle Eastern/ Latin American/African[5]	6,330	15,288	24,084	34,743
Other Ethnicity				
New Zealander	...	...	...	429,429
Other 'Other' Ethnicity	267	516	801	1,494
Total, Other Ethnicity	267	516	801	430,881
Total People Stated	3,345,741	3,466,515	3,586,641	3,860,163
Total People, Not Elsewhere Included[6]	28,221	151,788	150,705	167,784
TOTAL PEOPLE	**3,373,926**	**3,618,303**	**3,737,277**	**4,027,947**

1. Includes all of the people who stated each ethnic group, whether as their only ethnic group or as one of several ethnic groups. Where a person reported more than one ethnic group, they have been counted in each applicable group.
2. Changes to the ethnicity question used in the 1996 Census have resulted in some data that is not consistent between 1996 and 2001, or between 1996 and 2006. For further information, refer to the ethnicity variable on the 2006 Census Information About Data webpage: www.stats.govt.nz/census/.
3. The ethnicity data in this table for 1991 and 1996 has been output using up to three responses. The 2001 and 2006 data has been output using up to six responses.
4. All figures are for the census usually resident population.
5. Middle Eastern, Latin American and African was introduced as a new category for the 2006 Census. Previously Middle Eastern, Latin American and African responses were allocated to the Other Ethnicity category
6. The 1991 data includes Black (undefined), Other (undefined) and Not Specified. The 1996 and 2001 data includes Black, Other not further defined, Response Unidentifiable, Response Outside Scope and Not Stated. The 2006 data includes Don't Know, Refused to Answer, Response Unidentifiable, Response Outside Scope and Not Stated.

Statistics New Zealand 2012a

Table 2. **Seven largest Asian ethnic groups,** 2001–2006 censuses

Ethnic group	2001 count	2006 count	Percentage change, 2001–2006
Chinese	105,057	147,570	40.5
Indian	62,190	104,583	68.2
Korean	19,026	30,792	61.8
Filipino	11,091	16,938	52.7
Japanese	10,023	11,910	18.8
Sri Lankan	7,011	8,310	18.5
Cambodian	5,268	6,918	31.3

Statistics New Zealand 2012b

Table 3. Ethnic group (total responses), 1991–2006 censuses

ETHNIC GROUP	CENSUS YEAR			
	1991	1996	2001	2006
ASIAN				
Chinese nfd	44,136	78,663	100,680	139,728
Indian nfd	29,823	40,401	60,210	97,443
Korean	930	12,753	19,026	30,792
Filipino	4,920	8,190	11,091	16,938
Japanese	2,970	7,458	10,023	11,910
Sri Lankan nfd	2,406	4,077	6,042	7,041
Cambodian	4,320	4,407	5,265	6,915
Thai	1,047	2,838	4,554	6,057
Fijian Indian	780	2,970	1,983	5,616
Taiwanese	...	2,718	3,771	5,451
Vietnamese	2,673	2,886	3,462	4,770
Malay	1,383	2,937	2,052	3,537
Indonesian	861	1,662	2,073	3,261
Afghani	117	258	807	2,538
Asian nfd	495	1,995	3,927	2,160
Pakistani	291	660	1,017	2,052
Eurasian	1,224	...	...	1,617
Bangladeshi	132	1,125	1,143	1,488
Malaysian Chinese	60	357	489	1,353
Laotian	1,197	1,278	1,401	1,344
Other Asian	1,476	2,949	3,864	6,504
TOTAL PEOPLE, ASIAN	99,756	173,502	238,179	354,552

Statistics New Zealand 2012a

Table 4. Estimated subnational ethnic population (RC,TA) by age and sex at 30 June 1996, 2001 and 2006

AGE	Total All Ages					
SEX	Total Sex					
ETHNICITY	**TOTAL PEOPLE, ETHNICITY**			**ASIAN**		
Year at 30 June	1996	2001	2006	1996	2001	2006
REGION						
Northland	140700	144400	152700	1910	2310	3110
Auckland	1114700	1216900	1371000	116600	175100	268600
Waikato	359900	369800	395100	9830	13400	20600
Bay of Plenty	230600	246900	265300	4320	5780	8910
Gisborne	47200	45500	46000	620	700	900
Hawke's Bay	146600	147300	152100	2620	3250	3920
Taranaki	109000	105700	107300	1420	1650	2430
Manawatu–Wanganui	234500	227500	229400	6740	7390	9130
Wellington	426900	440200	466300	25600	31300	40800
Tasman	38800	42400	45800	290	430	620
Nelson	41200	42900	44300	930	990	1210
Marlborough	39200	40700	43600	300	440	730
West Coast	33200	31100	32100	250	270	410
Canterbury	480400	496700	540000	16600	21900	32800
Otago	189300	188300	199800	5940	6630	8860
Southland	99000	93300	93200	860	930	1320
Area Outside	780	760	650	10	10	10
Total North Island	2810100	2944300	3185100	169600	240900	358400
Total South Island	921100	935400	998800	25200	31600	45900

Statistics New Zealand 2012a

Appendix 1. Lantern Festival programme 2012. Main Stage, Albert Park, Auckland*

Friday 3 February
5.00 pm   Contemporary Pop Band – Social Horizon Music Band
5.15   Cantonese Opera – Audrey Chan
5.30   *Hong Kong Melody Makers Student A Capella*
5.45   *Taizhou Luantan Opera*
6.05   Group Folk Dance – Dong Fang Dance Group
6.20   Traditional Chinese Instrument Play – Blossom Arts Association of Auckland
6.40   *Sanlin Dragon and Lion Dance from Shanghai*
7.05   Male Folk Song – Qi Zhilin
7.20   Diablo Performance – Auckland Diablo Group
7.30   *Confucius Institute*
8.00   OFFICAL OPENING
8.20   *Sanlin Dragon and Lion Dance from Shanghai*
8.40   *Hong Kong Student A Capella*
8.55   *Taizhou Luantan Opera*
9.15   *Confucius Institute*
9.45   *Long Shen Dao Reggae Band from Beijing*
10.30   Main Stage performances ends

Saturday 4 February
5.00 pm   Group Folk Dance – North Shore Chinese Friendship Association
5.15   Chinese Folk Dance – Parnell District School
5.30   *Hong Kong Melody Makers Student A Capella*
5.45   *Taizhou Luantan Opera*
6.05   *Countertenor Xiao Ma and Guzheng*
6.25   *Confucius Institute*
6.45   Group Folk Dance – Mayday Oriental Dance Group
7.00   Chinese Traditional Musical Play – Gone With Wind Guzheng Group
7.20   Group Folk Dance – Macang Dance Group
7.35   Diablo Performance – Auckland Diablo Group
7.45   *Countertenor Xiao Ma and Guzheng*
8.05   *Sanlin Dragon and Lion Dance from Shanghai*
8.25   *Taizhou Luantan Opera*
8.45   *Hong Kong Melody Makers Student A Capella*
9.00   *Sanlin Dragon and Lion Dance from Shanghai*
9.20   *Confucius Institute*
9.40   *Long Shen Dao Reggae Band from Beijing*
10.30   Main Stage performances ends

Sunday 5 February

5.00 pm	Chinese Folk Dance – Panmure Chinese Association
5.15	Group Folk Dance – Blue Sky Dance Group
5.30	*Hong Kong Melody Makers Student A Capella*
5.45	*Taizhou Luantan Opera*
6.05	*Confucius Institute*
6.25	Contemporary Beijing Opera – New Zealand Beijing Opera Association
6.40	Diablo Performance – Auckland Diablo Group
6.50	Female Solo Pop Song – Kong Jingting
7.05	*Sanlin Dragon and Lion Dance from Shanghai*
7.30	*Hong Kong Melody Makers Student A Capella*
7.45	*Countertenor Xiao Ma and Guzheng*
8.05	*Taizhou Luantan Opera*
8.25	Chinese Folk and Standard Ballroom Dance – Yue Feng Dancemaker Production
8.40	Oriental Fashion Show – Mulan Fashion Show Group
8.55	*Countertenor Xiao Ma and Guzheng*
9.15	*Confucius Institute*
9.35	*Long Shen Dao Reggae Band from Beijing*
10.15	Fireworks
10.30	Lantern Festival ends

* Items in italics indicate international acts.

Appendix 2. Diwali (Auckland 2011)

Saturday 8 October
Local artists
Noon – 9 pm, Aotea Square main stage, Queen St stage, Town Hall stage
Manipuri Dancers
12.30 pm, 4.30 pm, 6.20 pm, Aotea Square main stage, Queen St stage
Diwali Active Yoga
12.30 pm, 2 pm, Aotea Square grass area
Indian Classical performers
12.30 pm – 6.30 pm, Classical stage, AirNZ Foyer, Aotea Centre
Live Sitar and Tabla group
1.30 pm, Aotea Square main stage
Radio Tarana Bollywood Dance competition
2 pm, Aotea Square main stage
Official opening
4 pm, Aotea Square main stage
The Indian Puppeteers
4.30 pm, 6 pm, 7 pm, Puppetry stage, grass area, Aotea Square
Diwali Workshops
Smita Upadhye – Rangoli making
Noon, 5 pm, Aotea Centre, Blues Bar
Basant Madhur – Tabla workshop
4.30 pm, Aotea Centre, Classical stage
Live Gujarati Folk band – Surganga
5 pm, Queen St stage
Live Sitar and Tabla group
6.20 pm, Classical stage, AirNZ Foyer, Aotea Centre
Bridal Fashion Show
5.30 pm, 6 pm, Queen St stage, Classical stage
Sargam School of Indian Music
5.50 pm, Classical Stage, AirNZ Foyer, Aotea Centre
Live Gujarati Folk band – Surganga
7 pm, Aotea Square main stage
International sand artist
Ranjan Kumar Ganguly, Aotea Square south
Digital Art Live – Sparkly Spices
Kritteka Gregory, Owens's foyer, Aotea Centre

Appendix 3. Southeast Asian Night Market 2011. Programme, Saturday 16 April

Stage 1 – Frank Kitts Park
Country/Segment
4 pm Opening by children
4.20 pm Golden Burma
4.40 pm Wonderful Indonesia
5.05 pm Malaysia Truly Asia
5.30 pm 'WOW' Philippines
6 pm FORMAL OPENING
6.30 pm Uniquely Singapore
6.55 pm Glorious Vietnam
7.05 pm Smiling Thailand
7.25 pm Wonderful Indonesia
7.45 pm Malaysia Truly Asia
8.05 pm 'WOW' Philippines
8.25 pm Uniquely Singapore
8.50 pm Smiling Thailand
9.10 pm Glorious Vietnam
9.40 pm Finale - ASEAN Fashion
9.30 pm ASEAN Singers

Stage 2 – Shed 6
Country/Segment
4.20 pm Dances from Thailand
4.40 pm Indonesian Puppetry and Gamelan
5.35 pm ASEAN Band
6 pm FORMAL OPENING ON STAGE 1
6.30 pm Live Band – Philippines
6.55 pm Thai Kick Boxing Demonstration
7.15 pm Snake Charmers Belly Dancers
7.40 pm Indonesian Puppetry and Gamelan
8.35 pm Live Band – Philippines
8.55 pm Malaysia Medley
9.15 pm Stage 2 Closes

Upper Frank Kitts Park – Traditional South East Asia Games
Games
4.15 pm Bakiak (Giant Sandals) – Indonesia
4.45 pm Jumping Thais – Thailand
5.15 pm Buko (Coconut Husk Race) – Philippines
6 pm FORMAL OPENING ON STAGE 1
6.30 pm Capteh (Chinese Hacky Sack) – Singapore
6.50 pm Gelasin (Fortress Game) – Indonesia
7.15 pm Snake Game – Thailand
7.50 pm Games area closes

Endnotes

1. Nancy L. Green, 'The comparative method and poststructural structuralism: New perspectives for migration studies', *Journal of American Ethnic History* 13, no. 4, 1994, 3–22.
2. Green, 'The comparative method and poststructural structuralism', 13.
3. See Jacob Edmond, Henry Johnson and Jacqueline Leckie (eds), *Recentring Asia: Histories, encounters, identities*, Leiden: Global Oriental, 2011.
4. See, for example, James Belich, *Making Peoples: A history of the New Zealanders*, Auckland: Allen Lane, 1996; Stuart William Greif, *Immigration and National Identity in New Zealand: One people, two peoples, many peoples?*, Palmerston North: Dunmore Press, 1995; Jane Roscoe, *Documentary in New Zealand: An immigrant nation*, Palmerston North: Dunmore Press, 1999.
5. See further Janine Hayward, 'Biculturalism', Te Ara – the Encyclopedia of New Zealand: www.TeAra.govt.nz/en/biculturalism; Richard Mulgan, *Māori, Pākehā and Democracy*, Auckland: Oxford University Press, 1989; Andrew Sharp, 'Why be bicultural?' in Margaret Wilson and Anna Yeatman (eds), *Justice and Identity: Antipodean practices*, Wellington, Bridget Williams Books Ltd, 1995, 116–33; Raj K. Vasil, *Biculturalism: Reconciling Aotearoa with New Zealand*, Wellington: Institute of Policy Studies, Victoria University Press, 1988. Compare other versions of biculturalism in countries such as Belgium, Vanuatu and Switzerland. See, for example, Dennis M. Rutledge (ed.), *Biculturalism, Self-Identity and Societal Transformation*, Bingley: Emerald JAI, 2008.
6. Arjun Appadurai, *Modernity at Large: Cultural dimensions of globalization*, Minneapolis: University of Minnesota Press, 1996; Homi Bhabha, 'Postcolonial authority and postmodern guilt', in Lawrence Grossberg, Cary Nelson and Paula Treichler (eds), *Cultural Studies*, London: Routledge, 1992, 55–66; 'Culture's in-between', in Stuart Hall and Paul du Gay (eds), *Questions of Cultural Identity*, London: Sage Publications, 1996, 53–60.
7. Ali Rattansi, *Multiculturalism: A very short introduction*, Oxford: Oxford University Press, 2011.
8. John Armstrong and Audrey Young, 'Who wants a PM who's down in the mouth?', *New Zealand Herald*, 19 November 2011, www.nzherald.co.nz/election-2011/news/article.cfm?c_id=1503012&objectid=10767097
9. Peter Dunne, 'Press release: Dunne: NZ needs a multiculturalism Act', 11 May 2011, www.scoop.co.nz/stories/PA1105/S00236/dunne-nz-needs-a-multiculturalism-act.htm; compare with Joelle Dally, '"Counter-protest" against racism', *The Press*, 22 March 2013, www.stuff.co.nz/the-press/news/8457819/Counter-protest-against-racism
10. Brian Wearing, 'New Zealand's immigration policies and Immigration Act (1987): Comparisons with the United States of America', in Ivan Light and Parminder Bhachu (eds), *Immigration and entrepreneurship: Culture, capital, and ethnic networks*, New Brunswick: Transaction, 1993, 307–27.
11. Henry Johnson and Brian Moloughney (eds), *Asia in the Making of New Zealand*, Auckland: Auckland University Press, 2006.

12 Paola Voci and Jacqueline Leckie (eds), *Localizing Asia in Aotearoa*, Wellington: Dunmore Publishing, 2011; Edwina Pio, *Longing and Belonging: Asian, Middle Eastern, Latin American and African peoples in New Zealand*, Wellington: Dunmore Publishing, 2010; Appadurai, *Modernity at Large*.
13 Compare with Dunne, 'Press release'; David Theo Goldberg (ed.), *Multiculturalism: A critical reader*, Oxford: Blackwell, 1994; Stephen May (ed.), *Critical Multiculturalism: Rethinking multicultural and antiracist education*, London: Falmer Press, 1999; Bhikhu C. Parekh, *Rethinking Multiculturalism: Cultural diversity and political theory*, Cambridge, Mass.: Harvard University Press, 2000; Rattansi, *Multiculturalism*; Mervin Singham, 'Multiculturalism in New Zealand – the need for a new paradigm', in *Aotearoa Ethnic Network Journal* 1, 2006, 33–37; Paul Spoonley and Andrew Trlin, *Making Sense of Multicultural New Zealand*, Palmerston North: New Settlers Programme, Massey University, 2004.
14 Statistics New Zealand, 'QuickStats about culture and identity: Asian',: www.stats.govt.nz (2012b).
15 See Tables 2 and 3 in Statistics New Zealand 'QuickStats about culture and identity'.
16 Manying Ip and David Pang, 'New Zealand Chinese identity: Sojourners, model minority and multiple identities', in James H. Liu, Tim McCreanor, Tracey McIntosh and Teresia Teaiwa (eds), *New Zealand Identities: Departures and destinations*, Wellington: Victoria University Press, 2005, 186.
17 The Asia New Zealand Foundation is a non-profit and non-partisan organisation established in 1994 as a partnership between public and private sectors. Its funding is sourced from public, philanthropic and corporate sponsors.
18 Compare with Appadurai, *Modernity at Large*; Carol A. Breckenridge (ed.), *Consuming Modernity: Public culture in a South Asian world*, Minneapolis: University of Minnesota Press, 1995; Jürgen Habermas, *The Structural Transformation of the Public Sphere: An inquiry into a category of bourgeois society*, trans. Thomas Burger, Cambridge: Polity, 2008.
19 Appadurai, *Modernity at Large*.
20 Annual Report of the Asia New Zealand Foundation, Wellington: Asia New Zealand Foundation, 2009, 4.
21 Brunton Colmar, 'New Zealanders' perceptions of Asia and Asian peoples in 2010', Wellington: Asia New Zealand Foundation, 2011, 9. See also Paul Spoonley and Phillip Gendall, 'Welcome to our world: Attitudes to immigrants and immigration', in Andrew Trlin, Paul Spoonley, Richard Bedford (eds), *New Zealand and International Migration: A digest and bibliography, No. 5*, Auckland: Massey University, 2010, 136–58.
22 Compare with Henry Johnson, 'Performing identity, past and present: Chinese cultural performance, New Year celebrations, and the heritage industry', in Charles Ferrall, Paul Millar and Keren Smith (eds), *East by South: China in the Australasian Imagination*, Wellington: Victoria University Press, 2005, 217–42; Siong Ngor Ng, 'The Chinese community in Auckland: A musical ethnography and musical history', MA dissertation, University of Auckland, 2000, 99.

23 Tony Mitchell, *Popular Music and Local Identity: Rock, pop and rap in Europe and Oceania*, London: Leicester University Press, 1996, 85.
24 Cf. Edward W. Said, *Orientalism*, New York: Pantheon Books, 1978.
25 Cf. Hal Foster, *Vision and Visuality*, Seattle: Bay Press, 1995; John Urry, *The Tourist Gaze: Leisure and travel in contemporary societies*, London: Sage Publications, 1990.
26 Andrew Heywood, *Political Ideologies*, 3rd ed., Palgrave Macmillan, 2003, 67.
27 Heywood, *Political ideologies*, 67.
28 Compare with Parekh, *Rethinking Multiculturalism*; and Goldberg (ed.), *Multiculturalism*.
29 See, for example, Goldberg, *Multiculturalism*; May, *Critical Multiculturalism*; Rattansi, *Multiculturalism*.
30 See, for example, Allen Bartley and Paul Spoonley, 'Constructing a workable multiculturalism in a bicultural society', in Michael Balgrave, Merata Kawharu and David Williams (eds), *Waitangi Revisited: Perspectives on the Treaty of Waitangi*, Auckland: Oxford University Press, 2005, 136–48; Ron Johnston, Phillip Gendall, Andrew Trlin and Paul Spoonley, 'Immigration, multiculturalism and geography: Inter-group contact and attitudes to immigrants and cultural diversity in New Zealand', *Asian and Pacific Migration Journal* 19, no. 3, 2010, 343–69; Singham, 'Multiculturalism in New Zealand'; Spoonley and Trlin, *Making Sense of Multicultural New Zealand*; Compare with James H. Liu, Tim McCreanor, Tracey McIntosh and Teresia Teaiwa, (eds), *New Zealand Identities: Departures and destinations*, Wellington: Victoria University Press, 2005.
31 See Steven Young, www.stevenyoung.co.nz
32 New Zealand Federation of Ethnic Councils Inc. 'Press release: Federation seeks a multicultural Act for NZ', 3 March 2008, www.scoop.co.nz/stories/PO0803/S00024.htm
33 New Zealand Federation of Ethnic Councils, 'Press release'.
34 New Zealand Travel Guide, www.tourism.org.nz/people-and-history.html
35 Multicultural Services Centre, www.msc.wellington.net.nz
36 Rattansi, *Multiculturalism*, 17.
37 Michelle Duffy, 'The performance of identity: The community music festival in Australia', paper presented at the Institute of Australian Geographers 'Identities in Action!' conference, 10–12 December, 1999; 'Lines of drift: Festival participation and performing a sense of place', *Popular Music* 19, no.1, 2000, 51–64; 'Possibilities: The role of music and emotion in the social dynamics of a music festival', paper presented at the WSEAS International Conference on Cultural Heritage and Tourism (CUHT'08), Heraklion, Crete Island, Greece, 22–24 July 2008; Alessandro Falassi, (ed.), *Time out of Time: Essays on the festival*, Albuquerque: University of New Mexico Press, 1987; Donald Getz, 'Assessing the economic impact of festivals and events: Research issues', *Journal of Applied Recreation Research* 16, no.1, 1991, 61–77; 'The nature and scope of festival studies', *International Journal of Event Management Research* 5, no.1, 2010: www.ijemr.org/docs/Vol5-1/Getz.pdf; Donald Getz and Tommy D. Andersson, 'Sustainable festivals: On becoming an institution', *Event Management* 12, 2008, 1–17; Percy M. Young et al. 'Festival', in *Grove Music*

      Online, Oxford Music Online, 2011: www.oxfordmusiconline.com/subscriber/article/grove/music/49527
38 Michelle Duffy, 'Performing identity within a multicultural framework', *Social and Cultural Geography* 6, no. 5, 2005, 679.
39 For example, Johnson 'Performing identity, past and present'; Henry Johnson '"Happy Diwali!" Performance, multicultural soundscapes and intervention in Aotearoa New Zealand', in *Ethnomusicology Forum* 16, no. 1, 2007, 71–94; J. Mackley-Crump, 'The festivalisation of Pacific cultures in New Zealand: Diasporic flow and identity within "a sea of islands"', PhD dissertation, University of Otago, 2012.
40 Johnson, 'Performing identity, past and present'.
41 Asia New Zealand Foundation, 'Behind the scenes at the lantern festival': www.asianz.org.nz
42 Lincoln Tan, 'Lantern festival sets park aglow', *New Zealand Herald*, 6 February 2012: www.nzherald.co.nz/chinese-in-nz/news/article.cfm?c_id=147&objectid=10783667
43 Anonymous, 'When Asian lights draw 40,000 in', *The Press*, 13 February 2012, 2.
44 Siong Ngor Ng, 'The Chinese community in Auckland: A musical ethnography and musical history', 2004, n.p.; UNESCO, www.portal.unesco.org/culture/en/ev.php-URL_ID=21747&URL_DO=DO_TOPIC&URL_SECTION=201.html
45 Ng, 'The Chinese community in Auckland'.
46 Johnson, '"Happy Diwali!"'.
47 Sekhar Bandyopadhyay (ed.), *India in New Zealand: Local identities, global relations*, Dunedin: Otago University Press, 2010.
48 Bandyopadhyay *India in New Zealand*; Jacqueline Leckie, *Indian Settlers: The story of a New Zealand South Asian community*, Dunedin: Otago University Press, 2007.
49 New Zealand Federation of Ethnic Councils, 2013: www.nzfmc.org.nz
50 Bandyopadhyay, *India in New Zealand*.
51 Compare with Stephen Shaw, Susan Bagwell and Joannna Karmowska, 'Ethnoscapes as spectacle: Reimaging multicultural districts as new destinations for leisure and tourism consumption', in *Urban Studies* 41, no. 10, 2004, 1983–2000.
52 ANZF includes a quiz on its website that has been written as a short resource consisting of eight questions and answers for teachers and/or students as a way of offering an educational aspect of the Southeast Asian Night Market. There are also school-oriented materials for teachers and students to utilise in connection with the other festival that ANZF partly organises.
53 Asia New Zealand Foundation, 'Press release', Wellington: Asia New Zealand Foundation, 13 August 2008a.
54 Anon., 'Asian sensation', *Dominion Post*, 18 August 2008, 3.
55 Darren Hughes, 'Speech: New Zealand government', 18 August 2008.
56 Interestingly, on the same day, the local Polish community in Lower Hutt held their annual public festival in a similar style, which included the Lublin Dance Company, Orleta Polish Song and Dance Ensemble, the Polish Church Choir and

Koledzy. See Anon., 'Free', *Dominion Post*, 20 March 2010, 19. The annual event, which has been running for over 15 years (see www.polishcommunity.org.nz), received little media attention, and lacked such intervention as found with the Southeast Asian Night Market.

57 Asia New Zealand Foundation, 'Press release', Wellington: Asia New Zealand Foundation, 16 March 2010.
58 Annual Report of the Asia New Zealand Foundation, Wellington: Asia New Zealand Foundation, 2011, 5.
59 Statistics New Zealand, 'Census data'; Statistics New Zealand, 'QuickStats about culture and identity: Asian', (2012b) www.stats.govt.nz
60 Simon Collins, 'The Kiwi and the dragon China and us', *New Zealand Herald*, 9 April 2011: www.nzherald.co.nz/nz/news/article.cfm?c_id=1&objectid=10718165
61 Parekh, *Rethinking multiculturalism*, 224.
62 Asia New Zealand Foundation, *Annual Report of the Asia New Zealand Foundation*, 2006, 5-6. ANZF's Annual Report of 2007–08 notes that at the Lantern Festivals in Auckland and Christchurch an 'average 60 percent of attendees had learnt something about Chinese culture'; and at Diwali in Auckland and Wellington an 'average 64 percent of attendees had learnt something about Indian culture' (Asia New Zealand Foundation 2008b, 20).
63 Shaw, Bagwell, and Karmowska, 'Ethnoscapes as spectacle'.
64 Compare to Greg Richards, and Julie Wilson, 'The impact of cultural events on city image: Rotterdam, cultural capital of Europe 2001', *Urban Studies* 41, no. 10, 2004, 1931–51.

Bibliography

Anon. 'Asian sensation', *Dominion Post*, 18 August 2008, 3.
Anon. 'Free', *Dominion Post*, 20 March 2010, 19.
Anon. 'When Asian lights draw 40,000 in', *Press*, 13 February 2012, 2.
Appadurai, Arjun, *Modernity at Large: Cultural dimensions of globalization*, Minneapolis: University of Minnesota Press, 1996.
Armstrong, John and Young, Audrey, 'Who wants a PM who's down in the mouth?', *New Zealand Herald*, 19 November 2011: www.nzherald.co.nz/election-2011/news/article.cfm?c_id=1503012&objectid=10767097
Asia New Zealand Foundation, *Annual Report of the Asia New Zealand Foundation*, Wellington: Asia New Zealand Foundation, 2006.
Asia New Zealand Foundation, Press release, Wellington: Asia New Zealand Foundation, 13 August 2008a.
Asia New Zealand Foundation, *Annual Report of the Asia New Zealand Foundation*, Wellington: Asia New Zealand Foundation, 2008b.
Asia New Zealand Foundation, *Annual Report of the Asia New Zealand Foundation*, Wellington: Asia New Zealand Foundation, 2009.
Asia New Zealand Foundation, Press release, Wellington: Asia New Zealand Foundation, 16 March 2010.

Asia New Zealand Foundation, *Annual Report of the Asia New Zealand Foundation*, Wellington: Asia New Zealand Foundation, 2011.

Asia New Zealand Foundation, 'Behind the scenes at the lantern festival': www.asianz.org.nz

Bandyopadhyay, Sekhar (ed.), *India in New Zealand: Local identities, global relations*, Dunedin: Otago University Press, 2010.

Bartley, Allen and Spoonley, Paul, 'Constructing a workable multiculturalism in a bicultural society', in Michael Balgrave, Merata Kawharu and David Williams (eds), *Waitangi Revisited: Perspectives on the Treaty of Waitangi*, Auckland: Oxford University Press, 2005, 136-48.

Belich, James, *Making Peoples: A history of the New Zealanders*, Auckland: Allen Lane, 1996.

Bhabha, Homi, 'Postcolonial authority and postmodern guilt', in Lawrence Grossberg, Cary Nelson and Paula Treichler (eds), *Cultural Studies*, London: Routledge, 1992, 55-66.

Bhabha, Homi, 'Culture's in-between', in Stuart Hall and Paul du Gay (eds), *Questions of Cultural Identity*, London: Sage Publications, 1996, 53-60.

Breckenridge, Carol A. (ed.), *Consuming Modernity: Public culture in a South Asian world*, Minneapolis: University of Minnesota Press, 1995.

Colmar, Brunton, 'New Zealanders' perceptions of Asia and Asian peoples in 2010', commissioned by Asia New Zealand Foundation, Wellington: Asia New Zealand Foundation, 2011.

Dennis, Rutledge M. (ed.), *Biculturalism, Self-Identity and Societal Transformation*, Bingley: Emerald JAI, 2008.

Duffy, Michelle, 'The performance of identity: The community music festival in Australia', paper presented at the Institute of Australian Geographers 'Identities in Action!' Conference, 10-12 December 1999.

Duffy, Michelle, 'Lines of drift: Festival participation and performing a sense of place', *Popular Music* 19, no. 1, 2000, 51-64.

Duffy, Michelle, 'Performing identity within a multicultural framework', *Social and Cultural Geography* 6, no. 5, 2005, 677-92.

Duffy, Michelle, 'Possibilities: The role of music and emotion in the social dynamics of a music festival', paper presented at the WSEAS International Conference on Cultural Heritage and Tourism (CUHT'08), Heraklion, Crete Island, Greece, 22-24 July 2008.

Dunne, Peter, 'Press release: Dunne: NZ needs a Multiculturalism Act', 11 May 2011: www.scoop.co.nz/stories/PA1105/S00236/dunne-nz-needs-a-multiculturalism-act.htm

Edmond, Jacob, Johnson, Henry and Leckie, Jacqueline (eds), *Recentring Asia: Histories, encounters, identities*, Leiden: Global Oriental, 2011.

Falassi, Alessandro (ed.), *Time out of Time: Essays on the festival*, Albuquerque: University of New Mexico Press, 1987.

Foster, Hal (ed.), *Vision and Visuality*, Seattle: Bay Press, 1995.

Getz, Donald, 'Assessing the economic impact of festivals and events: Research issues',

Journal of Applied Recreation Research 16, no. 1, 1991, 61–77.
Getz, Donald, 'The nature and scope of festival studies', *International Journal of Event Management Research* 5, no. 1, 2010: www.ijemr.org/docs/Vol5-1/Getz.pdf
Getz, Donald and Andersson, Tommy D., 'Sustainable festivals: On becoming an institution', *Event Management* 12, 2008, 1–17.
Goldberg, David Theo (ed.), *Multiculturalism: A critical reader*, Oxford: Blackwell, 1994.
Green, Nancy L., 'The comparative method and poststructural structuralism: New perspectives for migration studies', *Journal of American Ethnic History* 13, no. 4, 1994, 3–22.
Greif, Stuart William, *Immigration and National Identity in New Zealand: One people, two peoples, many peoples?*, Palmerston North: Dunmore Press, 1995.
Habermas, Jürgen, *The Structural Transformation of the Public Sphere: An inquiry into a category of bourgeois society*, trans. by Thomas Burger, Cambridge: Polity, 2008.
Hayward, Janine, 'Biculturalism', Te Ara – the Encyclopedia of New Zealand: www.TeAra.govt.nz/en/biculturalism
Dally, Joelle, '"Counter-protest" against racism', *Press*, 22 March 2013: www.stuff.co.nz/the-press/news/8457819/Counter-protest-against-racism
Heywood, Andrew, *Political Ideologies*, 3rd edition, Palgrave Macmillan, 2003.
Hughes, Darren, 'Speech: New Zealand government', 18 August 2008.
Ip, Manying and Pang, David, 'New Zealand Chinese identity: Sojourners, model minority and multiple identities', in James H. Liu, Tim McCreanor, Tracey McIntosh and Teresia Teaiwa (eds), *New Zealand Identities: Departures and destinations*, Wellington: Victoria University Press, 2005, 174–90.
Johnson, Henry, 'Performing identity, past and present: Chinese cultural performance, New Year celebrations, and the heritage industry', in Charles Ferrall, Paul Millar and Keren Smith (eds), *East by South: China in the Australasian imagination*, Wellington: Victoria University Press, 2005, 217–42.
Johnson, Henry, '"Happy Diwali!" Performance, multicultural soundscapes and intervention in Aotearoa New Zealand', *Ethnomusicology Forum* 16, no. 1, 2007, 71–94.
Johnson, Henry and Moloughney, Brian (eds), *Asia in the Making of New Zealand*, Auckland: Auckland University Press, 2006.
Johnston, Ron, Gendall, Phillip, Trlin, Andrew and Spoonley, Paul, 'Immigration, multiculturalism and geography: Inter-group contact and attitudes to immigrants and cultural diversity in New Zealand', *Asian and Pacific Migration Journal*, 19, no. 3, 2010, 343–69.
Leckie, Jacqueline, *Indian Settlers: The story of a New Zealand South Asian community*, Dunedin: Otago University Press, 2007.
Liu, James H., McCreanor, Tim, McIntosh, Tracey, and Teaiwa, Teresia (eds), *New Zealand Identities: Departures and destinations*, Wellington: Victoria University Press, 2005.
Mackley-Crump, J., 'The festivalisation of Pacific cultures in New Zealand: Diasporic flow and identity within "a sea of islands"', PhD dissertation, University of Otago, 2012.

May, Stephen (ed.), *Critical Multiculturalism: Rethinking multicultural and antiracist education*, London: Falmer Press, 1999.
Mitchell, Tony, *Popular Music and Local Identity: Rock, pop and rap in Europe and Oceania*, London: Leicester University Press, 1996.
Mulgan, Richard, *Māori, Pākehā and Democracy*, Auckland: Oxford University Press, 1989.
Multicultural Services Centre: www.msc.wellington.net.nz
New Zealand Federation of Ethnic Councils Inc., 'Press release: Federation seeks a Multicultural Act for NZ', 3 March 2008: www.scoop.co.nz/stories/PO0803/S00024.htm
New Zealand Federation of Ethnic Councils, 2013: www.nzfmc.org.nz
Collins, Simon, 'The Kiwi and the dragon China and us', *New Zealand Herald*, 9 April 2011: www.nzherald.co.nz/nz/news/article.cfm?c_id=1&objectid=10718165
New Zealand Travel Guide: www.tourism.org.nz/people-and-history.html
Ng, James, *Windows on a Chinese Past*, 4 volumes. Dunedin: Otago Heritage Books, 1993-99.
Ng, Siong Ngor, 'The Chinese community in Auckland: A musical ethnography and musical history', MA dissertation, University of Auckland, 2000.
Ng, Siong Ngor, 'The Chinese community in Auckland: A musical ethnography and musical history', 2004, UNESCO: www.portal.unesco.org/culture/en/ev.php-URL_ID=21747&URL_DO=DO_TOPIC&URL_SECTION=201.html
Parekh, Bhikhu C., *Rethinking Multiculturalism: Cultural diversity and political theory*, Cambridge, Mass.: Harvard University Press, 2000.
Pio, Edwina, *Longing and Belonging: Asian, Middle Eastern, Latin American and African peoples in New Zealand*, Wellington: Dunmore Publishing, 2010.
Rattansi, Ali, *Multiculturalism: A very short introduction*, Oxford: Oxford University Press, 2011.
Richards, Greg and Wilson, Julie, 'The impact of cultural events on city image: Rotterdam, cultural capital of Europe 2001', *Urban Studies* 41, no. 10, 2004, 1931-51.
Roscoe, Jane, *Documentary in New Zealand: An immigrant nation*, Palmerston North: Dunmore Press, 1999.
Said, Edward W., *Orientalism*, New York: Pantheon Books, 1978.
Sharp, Andrew, 'Why be bicultural?', in Margaret Wilson and Anna Yeatman (eds), *Justice and Identity: Antipodean practices*, Wellington, Bridget Williams Books, 1995, 116-33.
Shaw, Stephen, Bagwell, Susan and Karmowska, Joannna, 'Ethnoscapes as spectacle: Reimaging multicultural districts as new destinations for leisure and tourism consumption', *Urban Studies* 41, no. 10, 2004, 1983-2000.
Singham, Mervin, 'Multiculturalism in New Zealand - the need for a new paradigm', *Aotearoa Ethnic Network Journal* 1, 2006, 33-37.
Spoonley, Paul and Gendall, Phillip, 'Welcome to our world: Attitudes to immigrants and immigration', in Andrew Trlin, Paul Spoonley, Richard Bedford (eds), *New Zealand and International Migration: A digest and bibliography, Number 5*, Auckland: Massey University, 2010, 136-58

Spoonley, Paul and Trlin, Andrew, *Making Sense of Multicultural New Zealand*, Palmerston North: New Settlers Programme, Massey University, 2004.
Statistics New Zealand, 2012a, Census data: www.stats.govt.nz
Statistics New Zealand, 2012b, 'QuickStats about culture and identity: Asian': www.stats.govt.nz
Tan, Lincoln, 'Lantern festival sets park aglow', *New Zealand Herald*, 6 February 2012: www.nzherald.co.nz/chinese-in-nz/news/article.cfm?c_id=147&objectid=10783667
Urry, John, *The Tourist Gaze: Leisure and travel in contemporary societies*, London: Sage Publications, 1990.
Vasil, Raj K., *Biculturalism: Reconciling Aotearoa with New Zealand*, Wellington: Institute of Policy Studies, Victoria University Press, 1988.
Voci, Paola and Leckie, Jaccqueline (eds), *Localizing Asia in Aotearoa*, Wellington: Dunmore Publishing, 2011.
Wearing, Brian, 'New Zealand's immigration policies and Immigration Act (1987): Comparisons with the United States of America', in Ivan Light and Parminder Bhachu (eds), *Immigration and Entrepreneurship: Culture, capital, and ethnic networks*, New Brunswick: Transaction, 1993, 307–27.
Young, Percy M. et al., 2011, 'Festival', in *Grove Music Online, Oxford Music Online*: www.oxfordmusiconline.com/subscriber/article/grove/music/49527
Young, Steven, 2012: www.stevenyoung.co.nz

Part III: Multiculturalism and Religion

6. Whither Cultural Acceptance?
Muslims and multiculturalism in New Zealand

ERICH KOLIG

My book *New Zealand's Muslims and Multiculturalism* (Leiden: Brill, 2010) discusses the effects of New Zealand's pragmatic brand of multiculturalism on the Muslim minority within a global context. About 46,000 Muslims form a small minority of around 1 per cent of the country's population. This is tiny, both numerically and proportionally to the total population, compared with the European Muslim diaspora. In some parts of Western Europe Muslims are a sizeable minority of 5 to 8 per cent; France alone allegedly has a Muslim population of four to five million, and Germany is home to about three to four million Muslims. In some Christian and mixed-religious countries Islam appears to be taking the position of second largest religion behind the majority religion.[1] Perhaps due to the small size of New Zealand's Muslim community, many of the problematic issues associated with multiculturalism and the accommodation of a Muslim minority elsewhere (such as extremism, parallel societies, lack of social cohesion and ghettoisation) do not seem to surface. Yet, questions of principle arise concerning integration, and pluralist accommodation of a minority's socio-cultural and religious needs.

Not only in numbers, but also in controversiality, European Muslims surpass New Zealand's Muslims. The concept of multiculturalism has a different focus in Europe. It refers primarily to the relationship between 'native' European society, grounded in a predominantly Christian background which metamorphosed into a dominant secularism in more recent times, and the Muslim minority, made up of various ethnic and national backgrounds who are committed to Islam in varying degrees. In this context, multiculturalism refers to the coexistence of two cultural blocs, which face each other with increasing unease.

The physical reality of multiculturalism has two major aspects: (i) the politicisation of Muslim presence and (ii) the influence, accommodation and absorption of Islam as culture. Debates about Muslim immigration and integration have been strongly politicised by political parties that have constructed their platforms around the rejection of the immigration of 'cultural aliens' in order to engage in the political process. Furthermore, the effect that Islam may have on European identity and traditional culture has also become a hotly debated issue. In Europe, Muslims traditionally represent stereotypical cultural Otherness (ignoring Jews, Roma and other religio-cultural minorities who, due to their small numbers, do not currently threaten dominant cultural and national identities in the same way). Islam is traditionally counterpoised to the Christian heritage, which is significant in the context of this chapter due to the formative influence Christianity had on European identity. Especially in very recent decades, however, strong processes of secularisation have changed that. Nonetheless, in a cultural sense, the perceived difference, almost of antinomic proportions, remains. The now very noticeable presence of Muslims has evoked various forms of 'cultural racism' that had previously been considered buried and forgotten. Muslims are being used for political mobilisation, especially in a negative sense, rekindling nationalist and culture-purist sentiments. As a consequence, Islamophobia has reared its ugly head in various forms, spanning politics and the arts, from Geert Wilders[2] to (some of) the Danish cartoons.[3] Even serious scholars (such as Bernard Lewis and Francis Fukuyama)[4] have warned of an impending loss of European culture and identity.

In government circles, as well, alarmist cries have increased in intensity, with declarations that multiculturalism as a policy has failed. German Chancellor Angela Merkel, France's (former) President Nicolas Sarkozy and the British Prime Minister David Cameron are just the most prominent leaders among a multitude of other European politicians who have expressed such views. They are often joined by sceptical social scientists.[5] Security concerns also tend to tarnish Muslims collectively with the brush of suspicion. Not surprisingly, hybridisation of identity appears to be making little headway against the persistence of an exclusively Muslim or ethnic identity.[6] As the well-known German-Muslim social scientist Bassam Tibi recently intimated in an interview, the attempts to form a Euro-Islam, a modernised, de-politicised, liberal version of Islam, have failed in the face of rising Muslim radicalisation.[7] However, rejection of the Muslim presence is balanced by many expressions of genuine acceptance, socio-political enfranchisement through integration, and the juridical and practical goodwill of liberal policies. Among the most prominent exponents of this attitude is the (former) Archbishop of Canterbury, Dr Rowan Williams, who called for the official recognition of the sharia in the UK.[8] As might have been expected, this sparked a lively and vitriolic debate as to whether such recognition is possible, or desirable, for Western secularised liberal democracies.

Australia and North America also have sizeable Muslim minorities, by far exceeding the numbers of New Zealand's Muslims. These minority Muslim populations are also showing some unsettling phenomena of mutual maladjustment, which is unheard of in this country.[9] On the basis of this international comparison, one must agree that New Zealand is fortunate to have one of the most peaceful and complacent Muslim minorities in the Western world. I see no reason to attribute this to the effectiveness of the intelligence services in screening immigrants and maintaining surveillance on residents and citizens, but am inclined to give credit mostly to Muslims individually, as well as to their leadership. Another reason may be that New Zealand immigration policies have favoured better-educated and economically better-situated immigrants.

Muslims en bloc have not come to the public's attention by making concerted, vociferous demands to have aspects of their culture officially recognised, or through their antagonistic, violent behaviour. There are very few incidents in which Muslims have drawn unfavourable attention to themselves. If it were not for the characteristic architecture of mosques and a distinctive female sartorial code, New Zealand majority society would hardly notice their presence. So far, and importantly, the acute danger of Islamic terrorism seems far removed from these shores.[10]

Muslims in New Zealand

This is simply to say that when comparisons are made with other Western countries with sizeable Muslim minorities, New Zealand is fortunate insofar as the Muslim presence has not been politicised and become an ideological issue to the degree that it has, for instance, in neighbouring Australia. In the absence of negative experiences of the kind already experienced in Australia, for example, Islamophobia has not arisen publicly to a very noticeable extent and is not openly expressed.[11]

Only a few years ago, however, it looked as if New Zealand was falling victim to an unpleasant paranoia about Muslims – but this proved to be a passing phase.[12] Perhaps as the fallout of 9/11 and 7/7, some of the press and television had engaged in promoting paranoia, voicing suspicion of New Zealand Muslims or attributing sinister motives to Islam per se, but the topic has now largely disappeared from the media. The few New Zealand politicians who had in the past expressed the odd Islamophobic view, warning against Muslim immigration and the inability of Muslims to assimilate and integrate, or voicing a mistrust of global Muslimhood and Islam in general, have disappeared from the parliamentary scene, and with their departure such views have largely been silenced.[13] Islamophobic views probably still exist residually but at least for the moment they have been deprived of a public platform. All in all it may be justified to think there is a good embracement of the idea of multiculturalism in this country. Despite such incidents as 9/11, the Bali bombing, and the London 7/7 public transport bombing, which did cause a stir, empathy with the US, Australia and the UK was not transferred to strong physical hostility towards Muslim residents in New Zealand. Despite an underlying sentiment that identifies Islam per se as radical (in other words, ascribing to it a propensity of extremism), Muslims in New Zealand have had nothing to fear. Excepting the odd act of vandalism on mosques, some verbal abuse of, mainly, Muslim women, and a few other unsavoury incidents, Muslims have not become victims of hostilities in this country.

There is just enough suspicion remaining to justify the work of the intelligence service, a revision of the Terrorism Suppression Act, and one or two university-based experts who combine the study of Islam and terrorism. The Ahmed Zaoui case[14] moved Muslims into the limelight for a while, partially highlighting residual Islamophobia, but in equal measure also bringing out majority society's positive sentiments, fair-mindedness and respect for human rights. Muslims have reciprocated by not voicing loud demands for cultural recognition and catering to their customary needs, though at times they have expressed protest in certain specific matters.[15] Overall, New Zealand's Muslims hardly contribute to the imaginary 'clash of civilisations'.[16]

New Zealand multiculturalist policy has been strongly supported by the restraint of the Muslim leadership. Its programmatic demands are moderate and flexible; and the protests against violations of Muslim sensitivities – such as cartoons lampooning the Prophet Muhammad – do not fall outside the parameters of legitimate free expression allowed to all citizens. I can only surmise that this may have something to do with the fact that much of the leadership has predominantly been in the hands of

Muslims of European and South Asian (Indian) extraction. These groups have a long history of being of minority status and living under pluralist conditions. In this regard, arrivals from the Arab world, the Middle East and Somalia who have come into the country in more recent years are more attuned to a social environment that is structured and dominated by Islamic requirements. With the recent influx of greater numbers of these Muslims, the balance may shift slightly. At times Muslim politics have assumed a different tone because Muslims from these societies are accustomed to the greater assertiveness of Muslim-ness in their home countries. On a more abstracted sociological level, however, Muslims in New Zealand have from the beginning bedded down an Islamic worship that to a large extent is detached from specific ethno-cultural backgrounds, to allow Muslims of diverse origins to embrace it; and have developed a style of devotion that is purged of many of the trappings that would have accentuated the cultural difference vis-à-vis the encapsulating Western culture. This also supported a process of privatisation of belief and worship detached from the public sphere. The earliest Muslims in fact kept their 'Muslim-ness' so discrete that most of their contemporaries seem to have been uncertain about it. More recent immigration, however, brings different conceptions of what it means to be Muslim. It is unclear whether this has to do primarily with ethnicity or with a general global climate of Islamic revivalism.

For a short while Muslims managed to have parliamentary representation in the previous Labour government under Helen Clark. Dr Ashraf Choudhary, an ex-academic, became a low-ranked Labour Party list MP. However, soon after entering parliament he lost the allegiance of Muslim voters when he supported Labour Party legislation allowing civil unions (and with it homosexual unions) and the Prostitution Law Reform Bill. Choudhary obviously put party loyalty above an Islamic agenda, and quite sensibly argued that Muslims, as a minority themselves, would be wise to support minority issues.

Despite being relatively well organised – through the national organisation Federation of Islamic Associations of New Zealand (FIANZ) and several regional associations – Muslims at this time have no official political mouthpiece at the national level. Their views are usually expressed in terms of quiet diplomacy and press releases. Muslims by and large have so far not been inclined to make demands through undemocratic political pressure, public spectacle or violence.

It is unlikely that Muslim influence on government policies will grow in the foreseeable future. Political participation and influence of Muslims and their organisations would potentially touch on sensitive matters. In 2005 the Exclusive Brethren (an exclusive religious group) were found to be attempting to influence elections by surreptitious and somewhat odious means.[17] As a result, New Zealand has been sensitised to religious organisations seeking to gain political influence. This country's Islamic organisations are not known to have ever attempted a similar strategy. However, in several respects some government policies and new legislation have been deeply unpopular among Muslim constituents. Sexual liberalisation, enacting new marriage laws, and military participation in the Afghan war are just some of the issues in which majority Muslim opinion, as far as it can be gauged, deviated significantly from the dominant political discourse. New Zealand's abstention from participating in the 2003 US-led invasion of Iraq was noted with satisfaction among Muslims,[18] as was the distancing from George W. Bush's administration pursued by the previous Labour-led government. New Zealand's Muslim organisations, though urging their members to participate in the democratic process, beyond expressing a view in the form of protest demonstrations or press releases, have done nothing to earn the nation's distrust. The decision by Prime Minister John Key and his government in 2011 to send fighting troops (SAS) to Afghanistan, and thus involve New Zealand in what essentially has become an Afghan civil war, may change the perception global Muslimhood has of New Zealand. The wider ramifications of this remain to be seen.

My task here is not to examine how Muslims feel in New Zealand, whether they are contented, respected as a minority, their needs well looked after, or the opposite. A consistent and dominant theme in migration studies and Muslim diaspora issues is the adaptability of 'Islamic faith and culture' to Western norms, conventions, customs and laws. This is to say, doctrinal issues of Islam appear to pose, and judging by actual experience *do* pose, problems of adaptation in a Western context. To discuss this in a more generalised sense means violating anthropological mantras of avoiding essentialisation, usually decried as illicit stereotyping; or to phrase it differently: it means discussing Muslims as a generic bloc, and in doing so ignoring national, ethnic and sectarian differences and other ideological nuances such as nominal, secularised or devout and fundamentalist attitudes in being Muslim.

Multicultural accommodation and conflict potential

How can a Muslim minority, in New Zealand as much as elsewhere, and in a more abstract sense how can Islam, as a minority culture and religion, be accommodated in a Western secularised, liberal democratic society? How can Western society with its emphasis on human rights, religious and cultural freedom – but also its anthropocentric secularism – be reconciled with Islamic culture, beliefs and customs, values, and the theocentric world view deeply rooted in the Islamic faith? What concessions do diasporic Muslims have to make? What demands are being placed on policies of multiculturalism, on cultural adaptation and the need for accommodation for minority cultures to exist in majority culture and dominant society? Despite a prevalent sense of cultural tolerance, or benign indifference, and legal provisions that ensure a certain degree of cultural accommodation, there are considerable difficulties and not-so-hidden pitfalls. New Zealand's Muslims have not en bloc demanded special recognition, but issues of their integration into a Western liberal secularist democracy are relevant, such as the extent of the cultural freedom guaranteed by multicultural policies and human rights. New Zealand's multicultural policy is mainly grounded in internationally formulated human rights provisions and in particular in the Bill of Rights Act 1990. The latter stipulates that 'assimilation' is no longer a legitimate goal. By guaranteeing religious and cultural freedom, however, this Act implicitly bears the risk of creating conflict with social and legal barriers; that is to say, with boundaries set by common conventions, social norms and existing domestic laws. In other words: how is multiculturalism for Muslims practically exercised in New Zealand to satisfy the Bill of Rights Act, yet without generating a so-called 'parallel society', negating integration, undermining social cohesiveness and breaking national rules of law and conventional behaviour?

In Stanley Fish's terminology, the practical result in New Zealand is a kind of 'boutique multiculturalism'.[19] That is to say, selected items that do not conflict with majority society laws, conventions and aesthetic regimes are acceptable, can be practised, and may even attract benevolent participation by members of the encapsulating dominant society. Such things as Chinese New Year, Diwali, song and dance, costumes and exotic cuisine add to the colour and diversity of New Zealand cultural life and do not challenge existing levels of tolerance or legal acceptability. Pasifika culture (and language) enjoys an even more privileged position and a great deal of sympathy, as it is closely linked with the cultural 'opening' brought about by biculturalism.

Accommodating halal requirements and wearing the hijab in public pose no problem – but wearing the burqa or the niqab does in certain situations.[20] Recognising polygyny is a problem for the state, as is gender inequality as defined by New Zealand law and social convention. Applying sharia jurisdiction is another potential problem, even in an extremely liberal, secularised and 'religion-blind' democracy such as New Zealand. Some countries make concessions in Private Law (inheritance, marriage, divorce, family matters); to my knowledge New Zealand law does not. The UK has admitted sharia courts (or tribunals) with limited jurisdiction to adjudicate in family matters, financial affairs and the like. Australian Muslim leaders made such a request in 2011, in the name of multiculturalism, to the Commonwealth government. It was immediately rebuffed by the Federal Attorney-General, who proclaimed that the sharia has no place in Australia.[21] One wonders what would be New Zealand's position if such a demand were to be made here. Of course, institutionalising something like this poses enormous difficulties, and in effect leads us to the debates associated with legal pluralism. The question would also have to be addressed: which kind of sharia[22] and to what extent is this possible without violating dominant juridical and constitutional doctrines? Jeremy Waldron[23] has powerfully argued that the maxim 'one law for all' is to be rejected by a liberal democracy in favour of a more sympathetic cultural accommodation. But how far can legal pluralism and recognition of an alternative justice system go, without seriously undermining national social cohesiveness and violating majority society's sense of equality and justice? What does that do to a society's fabric of social interaction?

In terms of multiculturalism in a Western liberal democracy, Muslims pose possibly the greatest challenge. Islam is a strong culture-producing matrix, encompassing potentially every aspect of social conduct of the devout in addition to vitally shaping value system, aesthetic and ethical views, and the world view in general. For Muslims everywhere, therefore, freedom of religion potentially means more than just the liberty of ritual and belief. This unique constellation is what Jocelyne Cesari has called Muslim exceptionalism.[24] In Islam, orthopraxy is as important as orthodoxy – that is, the right social conduct is as important as the right belief – so that the issue of freedom of religion intrudes strongly into social practice. Thus absolute religious freedom to be a Muslim, for the devout – not the 'secularised' Muslim of course – means to be able to adhere to certain behaviour, norms and values prescribed by particular schools or authorities in Islam. Some of these may be in conflict with Western standards. Globally, processes of re-moralisation of Muslim society,[25] which go hand in hand with fundamentalisation, also seem to lead to a tightening of the connection between orthodoxy and orthopraxy. This not only opposes to a considerable degree the forces of secularisation affecting Islam, it also runs counter to the West's dominant perception of what a religion should be. British legal expert Sebastian Poulter has paraphrased the position Muslims face in Western society succinctly: 'Muslims can only adhere to Islam as a religion and not as a total way of life.'[26] Poulter refers to the fact that secularisation in Europe has stripped formal, institutional religion of its erstwhile normative and social-controlling significance and religion-controlled social patterns have no validity any more. Sociologically speaking, Islam has to recast itself as one religion among others in a secular space. This may entail the need to discard certain cultural markers and characteristic religio-cultural features that spring from a basis in Islamic doctrine.

Linked with this is another important aspect of secularisation that affects Islam in Western society: that is the privatisation of religious belief.[27] In the absence of the dominant ideological force of Islam in the public space, as it exists ubiquitously and all-pervasively in the traditional Islamic world, whether or not to be a Muslim (in other words, to act as a Muslim) and to what extent, becomes a matter of personal choice.[28] The degree of intensity of participating in the faith and its rules passes into a person's individual discretion and deep into their private sphere.

The relevant questions go right to the heart of how a liberal democracy such as New Zealand arrives at practical and legal solutions to cultural difference. My concern in this chapter – and this is the purpose for drawing some comparisons between New Zealand and Europe – is with the boundaries of multiculturalism.[29] Modern Western liberal democracy and its state have forsworn cultural and religious intolerance towards resident minorities and maintain provisions (legal instruments and institutions) that guarantee the requisite forms of freedom demanded above all by human rights provisions. But these are not straightforward issues of simple tolerance. As assimilation of culturally distinct and different minorities is no longer legally enforceable – in fact is derided as cultural colonialisation – questions of integration and national identity come into focus. How far can the acceptance of cultural Otherness go – or to phrase it differently and more concretely: to what extent can the religious and cultural distinctiveness of Muslims be accommodated under a regime of Western secularised democratic liberalism without doing damage in some way to the encapsulating host society? Or at what point does the denial of concessions violate the rights of minorities? In a demographically and culturally mixed society such as New Zealand, it is not just a matter of sharing the same geographical space. The practical social interpenetration of Muslims (that is, the devout ones) with non-Muslims within a modern Western liberal democracy, and the secularised, legal framework it posits, its ethics and values, necessitate targeted responses from policies. I am concerned with policy outcomes based on liberal theory, rather than with philosophical and ethical principles of democratic liberalism, egalitarianism, illiberality of policy choices and the definition of common good.[30]

Tariq Ramadan[31] demands that tolerance should be replaced with recognition. Toleration is the charity of the powerful, he argues, but not a relationship among equals. However, policies of recognition pose a considerable problem. Celebrating diversity and avoiding moral judgment is very New Age and post-modernist, but lacks in practical reason. Since the nationalist–conformity discourse has been replaced with a liberal-democratic one, after initial enthusiasm a chasm of difficulties, both practical and philosophical, has opened up. Politically it has led to the open admission that cultural accommodation must have its limits.

The vexing question of cohesion and the spectre of parallel societies

Let me briefly address the question of social cohesion in a multicultural, pluralist society. As the Cantle Report[32] in the UK in 2001 made clear, there is a fear that multicultural liberalism creates parallel societies that are not just poorly integrated into the wider society and segregated but, as minorities, are actively hostile to each other and to the majority society. The meaning of being a citizen of a country is lost to separatist ethnic, religious and cultural identities. This seems to harbour palpable dangers. As Robert Putnam[33] has argued, one consequence of the entrenchment of socio-cultural distinctiveness and diversity is the loss of integrative potential, a diminution of social cohesiveness in a nation, and the loss of trust between communities.

In the political parlance and broader context of Europe, the issue of social cohesion is couched in the concept of integration. It is often said that Muslims lack 'integration-willingness'. Practically, this means that they form a separate section of society – a so-called parallel society – and have minimal interaction with the rest. Residential patterns of geographic segregation (ghettoisation), culture-and-language-preserving mechanisms, ethnic and religion-specific education, minimal everyday interaction with majority society, and disengagement with the democratic political process, tend to perpetuate a distinct Islamic minority culture and society. As the Cantle Report pointed out with some hyperbole, this may become a 'powder keg' situation exploding episodically into violent civil unrest.

Current human rights conventions and laws ensure that assimilation cannot be enforced to produce a homogenous citizenry that criminalises socio-cultural expressions that resist this kind of societal 'terra-forming'. However, the prevailing expectation still is of a polity and society in which members accept a common juridical framework, share a diffuse agreement on rights, duties and freedoms, and vaguely adhere to a common set of values, usually described as 'core' values.

Muslim immigrants have been accused of lacking loyalty to the nation or society in which they choose to reside, that their language of choice remains that of their country of origin or descent, and that they retain self-identification as Muslims rather than accepting the national identity. The question is whether these are valid indicators of lack of a society's cohesiveness and of the absence of a coherent polity. Where exactly is the tipping point when this freedom turns into social disintegration by way of creating a 'parallel society' that seriously erodes the wider society's cohesiveness? What are the markers and building blocks of such cohesiveness, and is social cohesion really needed in a modern, democratic liberal society that gives wide latitude to political and ideological sympathies, networks of personal loyalties, special interest groups, the growing numbers of multiple citizenship and mixed nationalities, fashionable tribal affiliations, international linkages through professional and political affiliations, the high degree of spatial mobility driven by economic interests, and internationalism, engendering the growing notion of global citizenship?

Multiculturalism and national identity

Globalisation has brought about increased migration and mobility. Together with a new global awareness, over time this will countervail sentimental patriotism, and change the face of identification with a nation-state.

The human rights ideology pervades international relationships as well as domestic matters, especially in Western liberal democracies. Following the racist atrocities of World War II, human rights were designed to protect individual rights. Human rights by extension now apply also to group rights and in this capacity manage to suppress the worst forms of ethnic-cultural-racist abuse. But the combination of codified rights, legally enforced tolerance and increased geographic mobility, also has more far-reaching effects. One important effect is on nationhood and the sense of national identity. Multiple forms of citizenship and hybrid individual and collective identities are emerging in ever growing numbers, as are new and more complex forms of loyalty that are less based on birth, historical and cultural nostalgia, or fervent nationalism – but which rely more on rational decisions. Over time, sensible pluralism and multiculturalism – at least in the West – are set to overcome the fears of loss of national identity and the need to cling to cultural purity.[34] Such fears, as expressed academically by Francis Fukuyama[35] and Samuel Huntington,[36] seem destined to become a by-product of this flow of social history.[37] However, a clear prognostication is not possible owing to the enormous complexity and the existence of counter-current processes. The long-term influence of more popularly based resistance to globalisation, such as the erection of cultural boundaries – so-called 'cultural closure' – remains to be seen. Despite its homogenisation – and perhaps because of it – globalisation seems to have released identities previously bottled up by national hegemony.[38] Ethnic and religious identities especially have gained in significance, as the many ethnic and religious conflicts world wide clearly demonstrate.[39]

These and other phenomena herald a fading of the national identity, at least in the traditional homogenous, monocultural form, and foreshadow problems for multicultural society. Bikkhu Parekh addresses the difficulties that a multicultural nation may increasingly face in trying to invoke a sense of cohesiveness:

Defining national identity in a multicultural society is an exceedingly difficult enterprise. It cannot, and should not be ethnically and culturally neutral, as it then satisfies nobody and lacks the power to evoke deep historical memories but neither should it be biased towards a particular community as it then de-legitimises and alienates others, nor should it be culturally eclectic as it then lacks coherence and focus.[40]

The public use of specific cultural markers and symbols may appeal to one section of multicultural society and may repel another. However, the multiplicity of ethnically and religiously specific imagery may challenge the conservative national identity, which some elements of the 'native' population may perceive as weakening or disappearing altogether.

Globally, there seems to be a strengthening of Muslim identity, bringing to the fore an increased pride in being Muslim. As the Muslim minority grows in Western Europe, almost inevitably, the desire to assimilate with the dominant culture shrinks proportionally. Huntington brings the issue to the point: 'People came to America because they wanted to become Americans. The Turks do not come to Germany because they want to become Germans.'[41] The immigrants' expectation is that their identity as Turks or Kurds of Islamic faith be respected and incorporated in a multi-formed, heterogeneous German national identity. Jonathan Friedman,[42] among others, answered this interesting question about the change in desired identity, by arguing that there is a global diminution of the Western hegemony, concomitant with a process in which the focus on material progressiveness is being replaced with a greater emphasis on culture and tradition. Some have even spoken of a 're-religionisation' and 're-spiritualisation' of the world – a kind of New Age response to the materialistically oriented rationalism that seems so far to have accompanied globalisation.[43]

The official pursuit of multiculturalism requires a shift in emphasis away from nationalism based on cultural specifics, and a growth of awareness that in a pluralist society the sense of nationhood, as much as social cohesion, can be based on common practical interests – rather than emotive factors of cultural or racial legacy, idealised traditions or divine providence. Diverse and discrete identities can then meld in a pragmatic manner in a society in which enforced nationalism and adherence to monocultural tradition is replaced by a maximum of cultural freedom. This may also mean revising the concept of citizenship and replacing it with a concept acknowledging a person's embeddedness in multiple webs of loyalty – even if it is not around a doctrine of cultural uniformity, or a strictly defined national identity and the maxim of 'one law for all'. However, even a very liberal democracy such as New Zealand will have to insist on the adherence to certain principles, in a legal, ethical and social sense, in order to facilitate the existence of a functioning society.

Balancing cultural freedom with securing integration will not be easy. I shall just refer to two cases in which monocultural insistence has led to drawing the boundaries in a rather parochial manner. France's prohibition on the Islamic face veil (burqa and niqab) demonstrates a heavy-handed enforcement of identity uniformity.[44] At the root is a conservative view of the importance of maintaining the national identity as secularised,[45] egalitarian and distinctly anti-religious. On this basis the prohibition of ostentatious religious phenomena in the public discourse is considered justified (hence the earlier prohibition of the hijab in the public education system). The ban on face veils is also supposed to strike a blow for women's liberation.[46] The relevant anti-liberal legislation, which now violates several values of freedom and personal choice, also breaks several laws, among them the European Union conventions on religious freedom and human rights laws, all of which are set aside in favour of the perceived importance of instilling an a-religious, secularist, gender-neutral and rationalist official national identity.

It is fair to assume that the deeper reason is a crisis of national identity. By projecting an image of the cultural enemy – the veiled Muslima, the poster representative of the dangerous Islamic Otherness with a whiff of terrorism – the reassuring superiority of monocultural French identity is underlined. In a similar way, the minaret prohibition in Switzerland also relates to issues of national identity transposed to the level of a picturesque land and cityscape. Swiss national identity draws on images of lovely small cities full of conservative and rustic alpine architecture, nestled among mountains, lakes and wholesome pastures. The alien and phallic images of minarets thrusting towards the sky, taller than church bell-towers, literally seem to stick out like sore thumbs, threatening the idyllic character of Swiss national culture.

The UK delivers another example of a national defence mechanism curtailing the freedom of being Muslim. Freedom of expression – including the right to peaceful protest – is a cherished public good in in all Western democracies. Despite several limitations on this freedom, imposed by law as well as convention, it is considered a cornerstone of a progressive, modern and enlightened society and polity. Yet it is far from being all-embracing or culture-blind, as the Luton case in the UK has demonstrated. In this case five Muslim demonstrators, who 'hurled abuse' at the British armed forces in a rowdy demonstration in 2009, were convicted of public order offences after appeal in the British High Court. In defiance of Article 10 of the European Convention on Human Rights, which guarantees the right to expression and protest, insulting the British army appears to be a punishable offence under a High Court judge's interpretation of British law. It does not require drawing a long bow to see that the British identity, which draws much on military prowess, is fiercely defending itself against corrosive attacks by a cultural Other.[47]

New Zealand's readiness to compromise and its policies of accommodation

New Zealand is formally bicultural, institutionally monocultural (with some exceptions), and demographically, to some noticeable extent, multicultural. On the one hand, the country's multiculturalism is of a pragmatic and officially undeclared kind, based on a diffuse sense of tolerance of – or, perhaps better, indifference to – cultural Otherness.[48] On the other hand, the country's multiculturalism is legally underpinned by the Bill of Rights Act 1990 and Human Rights Act 1993. In addition, New Zealand is a signatory to most, if not all, human rights compacts and declarations of the United Nations, which, when their stipulations are complied with, provide a sure foundation for multiculturalism.

New Zealand's populist multiculturalism expresses itself mainly in eating 'ethnic' food, enjoying ethnic festivities, music and dance on occasion, politely ignoring saris and hijabs in the streets, accepting halal meat and roti in supermarkets, and seeing building permits granted to mosques of distinctive Middle Eastern architecture. By and large this is not dissimilar to the situation in Western Europe.[49] Hidden behind such ostentatious cultural markers is the selective and largely inconsequential nature of cultural acceptance. Harmony and tranquillity are not disturbed as long as minorities make no more radical demands. In New Zealand's case obviously the line of acceptability of cultural Otherness does not coincide with where biculturalism and the acceptance of Māori culture is situated. Immigrant minorities evidently cannot expect the same level of accommodation as the tangata whenua, the indigenous people.[50] The West's general moral equipment at this time inclines the dominant culture to make greater concessions for indigenous minorities than for immigrant minorities of noticeably different cultural background.[51]

Yet, distinctions and divisions can be drawn often in unexpected and incongruous manners. While the Māori moko, for instance, can no longer be taken as an excuse for stigmatisation and social exclusion, wearing a Sikh turban apparently still can.[52] Similarly a newspaper columnist,[53] in analysing the hyperbolic praise by the media of the All Whites soccer team's performance at the 2010 FIFA World Cup in South Africa, concluded that New Zealand has not come to grips with multiculturalism – not as much, at least, as it has come to terms with biculturalism. His argument was based on the observation that one player, heaped with praise for scoring a goal, was repeatedly and emphatically referred to as Māori. Some of his team mates, judging by their names, were of an ethnicity or ethnic derivation other than Anglo-Celtic: one was clearly of Balkanese origin (the former Yugoslavia), another two seemed to be Germanic; but they were not referred to in these terms. However, this admits also to other interpretations: for instance, that this is a kind of racism in which 'whites' are simply subsumable under the dominant identity of 'New Zealander,' but 'brown people' are subject to definition by ethnicity.

On the other hand, the national mood – as far as can be gauged – is one of resignation to the impending 'browning' of New Zealand society. There is a distinct 'climate' of acquiescence to the fact that this will irreversibly change the national identity. Such a change has already been ushered in by the diminution of domestic hegemonic identity of Anglo-Celtism, as its monocultural monopoly is incrementally undermined by biculturalism, the latter increasingly enshrined in statutes over the last two decades and expressed in a multitude of official policies. (Usually the phraseology refers to the Treaty of Waitangi and what it requires in terms of cultural, economic and socio-political concessions.) On a less formal level, selected Māori cultural items have become so entrenched in the national cultural showcase as to now form an integral part of national identity.

There is also growing awareness, though seemingly meeting with less sympathy than the growth of the Polynesian component, that East and South Asian immigration is noticeably changing the ethnic composition.[54] Population projections make for interesting reading. The Māori population is projected to increase by an average of 1.4 per cent a year, from an estimated 620,000 in 2006 to 820,000 in 2026; the Asian population by 3.4 per cent a year from 400,000 to 790,000; the Pacific population by 2.4 per cent a year from 300,000 to 480,000; and the 'European or Other' population by 0.3 per cent a year from 3.21 million to 3.43 million. Given these growth rates, a very broad projection will comfortably predict that by 2050, the category 'Europeans' will be outnumbered by the other categories combined. This will undoubtedly make a difference to national identity.

Defining a new national identity multiculturally may not herald a 'catastrophic' diminution, let alone disappearance, of the current publicly dominant culture that is West-European in origin. Cultural assimilation rates, if such processes were measurable, may present quite a different statistical picture. In other words, the cultural minorities may successively and incrementally assimilate to the dominant culture so that when they have reached numerically majority status they are no longer, at least superficially, distinguishable in a cultural sense. In a society and state in which multicultural policies are applied in a sustained manner, assimilation pressure does not primarily arise from coercive measures, but from the assimilative pull any dominant culture is likely to exercise. What applies here is Antonio Gramsci's argument about how hegemony is achieved: a client culture is assimilated by ideological persuasion, the promise of enfranchisement and perhaps by the apparent attractiveness of the dominant culture, rather than coercion in the 'classical' Marxist sense of class struggle and ideological domination by force.

In recent years, however, pressure to assimilate has again increased in Europe and Australia, especially through a tightening of immigration laws. Some spectacular cases of maladjustment of Muslims have encouraged a revision of rules relating to immigrants and asylum seekers. Language and history tests for citizenship have been introduced.[55] In some European countries even, training courses for Muslims intending to migrate to Europe are being mooted, with the putative aim of preparing Muslims for key components of Western culture such as gender equality, sexual liberalism, sartorial code, democracy, freedom of expression and the like. The debate on differentiated forms of citizenship and greater instrumentalisation of policies of cultural recognition is increasingly overshadowed by the rhetoric of a strictly uniform citizenship.[56] The rhetoric of national cultural uniformity has been ratcheted up, especially by some political parties, which find increasingly popular support. European countries, where this has been tolerated before, are tightening restrictions on underage and enforced marriage, punishing Muslim domestic violence, defending Muslim women against sexual predation by Muslim men, more vigorously defending the right to offend Islam through the arts, and making access to citizenship and residency more difficult.

Such measures, however, have a hollow ring in New Zealand, as immigration laws are already stringent and even intending asylum seekers are carefully vetted. On the other hand, New Zealand does not want to be seen to target a particular racial, religious or ethnic group in a legislatively discriminative way. Successive New Zealand governments have demonstrated great pragmatism in cultural accommodation, by employing a specifically targeted, case-by-case approach to ethnic-religious issues. In doing so they have, de facto, set aside debates on the ethical and philosophical foundations of policies in favour of practical realism. A consistently underlying theme implicit in policies and practical decisions is that, by virtue of being the tangata whenua, Māori merit special concessions not extensible to other minorities. Although this has not been officially framed in any way, the Pasifika minority also receives favourable treatment at times.

To take a cynical view, making concessions to non-majority cultures and religions seems to depend to a considerable extent on political opportunism and the calculation of political pay-offs and risks, and rather less on a measured consideration of principle. Let me cite just two examples where government concessions provoked interpretations of this kind. One example of such piecemeal, opportunistic cultural deal-making is the temporary and ad hoc changes made to New Zealand's political culture in order to appease visiting Chinese dignitaries. The freedom of expression, and the freedom to protest, at times get seriously restricted – in view of the fact, as some interpret it, that economic linkages with China are of immense importance.[57] Another incident relates to the television docu-drama *Death of a Princess* in 1980. A joint Anglo-American production allegedly about a real incident in Saudi Arabia in which a Saudi princess was put to death for adultery, the film created international controversy. Saudi Arabia tried to ban it, a move that was respected by some countries and not by others. The New Zealand government banned it from screening on television,[58] causing speculation as to whether the government was giving in to protests from New Zealand Muslims or to threats from Saudi Arabia. In a less cynical view, reasons for these and similar cultural concessions can be found in a genuine humanist desire to enfranchise cultural Otherness and to show regard for its sensitivities.

So far, finding compromises in particular cases has not posed serious problems in New Zealand. The most compelling instance to date in which Islamic religious requirement collided with Western conventions was the so-called 'burqa affair' I have described elsewhere.[59] Two Muslim women, invoking their religious rights under the Bill of Rights Act, wished to remain completely veiled before a court of law. This was seen as unacceptable, out of tune with court protocol, and detrimental to conducting a fair trial. Eventually, a compromise was reached to the satisfaction of most, including the two women. The case ignited a debate on which cultural features are religiously prescribed – falling under the aegis of the doctrine of religious freedom including the freedom of practice – and which are 'merely' customary (without backing of Islamic canonical law). The compromise reached in the burqa case in the end did not directly address, or resolve, this debate. It provided, instead, a cautious middle path, offering a hybrid response that avoided a clear determination.

Islamic head-dress and veiling do emerge as focal points when cultural interests clash. A Muslim woman filed a complaint with the Human Rights Commission over her removal from the public gallery of a Hastings courtroom for refusing to take off her headscarf.[60]

The judge subsequently apologised and admitted that he had acted in error being under a false impression. In July 2011 the refusal by Auckland and Wellington public transport drivers to allow veiled Muslim women onto their buses led to considerable publicity in the media. Appropriate apologies to the affected women were made – though perhaps only after intervention of the Saudi ambassador. The bus drivers were cautioned, and the media expressed sympathy for the women and for the Islamic

Yasmeen Ali was expelled from a Hastings courtroom because the judge mistook her hijab (head covering) for a sign of protest (September 2009). *Hawke's Bay Today*

dress code in general, in the name of cultural freedom and New Zealand's multiculturalism.[61] New Zealand, on the whole, is supportive of cultural diversity and loath to legislate to restrict cultural freedom, although tacitly, Muslims are expected to respect limitations voluntarily. When this fails, domestic criminal law is meant to prevail in cases of conflict. But it seems that legislating with the specific aim of circumscribing customs is seen to be in conflict with religious freedom and human rights. All the more notable is the exception made with female genital 'mutilation'.[62] It is forbidden by New Zealand law, while a small minority of Muslims believe it is a shariatic requirement. The prohibition, theoretically at least, is against human rights insofar as it is gender discriminative, since male circumcision is allowed. The reason for this specific prohibition may be sought in the influence of the feminist lobby seeking to liberate women from what it sees as male-instigated cultural oppression. The accuracy of this assessment is debatable.

Normally when conflicts arise, a case-by-case solution is sought. For instance in the Danish cartoon affair, when two or three New Zealand newspapers insisted on publishing the images when it was already common knowledge just how much offence they had given, resident Muslims expressed strong discontent.

From the Muslim perspective this was a blasphemous act that put it beyond the right of freedom of expression, with which they are normally prepared to live. Muslims are well aware that the Western-cherished freedom of expression has its limitations, as there are many areas and issues that cannot be freely addressed. Yet, in this case, they seemed to believe that as far as their sensitivities were concerned, no restrictions applied. In the event the government of the day sought to broker an informal agreement between Muslim representatives and the relevant newspaper editors. Editors promised to exercise better discretion in such matters of cultural sensitivity and to show more respect to Muslim beliefs; Muslim leaders were reminded of the basic rights of freedom of expression and freedom of the media, which hold great currency in this country.

New Zealand tends to make concessions on a case-by-case basis without giving alien cultural customs official status or enacting exemption laws. For instance, unlike the UK, no exemption rules exist freeing Sikhs from protective helmet laws, or allowing turbans in conjunction with police and military uniforms.[63] In this light, somewhat more surprising was the modification of the Animal Welfare Commercial Slaughter Code as originally proposed in May 2010, in order to accommodate Jewish religious

Muslims marching in Queen Street, Auckland, on 5 February 2006, in protest against the publication of Danish cartoons in two New Zealand newspapers.
New Zealand Herald

custom. In its original form it effectively prohibited the Jewish *shechita* (kosher) slaughter method, which does not allow pre-slaughter stunning. The method had previously been exempted from restrictive rules but this was now to be rescinded.[64] After Jewish protests the ministry announced the case would go to court, only to reverse itself shortly afterwards, declaring that the Jewish exemption would be allowed to continue in the new code. A legal expert had hinted that in a courtroom contest, the religious rights of Jews based on human rights and the New Zealand Bill of Rights would win over the Animal Welfare Code.[65] One can only surmise that vigorous behind-the-scene lobbying led to the ministry's capitulation. This case can be compared with the introduction of the halal slaughter method in New Zealand in the 1970s. It was strongly opposed by Christians, farmers and wide sections of society, and would likely not have been implemented had it not been appended with pre-slaughter stunning procedures, and, moreover, deemed desirable for reasons of dire economic necessity. It was a decision hardly made in support of cultural and religious freedom.

In 2009, the Department of Corrections revealed that all meat served to prisoners had undergone halal slaughter.[66] As I was informed this was to provide for any Muslim inmates because human rights law requires that food must be religiously acceptable. The department also offers vegetarian and vegan diets, but apparently no kosher food. Perhaps revealing a modicum of Christian bias, despite a general alcohol prohibition in prisons, wine for the celebration of the Eucharist is allowed.[67]

An example of multiculturally softened cultural boundaries was seen in August 2009, when a Pacific Islander slaughtered and cooked his dog in the backyard.[68] It provoked some public outrage – based of course on ignorance of the fact that in many parts of the world (historically and even today) dogs are considered food. The Tongan family was given a warning. I recall Muslims of my acquaintance complaining that they could not slaughter sheep in private at Eid al Adha celebration (which is meant to commemorate Abraham's sacrificial act), as that would bring them in conflict with the police.

In August and September 2010 a case of a cultural claim colliding with New Zealand law provided media copy across the world. A Turkish man, described as a South Taranaki kebab shop owner, was charged with assault against his wife, having allegedly beaten her in the street in front of the shop.[69] The man's defence was that they actually had performed a traditional Turkish dance called *kolbasti*, which allegedly portrays what might be called 'police brutality' with some vigorous and seemingly aggressive moves. The whole family claimed they like to dance, saying it was their 'culture'. The judge asked the prosecutors to view some videos of *kolbasti*. Ultimately, about a month later, the judge decided that the family's account – that they were dancing – was mendacious; the man's behaviour was judged an assault and he was fined. It is unclear whether this verdict is just or unjust in a multiculturalist sense, and whether what appeared to outsiders to be a brutal attack really was no more than a very vigorous form of choreography; or to what extent the man had taken 'artistic licence' to elaborate on the dance moves.

The *kolbasti* case raises the question of to what extent a court is able, and empowered, to distinguish between cultural tradition and criminal behaviour. In this case the issues concerned an ethnic custom and not Islam itself. Some Islamic customs and potential demands can be accommodated relatively easily as individual need arises. For example, although it is unlikely that the religious holiday Eid[70] will in the foreseeable future have the same national holiday status as Christmas or Easter, Sabbatarian wishes can be accommodated and are supported by legislation that ensures individual cultural rights are observed if the persons concerned so desire. Similarly, if gender segregation in education is desired by Muslims (or others), they are free to organise religiously based private schooling beyond the usual *tafsir* (Quran) classes. After accreditation of the curriculum, such schools can then be integrated with the public system and receive state funding support, just as Catholic or other private schools do (some of which are also gender segregated). Auckland's Zayed College for Girls, after initial difficulties, achieved this in June 2010. This is the second Islamic school to have been integrated into the New Zealand public education system.[71]

Excepting indigenous culture and its rights, New Zealand has shown little ambition to regulate multiculturalism, to an extent that places minority community rights somewhat outside national law and national norms. This country also shuns categorising individuals, regardless of whether they wish to belong to a particular class or not. It is not clear whether or not this stems from the insight that, when there is no freedom of choice and an absence of flexibility, classification can become a possible source of negative discrimination. European Muslim leaders appear divided over the merits of a classificatory system that provides them with a particular legal framework.[72] Perhaps having in mind the Islamic *dhimma* system or the Malaysian multicultural system, both of which carve cultural, religious and socio-political differences deeply into a nation, some seem to fear legal classification can easily be turned to negative discriminative purposes.[73] New Zealand's penchant to leave multiculturalism as a grey area and to deal with situations as they arise on a case-by-case basis – retaining flexible borders of toleration of foreign cultural patterns, making some concessions and remaining steadfast in other areas – so far has served the country well. Internationally, New Zealand is cited as a beacon of multiculturalism and enlightened pluralist tolerance in a globalising world.

A communitarian approach – as it is applied only to Māori ethnicity – works with group identity and defined cultural patterns to create culture-specific spaces. Its disadvantage is that it can inflect to collective ostracism, discrimination, cultural stagnation and lack of state protection for individual interestedness and rights, when these deviate from defined minority norms. Culturally grounded illiberality, if and when it acts out minority cultural beliefs and practices but conflicts with majority culture laws and values, poses, then, a particular problem which needs to be overcome with certain provisos such as: that exceptionary accommodations and their consequences may not contradict basic human rights, constitutional and statutory provisions etc. Although some theorists such as Parekh and Kymlicka have argued that dominant society's liberality should find ways to accommodate minority groups' illiberality, this is utopian thinking.[74] Yet, in a small measure it does exist in New Zealand's accommodation of Māori exceptionalism, for instance in allowing a Māori politician to be openly racist with impunity.

New Zealand, when it comes to its (non-Māori) minority groups, espouses so-called liberal thought and liberal theory par excellence. This approach is based on the notion that minority groups are aggregates of individuals who innately have, and are entitled to, their own discreet interestedness, and have to be treated on an individual basis. It views cultural minorities as composed of individuals who personally 'suffer' from an inability to agree with majority culture in all respects. Combined with a deliberative democratic process and its legal instruments (such as the Bill of Rights) and based on a maxim of 'best practice individual freedom', multiculturalism creates – often rather arbitrarily – exceptions and concessions, but by and large refuses to enshrine *a priori* the collective cultural rights of defined groups in law. On a basis of a liberal orientation the political and legal process then accommodates small-scale cultural differences when it feels it can do so without political damage, and without seriously violating its own interests, dogmas and core values.

Endnotes

1. The figures are only estimates as secularised Western society does not keep accurate statistics on people's religious affiliation, considering it a very private matter as well as irrelevant to the state's business. With regard to citations throughout the chapter, note that news events if considered of some importance are reported by several media and recorded in several web sites. When of international significance they are likely to be reported in several languages and at more or less different times (not only due to date differences); for the purposes of this paper only one source is referred to as an example for a news event. But search engines can usually dredge up a plethora of relevant information sources.
2. Wilders' Freedom Party, campaigning on a platform of stopping Muslim immigration, is a sizeable factor in the Dutch parliamentary composition. Other European countries have similar political parties, although no leader comes near Wilders' flamboyance and notoriety.
3. See Jytte Klausen, *The Cartoons that Shook the World*, New York: Yale University Press, 2010. Not all of the 12 cartoons originally published by *Jyllands Posten* are objectionable to Muslims, mainly because the pictorial representation of the Prophet is considered blasphemous. Theo van Gogh's murder seems to have been motivated by hatred of his anti-Muslim film, made in cooperation with Ayaan Hirsi Ali, the well-known anti-Islam and ex-Muslim feminist.

4   See Bernard Lewis, Interview, October 2004: www.weeklystandard.com; and Francis Fukuyama, 'Identity, immigration, and liberal democracy', *Journal of Democracy* 1, 2006, 5–20: www.lacomunitatinconfessable.cat/wp-content/uploads/2009/06/7049410-fukuyama-francis-identity-immigration-democracy-artigo.pdf
5   Examples of multicultural-sceptic writings from the UK include the Cantle Report, *Community Cohesion: A report of the independent review team chaired by Ted Cantle*, UK Home Office, London, n.d.; from Germany, Thilo Sarrazin, *Deutschland schafft sich ab*, Munich: DVA-Randum, 2010, a hugely controversial book; and Ernst Hofbauer, *Inshallah Österreich*, Vienna: Universitas, 2009. See also Derek McGhee, *The End of Multiculturalism?*, Maidenhead: McGraw Hill, 2008; and Vertovec, Steven and Wesselsdorf, Susanne (eds), *The Multiculturalism Backlash: European discourses, policies and practices*, London, New York: Routledge, 2010.
6   For an Austrian example see Erich Kolig, 'Freedom, identity construction and cultural closure', in Elizabeth Rata and Roger Openshaw (eds), *Public Policy and Ethnicity: The politics of ethnic boundary making*, Basingstoke: Routledge, 2006a.
7   N.N., 'Prof. Tibi Bassam: "Die Islamisten sind staerker als wir Reformer"', 16 May 2011: www.EuropeNews43302.html
8   Rowan Williams, 'Archbishop's Lecture – civil and religious law in England: A religious perspective', 7 February 2008: www.archbishopofcanterbury.org/articles.php/1137/archbishops-lecture-civil-and-religious-law-in-england-a-religious-perspective
    According to blogsites the UK, in 2009, had about 85 sharia courts which could operate legally as long as they stayed juridically within a certain framework. See Erich Kolig, 'To shari'aticize or not to shari'aticize: Islamic and secular law in liberal democratic society', in Rex Ahdar and Nicholas Aroney (eds), *Shari'a in the West*, Oxford: Oxford University Press, 2010, 255–77.
9   For a New Zealand–Australia comparison see Erich Kolig and Nahid Kabir, 'Not friend, not foe: The rocky road of enfranchisement of Muslims into multicultural nationhood in Australia and New Zealand', *Immigrants and Minorities* 26/3, 2008, 266–300. Australian Muslims make up about 2 per cent of the total population.
10 This chapter was written in 2011, before the so-called Islamic State (or Isis) acquired the global internet reach it has in 2014, using it to disseminate propaganda and recruit with considerable efficacy. Among other things this has raised the issue about returning 'foreign fighters' and domestic terrorism. See also e.g. 'Maori Muslim backs Islamic State' (*NZ Sunday Star-Times*, 2 November 2014). It may also change state responses to this perceived threat.
11 Erich Kolig, 'Is multiculturalism working in New Zealand?', in Farid Hafez (ed.), *Jahrbuch für Islamophobieforschung*, Vienna: New Academic Press, 2012.
12 Erich Kolig, 'Islam and orientalism in New Zealand', in Erich Kolig, Vivienne S.M. Angeles and Sam Wong (eds), *Identity in Crossroad Civilisations: Ethnicity, nationalism and globalism in Asia*, Amsterdam: Amsterdam University Press, 2009b, 219–40.

13 I do not wish to name them here. For one case see Rex Ahdar, 'Religious liberty in a temperate zone', *Emory International Law Review* 21, 2007, 205–38.
14 Kolig, 2009b, 'Islam and orientalism'; Najib Lafraie, 'Ahmed Zaoui, a victim of 9/11', *New Zealand Journal of Asian Studies* 8, 2006, 110–33.
15 The Danish cartoon affair sparked some protests, and so did the planned showing of the film *Death of a Princess*. Muslim organisations have also expressed views on the Afghanistan and Iraq invasions and other issues; but in doing so have always used measured tones. In this they have often been supported by Christian organisations.
16 See Samuel Huntington, *The Clash of Civilizations and the Remaking of World Order*, New York: Simon & Schuster, 1996.
17 See e.g. Rex Adhar, 'Religious liberty in a temperate zone', *Emory International Law Review* 21, 2007, 206.
18 The fact that the Labour government dispatched a reconstruction (non-fighting) team to Basra remained largely ignored by the public.
19 Stanley Fish, 'Boutique multiculturalism, or why Liberals are incapable of thinking about hate speech', *Critical Inquiry* 23, 1997, 378–95.
20 See Erich Kolig, 'Muslim traditions and Islamic law in New Zealand: The "burqa case" and the challenge of multiculturalism', in Henry Johnson & Brian Moloughney (eds), *Asia in the Making of New Zealand*, Auckland: Auckland University Press, 2006b, 204–24; also the case of so-called 'maskophobia' reported for example on ONE News, 5 May 2011 under '"Maskophobia" claims rubbished after burqa incident'.
21 Patricia Karvelas, 'Muslims to push for sharia', *The Australian Online*, 17 May 2011; and 'Imam wants sharia law here, but A-G says no way', *The Australian Online*, 18 May 2011b.
22 Sharia exists in many different versions. See for instance Erich Kolig, 'To shari'aticize or not to shari'aticize: Islamic and secular law in Liberal democratic society', in Rex Ahdar and Nicholas Aroney (eds), *Shari'a in the West*, Oxford: Oxford University Press, 2010, 255–77; and Abbas Amanat and Frank Giffel (eds), *Islamic Law in Contemporary Context: Shari'a*, Stanford: Stanford University Press, 2007.
23 Jeremy Waldron, 'One law for all? The logic of cultural accommodation', *Washington and Lee Law Review* 59, 2002, 3–34.
24 Jocelyne Cesari, 'Muslim identities in Europe: The snare of exceptionalism', in Aziz al Azmeh and Effie Fokas (eds), *Islam in Europe: Diversity, identity and influence*, Cambridge: Cambridge University Press, 2007, 49–67.
25 Jocelyne Cesari, *When Islam and Democracy Meet*, New York: Palgrave Macmillan, 2004.
26 Sebastian Poulter, *Ethnicity, Law and Human Rights: The English experience*, Oxford: Oxford University Press, 1998.
27 Olivier Roy in *Secularism Confronts Islam* (New York: Columbia University, 2007) claims this process is well under way in France.
28 Like others Islam effectively has to become a 'silent religion'. See Thomas

Luckmann, *The Invisible Religion*, New York: Macmillan, 1967.
29 See also Erich Kolig, 'Romancing culture and its limitations: Policies of cultural recognition, multiculturalism and cultural boundaries in New Zealand', in Roger Openshaw and Elizabeth Rata (eds), *The Politics of Conformity in New Zealand*, Auckland: Pearson, 2009a.
30 There is a considerable body of literature on this subject, which I do not propose to review here. For instance (to mention only a few) Will Kymlicka, *Liberalism, Community and Culture*, Oxford: Oxford University Press, 1989; Will Kymlicka, *Multicultural Citizenship: A liberal theory of minority rights*, Oxford: Oxford University Press, 1995a; Will Kymlicka, *The Rights of Minority Cultures*, Oxford: Oxford University Press, 1995b; Jacob T. Levy, 'Classifying cultural rights', in Ian Shapiro & Will Kymlicka (eds), *Ethnicity and Group Rights*, New York, London: New York University Press, 22–25; and Bhiku Parekh, *Rethinking Multiculturalism: Cultural diversity and political theory*, Hampshire: Macmillan, 2000.
31 In his latest book, Tariq Ramadan, *The Quest for Meaning: Developing a philosophy of pluralism*, London: Allen Lane, 2010.
32 Cantle Report, *Community Cohesion: A report of the independent review team chaired by Ted Cantle*, UK Home Office, London, n.d. It was commissioned in response to the 'race riots' earlier in 2001.
33 See for example Robert Putnam (ed.), *Democracies in Flux*, Oxford, New York: Oxford University Press, 2002; and his *Bowling Alone* (2000) and *E Pluribus Unum* (2007).
34 See Arjun Appadurai, *Fear of Small Numbers: An essay on the geography of anger*, Durham, London: Duke University Press, 2006, 8. His analysis on the possible fate of ethnic and cultural minorities being threatened by paroxysms of violence in the name of cultural purism and ethnonationalism contains some remarkable leaps of generalisations. Obviously, in this paper I am not talking about Rwanda, Yugoslavia or fringe Nazism. Appadurai curiously ascribes such features of violent xenophobism to countries like the Netherlands, France and Austria – normally considered in the vanguard of liberal democracies.
35 Francis Fukuyama, 'A year of living dangerously', *Wall Street Journal* 2, 2005, 5; Francis Fukuyama, 'Identity, immigration, and Liberal democracy', *Journal of Democracy* 17, 2006, 5–20. His argument addresses the concern that massive Muslim immigration in the West brings about a shift in cultural identity.
36 Samuel Huntington, *Who Are We? The challenges to America's national identity*, New York: Simon & Schuster, 2004. In this case the author bemoans the mass immigration of Hispanics into the US and the impending loss of the traditional (Protestant Anglo-Saxon-based) identity heritage it threatens.
37 Lewis has expressed similar fears with regard to Europe, reported several times in the *Jerusalem Post*. See Bernard Lewis, *Jerusalem Post*, 2 November 2009: www.jpost.com; and Caldwell (2004) and Machlis (2007). Earlier on he had already predicted that 'by century's end Europe would be Islamic' (Lewis, October 2004: www.weeklystandard.com).

38 Ralph Grillo, R.D., 'Cultural essentialism and cultural anxiety', *Anthropological Theory* 3, 2003, 157–73; Simon Harrison, 'Cultural boundaries', *Anthropology Today* 15, 1999, 10–13; Jonathan Friedman, *Cultural Identity and Global Process*, London: Sage, 1994; Jonathan Friedman, 'Preface', in Elisabeth Rata and Roger Openshaw (eds), *Public Policy and Ethnicity*, Basingstoke: Palgrave Macmillan, 2006, xi–xxv.
39 The Balkans and Rwanda provide the most 'impressive' examples of recent times. At the time of writing in June 2010 the conflict between Sunni Uzbeks and Sunni Kyrgis in Kyrgistan had just erupted. In a sense the squabbling between Pākehā and Māori over assets and rights can also be seen as a related phenomenon. Other examples are the rancour between diasporic Turks and Kurds in Germany erupting at times into violent clashes, and the constant murderous altercations between Sunni and Shia and Ahmadis in Pakistan. These are just a very few examples.
40 Bhiku Parekh, 'Defining national identity in a multicultural society', in Edmund Mortimer (ed.), *People, Nation and State: The meaning of ethnicity and nationalism*, London, New York: Tauris, 1999, 66–74.
41 Samuel Huntington, *Who Are We? The challenges to America's national identity*, New York: Simon & Schuster, 2004, 191.
42 Jonathan Friedman, 'Preface', in Elisabeth Rata and Roger Openshaw (eds), *Public Policy and Ethnicity*, Basingstoke: Palgrave Macmillan, 2006, xi–xxv.
43 See Erich Kolig, 'De-Talebanising Islam and creating inter-cultural spaces'. Paper given in abbreviated form at the Islam Research Centre colloquium, Otago University, July 2009. Erich Kolig, 'De-Talebanizing Islam and creating inter-cultural spaces', in Paul Morris, William Shepard, Toni Tidswell and Paul Trebilco (eds), *The Teaching and Study of Islam in Western Universities*, London: Routledge, 2013.
44 While France and Belgium are already enforcing this law, other European countries are considering similar laws.
45 *Laïcité* in France is law-based and therefore is amenable to be enforced by law.
46 This is based on the tenuous argument that veiling is a symbol for patriarchy, androcracy and male oppression. See Erich Kolig, *Conservative Islam*, Lanham MD: Lexington, 2012, 185–226.
47 Later this protest (in May 2013) was followed by the gruesome murder of a British soldier in broad daylight by two Muslims protesting the (alleged) role of the British army in oppressing Muslims.
48 Xenophobia traditionally was directed more towards the Chinese and less towards Muslims who, until recent years, were practically invisible (both optically and socially) in New Zealand society.
49 In the UK it has been called the Three S multiculturalism (for saris, samosas and steelbands) or the Three C multiculturalism (for costumes, cooking and concerts). See James Donald & Ali Rattansi, *'Race', Culture and Difference*, Newbury Park, CA: Sage, 1992; Sneja Gunew, *Haunted Nations: The colonial dimensions of multiculturalism*, London: Routledge, 2004.
50 See Bashir Bashir and Will Kymlicka, 'Introduction: Struggles for inclusion and reconciliation in modern democracies', in Will Kymlicka & Bashir Bashir (eds),

The Politics of Reconciliation in Multicultural Societies, Oxford, New York: Oxford University Press, 2008, 1–24.
51 Exceptions seemingly do still occur. For instance, a case was reported by the *Otago Daily Times* (N.N., 17 February 2005, 3) of a Māori woman losing out on employment as a waitress because of her moko. Nightclub security, on the other hand, have been advised when admitting people to differentiate between the moko, as a marker of Māori identity, and other tattoos which may provide legitimate grounds for refusing entry.
52 The private Auckland club that had earlier barred a Sikh from entering – to participate in a ceremony in his honour – because of its rule of 'no head-gear', reaffirmed this rule despite protests by a vote in June 2010 (Lincoln Tan, *New Zealand Herald*, 14 June 2010). Club members were well aware of the rule's discriminative effect, as two years earlier a problem arose over a Muslim hijab-wearing woman being similarly barred. The turban case was allegedly referred to the Human Rights Commission but no further action was taken.
53 Falcous, *Otago Daily Times*, 30 June 2010, 15.
54 Colmar Brunton, *New Zealander's perceptions of Asia and Asian peoples in 2010*, Asia Research Foundation: www.asiaNew Zealand.org.New Zealand/our-work/knowledge:research/research-reports/social-research/perceptions-study. The report speaks of an increase in the appreciation of Asians and that a majority of respondents expressed this. However, this does not have the same aroma of realism as the picture conveyed by news journalism.
55 It was reported in the *Press* (in January 2008; again by *Otago Daily Times*, 22 January 2013, 3) that 'Kiwis' undergoing the recently introduced Australian citizenship test did very poorly in cultural and history questions.
56 On a pessimistic note, Kymlicka claims that the time for advances on minority rights is past. See Will Kymlicka, *Multicultural Odysseys: Navigating the new international policies of diversity*, Oxford, New York: Oxford University Press, 2007, 315.
57 On several occasions when Chinese state visits occurred, anti-Chinese demonstrations by Falun Dafa (also known as Falun Gong) members, who for the most part are Chinese refugees, and people protesting for a 'free Tibet' have been blocked or dispersed by police and security, apparently in violation of fundamental rights.
58 See William Shepard, 'Muslims in New Zealand', in Yvonne Yazbek Haddad and Jane I. Smith (eds), *Muslim Minorities in the West: Visible and invisible*, Lanham: Altamira Press, 2002, 233–54.
59 Erich Kolig, 'Muslim traditions and Islamic law in New Zealand'.
60 N.N., 'Muslim woman furious at courtroom ban', *New Zealand Herald*, 2 September 2009: www.nzherald.co.nz/nz/news/article.cfm?c_id=1&objectid=10594811
61 Both TVNZ and TV3 broadcasted relevant items; the latter went to great lengths to condemn intolerant attitudes to Islamic dress. Interestingly, a new psychological concept cropped up in the debate: maskophobia. The fear of masks had allegedly

motivated the drivers to deny the veiled women access to the bus. See for instance '"Maskophobia" claims rubbished after burqa incident', *ONE News online*, 5 May 2011; and N.N., 'Bus drivers warned after veil incidents', *NZ Herald online*, 5 July 2011.

62 Elizabeth McDonald, 'Circumcision and the criminal law: The challenge for a multicultural state', *New Zealand Universities Law Review* 21, 2004, 233–67.

63 In 2009 a Sikh policeman received personal permission to wear a uniform turban. This was a strictly personal exemption from ordinary dress rules and not meant to set a precedent. Uniform rules of the police force have not been changed.

64 According to this method, prescribed by *kashrut* (Jewish dietary law), an animal must be bled and slaughtered when still alive and fully conscious. The new code (Animal Welfare [Commercial Slaughter] Code of Welfare 2010) stipulated stunning before actual slaughter. Halal slaughter does not exclude stunning on principle. The orthodox Jewish community objected to the change in slaughter regulations and the case was to go to court in 2011. Subsequently, the minister withdrew the regulatory change allowing the continuation of *shechita* slaughter.

65 www.stuff.co.New Zealand/dominion-post/national/3788878/Jewish-community-upset-at-ban-on-kosher-killing

66 'Only halal-certified meat served to prisoners', *Otago Daily Times*, 9 October 2009. An enquiry in January 2011 to the Minister of Corrections was acknowledged and referred on to the Corrections Department, who responded on 2 March.

67 Corrections Amendment Bill (no. 2), February 2009. Sacramental wine has already been permitted by the Corrections Department (since 2004) on the basis of a re-interpretation of an earlier act.

68 'Tongan family "barbecued" dog in back yard earth oven': www.dogs.suite101.com/article.cfm/immigrant_tongan_family_eats_its_pet_dog

69 www.stuff.co.New Zealand/national/crime/4181362/Judge-rejects-dance-defence

70 Eid al Fitr and Eid al Adha.

71 The other is Al-Madinah School, also in Auckland.

72 Jytte Klausen, *The Islamic Challenge: Politics and religion in Western Europe*, Oxford, New York: Oxford University Press, 2005; Jörgen Nielsen, 'The question of Euro-islam: Restriction or opportunity', in Aziz Al-Azmeh and Effie Fokas (eds), *Islam in Europe*, Cambridge: Cambridge University Press, 2007, 34–48.

73 Shortly before the regime's demise, the Taliban announced that Afghanistan (following the classical *dhimma* system) would introduce a badge system for religious minorities and that this would be for their protection. The world responded with loud protests as this plan was too reminiscent of Nazism's treatment of (so-called undesirable) minorities.

74 For instance, curbing speech that Muslims consider blasphemous while allowing Muslims to critique and protest against Western norms is unlikely to happen in the foreseeable future – even despite the fact that freedom of expression is not unlimited even in the most liberal of Western democracies. Attempts to punish apostasy, blasphemy, heresy and social misdemeanour in accordance with conservative interpretations of sharia (and its hudud provisions) are also unlikely to be tolerated by majoritarian law.

Bibliography

Ahdar, Rex, 'Religious liberty in a temperate zone', *Emory International Law Review* 21, 2007, 205-38.

Amanat, Abbas and Giffel, Frank (eds), *Islamic Law in Contemporary Context: Shari'a*, Stanford: Stanford University Press, 2007.

Appadurai, Arjun, *Fear of Small Numbers: An essay on the geography of anger*, Durham, London: Duke University Press, 2006.

Bashir, Bashir and Kymlicka, Will, 'Introduction: Struggles for inclusion and reconciliation in modern democracies', in Will Kymlicka & Bashir Bashir (eds), *The Politics of Reconciliation in Multicultural Societies*, Oxford, New York: Oxford University Press, 2008, 1-24.

Colmar Brunton, *New Zealander's perceptions of Asia and Asian peoples in 2010*, Asia Research Foundation: www.asiaNew Zealand.org.New Zealand/our-work/knowledge:research/research-reports/social-research/perceptions-study

Caldwell, Christopher, 'Islamic Euope?', *Weekly Standard*, vol. 10/4, 4 October 2004: www.weeklystandard.com/Content/Public/Articles/000/000/004/685ozxcq.asp

Cantle Report, *Community Cohesion: A report of the independent review team chaired by Ted Cantle*, UK Home Office, London, n.d.

Cesari, Jocelyne, 'Muslim identities in Europe: The snare of exceptionalism', in Aziz al Azmeh and Effie Fokas (eds), *Islam in Europe: Diversity, identity and influence*, Cambridge: Cambridge University Press, 2007, 49-67.

Cesari, Jocelyne, *When Islam and Democracy Meet*, New York: Palgrave Macmillan, 2004.

Curtis, Sarah, 'Tongan family barbecued dog in backyard earth oven': www.dogs.suite101.com/article.cfm/immigrant_tongan_family_eats_its_pet_dog

Donald, James and Rattansi, Ali, *'Race', Culture and Difference*, Newbury Park, CA: Sage, 1992.

Falcous Mark, 'New look, same Kiwi identity', *Otago Daily Times*, 30 June 2010, 15.

Fish, Stanley, 'Boutique multiculturalism, or why Liberals are incapable of thinking about hate speech', *Critical Inquiry* 23, 1997, 378-95.

Fisher, Amanda, 'Jewish community upset at ban on kosher killing', *Dominion Post*, 9 June 2010: www.stuff.co.New Zealand/dominion-post/national/3788878/Jewish-community-upset-at-ban-on-kosher-killing

Friedman, Johnathan, 'Preface', in Elisabeth Rata and Roger Openshaw (eds), *Public Policy and Ethnicity*, Basingstoke: Palgrave Macmillan, 2006, xi-xxv.

Friedman, Johnathan, *Cultural Identity and Global Process*, London: Sage, 1994.

Fukuyama, Francis, 'Identity, immigration, and Liberal democracy', *Journal of Democracy* 1, 2006, 5-20: www.lacomunitatinconfessable.cat/wp-content/uploads/2009/06/7049410-fukuyama-francis-identity-immigration-democracy-artigo.pdf

Fukuyama, Francis, 'Year of living dangerously', *Wall Street Journal* 2, 2005, 5: www.collier.ukzn.ac.za/Chomsky/OpinionJournal%20-%20FF-AT%20WAR.pdf

Grillo, Ralph R.D., 'Cultural essentialism and cultural anxiety', *Anthropological Theory* 3, 2003, 157-73.

Harrison, Simon, 'Cultural boundaries', *Anthropology Today* 15, 1999, 10–13.
Harvey, Sarah, 'Only halal-certified meat served to prisoners', *Otago Daily Times*, 9 October 2009: www.odt.co.nz/news/national/77325/only-halal-certified-meat-served-prisoners
Hoftbauer, Ernst, *Inshallah Österreich*, Vienna: Universitas, 2009.
Horowitz, David, 'Historian Bernard Lewis diagnoses the fundamental cause of the region-wide explosion of protest, and discusses Western notions of a quick fix', *Jerusalem Post*, 2 November 2009: www.jpost.com
Horowitz, David, 'A mass expression of outrage against injustice', *Jerusalem Post*, 25 February 2011: www.jpost.com
Huntington, Samuel, *The Clash of Civilizations and the Remaking of World Order*, New York: Simon & Schuster, 1996.
Huntington, Samuel, *Who Are We? The challenges to America's national identity*, New York: Simon & Schuster, 2004.
International Express, 22 February 2011, 7.
Karvelas, Patricia, 'Muslims to push for sharia', *Australian Online*, 17 May 2011.
Karvelas, Patricia, 'Imam wants sharia law here, but A-G says no way', *Australian Online*, 18 May 2011.
Klausen, Jytte, *The Islamic Challenge: Politics and religion in Western Europe*, Oxford, New York: Oxford University Press, 2005.
Klausen, Jytte, *The Cartoons that Shook the World*, New York: Yale University Press, 2010.
Kolig, Erich, 'De-Talebanizing Islam and creating inter-cultural spaces', in Paul Morris, William Shepard, Toni Tidswell and Paul Trebilco (eds), *The Teaching and Study of Islam in Western Universities*, London: Routledge, 2013, 113–35.
Kolig, Erich, 'Is multiculturalism working in New Zealand?', in Farid Hafez (ed.), *Jahrbuch für Islamophobieforschung*, Vienna: New Academic Press, 2012, 177–96.
Kolig, Erich, *Conservative Islam: A cultural anthropology*, Lanham MD: Lexington, 2012.
Kolig, Erich, *New Zealand's Muslims and Multiculturalism*, Leiden: Brill, 2010.
Kolig, Erich, 'To shari'aticize or not to shari'aticize: Islamic and secular law in Liberal democratic society', in Rex Ahdar and Nicholas Aroney (eds), *Shari'a in the West*, Oxford: Oxford University Press, 2010, 255–78.
Kolig, Erich, 'Romancing culture and its limitations: Policies of cultural recognition, multiculturalism and cultural boundaries in New Zealand', in Roger Openshaw and Elizabeth Rata (eds), *The Politics of Conformity in New Zealand*, Auckland: Pearson, 2009a, 63–88.
Kolig, Erich, 'Islam and orientalism in New Zealand', in Erich Kolig, Vivienne, S.M. Angeles and Sam Wong (eds), *Identity in Crossroad Civilisations: Ethnicity, nationalism and globalism in Asia*, Amsterdam: Amsterdam University Press, 2009b, 219–40.
Kolig, Erich and Kabir, Nahid, 'Not friend, not foe: The rocky road of enfranchisement of Muslims into multicultural nationhood in Australia and New Zealand', *Immigrants and Minorities* 26, 2008, 266–300.

Kolig, Erich, 'Freedom, identity construction and cultural closure', in Elizabeth Rata and Roger Openshaw (eds), *Public Policy and Ethnicity: The politics of ethnic boundary making*, Basingstoke: Routledge, 2006a, 25-39.

Kolig, Erich, 'Muslim traditions and Islamic law in New Zealand: The "burqa case" and the challenge of multiculturalism', in Henry Johnson & Brian Moloughney (eds), *Asia in the Making of New Zealand*, Auckland: Auckland University Press, 2006b, 204-24.

Kymlicka, Will, *Liberalism, Community and Culture*, Oxford: Oxford University Press, 1989.

Kymlicka, Will, *Multicultural Citizenship: A liberal theory of minority rights*, Oxford: Oxford University Press, 1995a.

Kymlicka, Will, *The Rights of Minority Cultures*, Oxford: Oxford University Press, 1995b.

Kymlicka, Will, *Multicultural Odysseys: Navigating the new international policies of diversity*, Oxford, New York: Oxford University Press, 2007.

Lafraie, Najib, 'Ahmed Zaoui, a victim of 9/11', *New Zealand Journal of Asian Studies* 8, 2006, 110-33.

Levy, Jacob T., 'Classifying cultural rights', in Ian Shapiro & Will Kymlicka (eds), *Ethnicity and Group Rights*, New York, London: New York University Press, 1997, 22-25.

Lewis, Bernard, Interview, October 2004: www.weeklystandard.com

Luckmann, Thomas, *The Invisible Religion*, New York: Macmillan, 1967.

Machlis, David, 'Muslims "about to take over Europe"', *Jerusalem Post online*, 29 January 2007.

McDonald, Elizabeth, 'Circumcision and the criminal law: The challenge for a multicultural state', *New Zealand Universities Law Review* 21, 2004, 233-67.

McGhee, Derek, *The End of Multiculturalism?*, Maidenhead: McGraw Hill, 2008.

N.N., 'Muslim woman furious at courtroom ban', *New Zealand Herald*, 2 September 2009: www.nzherald.co.nz/nz/news/article.cfm?c_id=1&objectid=10594811 (NN stands for *nomen nescio* or anonymous.)

N.N., 'Prof. Bassam Tibi: "Die Islamisten sind staerker als wir Reformer"', *Kleine Zeitung*, 13 May 2011: www.kleinezeitung.at/nachrichten/politik/2742686/islamisten-sind-staerker-reformer.story

N.N., 'Refused job due to Māori moko, woman says', *Otago Daily Times*, 17 February 2005, 3.

N.N., 'Bus drivers warned after veil incident', *NZ Herald online*, 5 July 2011: www.nzherald.co.nz/nz/news/article.cfm?c_id=1&objectid=10736411

Nielsen, Jörgen, 'The question of Euro-Islam: restriction or opportunity', in Aziz Al-Azmeh and Effie Fokas (eds), *Islam in Europe*, Cambridge: Cambridge University Press, 2007, 34-48.

Parekh, Bhikku, *Rethinking Multiculturalism: Cultural diversity and political theory*, Hampshire: Macmillan, 2000.

Parekh, Bhiku, 'Defining national identity in a multicultural society', in Edmund Mortimer (ed.), *People, Nation and State: The meaning of ethnicity and nationalism*, London, New York: Tauris, 1999, 66-74.

Poulter, Sebastian, *Ethnicity, Law and Human Rights: The English experience*, Oxford: Oxford University Press, 1998.
Putnam, Robert, (ed.), *Democracies in Flux*, Oxford, New York: Oxford University Press, 2002.
Putnam, Robert, *Bowling Alone: The collapse and revival of American community*, New York: Simon & Schuster, 2000.
Putnam, Robert, 'E pluribus Unum: Diversity and community in the twenty-first century', *Scandinavian Political Studies* 30/2, 2007, 137–74.
Ramadan, Tariq, *The Quest for Meaning: Developing a philosophy of pluralism*, London: Allen Lane, 2010.
Roy, Oliver, *Secularism Confronts Islam*, New York: Columbia University, 2007.
Sarrazin, Thilo, *Deutschland schafft scih ab*, Munich: VDA Random, 2010.
Shepard, William, 'Muslims in New Zealand', in Yvonne Yazbek Haddad and Jane I. Smith (eds), *Muslim Minorities in the West: Visible and invisible*, Lanham: Altamira Press, 2002, 233–54.
Smith, Jared, 'Judge rejects dance defence', *Taranaki Daily News*, 30 September 2010: www.stuff.co.New Zealand/national/crime/4181362/Judge-rejects-dance-defence
Sneja Gunew, *Haunted Nations: The colonial dimensions of multiculturalism*, London: Routledge, 2004.
Tan, Lincoln, 'Cossie club votes to keep ban on turbans', *New Zealand Herald online*, 14 June 2010: www.nzherald.co.nz/nz/news/article.cfm?c_id=1&objectid=10651716
Vertovec, Steven and Wesselsdorf, Susanne (eds), *The Multiculturalism Backlash: European discourses, policies and practices*, London, New York: Routledge, 2010.
Waldron, Jeremy, 'One law for all? The logic of cultural accommodation', *Washington and Lee Law Review* 59, 2002, 3–34.
Williams, Rowan, 'Archbishop's Lecture – civil and religious law in England: A religious perspective', 7 February 2008: www.archbishopofcanterbury.org/articles.php/1137/archbishops-lecture-civil-and-religious-law-in-england-a-religious-perspective

7. The New Asian Faces of Kiwi Christianity

ANDREW BUTCHER AND GEORGE WIELAND

Visitors strolling along Auckland's Queen Street on a Sunday morning may pause to glance up at the imposing columns of the iconic Auckland Baptist Tabernacle. This building, opened in 1881, is testimony to the faith of nineteenth-century British settlers nurtured by pastors dispatched from England, such as Thomas Spurgeon, son of the famous London preacher Charles Spurgeon. Those visitors who step inside during the Sunday morning service are immediately struck by the fact that although people of British and other European descent are present in the congregation, they are outnumbered by Chinese, Korean, Japanese, Indian and other Asian worshippers, along with people from Africa, South America, the Middle East and elsewhere. As this diverse congregation disperses, a music group sets up in preparation for a service in Mandarin, conducted by a Malaysian Chinese pastor. The Chinese group hands over in turn to a Korean congregation; and finally there is another English language service, recently started specifically to meet the needs of international students and other immigrants, most of whom have arrived from various parts of Asia. These are some of the new and, for many visitors, surprising Asian faces of Kiwi Christianity. When such surprise is expressed it is often twofold: first, that such a significant proportion of Auckland's population comprises people of Asian origin; and second, that many of those Asians are Christian. The goal of this chapter is to increase awareness of both those aspects of the contemporary reality, particularly of Auckland but also of New Zealand more generally.

It might be claimed that New Zealand has been 'multicultural' for the past two hundred years, in the sense that there has been a multiplicity of cultures in these islands. It must also be acknowledged that for most of this time the dominant culture has been Anglo-Celtic. Whether expressed in English Anglicanism or Methodism, Scots Presbyterianism or Irish Catholicism, those Anglo-Celtic cultural streams are profoundly influenced by Christianity. The contribution of this Christian world view, traditions and practice, along with that of religion generally, has not received the attention it merits in accounts of the making of New Zealand and its national identity by major historians such as Sir Keith Sinclair, Jamie Belich and Michael King.[1] For a more adequate appreciation of New Zealand's history and current reality this lacuna must be addressed.

The expression of religion, in buildings, diet and dress, is a distinctive marker of the social changes in New Zealand. In New Zealand's major cities, mosques and temples can be found alongside cathedrals and quaint churches. In ceremonies of national mourning, prayers will be given not only by the Anglican Bishop but also often by representatives of other faiths.[2] In the public perception much of this represents 'new' religion to New Zealand (religions other than Christianity) and is associated with the concomitant increase of numbers of migrants from 'non-Christian' (in common perception, non-Western) countries. In this respect immigration from Asia, which began in the mid-nineteenth century but has accelerated and diversified in recent decades, has differed from previous waves of migration from largely Christian Europe and, in the 1970s, from the Pacific with its strong cultures of church participation;[3] 80 per cent of Pacific peoples in New Zealand are Christian. With Pacific peoples being such an integral part of New Zealand culture now, it is easy to forget that 30 years ago they were the new migrants bringing their styles and culture to New Zealand. Asian migrants, on the other hand, come from a part of the world that is not usually considered Christian, and with the rapid increase in Asian migration to New Zealand there has also been a rapid rise in religions other than Christianity.

Less widely noticed is that among Asian immigrants are many whose religion is Christianity, who bring to New Zealand expressions of Christianity that have taken root in contexts shaped by Asian cultural, religious and socio-economic realities. These Asian immigrants now encounter rather different forms of Christian faith and tradition, in a westernised culture that may be nominally Christian. Kevin Ward has described this culture as 'the new world of post Christian, postmodern and post secular New Zealand'.[4]

When Asian migrants arrive in New Zealand, they bring with them not only their particular religious practices: these may reflect cultural norms and practices as much as they may reflect denominational traditions. They also bring particular theological beliefs that may differ from the beliefs of host country populations. Host community Christian populations also share diverse theological viewpoints and religious practices, and while this diversity may likewise reflect cultural norms as much as denominational traditions, these host community practices and beliefs are often not critiqued in the same way as migrant expressions of Christianity. The lack of critical self-reflection of host community practices and beliefs may be one reason for the resistance toward migrant populations' expressions of Christianity. Instead this chapter emphasises that there is no simple dichotomy between 'Asian Christianities' and 'non-Asian Christianities'. Theological belief and practice do not divide neatly along this or other lines. This dichotomy is a useful marker but it should not be read as constituting anything more than that.

This chapter challenges some of the assumptions behind Asian migrants to New Zealand, their religious practices and their impact upon Christianity in New Zealand. To begin, contemporary debates and migration and religion, through academic literature and public commentary, are briefly considered. This is followed by an overview of migrants and migration to New Zealand, noting changes across time. In this section the various responses to migrants in New Zealand, particularly those that see migrants as a threat to a 'New Zealand' way of life *vis-à-vis* Christianity, are also noted. Then the chapter considers the debate about migrants and the 'decline' of Christianity in New Zealand and whether this has merit. Census data provides a statistical overview of migrants to New Zealand and their religious affiliations, though this only provides a partial reading of religious affiliation and expression.

Contemporary debates about migration and religion

The extent to which minority populations can have and exercise rights, practices and values dominates recent scholarship on migration and political theory.[5] Much of the impetus behind this scholarship has been driven by the twin realities of the ubiquity of international migration (and the attendant increased ethnic diversity of populations) and the risks perceived in this movement of people – for example on the threat it may pose to the nation-state and its values.

Demographic changes in New Zealand, alongside other countries including the UK, France, Canada and the US, all provoke a myriad of questions relating to the impact of migrants on host country institutions and ideals. In many of these countries, with respect to religion, the focus has been on Muslim migrants,[6] particularly in light of the terrorist attacks on the US on 11 September 2001 and the aftermath. Many studies of immigration have focused on the problematic integration of Muslim communities and government strategies for improving integration policies of these communities. In these contexts, 'good citizenship' is often seen as a measure of 'Europeanisation,' which in popular debate 'is often understood as assimilation into a Judeo-Christian culture or, at the least, the abandonment of public signifiers associated with Islam'.[7] Many Muslim practices are 'often seen as antithetical to European values of gender equality and emblematic of the perceived anti-liberal, anti-democratic influence of Islam'.[8] The rise in 'right-wing' parties in the UK and in the European Parliament may be seen as one response to these challenges.[9]

In the UK, for example, the role of migration, migrants and asylum seekers has concerned Christian writers and others also because of the challenges for pastoral care these new populations bring to Christian communities and practice. The significant increase of Polish migrants in Catholic churches there, following the entry of Poland into the European Union is one example.[10] These migrant populations challenge notions of nationality and the practice of Christianity.[11]

The relationship between migration and religion has taken on an unprecedented prominence in many Western countries, not only in scholarship but also in public and political discourse. In both the US and the UK, that convergence may be seen in relation to Muslim migrants (and citizens of those countries who are Muslim) and their perceived association with terrorism. In England, two former Archbishops of Canterbury (the head of the Church of England) have participated in this debate. Former Archbishop Lord George Carey noted in early 2010 that 'migration threatens the DNA of our nation':

> ... the last thing any of us want is ghettos. And while we don't expect groups to assimilate, there must be a willingness on [migrants'] part to integrate with the rest of British society ... [T]hose who seek to live in this country recognise that they are coming to a country with a Christian heritage and an established Church. Just as we should expect immigrants to subscribe to democratic principles, abide by our laws, speak English, support freedom of speech and a free press, so they should also respect the Christian nature and history of our nation with its broad, hospitable Establishment.[12]

This is somewhat in tension with a speech in 2008 by Carey's successor, Archbishop Lord Rowan Williams, about the role of sharia law in the jurisprudence of England.[13] The arguments or criticisms of that speech will not be discussed in this chapter,[14] but these two contributions are significant for how both religion and migration are now considered in public discourse. While the convergence between ethnicity and religion is not unique in many parts of the world, for many Western developed nations religion has dominated the private rather than public space. This is particularly so for New Zealand, where religion has historically played a very small role in public life or discourse.

In New Zealand, practical issues around the establishing and use of Muslim prayer rooms in universities, for example, is a salient and controversial issue. The University of Otago spent at least two years deciding where, how and when to create a prayer space for Muslim students, which they have done by converting two small rooms (one for men and the other for women) in the basement of one of the university's older buildings. Other universities and educational institutions face similar issues.[15] These challenges also extend to the development of public policy.[16]

Migrants and migration in New Zealand

New Zealand has not been immune to these international debates about migration and its impact on values. If anything, New Zealand faces these issues more starkly than other countries because of its comparatively small population. Traditionally, New Zealand sourced immigrants from English-speaking Anglo-Celtic countries, notably Great Britain. Alongside this, there were smaller numbers of Germans, Greeks, Yugoslavians, Dutch and Dalmatians and, from the 1960s, a growing number of migrants from the Pacific.

In 1987, following a major immigration policy change, New Zealand diversified its source countries and an increasing number of migrants came to New Zealand from Korea, Hong Kong, Taiwan, Southeast Asia and later, the People's Republic of China. Between 1986 and 2006, New Zealand's resident population that had been born in countries in Asia increased almost sevenfold from 32,685 to 248,364. In 2006 the population that identified with Asian ethnicities (including the New Zealand-born) increased by 550 per cent in the same period.[17] The Chinese and Indian components of the Asia-born population increased even more – over 800 per cent during that 20-year period. In 2006 nearly 20 per cent of the Chinese and Indian populations in New Zealand were local-born, reflecting their longstanding presence in New Zealand, in some cases going back to the nineteenth century.

Over one-fifth of all Asians in the 2013 census (105,729) had been born in New Zealand. New Zealand's major metropolitan and migrant-receiving city, Auckland, saw the most substantial change, to the extent that the Asian 'face' of Auckland foreshadowed the changing demographic realities of New Zealand in the twenty-first century. About two-thirds of all Asian migrants settle in Auckland; the 2013 census showed that 39 per cent of Aucklanders had been born overseas,[18] an increase from a quarter born overseas at the 2006 Census.[19] In 2013 New Zealand had a net permanent and long-term (PLT) migrant gain (i.e. of 12 months or more) of 22,468. Seventy-five per cent of this was accounted for by roughly equal numbers from China, India and the United Kingdom, and another 20 per cent by approximately equal numbers from Germany and the Philippines.[20]

A combination of a number of factors, including immigration, growth in the number of New Zealanders who identify with more than one ethnicity (for example, children born to parents of two different ethnicities) and the age structures of New Zealand's different ethnic populations, means that New Zealand society will become even more ethnically diverse in the next 20 years. Using projections based on the 2006 census results, Statistics New Zealand estimated that, in the years between 2006 and 2026, New Zealand's Pacific population would increase by around 60 per cent, the Māori population by 31 per cent, the European or Other population by 7 per cent and the Asian population by 95 per cent. These projections will mean that by 2026 there will be almost as many people in the Asian ethnic population as there will be in the Māori population. The Asian share of New Zealand's population will have increased from 1.7 per cent of New Zealand's total population in 1986, to a projected figure of 16 per cent in 2026.[21]

The reception of immigrants to New Zealand has been very mixed. Anglo-Celtic migrants have tended to be more readily accepted than migrants from non-English speaking countries, especially those in Asia. There is a long history of discrimination against Asians, both Chinese[22] and Indian[23] migrants to New Zealand. While New Zealanders are warming towards Asian peoples, there is a significant body of literature that demonstrates that discrimination and social exclusion against migrants and refugees to New Zealand is wide and deep.[24]

In New Zealand, Winston Peters, populist politician and leader of the New Zealand First Party (in Parliament from 1995 to 2008 and since late 2011)[25] was speaking for a number of his constituents and others when he noted in the early 2000s that New Zealand's immigration policy was 'sowing the seeds of sectarianism', and that Asian immigrants in particular threatened to turn New Zealand into a 'hell-hole of ethnic and religious conflict' and 'communal violence ... like Kosovo, Sri Lanka or Northern Ireland'.[26] Similar statements were made by other public commentators, such as former *New Zealand Herald* columnist Garth George:

If I am a racist because I prefer New Zealand to be populated principally by Pakeha, Maori and Pacific Islanders, I'll wear the epithet like a rosette. Because that's the bottom line, isn't it? We are New Zealanders and we want our population mix and our society to stay pretty much the way it is. We don't want to have to assimilate alien cultures, many of which obviously don't want to be assimilated. I am careful whom I invite into my home. Because it is my home I am entitled to be choosy. And New Zealand is as much my home as the house I live in. The Government, on my behalf and not before time, has decided to go back to being choosy about who gets invited to come to stay. Manying Ip [Professor of Asian Studies at the University of Auckland] says migrants from Asia have options other than New Zealand. Good. Other countries are welcome to them.[27]

The leader of the Destiny Church, Bishop Brian Tamaki asserted:

Ironically, we need only look to our motherland for an example of a nation that has compromised its Christian heritage and opened its borders in pursuit of religious diversity. Today, Londoners live in constant fear of terrorism ... Of course, immigrants who come to New Zealand have every right to pursue their religion of choice. But they should come understanding that New Zealand is a Christian nation and that as such, it is their responsibility to respect our nation's Christian founding values. Many other countries are perfectly secure and have no problems stating their religious allegiance.[28]

Admittedly, these quotes come from two of the more vocal and extreme elements of public commentary, but they express what is also revealed in social surveys: that there is a significant disquiet about New Zealand's immigrant Asian populations.[29] Tamaki's quote indicates that much of that disquiet relates to the threat to New Zealand's perceived Christian heritage and values. Tamaki is not alone in his views. Joris de Bres, the former New Zealand Race Relations Commissioner, mentioned to one of us (Butcher) that the level of criticism that he and co-author Professor Paul Morris received regarding New Zealand's National Statement on Religious Diversity[30] was particularly vitriolic from Christians.[31]

Migrants and the 'decline' of Christianity in New Zealand

The religious landscape in New Zealand is changing as indicated in the various religious 'ethnoscapes' in Auckland. These are outlined by Ward Friesen:

> *The term 'ethnoscape' has been used in the social sciences literature to describe the impacts that new migrant populations make in a host society. This ranges from things visible in the landscape such as people, housing, shops, restaurants and temples, through to the less visible aspects such as language and changing attitudes, with the latter often being represented by media coverage. In between are the visible but transitory phenomena such as festivals and markets. Paralleling the increase in Asian populations in Auckland have been rapidly changing ethnoscapes.*[32]

Debates surrounding social cohesion are often in response to these changes. A 'socially cohesive society', according to Canadian Jane Jenson, is one where all groups have a sense of 'belonging, participation, inclusion, recognition and legitimacy.'[33] The measuring of social cohesion of migrants is characterised and measured in various ways in New Zealand[34] and abroad.[35] However, the question of what sort of 'social cohesion' is required for contemporary society remains unresolved: to what extent does social cohesion depend on the social exclusion of particular groups of people or practices? Where does the dividing line lie between 'them' and 'us', 'we' and 'you'?[36]

Aspiring to, or developing indicators to measure a socially cohesive society is irrelevant when there is an assumption that everyone who lives in a population generally adheres to the same values and aims. While much of the debate in New Zealand regarding social cohesion has taken place within policy and academia, there are also reasons for churches and church leaders to be interested in these areas. Often this interest takes the form of anxiety around the extent to which increased immigration, diversification of ethnic populations and decline in church attendance are all contributing to the 'death' of Christianity in many Western countries or, at the very least, the decline of Christian congregations.

Asian migrants are easy and obvious scapegoats for what is seen as a decline in Christian New Zealand. The reasons for the decline could echo what Callum Brown in his provocative book *The Death of Christian Britain* suggests:

> *Indeed, one of the hallmarks of Britain in the year 2000 is the recent growth of ethnic diversity, largely through immigration, and the rise of a multi-faith society, in which Christianity has been joined by Islam, Hinduism and the Sikh religion, amongst others. However, what has been noticeable to all observers is that the strength of attachment to other religions has not, in the main, suffered the collapse that has afflicted the bulk of the Christian churches. In the black and Asian communities of Britain, non-Christian religions in general are thriving. Moreover, one of the few sections in our society where Christian churches are thriving is in the predominantly black communities. Yet, it must be emphasised that the haemorrhage of British Christianity has not come about as a result of competition from or conversion to other churches. No new religion, no new credo, not even a state-sponsored secularism, has been there to displace it.*[37]

Historian John Stenhouse asserts that religion has 'played a central role in the making of New Zealand society and culture'.[38] The role of religion in the settlement experiences of migrants, within particular religious communities, is well canvassed in international and New Zealand literature.[39] Religious beliefs, like migrants' experiences, are transnational: they cross borders, are easily transportable and often access international as well as local and national networks.

A further assumption behind some of the criticisms of Asian migrants vis-à-vis New Zealand's Christianity is that Christianity is somehow a Western religion, expressed in English by people who share a broadly common Anglo-Saxon ethnic heritage. As Philip Jenkins has shown,[40] Christianity's roots are in the Middle East, now dominated by Muslim populations. It is a recent phenomenon in historical terms for Christianity to be associated with the 'West'. A country like the Republic of Korea for example, sees itself as a mission-sending country. This is one reason why a disproportionate number of Korean migrants in New Zealand (compared to the population of Korea generally) are Christian.[41]

To what extent can these changes in New Zealand's religious landscape be attributed to the ethnic diversification of New Zealand's population? A look at some figures is instructive here. The 2013 census data illustrates an overall decline in the number of people identifying themselves as Christian, from 55.6 per cent in 2006 to 48.9 per cent in 2013. Between 2001 and 2006 the traditional Christian denominations either decreased (Anglican and Presbyterian) or grew only slightly (Catholics and Methodists), and there were significant increases for those affiliating with 'Orthodox', 'Evangelical', 'Born Again', 'Fundamentalist' and 'Pentecostal' religions.[42] By the 2013 census most denominations (except 'Christians not further defined') experienced decreases, though data is not available for the categories in which there were recorded increases in 2006.

In 2005 Peter Lineham estimated 'Pentecostals' to be about 10 per cent of nominal Christians, 30 per cent of churchgoers, and 3.5 per cent of the total population.[43] Census figures do not show what percentage of Christians regularly attend church, which may be charitably estimated to be at about 8–10 per cent, and does not include those who make an annual church visit at Christmas time.[44] If one measure of a 'Christian country' is that at least 55 per cent of its population practices Christianity,[45] New Zealand has now become the only non-Christian country in the Pacific region.

New Zealand census data further shows that there has also been an increase in other religions, attributed to the increase in migrants from Asia. As shown in Figure 1, there have been increases in those identifying as Buddhist (1.3 per cent in 2006 to 1.4 per cent in 2013), Hindu (1.6 per cent in 2006 to 2.1 per cent in 2013) and Muslim (0.9 per cent in 2006 to 1.2 per cent in 2013). In 2013 a sizeable majority of those Hindus (42.4 per cent), Buddhists (65 per cent) and Muslims (26.5 per cent) were born in Asia. In comparison, 25 per cent of New Zealand's Muslim population was New Zealand-born, which is similar to the New Zealand-born Buddhist population (27 per cent), though higher than the New Zealand-born Hindu population (20.5 per cent) in the same year. These figures are comparable to 2006, when 22.7 per cent of Muslims were New Zealand-born, 21 per cent of Hindus and 27 per cent of Buddhists. The relatively high number of New Zealand-born among Hindus and Muslims most likely reflects the long-standing South Asian communities in New Zealand. In 2006, Asia-

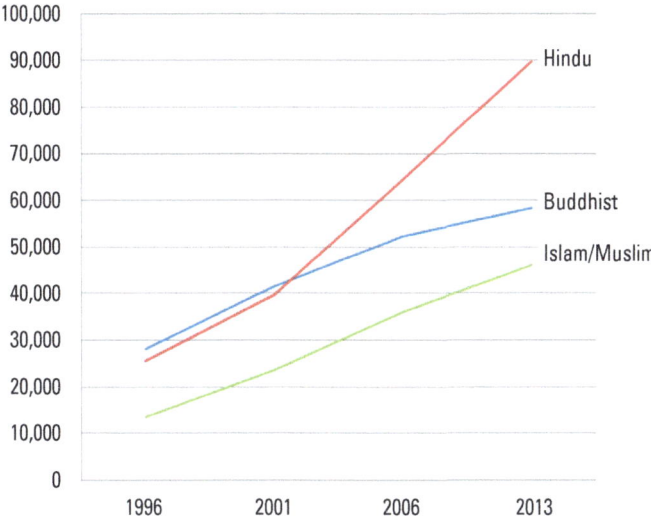

Figure 1. Growth of Buddhism, Hinduism and Islam, 1996–2013.

born Christians in New Zealand made up 3.8 per cent of the total Christian population, increasing to 5.5 per cent in 2013. During the same period, New Zealand-born Christians decreased from 76 per cent of the total Christian population to 72.9 per cent. This matched an overall decline in people who identified with the Christian religion, from 2,082,942 (55.6 per cent) in 2006 to 1,096,398 (48.9 per cent) in 2013. Concomitant with this was an increase in people identifying with 'no religion', from 1,297,104 (32 per cent of the total population) to 1,635,345 (38.6 per cent). Of these, the vast majority (80.9 per cent) were New Zealand-born.

New Zealand's Muslim population is relatively small internationally. At the 2013 census just over 1 per cent of New Zealanders identified as Muslim, compared to 2 per cent for Hindu, 44 per cent for Christian and 39 per cent for 'no religion', of which the majority were 'European New Zealanders' and 'New Zealanders'.[46] By contrast, in the UK the Muslim population was 4.6 per cent of the total population in 2010 and is projected to reach 8.2 per cent in 2030, while in the US the Muslim population is anticipated to increase from 0.8 per cent of the total population to 1.7 per cent.[47]

The differences in religious affiliation between New Zealand and other countries extend to Christianity also.[48] There are different measures of religious affiliation between countries,[49] so any data comparison is only indicative, rather than conclusive. Nevertheless, New Zealand has

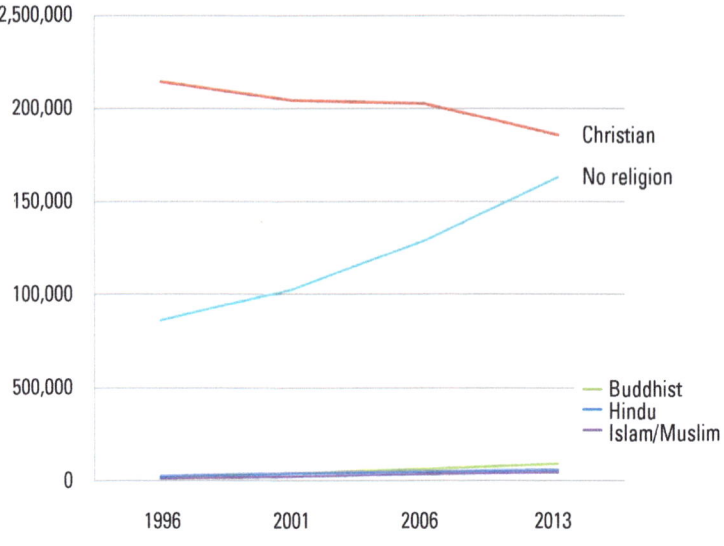

Figure 2. Trends in religious affiliation, 1996–2013

a significantly smaller Christian population (53 per cent in 2006) than Australia (64 per cent in 2006),[50] England and Wales (78 per cent in 2001),[51] Canada (78 per cent in 2001),[52] or the US (76 per cent in 2008).[53]

As Figure 2 illustrates, concomitant with a relatively small decline in people who affiliate as Christian there has been a much greater increase of people who affiliate with 'no religion'. Clearly, one is not the mirror of the other.

Figures 3 and 4 illustrate further the ethnic diversification of Christians in New Zealand. Figure 3 shows that in 1996 an overwhelming 76 per cent of Christians were European, with only 2.07 per cent identifying as Asian. By 2013 (Figure 4) Europeans still comprised the majority of Christians, but at a reduced 68 per cent (a drop of about 1 per cent per year over the previous decade), while Māori were 11.1 per cent, Pacific peoples 10.6 per cent, Asians 6.6 per cent, Middle Eastern, Latin American and African 1.2 per cent, and other ethnicities 1 per cent.[54]

The picture becomes more interesting when analysed by birthplace (Figure 5). While migration from Asia may be cited as one factor in an increase in Christian religions (such as Filipinos joining the Catholic church, or Koreans joining the Presbyterians) that is not the sole reason for the increase. An indeterminate increase is also attributable to some local-born Asians affiliating with Christianity.

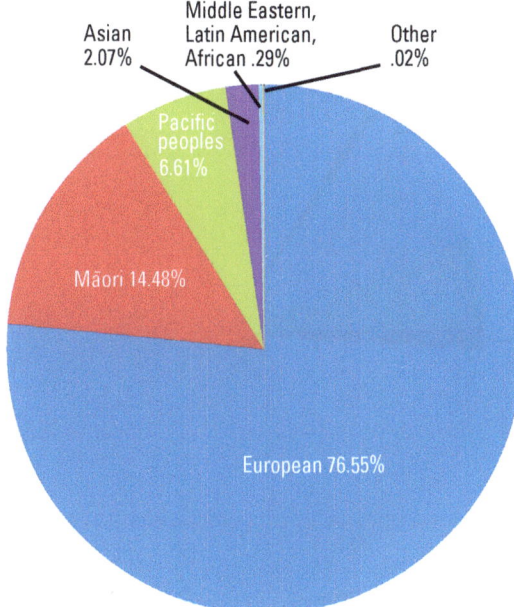

Figure 3. Total people, Christian religion, by ethnicity, in New Zealand, 1996 census

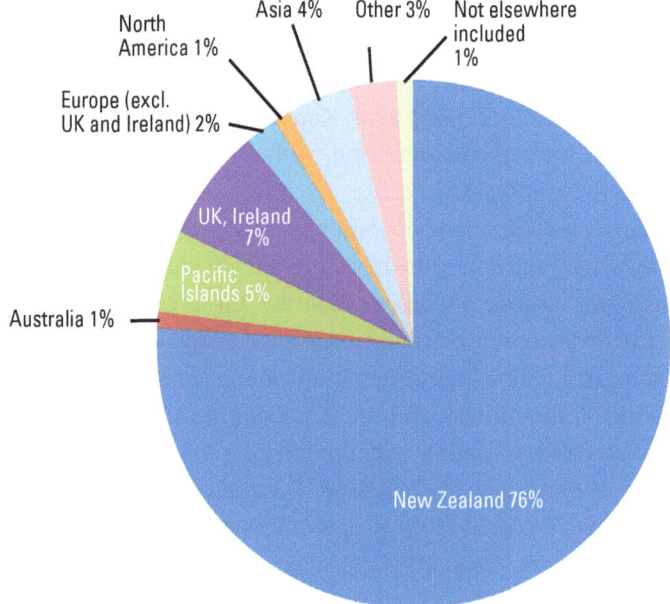

Figure 4. Religious affiliation (Christian), by birthplace, in New Zealand, 2006 census

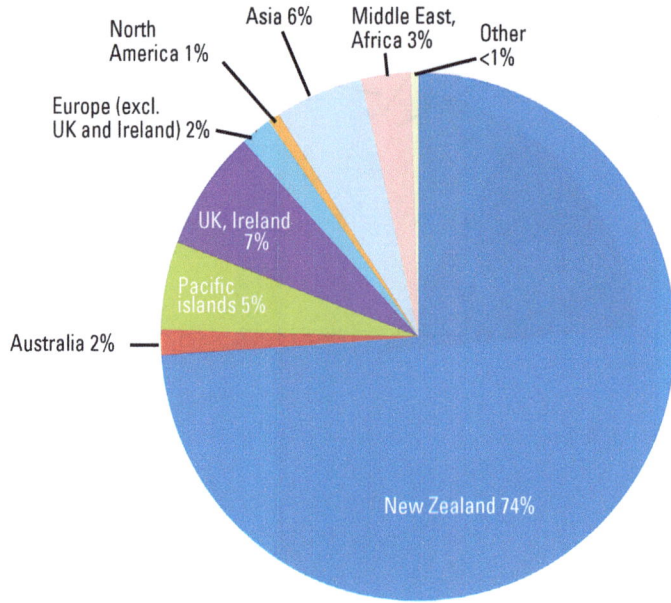

Figure 5. Religious affiliation (Christian), by birthplace, 2013 census

In 2013 the four largest Asian ethnic groups (with over 20,000 people) who identified as Christian were, in descending order: Filipino (37,617), Chinese (34,137), Indian (22,626) and Korean (20,010). This reflects migration trends in the intercensal period, with a significant increase in Filipino migrants to New Zealand.

Although the overall Christian population in New Zealand is decreasing, that cannot be wholly attributed to new migrant populations. The new migrant populations are clearly responsible for the increases in other religions, but the decrease in Christianity in New Zealand may also be the result of problems of attrition and/or retention among New Zealand's non-migrant Christian communities, and an increasing number of sceptical European New Zealanders stating that they belong to no religion. One might also infer that the growth of 'Orthodox', 'Evangelical' and 'Pentecostal' denominations could be as a result of new migrant populations as well as the 'natural' growth or changing denominations among non-migrant Christians.

The statistics suggest that the reading of migration threatening Christianity in New Zealand is not that simple. Such statistics are not unique.

Other Western countries, including Australia, the UK and Germany, are all facing declining church attendance (albeit to different degrees), while in other parts of the world, including the Republic of Korea and China, the Christian church is growing, though it is far from a majority religion. Inconsistency in recorded data on religious belief and practice from one country to another makes drawing comparisons on the basis of data alone very problematic.

Census data is a very rough guide to measuring Christianity in New Zealand. Statistics are of limited value for gauging the everyday experiences of believers, and for that reason care needs to be taken in interpreting this data. Christians, while confessing the same beliefs, practise their faith in very different ways, depending on their context and culture. We should not take the 'public' faces of Christianity in New Zealand and make them representative of all New Zealand Christians.

New Zealand's increasingly diverse society is changing how Christianity in New Zealand is practised. It is this diverse culture, with its bicultural foundations, its strong Pacific elements – particularly demonstrated in most Pacific people's dedication to their church – and New Zealand's growing Asian population, which makes Christianity in New Zealand unique. In 2005, New Zealand historian Peter Lineham described a journey down Chapel Road in Auckland:

Flat Bush has suddenly sprung up in the last five years as an overflow from the huge growth of new housing in the Howick area, primarily accommodating Asian people. The little chapel [that gave Chapel Road its name] still stands, now a joint Anglican–Methodist church halfway down the road that takes its name from it, but at the other end is the exotic Botany Downs shopping centre, a Truman Show-like phenomenon, looking like it has dropped as a unit from the sky, a whole plastic town centre modelled on traditional towns. The central focus of Chapel Road is the enormous, almost completed Buddhist Temple. On the other side of the road is a new co-educational Catholic School, reflecting a huge boom in Catholic education and in baptisms into the Catholic Church by Asians concerned at the violent tone of New Zealand. Other sites down the road have been purchased by Baptist churches, and doubtless the fine facilities of the new secular high school are rented out to a Pentecostal Church group on Sundays. It is boom time in Flat Bush and religion is booming there as well, but not in the little chapel. There is a plan for Anglicans and Methodists to build a big new church, but they are struggling to find the money. Meanwhile the Presbyterians have made a separate move. Their old Pakuranga congregation, famous for its evangelical and conservative tradition, has rebuilt just around the corner from Chapel Street and has attracted a large congregation including many Asian people with a formula that has something of the Pentecostal flavour mixed in.[55]

In the intervening period between then and 2014 the situation on Chapel Road has changed. The local Anglican Church is finding its place in that growing community and is actively engaging with its local Asian populations. Across the road, the diverse Catholic congregation meeting in the Sancta Maria College has ambitious plans for a new church building. Around the corner a new intentionally multicultural Baptist church has begun to meet in Ormiston College. There are signs that Asian immigration is bringing an infusion of new life to more established New Zealand churches and denominations that are willing to adapt and embrace the opportunities.

Conclusion

Migration is recognised as being part of New Zealand's identity- and nation-building project. Increasingly this project is being shaped by migration from Asia to New Zealand and the growth of New Zealand-born Asian communities. With that growth in New Zealand's Asian populations is a concomitant growth in New Zealand of the religions that they practise. Religion plays a more significant role than is often acknowledged in the making of New Zealand, and in ways that are perhaps surprising. Recent years have seen a decrease in the proportion of New Zealand's population that claims to practise Christianity, together with a growth in the numbers of adherents of religions other than Christianity. When these observations are placed alongside the marked increase in Asian immigration, it would be easy to infer that New Zealand's traditionally 'Christian character' is being 'diluted' by Asian immigration. A more nuanced reading of the evidence is required. Many Asian immigrants are Christian, and Asians comprise a growing proportion of the total number of New Zealanders who identify as Christian. Forms and expressions of Christianity developed in various Asian contexts are an increasingly significant component of New Zealand's Christian population, and of New Zealand society as a whole.

Endnotes

1. John Stenhouse, 'Religion and Society', in Giselle Byrnes (ed.), *The New Oxford History of New Zealand*, Melbourne, Oxford University Press, 2009, 313–47; See also Laurie Guy, *Shaping Godzone: Public issues and church voices in New Zealand, 1840–2000*, Wellington: Victoria University Press, 2011.
2. For example the widely praised national memorial service on 18 March 2011 for the victims of the Christchurch earthquakes included Muslim, Buddhist and Hindu prayers along with Christian contributions. See Catherine Masters, 'Christchurch earthquake: City unites on day of healing', *New Zealand Herald*, 15 March 2011: www.nzherald.co.nz/nz/news/article.cfm?c_id=1&objectid=10713470
3. For discussion on Pacific peoples and Christianity in New Zealand, see Feiloaiga Taule'ale'asusumai, 'New religions, new identities: The changing contours of religious commitment', in Cluny Macpherson, Paul Spoonley, and Melanie Anae (eds), *Tangata O Te Moana Nui: The evolving identities of Pacific peoples in Aotearoa New Zealand*, Palmerston North: Dunmore Press, 2001, 181–97; and Cluny Macpherson, 'From Pacific Islanders to Pacific people and beyond', in Spoonley et al (eds), *Tangata, Tangata: The changing ethnic contours in New Zealand*, Southbank, Vic: Dunmore Press, 2004 (135–56).
4. Kevin Ward, 'Is New Zealand's future churchless?', *Stimulus: The New Zealand journal of Christian thought and practice*, 12. 2, 2004, 7: www.knoxcentre.ac.nz/wp-content/uploads/2012/04/Ward-Is-New-Zealands-Future-Churchless-2004.pdf
5. For example see Paul Bramadat and Matthais Koenig (eds), *International Migration and the Governance of Religious Diversity*, Ontario: Queen's School of Policy Studies and Metropolis, 2009; David Bromell, *Ethnicity, Identity and Public Policy: Critical perspectives on multiculturalism*, Wellington: Institute of Policy Studies, 2008; Will Kymlicka, *Politics in the Vernacular: Nationalism, multiculturalism and citizenship*, New York: Oxford University Press, 2001.
6. Paul Bramadat, 'Religious diversity and international migration: national and global dimensions', in Bramadat and Koenig, *International Migration and the Governance of Religious Diversity*, 1–26.
7. Irene Bloemraad, Anna Kortewag and Gokce Turdakul, 'Citizenship and immigration: Multiculturalism, assimilation and challenges to the nation-state', *Annual Review of Sociology* 34, 2008, 153–79, 169.
8. Bloemraad, Kortewag and Turdakul, 'Citizenship and immigration', 163.
9. Paul Bramadat, 'Religious diversity and international migration'.
10. See for example 'Polish influx changing the face of UK Catholic church': www.dw.de/dw/article/0,,6005169,00.html. In the New Zealand Catholic Church a recent Bishops' Statement acknowledges the challenge of '[c]reating inclusive and connected communities as Catholic immigrants arrive in New Zealand parishes': www.catholic.org.nz/nzcbc/fx-view-article.cfm?ctype=BSART&loadref=83&id=158_

11 See for example Nick Spencer, *Asylum and Immigration: A Christian perspective on a polarised debate*, Cambridge: Jubilee Centre, 2004; Andrew Bradstock and Arlington Trotman, *Asylum Voices: Experiences of people seeking asylum in the United Kingdom*, London: Churches Together in Britain and Ireland, 2003.
12 George Carey, 'Migration threatens the DNA of our nation', *The Times*, 7 January 2010: www.timesonline.co.uk/tol/comment/columnists/guest_contributors/article6978389.ece
13 Rowan Williams, 'Archbishop's Lecture – civil and religious law in England: A religious perspective', Foundation lecture, Temple Festival Series, Royal Courts of Justice, London, 7 February 2008): www.archbishopofcanterbury.org/articles.php/1137/archbishops-lecture-civil-and-religious-law-in-england-a-religious-perspective
14 Note the Archbishop's response to criticism of his speech at www.archbishopofcanterbury.org/articles.php/1135/sharia-law-what-did-the-archbishop-actually-say
15 We are grateful to Greg Hughson, Chaplain, University of Otago, for helpful conversations about this.
16 Jonathan Boston, Paul Callister and Amanda Wolf, *The Policy Implications of Diversity*, Wellington: Institute of Policy Studies, 2006.
17 Richard Bedford and Elsie Ho, *Asians in New Zealand: Implications of a changing demography*, Wellington: Asia New Zealand Foundation, 2008, 11.
18 Royal Society of New Zealand, *Our Futures Te Pae Tawhiti: The 2013 census and New Zealand's changing population*, Wellington: Royal Society of New Zealand, 2014, 6.
19 Paul Spoonley and Andrew Butcher, 'Reporting superdiversity: The mass media and immigration in New Zealand', *Journal of Intercultural Studies* 30. 4, 2009, 355–72, 361–62.
20 Royal Society, *Our Futures*, 17.
21 Bedford and Ho, *Asians in New Zealand*, 31. Projections based on the 2013 census are not available at the time of writing.
22 Nigel Murphy, 'Joe Lum v. the Attorney General: the politics of exclusion', in Manying Ip (ed.), *Unfolding History, Evolving Identity: The Chinese in New Zealand*, Auckland: Auckland University Press, 2003, 46–48; Brian Moloughney and John Stenhouse '"Drug-besotten, sin-begotten fiends of filth": New Zealand and the Oriental Other', *New Zealand Journal of History* 33. 1, 1999, 43–64.
23 Manying Ip and Jacqueline Leckie, '"Chinamen" and "Hindoos": Beyond stereotypes to Kiwi Asians', in Paola Voci and Jacqueline Leckie (eds), *Localizing Asia in Aotearoa*, Wellington: Dunmore Publishing, 2011, 77–106; Jacqueline Leckie, 'A long diaspora: Indian settlement in Aotearoa New Zealand', in Shekar Bandyopadhyay (ed.), *India in New Zealand: Local identities, global relations*, Dunedin: Otago University Press, 2010, 45–63.
24 For discussion on these social surveys and public attitudes, see Andrew Butcher, 'Well, they're very good citizens: New Zealand's perceptions of Asians in New Zealand', *Sites: A Journal of Social Anthropology and Cultural Studies – Special*

Issue: Asia and Aotearoa in New Zealand 5. 2, 2008, 5–30; Paul Spoonley, Philip Gendall and Andrew Trlin, *Welcome to our World: The attitudes of New Zealanders to immigrants and immigration*, Palmerston North: New Settlers Programme Occasional Publication No. 14, Massey University, 2007.

25 Peters had previously served as a minister in the National-led governments of the late 1980s and early 1990s. For commentary on the role of Peters in the shaping of public discourse about immigrants in New Zealand, see Paul Spoonley and Andrew Trlin, *Immigration, Immigrants and the Media: Making sense of multicultural New Zealand*, Palmerston North: New Settlers Programme Occasional Publication No. 9, Massey University, 2004.

26 Cited in John Stenhouse, 'Introduction', in John Stenhouse and G.A. Wood (eds), *Christianity, Modernity and Culture: New perspectives on New Zealand history*, Hindmarsh: ATF Press, 2005, 9.

27 Garth George, 'Breathtaking hypocrisy in Labour's immigration U-turn', *New Zealand Herald*, 21 November 2002: www.nzherald.co.nz/nz/news/article.cfm?c_id=1&objectid=3005336

28 Brian Tamaki, *Destiny Church Perspectives Column*, 26 February 2007: www.destinychurch.org.New Zealand/content/view/58/75/

29 For discussion on the relationship between media in New Zealand and attitudes to immigrants and immigration, see Paul Spoonley and Andrew Butcher, 'Reporting superdiversity: The mass media and immigration in New Zealand', *Journal of Intercultural Studies* 30. 4, 2009, 355–72.

30 For the full text, see www.hrc.co.nz/race-relations/te-ngira-the-nz-diversity-action-programme/statement-on-religious-diversity

31 For one example of a Christian response, see Simon Collins, 'Denying state religion like treason, says Brian Tamaki', *New Zealand Herald*, 17 February 2007: www.nzherald.co.nz/religion-and-beliefs/news/article.cfm?c_id=301&objectid=10424395. For a summary by Professor Paul Morris of all responses see www.hrc.co.New Zealand/hrc_new/hrc/cms/files/documents/21-May-2007_14-09-44_19-Mar-2007_10-15-11_21_Feb_2007_Paul_Morris_Hamilton_Speech.doc

32 Ward Friesen, *Diverse Auckland: The face of New Zealand in the twenty-first century?*, Wellington: Asia New Zealand Foundation, 2008, 14.

33 In www.msd.govt.nz/documents/about-msd-and-our-work/publications-resources/journals-and-magazines/social-policy-journal/spj24/24-pages85-110.pdf 88

34 Paul Spoonley, Robin Peace, Andrew Butcher and Damien O'Neill, 'Social cohesion: A policy and indicator framework for assessing immigrant and host outcomes', *Social Policy Journal of New Zealand* 24, 2005, 85–110.

35 James Jupp, John Nieuwenhuysen and Emma Dawson (eds), *Social Cohesion in Australia*, Cambridge: Cambridge University Press, 2007; Jane Jenson, *Mapping Social Cohesion: The state of Canadian research*, CPRN Study F03, Ottowa: CPRN, 1998; Bloemraad, Kortewag and Gocke, 'Citizenship and immigration'.

36 Bloemraad, Kortewag and Gocke, 'Citizenship and immigration', 156.

37 Callum Brown, *The Death of Christian Britain*, New York: Routledge, 2001, 2–3.
38 John Stenhouse, 'Religion and society', in Giselle Byrnes (ed.), *The New Oxford History of New Zealand*, Melbourne: Oxford University Press, 2009, 329.
39 For example see Frank Pieke, *Community and Identity in the New Chinese Migration Order*, Centre of Migration, Policy and Society, University of Oxford, Working Paper No. 24, Oxford: University of Oxford, 2005: www.compas.ox.ac.uk/publications/Working%20papers/Frank%20Pieke%20WP0524.pdf
40 Philip Jenkins, *The Lost History of Christianity: The thousand-year golden age of the Church in the Middle East, Africa and Asia*, London: Lion, 2009.
41 Ward Friesen, *Diverse Auckland: The face of New Zealand in the twenty-first century?* Wellington: Asia New Zealand Foundation, 2008.
42 What the census refers to as 'religion' in this context might be better described as 'denomination'.
43 Peter Lineham, 'Among the believers', *Massey News*, April 2005: www.masseynews.massey.ac.nz/magazine/2005_Apr/stories/thoughts-1.html
44 Denis Welch, 'Jingle tills', *New Zealand Listener*, 206, 2006, 3476: www.listener.co.NewZealand/issue/3476/features/7758/jingle_tills.
45 The criterion adopted by, for example, Michael S. Smith, *Are Muslims Distinctive? A look at the evidence*, Oxford: Oxford University Press, 2011, 18.
46 Ibid.; www.stats.govt.nz/Census/2013-census/profile-and-summary-reports/quickstats-culture-identity.aspx
47 Pew Templeton Global Religious Futures Project, *The Future of the Global Muslim Population: Projections for 2010–2030*, Washington, DC: Pew Research Centre, 2011, 15: www.pewforum.org/2011/01/27/future-of-the-global-muslim-population-regional-europe/
48 Statistics New Zealand, '*Quick Stats about culture and identity*', *2006 Census*: www.stats.govt.NewZealand/NR/rdonlyres/5F1F873C-5D36-4E54-9405-34503A2C0AF6/0/quickstatsaboutcultureandidentity.pdf
49 The US, unlike New Zealand, does not ask a religious affiliation question as part of its ten-year census and relies on self-described religious affiliation.
50 Australian Bureau of Statistics, *2006 Census of Population and Housing*: www.abs.gov.au/AUSSTATS/abs@.nsf/Latestproducts/9BAACC26CC709706CA25729E0008A88F?opendocument
51 Office of National Statistics (UK), *Census 2001* and *Labour Force Survey 2003/2004*: www.ons.gov.uk/ons/index.html
52 Statistics Canada, *2001 Census of Population*: www12.statcan.gc.ca/english/census01/home/Index.cfm
53 Institute for the Study of Secularism in Society and Culture, *American Religious Identification Survey, 2008*: www.commons.trincoll.edu/aris/
54 It is possible that 'other ethnicity' records those who identified themselves as 'New Zealander'.
55 Peter Lineham, 'Wanna be in my gang?' *New Zealand Listener*, 195, 2004, 3357: www.listener.co.nz/issue/3357/features/2554/wanna_be_in_my_gang

Bibliography

Australian Bureau of Statistics, *2006 Census of Population and Housing*. www.abs.gov.au/AUSSTATS/abs@.nsf/Latestproducts/9BAACC26CC709706CA25729E0008A88F?opendocument

Bedford, Richard and Elsie Ho, *Asians in New Zealand: Implications of a changing demography*, Wellington: Asia New Zealand Foundation, 2008.

Bloemraad, Irene, Anna Kortewag and Yurdakul Gokce, 'Citizenship and immigration: Multiculturalism, assimilation and challenges to the nation-state', *Annual Review of Sociology* 34, 2008, 153–79.

Boston, Jonathan, Paul Callister and Amanda Wolf, *The Policy Implications of Diversity*, Wellington: Institute of Policy Studies, 2006.

Bradstock, Andrew and Arlington Trotman, *Asylum Voices: Experiences of people seeking asylum in the United Kingdom*, London: Churches Together in Britain and Ireland, 2003.

Bramadat, Paul and Matthais Koenig (eds), *International Migration and the Governance of Religious Diversity*, Ontario: Queen's School of Policy Studies and Metropolis, 2009.

Bramadat, Paul, 'Religious diversity and international migration: National and global dimensions', in Paul Bramadat and Matthias Koenig (eds), *International Migration and the Governance of Religious Diversity*, Ontario: Queen's School of Policy Studies and Metropolis, 2009, 1–26.

Bromell, David, *Ethnicity, Identity and Public Policy: Critical perspectives on multiculturalism*, Wellington: Institute of Policy Studies, 2008.

Brown, Callum, *The Death of Christian Britain*, New York: Routledge, 2001.

Butcher, Andrew, '"Well, they're very good citizens": New Zealand's perceptions of Asians in New Zealand', in Jacqueline Leckie (ed.), *Sites: A journal of social anthropology and cultural studies. Special Issue: Asia and Aotearoa in New Zealand*, 5, 2, 2008, 5–30.

Carey, George, 'Migration threatens the DNA of our nation', *The Times*, 7 January 2010: www.timesonline.co.uk/tol/comment/columnists/guest_contributors/article6978389.ece

Collins, Simon, 'Denying state religion like treason, says Brian Tamaki', *New Zealand Herald*, 17 February 2007: www.nzherald.co.nz/religion-and-beliefs/news/article.cfm?c_id=301&objectid=10424395

Friesen, Ward, *Diverse Auckland: The face of New Zealand in the twenty-first century?* Wellington: Asia New Zealand Foundation, 2008.

George, Garth, 'Breathtaking hypocrisy in Labour's immigration U-turn', *New Zealand Herald*, 21 November 2002: www.nzherald.co.nz/nz/news/article.cfm?c_id=1&objectid=3005336

Guy, Laurie, *Shaping Godzone: Public issues and church voices in New Zealand, 1840–2000*, Wellington: Victoria University Press, 2011.

Institute for the Study of Secularism in Society in Culture, *American Religious Identification Survey, 2008*: www.commons.trincoll.edu/aris/

Jenkins, Philip, *The Lost History of Christianity: The thousand-year golden age of the Church in the Middle East, Africa and Asia*, London: Lion, 2009.

Jenson, Jane, *Mapping Social Cohesion: The state of Canadian research*, CPRN Study F03, Ottawa: CPRN, 1998.

Johnson, Henry and Brian Moloughney (eds), *Asia in the Making of New Zealand*, Auckland: Auckland University Press, 2007.

Jupp, James, John Nieuwenhuysen and Emma Dawson (eds), *Social Cohesion in Australia*, Cambridge: Cambridge University Press, 2007.

Kymlicka, Will, *Politics in the Vernacular: Nationalism, multiculturalism and citizenship*, New York: Oxford University Press, 2001.

Lineham, Peter, 'Wanna be in my gang?', *New Zealand Listener*, 195, 3357, 2004: www.listener.co.nz/issue/3357/features/2554/wanna_be_in_my_gang

Lineham, Peter, 'Among the believers', Massey News, April 2005: www.masseynews.massey.ac.nz/magazine/2005_Apr/stories/thoughts-1.html

Macpherson, Cluny, 'One trunk sends out many branches: Pacific cultures and cultural identities', in Cluny Macpherson, Paul Spoonley and Melanie Anae (eds), *Tangata o te Moana Nui: The evolving identities of Pacific Peoples in Aotearoa New Zealand*, Palmerston North: Dunmore Press, 2001, 66–81.

Macpherson, Cluny and L. Macpherson, 'Evangelical religion among Pacific Island migrants: New faiths or brief diversions?' *Journal of Ritual Studies*, 15. 2, 2001, 27–37.

Macpherson, Cluny, 'From Pacific Islanders to Pacific People and beyond', in Paul Spoonley, Cluny Macpherson and David Pearson (eds), *Tangata, Tangata: The changing contours of ethnicity in Aotearoa New Zealand*, Victoria: Thomson Dunmore Press, 2004, 135–56.

Masters, Catherine, 'Christchurch earthquake: City unites on day of healing', *New Zealand Herald*, 15 March 2011: www.nzherald.co.nz/nz/news/article.cfm?c_id=1&objectid=10713470

Moloughney, Brian and John Stenhouse, '"Drug-besotten, sin-begotten fiends of filth": New Zealand and the Oriental Other', *New Zealand Journal of History*, 33. 1, 1999, 43–64.

Murphy, Nigel, 'Joe Lum v. the Attorney General: The politics of exclusion', in Manying Ip (ed.), *Unfolding History, Evolving Identity: The Chinese in New Zealand*, Auckland: Auckland University Press, 2003, 48–68.

Office of National Statistics (UK), *Census 2001 and Labour Force Survey 2003/2004*: www.ons.gov.uk/ons/index.html

Pieke, Frank, *Community and Identity in the New Chinese Migration Order, Centre of Migration, Policy and Society*, University of Oxford, Working Paper No. 24, Oxford: University of Oxford, 2005: www.compas.ox.ac.uk/publications/Working %20papers/Frank %20Pieke %20WP0524.pdf

Smith, Michael S., *Are Muslims Distinctive? A look at the evidence*, Oxford: Oxford University Press, 2011.

Spencer, Nick, *Asylum and Immigration: A Christian perspective on a polarised debate*, Cambridge: Jubilee Centre, 2004.

Spoonley, Paul and Andrew Butcher, 'Reporting superdiversity: The mass media and immigration in New Zealand', *Journal of Intercultural Studies*, 30. 4, 2009, 355–72.

Spoonley, Paul and Andrew Trlin, *Immigration, Immigrants and the Media: Making sense of multicultural New Zealand*, New Settlers Programme Occasional Publication No. 9, Palmerston North: New Settlers Programme, Massey University, 2004.

Spoonley, Paul, Philip Gendall and Andrew Trlin, *Welcome to our World: The attitudes of New Zealanders to immigrants and immigration*, New Settlers Programme Occasional Publication No.14, Palmerston North: New Settlers Programme, Massey University, 2007.

Spoonley, Paul, Robin Peace, Andrew Butcher and Damien O'Neill, *Immigration and Social Cohesion: Developing an indicator framework for measuring the impact of settlement policies in New Zealand*, Ministry of Social Development Working Paper 01/05, Wellington: Ministry of Social Development, 2005.

Spoonley, Paul, Robin Peace, Andrew Butcher and Damien O'Neill, 'Social cohesion: A policy and indicator framework for assessing immigrant and host outcomes', *Social Policy Journal of New Zealand*, 24, 2005, 85–110.

Statistics Canada, 2001 Census of Population: www12.statcan.gc.ca/english/census01/home/Index.cfm

Statistics New Zealand, 'Quick Stats about Culture and Identity', *2006 Census*: www.stats.govt.New Zealand/NR/rdonlyres/5F1F873C-5D36-4E54-9405-34503A2C0AF6/0/quickstatsaboutcultureandidentity.pdf

Statistics New Zealand, Tables on culture and identity from the 2001 Census: www.stats.govt.New Zealand/NR/rdonlyres/226BAFE2-4B1C-4A84-A2E9-B6D2E3FDB4AA/0/CulturalTable16.xls

Statistics New Zealand, F*inal Report of a Review of the Official Ethnicity Statistical Standard*, Wellington: Statistics New Zealand, 2009: www.stats.govt.nz/~/media/Statistics/Publications/Census/2011-Census/final-report-review-official-ethnicity-statistical-standard-2009.ashx

Stenhouse, John, 'Introduction', in John Stenhouse and G.A. Wood (eds), *Christianity, modernity and culture: New perspectives on New Zealand history*, Hindmarsh: ATF Press, 2005, 1–22.

Stenhouse, John, 'Religion and society', in Giselle Byrnes (ed.), *The New Oxford History of New Zealand*, Melbourne: Oxford University Press, 2009, 313–47.

Tamaki, Brian, *Destiny Church Perspectives Column*, 26 February 2007: www.destinychurch.org.New Zealand/content/view/58/75/

Taule'ale'asusumai, Feiloaiga, 'New religions, new identities: The changing contours of religious commitment', in Cluny Macpherson, Paul Spoonley and Melanie Anae (eds), *Tangata O Te Moana Nui: The evolving identities of Pacific Peoples in Aotearoa New Zealand*, Palmerston North: Dunmore Press, 2001, 181–97.

Ward, Kevin, 'Is New Zealand's future churchless?' *Stimulus: The New Zealand Journal of Christian thought and practice* 12. 2, 2004, 2–12: www.knoxcentre.ac.nz/wp-content/uploads/2012/04/Ward-Is-New-Zealands-Future-Churchless-2004.pdf

Welch, Denis, 'Jingle tills', *New Zealand Listener*, 206, 2006, 3476: www.listener.co.New Zealand/issue/3476/features/7758/jingle_tills

Williams, Rowan, 'Archbishop's Lecture – Civil and religious law in England: A religious perspective', Foundation lecture delivered at the Temple Festival Series, Royal Courts of Justice, London, UK, 7 February 2008: www.archbishopofcanterbury.org/articles.php/1137/archbishops-lecture-civil-and-religious-law-in-england-a-religious-perspective

8. (Mis)Reporting Islam
New Zealand Muslim women viewing 'us' viewing 'them'

STEPHANIE DOBSON

This chapter will explore some ongoing media representations of Muslims, and Muslim women in particular, from a New Zealand perspective. New Zealand is described as a 'tolerant' society, yet Muslims are often subject to significant 'othering' and essentialism reflected in popular and institutional discourses, like that exhibited within the mass media. This essentialism commonly takes the form of a type of discursive orientalism that utilises broad stereotypes regarding Muslims, and Muslim and Asian women. As New Zealand becomes more culturally diverse

The *Waikato Times* published this image of members of WOWMA (Women's Organisation of the Waikato Muslim Association), 'Connecting to NZ: Despite experiencing verbal and physical harassment in their adopted city ...'. From left, Anjum Rahman, Radiya Ali, Eman Hepburn, Khatra Omar, Aaminah Ghani, Afreen Azfar. (Fairfax Media/*Waikato Times*, 25 July 2011) Photographer: Chris Hillock, Copyright *Waikato Times*.

through processes of immigration and increasing numbers of minority New Zealand-born generations, are these New Zealanders, in particular Muslim groups, being adequately represented within the mass media?

It is not uncommon to come across dominant discourses that are inculcated into the general New Zealand populace, such as those stereotyping women who practice Islam. I have observed, for example, the fascination with – and critique of – the headscarf from among New Zealand's non-Muslim public. When I discuss my research there are always comments about hijab (head covering) such as: 'I don't mind the scarf, with the face showing, but I don't like it when they wear the things over their face. I like to see the face,' or, 'Why do they wear that here? They must be so hot.' I recently taught some students who asked me: 'Do they [the women research participants] get permission to talk to you?' After some initial confusion on my part, I realised that they were asking if the participants had to gain permission from a male spouse or family member to participate in the research.

This chapter takes the approach of exploring 'insiders', or emic, responses to popular media portrayals, in order to 'stand in the shoes of another' to understand the fundamental sense of insecurity and lack of belonging that these representations can create in individual women's lives. Through the personal narratives of some ethnically/culturally diverse Muslim and Asian women in New Zealand, I will explore the individually felt impacts of media representations that are reductive and marginalising for Muslim women. Although the women considered that racism and prejudice were just products of ignorance, the media was seen to be a significant factor in influencing these attitudes.

Theorising media subjectivity

Literature regarding subjective mass media reporting of Islam and Muslim groups often focuses on quantitative methods that analyse the content and discursive tone of various reports, including television and news sources.[1] These analyses provide insightful and convincing data to support the contention that significant othering and subtle discriminatory language and style are consistently employed. Gabriele Marranci considers that mass media are not necessarily consciously creating a stereotypical profile of Muslims, yet the transnational nature of the media system encourages tautologically repetitive stereotypes of an essential Muslim 'archetype.'[2] This suggests that media reporting is far from objective; indeed the mass media's apparent subjectivity may be representative of dominant social mores and discourses, which become normalised within 'objective' reporting.

This chapter examines this subjectivity and draws on the theoretical analyses of Teun A. van Dijk,[3] who critiques the taken-for-granted power frameworks of dominant groups and their discourses and how these are reproduced, given access and communicated in media reporting and other elite institutions. This discussion is also based on qualitative ethnographic data gathered from research with 27 Muslim women from the main urban centres of New Zealand between 2006 and 2009.[4] The participants are from several different national and ethnic origins. Over one-third of these women represent various Asian ethnic groups in New Zealand. The chapter draws significantly on their perspectives.

It is important, in multicultural societies like New Zealand, that minorities are equitably represented in various institutions including the media. Minelle Mahtani contends that ethnographic data is often missing from commentaries regarding media analyses, and that this absence needs to complement and give empirical substance to the quantitative content examinations: 'We also need to carry out more interviews with minorities and minority groups in general to discern thoughts and opinions about their representation in the media ... how negative images of themselves impact their self-identity and esteem.'[5] Equitable representation necessitates presenting the perspectives of minority New Zealanders, as well as comprehensively incorporating minority viewpoints in journalistic commentary to ensure informed content.

Qualitative research enables in-depth insights into real people's lives, and how media representations can affect individuals in multicultural societies. Van Dijk suggests that ethnographic narratives and ethnomethodology offer knowledge of social interactions and of how communicative factors and language are used in specific social and cultural contexts.[6] How do particular news stories and reporting styles impact on the daily lives of others? How does mainstream reporting reflect subtle representations of dominant attitudes and the ways these are normalised and disseminated as knowledge? Is mainstream media representative of all citizens, including those defined as minorities? The recent terrorist events beginning with 11 September 2001 have tended to further polarise representations of Islam and Muslims in relation to the 'West'. As Pnina Werbner states, 'September 11 ... seemed to threaten the social order of the world and ... generated a manichean discourse of good and evil.'[7] As a follow-on effect, minority Muslim citizens often find themselves subject to public perceptions informed by this discourse.

Discourse and media

Discourses can be broadly defined as language and ideas that are reproduced or normalised over time through reiteration. Van Dijk suggests they may be particular communicative occurrences or specific language use, in verbal or written form; or a particular group of related genres or collections, such as legal discourse.[8] The term 'discourse' may also be employed to describe a particular ideology or movement, but van Dijk considers confusing values or ideology with discourse as reductive, unless it is in reference to collections of verbal or written resources. Van Dijk identifies pictures, art, body expressions and postures as the semiotic forms of discourse communicated through nonverbal communication.[9] Some of the structural means through which various discourses are disseminated are media reports and/or verbal interactions, which may use particular language or syntax to communicate an idea or tone.

Allan Bell takes the notion of discourses further, suggesting they are social values and stories that are reproduced as fact.[10] In terms of news stories, Bell contends that these are not representative of impartial factual events, but are a constructed narrative dependent on wider contexts of social and political discourses, which are then reproduced as fact. News stories are value-laden and 'reflect ideologies and priorities held in society'.[11]

Van Dijk critiques the conflation of ideologies as discourse. He defines ideologies as 'basic systems of fundamental social cognitions ... and other social representations shared by members of groups ... [which] ... indirectly control the mental representations (models) that form the interpretation basis and contextual embeddedness of discourse and its structures'.[12] The particular notions that one group holds about another inevitably inform and comprise popular, and elite, discourses that influence institutions such as the media. Van Dijk argues for the presence of racist ideology and its consistent reproduction within discourse.[13] He defines racism as an extremely complex system of both social and cognitive factors. 'Social racism', according to van Dijk, is comprised of discriminatory and prejudiced behaviours at both local and global levels with unequal power dynamics mostly determined 'by dominant groups, organizations, and institutions';[14] 'cognitive racism' can be defined as learned knowledge of other people and groups, or as socially validated representations of what 'we' are in relation to 'them'.[15] Van Dijk contends that cognitive racism particularly informs discourse. The ideas that people hold about one another are learned, and are most often acquired through verbal and written forms of communication, which then further inform and validate the discourses of dominant groups.[16] In this sense, racist discourse, however subtle, is consistently expressed through the use of language and other means.

Van Dijk's concept of 'elite racism' is crucial to interrogating media discourse and the stereotypes reproduced in media reporting.[17] Elite racism suggests that learned ideologies regarding ethnic or religious minorities are given legitimated access through powerful elite institutions such as the media, who supply knowledge and meaning about events that happen in the world in ways that maintain dominant interests. Van Dijk implicates powerful political and corporate entities as having interests in media discourses and representations.[18] Analyses of post-Cold War strategic and economic goals in the Middle East and elsewhere help to contextualise elite representations of Muslims and Islam.[19]

Elaborating on this, David Edwards and David Cromwell present a disturbing investigation of the corporate media.[20] They contend that the notion of the 'free press' is misleading considering that the contemporary political economy is comprised of massive multinational corporations and that the media system is also part of this landscape:

> *Like military personnel, journalists also sign themselves over to authority. Executives are obliged by corporate law to maximise profits for shareholders – corporate journalists are not exempt from the need to prioritise the company's welfare (in an unforgiving political and economic environment) in everything they say and do. Thus, individuals may come and go but, year after year, in an all but unvarying pattern, news reports end up demonising official enemies, prettifying our government's crimes, and overlooking the corporate greed that informs so much politics. Like military personnel, reporters view what happens next as someone else's moral responsibility.*[21]

Commentators have observed how news items may be selectively reported. For example, Edwards and Cromwell examine the 1990–2003 sanctions in Iraq.[22] As well as contending with the violence of a brutal dictatorship and the trauma of war, the Iraqi people were subjected to extreme suffering under the sanctions. Edwards and Cromwell argue that media reporting perpetuated a one-sided version of events. They cite former British Prime Minister Tony Blair's reiteration, through the media, that the dire humanitarian situation in Iraq was due entirely to Saddam Hussein's conscious mishandling of the sanctions regime.[23]

Edwards and Cromwell examine the impact of the large-scale devastation of infrastructure in Iraq due to the bombing campaigns, arguing that the United Nation's (UN) Oil-for-Food Programme was severely hampered by this lack of infrastructure and by sanction-restricted resources, which hindered reconstruction. They cite Denis Halliday, former UN Assistant Secretary-General, who stated that a significant proportion of funds meant for the Oil-for-Food Programme was used to pay for various UN expenses as well as reparations and compensation claims.[24] Halliday and his successor Hans von Sponeck 'resigned in protest', although this received very little mention in the press.[25] Edwards and Cromwell argue that Western political and strategic interests manipulated media reporting of events in Iraq, in order to gloss over their part in creating the human insecurity that was the result of this tragic, complex and protracted situation.[26] Another commentator, John L. Esposito, considers that the occupation of Iraq compromised the human security of many Iraqi people, as well as – paradoxically – intensifying sectarianism and radicalisation.[27]

The one-sided manner of such reporting of international events suggests that political and economic perspectives influence the media. Moreover, these perspectives can foreground dichotomous representations. The research participants described the mass media as often characterised by biased perspectives that can create stereotypes and misrepresentations. One Somali woman in her twenties stated:

> *They just watch the TV and they will come to you and say this and this ... [but] ... we're really not in the environment [being reported about] to sort of make complete opinions ... we're not living there ... All the news ... [about Muslims] is actually [international] news ... like when you turn on Three News ... you see news from all over the world ... They're only going to show you what they want us to see ... To really make full judgement and opinion ... we really have to be living there and [have context] ... So that's the hard thing ... that media is controlling all of us. It doesn't matter which, whether it's about Islamic stories, or it's about anything else, that media is ... controlling us and saying this is right, this is wrong, and this is how people are sort of making judgements.*

How do these representations affect the participants in their everyday lives? The next sections will explore how (mis)representations have profound effects in the women's lives.

Living with media (mis)representations

This section explores how some Muslim and Asian women in New Zealand assess the mass media and how it can affect their experiences of daily life. The women in this research considered the media to be very problematic for them. They felt that certain ways of speaking about Muslims, which are prevalent in written and verbal news reports, as well as strategic uses of visual material, affected areas of social relations. A significant proportion of these women are from Asian and Middle Eastern ethnic groups, while some are 'white' converts to Islam. It is significant that all 27 women made very similar assessments of media discourse and representations of Muslim peoples and Muslim women. Furthermore, some of the women, including several of Asian descent, provided insightful comments about the links between ethnic and religious prejudice.

Regardless of their ethnicity, the women found that their Muslim identity could elicit specific kinds of prejudice and social exclusion. This suggests that religion has become a popular focus for prejudice and discrimination in New Zealand. The research participants had experienced this exclusion in, for example, employment discrimination and everyday social interactions. They considered that media reports often reproduce this prejudice either subtly or overtly in stories about Muslim people. Some of the women commented that the globalised nature of the media – because New Zealand media is also comprised of press stories from various international sources – enables a type of universalising global discourse about Islam and Muslims, despite Muslims being differentiated by diverse ethnic, cultural and other factors. The following narratives form a cross-section representing the main concerns the women had about the media. These commentaries highlight the problematic aspects, from the women's perspectives, of mass-media coverage of Muslims and Islam.

Essentialism and Violence

One woman of Indian origin observed that when she was growing up in New Zealand in the 1970s, religion was less of an issue than the colour of a person's skin. She considered that being Muslim tended to be viewed by the majority of New Zealanders as just part of the 'weird' or 'exotic' practices of particular ethnicities. Her memories are in contrast to today, where being Muslim has become the main issue: 'I think because now racism is being, you know, one of those taboo areas and people feel generally uncomfortable to say anything against another person's race, even though there is still quite a bit of it ... but ... religion becomes the new racism.' Another young woman, from Pakistan, said that the derogatory term 'Paki' for a Pakistani person has been translated into a derogatory term about being Muslim. She cited the use of language, such as 'mad Mullah', 'fanatic' or 'terrorist', which she had been confronted with in public contexts.

There was unanimous agreement that the coverage of terrorist activity, particularly since 2001, has tangible effects on the women's lives. The respondents critiqued the ways that media reports linked Islamic belief with terrorist activity. A convert to Islam in her forties observed:

The hardest thing we deal with now is terrorism. I mean that, without a doubt, that is the hardest thing that we deal with. You know, before 9/11 ... my husband used to wear a turban and things like that ... but now it's very, very hard ... to go around looking like [a Muslim] really because ... people ... they always think [negative things] ... which is fair enough too, because ... Muslim people are very unhappy about, you know, what's happened. [Pauses and sighs]. Yeah, but we all have struggles don't we?

A 19-year-old Malaysian woman related how she lived in fear of retaliation for terrorist actions happening elsewhere in the world:

There are a lot of ... ignorant people. I have friends, and people come up to them and say like: 'Oh yeah, yeah terrorists' and 'Did you bomb the two towers?' and all these kind of things, and these poor girls are like 'What?' You still get prejudice and you still get abuse. I [had] some guy screaming at me in the streets ... Although I'm used to it now, at the beginning you sort of get really scared ... and it just gets really scary, you know, to walk alone in the streets ... You always get targeted. You can easily spot the [Muslim woman].

The increasing associations of violence with Muslims caused considerable anxiety for the women. They considered that there was an over-abundance of negative coverage of anything remotely associated with Muslims, and observed that mass media most commonly presents Muslims as violent people with a violent religion. At the time of researching this chapter, the social protests against ruling regimes occurring in Middle Eastern countries, such as Tunisia and Egypt – the so-called 'Arab Spring' – were primetime news. I noted the use of language in some verbal news reports: protesters were often described using terms such as 'frenzied crowds', 'open war' and 'the mob', despite some protests being peaceful demonstrations of social resistance.

Krista E. Wiegand observes that Muslims are generally represented within a narrow bandwidth of conflict, based on a militant and radical perception of Islam. She cites contemporary conflicts, such as those involving the Taliban in Afghanistan and the Israeli-Palestinian tensions, as often being represented within 'religious identity' paradigms.[28] Wiegand argues for the necessity of supplying context in reporting on these conflicts. Factors such as economic interests, political bids for territory, transnational power dynamics, national sovereignty and other mitigating factors provide far more pertinent background to understanding conflict than just religious ideologies.[29] However, considering the international rhetoric of the 'War on Terror', this polarising approach is hardly surprising. Karim H. Karim writes: 'The adjective "Islamic" is frequently used by journalists to describe the criminal activities of terrorists in ways that would be inconceivable in referring to similar actions carried out by members of other religions, especially Christians and Jews.'[30]

John E. Richardson quantitatively analyses media sources of reference about Islam. He found that when Muslim sources were used in journalistic texts they were generally quoted only if providing a critical appraisal of Islam or Muslims' actions. Furthermore members of 'fundamentalist' or 'terrorist' groups were frequently quoted.[31] I noted a recent example of this in the *Otago Daily Times*, in a report sourced from Reuters. Under the heading of 'Ordered airport bombing', the article stated: 'Islamist rebel leader Doku Umarov said yesterday he had ordered a suicide bombing that killed 36 people at Russia's busiest airport last month.' The article went on to say that Umarov demanded 'an independent Muslim state governed by Sharia law' and threatened further attacks.[32] Other than this distressing news and some brief information about the location of the region in question, little context or further explanation was given.

Richardson established that the results of his quantitative survey reflect the power dynamics that determine who has representational access in deciding news content: most often 'non-Muslim bureaucratic sources'.[33] Similarly, journalists are given legitimacy to interpret events in value-laden narrative forms (such as using language like 'frenzied crowds' or 'the mob') that preclude the possibility of more objective reporting.

On the question of news content about Muslims, one young woman from Afghanistan commented: 'In terms of Muslims [there's] lots of propaganda … that's been shown on big screen TV. I don't like that.' A New Zealand woman of Fiji-Indian descent observed:

> *I think the difference is that in other groups extremists are not portrayed as the majority and that's the problem with Islam; there's no distinction made. Which, of course, puts us in a very difficult position because, one: we have no intention or desire to defend extremism within our own community, but at the same time we find ourselves being labelled sort of within that same [paradigm]. In other words, issues are … generalised rather than localised.*

The lack of accurate knowledge about the diverse people that practise Islam is neglected, with a subsequent absence of positive reports to offset the negative ones. In reality, Muslims involved in conflict or violent activities represent a very small percentage of the Muslims in the world. The respondents considered the emphasis given to this small minority contributes to the lack of accurate public knowledge of the peaceful, heterogeneous Muslim majority that practise Islam.

Regarding these issues, Wiegand suggests that some Western commentators construct Islamic revivalism as a movement that is ethnically unified so that religious identity is emphasised over social factors such as ethnicity or nationality. She argues that revivalist groups have their own agendas, often in response to repressive postcolonial conditions, despite the utopian assumption that Islam unifies various Muslim ethnicities.[34] Wiegand draws on the case of diverse ethnic communities in Central Asia following the dissolution of the Union of Soviet Socialist Republics (USSR), pointing out that ethnic identity and competition for resources tend to be divisive factors in many cases of regional conflict, which negates the influence of Islam per se as the cause of conflict, let alone as a unifying factor.[35]

The research participants asserted that it was important for journalists to undertake considered, well-researched reporting. When watching media reports the public can be left with an overall impression of conflict being solely the fault of religious motivations or ideology, yet there are often other complex factors that influence the occurrence of social, political and economic instability. The emphasis on Islam can sometimes be misleading.

Gender and oppression

Popular stereotypes of so-called oppressed and vulnerable Muslim women are themes also found regularly in media stories. The women considered that preoccupation with the head covering (hijab) was unnecessary and essentialising, as expressed by a woman of Fiji-Indian and Dutch descent:

> We have a deplorable media, which I mean is very limited in its scope and its content, but also it's the only way in which most people receive information about Islam. So, you know, you can ... live in your country for ten years; there's one bad, for example, 60 Minutes *programme and the next day ... it's just so much harder. And, of course, for Muslim women ... for those of us who choose to visibly dress, you know, as such, it just means that you become the focus of that ... The problem is that the ideas that people have [about] people who dress like this tend to be negative. I mean we've talked ... to groups about the Airport Bookshop ... and there's like this whole row of books about Muslim women, you know, so* Not Without My Daughter *... The stuff that's available ... on an informal level ... all tends to be reasonably negative. Not necessarily untrue, but the fact is that the world of Islam is portrayed from only one point ... not other perspectives ... It tends to be based on the idea of the inequality of women and the repression of women.*

One example of these misconceptions received considerable attention in the press in May 2011. Two drivers for the company NZ Bus, in separate incidents, refused to let a burqa-wearing woman on their bus (the burqa is a type of covering that provides full covering for the face and body). Belinda McCammon of the *Sunday Star Times* reported that one of the women, a 'Saudi Arabian student was left crying on an Auckland street when the bus driver refused to let her board because of her veil'.[36] McCammon provided a more informed report that drew on the perspectives of Muslim women at an event – 'Hijab in the West', hosted by Auckland University and organised by the Young Muslim Women's Association – in which she quoted a woman who said: '... when we see a Muslim woman who is covered – it is associated with terrorism and oppression.'[37]

This article by McCammon contrasted with the editorial in the *Dominion Post*: 'Wrong to besmirch our stance on religion'.[38] The editorial questioned the drivers' acts of prejudice but also used particular language and tone. The editorial commented on the statements made by the first victim's husband (who intended to lodge a complaint with the Human Rights Commission), stating:

> *That will grate with many Kiwis, given the national origin [Saudi Arabia] of the man levelling the charge … New Zealand may have some way to go before it is a truly accepting society, and there will always be individuals whose souls are darkened by prejudice and intolerance. But Dr Aljabri should consider this before he judges too harshly: Saudi Arabia has religious police; New Zealand has human rights commissioners.*[39]

This suggests an 'us' and 'them' mentality. The use of the word 'our' in the title implies a unilateral stance or opinion. The editorial also suggested that the parties involved would be better to relativise the incident, that is, to compare New Zealand to Saudi Arabia, rather than challenge the xenophobic attitudes present in New Zealand. The editorial drew on gendered stereotypes of Muslim women, stating that women in Saudi Arabia 'are treated as the personal property of their menfolk',[40] an emotive and stereotypical comment that needs further factual explanation than that provided in the editorial. This perception – a common one that was articulated by the students discussed earlier – tends to be applied to all Muslims.

Van Dijk, in his discussion of institutional, or 'elite' racism evidenced in news sources, examines the use of syntax, lexical style and semantics to communicate a particular stance or discourse.[41] He argues:

> *[Media sources] systematically favour 'us' and problematise 'them' … Thus, on the whole, 'their' negative actions are made more prominent (e.g. by topicalisation, first page coverage, headlining, rhetorical emphasis), whereas 'our' negative actions are de-emphasised by denials, euphemism, mitigation or other strategies for avoiding negative self-presentation.*[42]

This 'us' and 'them' mentality was cited as being particularly distressing for the women interviewed. A New Zealand-born woman of Fiji-Indian descent commented:

> *I mean listening to talkback [radio] will break your heart. You're just thinking, oh my God, I'm not going out in the street again, you know. They had a poll on 'should we ban all Muslim immigration?' … Now change the word to Jewish and … is this acceptable? … As Muslim women, I think we're finding that veneer of civility being removed. [This] makes it much harder because it allows certain elements of prejudice into public discourse.*

Many of the women in this study were born in New Zealand, while others were recent immigrants. They all expressed a desire to be seen as 'valuable citizens contributing to New Zealand'. The practice of hijab, particularly the wearing of face-covering clothing, is usually perceived and represented as imported and 'foreign' to New Zealand – a 'backward' and 'unprogressive' female practice. The problematising of hijab, apparent in the media concentration of articles about it, is considered by Katherine H. Bullock and Gul Joya Jafri as failing 'to rupture the Orientalist discourse on Muslim women',[43] or, in other words, as perpetuating essentialist and stereotypical notions about covered women. The association of hijab with oppression, the eroticised exotic woman and extremism continues to inform the misrepresentation of Muslim New Zealanders.[44]

New Zealand's increasingly multicultural social landscape necessitates that clothing choices worn by different New Zealanders are accepted as legitimate Kiwi practices. A New Zealand-born convert to Islam related an incident where she had taken a local taxi to a destination. The taxi driver had looked at her headscarf and made the comment that she spoke very good English, for a foreigner. This woman found herself in a quandary as to whether she should just ignore the driver, or explain that she is a New Zealander who practises a particular religion. This popular essentialism of the foreign, headscarf-wearing 'other' emphasises the broader identity discourse in New Zealand as to who qualifies as a Kiwi. The comments I received from non-Muslim New Zealanders, which I quoted at the outset of this chapter, insinuate that this form of dress is not a 'Kiwi' practice, particularly when it is perceived as representative of various notions about the supposed misogyny and violence of Islam.

As Bullock and Jafri found in their study of how the media are perceived by Canadian Muslim women,[45] this focus on the stereotypical perceptions of the veil neglect the complex and varied reasons for women covering themselves in New Zealand. My research respondents cited a number of complex and personal reasons for covering, including faith, resisting sexual objectification, feeling a psychological and ontological strength from practising embodied faith, as well as veiling providing a 'buffer' to mitigate their minority status in an occasionally hostile society. Needless to say, the women's reasons for covering are not explained by the stereotypes described earlier. The participants did not suggest that negative things do not happen to Muslim women in the world, but that blaming Islam for this was inaccurate and neglected unequal, gendered cultural aspects of the different peoples that practise Islam. Some of the women also pointed out that violence against women happens in every culture and nation in the world and is not exclusive to particular social or religious groups. Indeed, the instances of prejudice and aggression experienced by a lot of women who cover in their daily lives, suggests that aggressive or hostile behaviour towards women is an unfortunate aspect of New Zealand society as well.

Moving forward

Bullock and Jafri comment, 'Although "the media" is not a monolithic, undifferentiated entity that necessarily intends overtly to exclude Muslim women, there are dominant and recurrent themes of Muslim women that prevail.'[46] This chapter has explored the international nature of the mass media in New Zealand, and the fact that many stories about Muslims and Islam are foreign in nature – as well as often tautologically reiterating Orientalist stereotypes – and serve to misrepresent the approximately 1.5 billion people around the world that practise Islam.

Some of the women participants suggested that reports of Muslim women and men involved in, for example, women's activism and human rights groups internationally could be constructive in demonstrating that Muslims are engaged in promoting women's rights and activating against injustices. The women felt that this might help to counter the concentration of violent reports about Muslims that 'project very circumscribed understandings of Muslims'.[47] Balance in reporting, and the inclusion of positive activities of Muslims, would help to show the affirmative impact that Islamic belief and Muslim social consciousness can have, particularly considering that Muslim women's activism and campaigning for human rights is a strong presence internationally.[48]

While fair balance in reporting was considered essential, some women also felt that Muslim people needed to work harder to connect with wider society in New Zealand to promote informed understanding of Muslims and their practice of Islam. One woman of Indian origin said: 'I think we've got a lot of responsibility, especially for those of us who have confidence in our identity as New Zealanders. We *have* to do it, you know ... I really feel [that].' As well as advocating for fairer reporting, some women considered that undertaking more public relations work would help to improve media subjectivity, while others felt that the inclusion of more Muslim people in key journalistic or media advisory roles would help to provide more informed analyses of Islamic beliefs and practices. Advocating for women's rights and accurate representation in various institutions was also considered an effective approach. Needless to say, the restricted notions of Islam and Muslim women in popular and mass-media discourses were analysed, critiqued and challenged by the women taking part in this research.

As a final consideration, one woman commented: 'I don't think I'm trying to fit into New Zealand society, I think I'm already a part of New Zealand society.' For the women in this research, their self-conception does not equate with the Orientalist stereotypes elaborated on in this discussion. These stereotypes, repeated consistently in elite institutions such as mass media and popular discourses, hamper Muslim women's sense of belonging as New Zealand citizens, significantly defining who is a Kiwi and who is not. They may also limit access for more informed and holistic understandings and interactions.

Endnotes

1 See for example, Ghazi-Walid Falah, 'The visual representation of Muslim/Arab women in daily newspapers in the United States', in Ghazi-Walid Falah and Caroline Nagel (eds), *Geographies of Muslim Women: Gender, religion, and space*, New York and London: The Guilford Press, 2005, 300–20; Elizabeth Poole, 'Framing Islam: An analysis of newspaper coverage of Islam in the British Press', in Kai Hafez (ed.), *Islam and the West in the Mass Media: Fragmented images in a globalizing world*, Cresskill, New Jersey: Hampton Press, 2000, 157–79; John E. Richardson, 'Who gets to speak? A study of sources in the broadsheet press', in Elizabeth Poole and John E. Richardson (eds), *Muslims and the News Media*, London: I.B. Taurus, 2010, 103–15.
2 Gabriele Marranci, *The Anthropology of Islam*, Oxford and New York: Berg, 2008, 93.
3 Teun A. van Dijk, *Racism and the Press*, London and New York: Routledge, 1991; 'Discourse semantics and ideology', *Discourse & Society* 6, 1995, 243–89; 'Discourse, power and access', in Carmen Rosa Caldas-Coulthard and Malcolm Coulthard (eds), *Texts and Practices: Readings in critical discourse analysis*, London and New York: Routledge, 1996, 84–104; 'The study of discourse', in Teun A. van Dijk (ed.), *Discourse as Structure and Process. Discourse Studies: A multidisciplinary introduction volume 1*, London, Thousand Oaks and New Delhi: Sage Publications, 1997, 1–34; 'Discourse and racism', in David Theo Goldberg and John Solomos (eds), *A Companion to Racial and Ethnic Studies*, Oxford and Malden, MA: Blackwell Publishers, 2002, 145–59.
4 The author is grateful to all of the women who participated in this research and gave so freely of their thoughts and opinions. Thanks also to the Asian Studies

Research Centre at the University of Otago for a Student Summer Bursary (2005–06), which partially funded the field research.
5 Minelle Mahtani, 'Representing minorities: Canadian media and minority identities', *Canadian Ethnic Studies/Études ethniques au Canada* 33, no. 3, 2001, 99–187, 120.
6 Van Dijk, 'The study of discourse', 25–26.
7 Pnina Werbner, 'The predicament of diaspora and millennial Islam: Reflections in the aftermath of September 11', *Social Science Research Council/After Sept. 11*, 1–16, Brooklyn, New York: Social Science Research Council, n.d.: www.essays.ssrc.org/sept11/essays/werbner_text_only.htm, 4.
8 Van Dijk, 'Discourse and racism', 146–47.
9 Ibid., 147.
10 Allan Bell, *The Language of News Media*, Oxford and Cambridge, MA: Blackwell, 1991.
11 Ibid., 156.
12 Van Dijk, 'Discourse semantics and ideology', 243.
13 Van Dijk, 'Discourse and racism', 146.
14 Ibid.
15 Ibid.
16 Ibid.
17 Van Dijk, *Racism and the Press*, 43.
18 Ibid.
19 See for example, Yvonne Yazbeck Haddad, 'American foreign policy in the Middle East and its impact on the identity of Arab Muslims in the United States', in Yvonne Yazbeck Haddad (ed.), *The Muslims of America*, New York and Oxford: Oxford University Press, 1991, 217–35; Carol A. Stabile and Deepa Kumar, 'Unveiling imperialism: Media, gender and the war on Afghanistan', *Media, Culture and Society* 27, 2005, 765–82.
20 David Edwards and David Cromwell, *Guardians of Power: The myth of the liberal media*, London and Ann Arbor, MI: Pluto Press, 2006.
21 Ibid., 174.
22 Ibid., 13–31.
23 Ibid., 15.
24 Ibid., 16–18.
25 Ibid., 18.
26 Ibid., 22.
27 John L. Esposito, foreword by Karen Armstrong, *The Future of Islam*, Oxford and New York: Oxford University Press, 2010, 83.
28 Krista E. Wiegand, 'Islam as an ethnicity? The media's impact on misperceptions in the West', in Kai Hafez (ed.), *Islam and the West in the Mass Media: Fragmented Images in a Globalizing World*, Cresskill, New Jersey: Hampton Press, 2000, 235–51, 236.
29 Ibid., 236.
30 Karim H. Karim, 'American media's coverage of Muslims: The historical roots of contemporary portrayals', in Elizabeth Poole and John E. Richardson (eds),

Muslims and the News Media, London: I.B. Taurus, 2010, 116–27, 118.
31　Richardson, 'Who gets to speak? A study of sources in the broadsheet press', 115.
32　'Ordered airport bombing', *Otago Daily Times* (from Reuters), 9 February 2011, 8.
33　Richardson, 'Who gets to speak? A study of sources in the broadsheet press', 115.
34　Wiegand, 'Islam as an ethnicity?' 240.
35　Ibid., 243–45.
36　Belinda McCammon, 'Women in bid to lift veil of ignorance', *Sunday Star Times*, 10 July 2011, A3.
37　Ibid.
38　Editorial: 'Wrong to besmirch our stance on religion', *Dominion Post*, 6 July 2011, B4.
39　Ibid.
40　Ibid.
41　Van Dijk, 'Discourse, power and access', 93–94.
42　Ibid.
43　Katherine H. Bullock and Gul Joya Jafri, 'Media (mis)representations: Muslim women in the Canadian nation', *Canadian Woman Studies/Les Cahiers De La Femme* 20, no. 2, 2001: 35–40, 36.
44　Katherine H. Bullock and Gul Joya Jafri, 'Media (mis)representations', 36.
45　Ibid., 37.
46　Ibid., 36.
47　Ghazi-Walid Falah, 'The visual representation of Muslim/Arab women in daily newspapers in the United States', 318.
48　See for example the edited collection by Nadje Al-Ali and Nicola Pratt (eds), *Women and War in the Middle East*, London and New York: Zed Books, 2009.

Bibliography

Al-Ali, Nadje and Nicola Pratt (eds), *Women and War in the Middle East*, London and New York: Zed Books, 2009.

Bell, Allan, *The Language of News Media*, Oxford and Cambridge, MA: Blackwell, 1991.

Bullock, Katherine H. and Gul Joya Jafri, 'Media (mis)representations: Muslim women in the Canadian nation', *Canadian Woman Studies/Les cahiers de la femme* 20, no. 2, 2001: 35–40.

Editorial: 'Wrong to besmirch our stance on religion', *Dominion Post*, 6 July 2011, B4.

Edwards, David and David Cromwell, *Guardians of Power: The myth of the liberal media*, London and Ann Arbor, MI: Pluto Press, 2006.

Esposito, John L., foreword by Karen Armstrong, *The Future of Islam*, Oxford and New York: Oxford University Press, 2010.

Falah, Ghazi-Walid, 'The visual representation of Muslim/Arab Women in daily newspapers in the United States', in Ghazi-Walid Falah and Caroline Nagel (eds), *Geographies of Muslim Women: Gender, religion, and space*, New York and London: Guilford Press, 2005, 300–20.

Haddad, Yvonne Yazbeck, 'American foreign policy in the Middle East and its impact on the identity of Arab Muslims in the United States', in Yvonne Yazbeck Haddad (ed.), *The Muslims of America*, New York and Oxford: Oxford University Press, 1991, 217-35.

Karim, Karim H., 'American media's coverage of Muslims: The historical roots of contemporary portrayals', in Elizabeth Poole and John E. Richardson (eds), *Muslims and the News Media*, London: I.B. Taurus, 2010, 116-27.

Mahtani, Minelle, 'Representing minorities: Canadian media and minority identities', *Canadian Ethnic Studies/Études ethniques au Canada* 33, no. 3, 2001, 99-187.

Marranci, Gabriele, *The Anthropology of Islam*, Oxford and New York: Berg, 2008.

McCammon, Belinda, 'Women in bid to lift veil of ignorance', *Sunday Star Times*, 10 July 2011, A3.

'Ordered airport bombing', *Otago Daily Times* (from Reuters), 9 February 2011, 8.

Poole, Elizabeth, 'Framing Islam: An analysis of newspaper coverage of Islam in the British press', in Kai Hafez (ed.), *Islam and the West in the Mass Media: Fragmented images in a globalizing world*, Cresskill, New Jersey: Hampton Press, 2000, 157-79.

Richardson, John E., 'Who gets to speak? A study of sources in the broadsheet press', in Elizabeth Poole and John E. Richardson (eds), *Muslims and the News Media*, London: I.B. Taurus, 2010, 103-15.

Stabile, Carol A. and Deepa Kumar, 'Unveiling imperialism: Media, gender and the war on Afghanistan', *Media, Culture and Society* 27, 2005, 765-82.

van Dijk, Teun A., *Racism and the Press*, London and New York: Routledge, 1991.

— 'Discourse semantics and ideology', *Discourse & Society* 6, 1995, 243-89.

— 'Discourse, power and access', in Carmen Rosa Caldas-Coulthard and Malcolm Coulthard (eds), *Texts and Practices: Readings in critical discourse analysis*, London and New York: Routledge, 1996, 84-104.

— 'The study of discourse', in Teun A. van Dijk (ed.), *Discourse as Structure and Process. Discourse studies: A multidisciplinary introduction volume 1*, London, Thousand Oaks and New Delhi: Sage Publications, 1997, 1-34.

— 'Discourse and racism', in David Theo Goldberg and John Solomos (eds), *A Companion to Racial and Ethnic Studies*, Oxford and Malden, MA: Blackwell Publishers, 2002, 145-59.

Werbner, Pnina, 'The predicament of diaspora and millennial Islam: Reflections in the aftermath of September 11', *Social Science Research Council/After Sept. 11*, 1-16, Brooklyn, New York: Social Science Research Council, n.d. www.essays.ssrc.org/sept11/essays/werbner_text_only.htm

Wiegand, Krista E., 'Islam as an ethnicity? The media's impact on misperceptions in the West', in Kai Hafez (ed.), *Islam and the West in the Mass Media: Fragmented images in a globalizing world*, Cresskill, New Jersey: Hampton Press, 2000, 235-51.

Part IV: Belonging

9. Immigrant Economies in Action
Chinese ethnic precincts in Auckland

PAUL SPOONLEY, CARINA MEARES
AND TRUDIE CAIN

Introduction

New Zealand has a history of radical policy shifts – the 1890s expansion of political enfranchisement and the post-1935 extension of welfare provisions and principles are two obvious examples. The mid-1980s, however, were also notable as a period of significant change. The development of an economically focused neo-liberalism was accompanied, somewhat paradoxically, by the recognition of group rights and the promotion (perhaps unintended in certain areas) of ethnic diversity. The most apparent was the recognition of Māori as tangata whenua and the rights that flowed from this. The project of building a 'Britain in the South Seas'[1] and the assumptions of a singular nation as the basis of a settler state were subverted in interesting ways by the constitutional status given to the Treaty of Waitangi, the rights of iwi as treaty partners, and the bicultural imperatives imposed on the state and service providers from the 1980s.

Another important shift in the nature of this nation-building project occurred as a result of the final dismantling of the 'white New Zealand' immigration policy, although this has only since become evident. Policy and legislative changes occurred in 1986–87, and there was a vigorous and very negative political and public response in the mid-1990s to this initial period of immigrant diversification. Despite this, by the turn of the century the diversity of immigrant flows meant that New Zealand had rapidly caught up with Australia and Canada in terms of the proportion of resident immigrant populations and the extent of cultural diversity. New Zealand had always used immigration as a means of populating the country and obtaining certain skills, but immigrants in colonial New Zealand came mostly from Britain and Ireland. By 1996 this had changed dramatically, and traditional source-country arrivals were easily outnumbered by those arriving from new sources. Colonial New Zealand had worked hard to exclude those who were seen as a 'racial threat',[2] especially those from Asia.

A century later, immigrants arriving from Asia constituted some of the largest new settler groups.

The immigrant communities that arrived post 1987 have had a significant impact on various aspects of New Zealand life, from the debate about multiculturalism in a bicultural context through to the operations of key institutions, such as the education system. Among the most visibly different immigrant communities are those from Asia. This chapter focuses on one Asian community – the Chinese – and one manifestation of their impact on the cityscape of Auckland – ethnic precincts. What shape do these precincts take? What do they represent both to the immigrant community involved and to other communities within the region? What are the policy and political implications of these shifts in community make-up and the various manifestations of this new diversity, including ethnic precincts? Some of these questions will be answered here, but others remain unanswered due to the newness of these developments, a limited evidence base, and the fact that a range of actors are influential including individuals and organisations from within the communities concerned as well as key regulatory agencies, such as the Auckland Council.

A primary focus on Chinese immigrants and Chinese (or Chinese-dominated) ethnic precincts is a function of the research that we have done[3] and the size of the Chinese community in Auckland. That said, there are important qualifications to the label 'Chinese'. First, the large Chinese community (171,000 in Auckland in 2013) is made up of distinct components – those from Hong Kong and Taiwan who dominated arrivals during the 1990s, and those from China who have arrived since 2000. Also included are smaller communities from Malaysia and Singapore, as well as the New Zealand-born – the children of recent arrivals as well as those whose families have been in the country since the late 1860s. Second, in all of the ethnic precincts that we have looked at, while the Chinese dominate, there are also business operators from other parts of Asia. We will signal this co-location and intermixing where it occurs.

Similarly, we also acknowledge that there are difficulties in collectively referring to the combined population of immigrants from various parts of Asia. The use of the label 'Asia' and 'Asian' can be problematic: first, because of its normative and sometimes pejorative[4] use, and second, because it tends to collapse and racialise communities whose linguistic, cultural and religious histories (including migration to New Zealand) are very different.[5] With this in mind, we have attempted to be as precise as possible in our references to new settlers.

Immigrant diversity and ethnic precincts

The arrival of culturally and visibly different communities in destination cities, and their concentration in particular locations within those cities, has long aroused the interest of social scientists. The Chicago School in the 1920s provided an early exemplar, although their focus was on the spatial segregation of minorities and the non-assimilation of ethnic communities.[6] This interest was re-ignited in the post-war period as labour migration to metropolitan centres produced new political and economic relations with accompanying spatial concentrations.[7] By the late 1980s, the migration of skilled and entrepreneurial immigrants led to further academic interest, both in areas of residential concentration (what Li has called 'ethno-burbs')[8] and the development of ethnic enclaves or ethnic precincts – areas of ethnic business concentration. The latter is our interest here, and specifically in relation to the development of Chinese ethnic precincts in Auckland.

Ethnic precincts raise some interesting questions, first with respect to their nature and second in relation to the reasons for their development. When we refer to ethnic precincts in the Auckland context, we define them as the co-location of businesses owned by members of the same or other minority ethnic communities. In the present chapter, we are particularly interested in the concentrations of Chinese businesses, although such concentrations tend also to involve members of other Asian communities. As later sections will illustrate, the precincts involve upwards of 50 businesses, of which more than two-thirds are run by Asian or Chinese. Ethnic precincts normally involve a range of business types but there is nearly always a predominance of food stores. These include restaurants and fast-food outlets as well as suppliers of food, from supermarkets to fresh food outlets – butchers, greengrocers – and Asian food specialty shops. Alongside these tend to be a range of businesses from services such as hairdressers, travel or real estate agents, to medical supplies or video rental agencies. Some involve products and services that are specific to Asian communities, while others include elements that are recognisable to non-Asian customers. It is the co-location of these immigrant and ethnic businesses, and their visibility both in terms of who runs them as well as their products and signage, which makes them a significant development in the cityscapes of contemporary New Zealand.

These ethnic precincts have emerged as a product of recent waves of migration from Asia and, as with ethnic precincts in other destination cities, they perform a number of functions. They are an important 'first access point and source of support'[9] for new arrivals. Given the significant cultural and linguistic differences between immigrants from Asia and most long-term resident New Zealand communities, ethnic precincts offer the known and familiar in terms of what is for sale and the way it is sold, including the language and assumptions involved in commercial exchange. Ethnic precincts are a focal point for recent immigrants as a place of 'meeting, shopping and eating'.[10] They also provide a supportive and familiar environment for business establishment, revolving as they do around cultural and community/familial networks. They offer access to known and trusted ethnic networks and knowledge, including capital, labour, supplies, prospective customers and information.[11] Equally, they are important sites of employment, especially for those new immigrant job-seekers who lack local labour-market experience, or the skills and qualifications recognised and valued by non-Asian employers. In these various ways, ethnic precincts represent that which is familiar for significant new communities of immigrants, and are a means of business establishment, employment or consumption. They also raise some important questions about immigrant settlement and acceptance within the resident community.

The key question is whether ethnic precincts represent the outcomes of immigrant choice or whether they are the product of discriminatory processes. In answering this question, further debate is generated about whether ethnic precincts inhibit or contribute to positive settlement outcomes. In addressing both of these questions, Waldinger, Ward, Aldrich and Stanfield suggest that both ethnic-specific and socio-cultural factors need to be considered;[12] such factors include the decisions made by immigrants, along with political and economic factors.[13] Kloosterman and Rath extend this analysis, suggesting in their mixed embeddedness approach that immigrants are located in ethnic social and business networks while also contending with the social and economic structures of their new location.[14] In the New Zealand context, the immigration environment has been influenced by neo-liberal imperatives.[15] Consequently, immigrant agency is emphasised and there is minimal market intervention or settlement support, little assistance for business establishment and entrepreneurialism, and a general lack of government recognition at both local and national level of ethnic-specific dynamics and outcomes.

Within this particular context, the ethnic embeddedness of immigrants – what Portes calls 'relational embeddedness'[16]– plays an important role, producing a particular set of vertical and horizontal linkages with the wider community. The former is reflected in interviews we carried out with Chinese and Korean business owners in Auckland, many of whom disclosed their unwillingness to participate in representative business organisations because of what they perceive as a lack of understanding or responsiveness to their particular (ethnic) practices or beliefs.[17] Similarly, with regard to policy and funding decisions, local authorities have, until recently, failed to fully account for ethnic diversity, including the development of ethnic precincts. The result is that immigrant agency is privileged in a regulatory environment that encourages individual responsibility and business establishment. As Pang and Rath note, '[d]ifferent markets obviously offer different opportunities and obstacles, demand different skills, and lead to different outcomes in terms of business success or – at higher levels of agglomeration – a different ethnic division of labour.'[18]

In New Zealand, as in other destination countries and cities, there is a new-found interest in the co-location of immigrant businesses, especially in relation to the visibility of both the immigrants and business concentration. These developments raise some important empirical and policy questions about what they represent – economic and labour market discrimination, constrained options and outcomes – and what therefore is the most appropriate policy response. Asian, and specifically Chinese-dominated, ethnic precincts are a relatively new phenomenon in a New Zealand context. They are a product of the last two decades, and there is relatively little known about what they represent, how they function, and what is the best policy response. This chapter explores these issues.

Monocultural Auckland to 'superdiver-city'

For the first century of New Zealand's settlement history (1840 through to the mid-twentieth century), immigration was dominated by arrivals from Britain and Ireland. As Belich notes, there was a strong emphasis on 'racial homogeneity, symbolised by the slogan "98.5 per cent British"', in this case relating to what he calls the period of recolonisation (1880s–1960s).[19] The major exception to this was the arrival of the Chinese from the 1860s; however, they were subjected to extensive discrimination and controls, both in terms of entry to New Zealand and to their rights once they were here. The number of Chinese grew through the 1870s and the perceived threat to 'racial homogeneity' resulted in a series (33 in total) of Acts to restrict their arrival and activities. The first piece of legislation was the Chinese Immigrants Act 1881, which limited Chinese arrivals to one person for every ten tons of the ship's weight, combined with an arrival tax of £10.

This was followed by a series of other discriminatory and exclusionary acts (Immigration Restriction Act, 1899; Chinese Immigrants Amendment Act, 1907; Immigration Restriction Amendment Act, 1908; Immigration Restriction Amendment Act, 1920).[20] Such discriminatory immigration policies toward those from Asia, coupled with the privileging of arrivals from Britain resulted in a very monocultural New Zealand.

The first major challenge to this white (British) immigration policy occurred not through any deliberate decision by the government, but as a result of the labour needs of urban-based industries from the 1960s. Local and traditional immigrant sources could not provide the numbers of semi- and unskilled labourers required during a period of major expansion, and so immigrants from the Pacific were used to provide a new labour source. This involved informal and, at times, illegal labour migration, especially from Samoa and Tonga. In the case of the Tokelaus, Niue and the Cook Islands, the government played an active part in the relocation of Pacific peoples to New Zealand.[21] Migration from the Pacific transformed a number of New Zealand cities, notably Auckland, as visibly different immigrants arrived and settled in the inner city and newly developed outer suburbs such as Ōtara. The reaction in the 1970s, especially as economic difficulties were encountered, was substantial and predominantly negative. However, while this period from 1973 to the late 1980s was deeply unsettling and resulted in a series of discriminatory Acts (e.g. the Citizenship (Western Samoa) Act 1982) and campaigns against Pacific-born overstayers by police and immigration, the numbers of Pacific-born immigrants continued to expand, especially in Auckland.[22] In 1971 there were 1273 Tongans and Samoans (who had been born in their respective countries) residing in New Zealand. By 2001 there were 18,054 Tongans and 47,118 Samoans who had migrated to New Zealand, now supplemented by those born in New Zealand (providing ethnic total populations of 40,700 and 115,017 respectively). By 2001, 80 per cent of New Zealand Tongans lived in Auckland along with two out of three Samoans.[23] Along with the changes that had occurred in the 1970s and 1980s as Māori asserted their political and treaty rights, New Zealand – especially Auckland – was now significantly less monocultural than it had been mid-century.

The next stage of disassembling this monoculturalism occurred in the wake of the changes to immigration legislation and policy in 1986–87, when the source country preference was finally abandoned. By 2000 New Zealand had fully adopted the points system that had been developed in Canada and Australia. Under this system, points were allocated to prospective immigrants for certain characteristics considered desirable to the economy, including educational credentials and employment experience. The result was the diversification of immigration flows, including significantly increasing numbers from Asia. Through the 1990s, this included the arrival of Koreans, Hong Kong Chinese and Taiwanese. As with Pacific immigrants, Auckland was a particular beneficiary of these flows (see Table 1). The rapid growth in the number of immigrants from 1986 through to 1996 is apparent. In 1986, prior to the changes, there were 5298 overseas-born Asians; by 1996, this had grown to 39,113.

This growth did not go unnoticed and there was a strong and negative political reaction between 1993 and the general election in 1996, with the newly established political party New Zealand First being a major contributor to, as well as beneficiary of, public concern about the diversification of immigration. The arrivals slowed in the late 1990s, partly in response to the racism directed towards them, but also as a result of the downturn in Asian economies. After 2000, the numbers again increased, but this time the migration was dominated by newcomers from China and India (the latter are not included in the figures here). More than 80 per cent of these new arrivals were from mainland China, with a doubling in the numbers from this source in the five years between 2001 and 2006. This dominance can be seen in the 2006 census figures in Table 1.

Table 1. Auckland's resident Chinese population by birthplace 1986–2006

YEAR	BIRTHPLACE						
	China	Hong Kong	Taiwan	Malaysia	NZ	Others*	TOTAL
1986	1668	561	39	597	5250	2433	10,548
1991	4110	2850	2838	3681	6306	3891	23,676
1996	12,054	8868	7965	4596	10,293	5928	49,704
2001	26,547	8406	8562	4953	13,203	6459	68,130
2006	53,694	5280	7323	6003	17,682	7443	97,425

*Note: This category includes all those born in countries other than those listed in the table.
Source: New Zealand Census of Population and Dwellings, 1986, 1991, 1996, 2001 and 2006

Consequently, alongside the large communities of Pacific peoples, Auckland became home to significant numbers of Asians by 2006. Indeed, the Asian population of Auckland now makes up a larger percentage of the city's population than the Pacific or Māori populations, and it is projected to grow further to comprise more than a quarter of the city's population within the next decade. As such, the city can lay claim to being a superdiverse metropolis, one that has important transnational links with the rest of the Pacific and Asia.

There have been a range of outcomes from the growth of this diversity, from the increased levels of familial and community links and transborder activity with Asia and the Pacific, to the new concentrations of immigrant/ethnic communities in particular streets or suburbs (ethno-burbs). The focus here is on one aspect of the changing cityscape: the concentration of economic activities and, most notably, retailing. The appearance of these ethnic precincts is a new development. Historically, there were modest groups of Chinese businesses in Greys Avenue and Ōtāhuhu in Auckland. But what has emerged in the first decade of the twenty-first century involves much larger concentrations of businesses that are visibly different in relation to other retail centres in Auckland. Not only are the owners/operators of these businesses ethnically different, the language used in transactions (Mandarin and to a lesser extent, Cantonese) and the signage (Chinese script) disrupts the dominant assumptions and practices of retail trading in the city. The products and services reflect the ethnic/national origins and inclinations of the business operators and many of the consumers – and the supply chains and networks that underpin what appears on a shelf in one of Auckland's ethnic precincts – to the bemusement and sometimes consternation of some members of other ethnic groups.

Ethnic precincts in Auckland

Ethnic precincts began to emerge in the mid- and late 1990s but grew in size and significance after 2000, when, it appears, the size of the resident Chinese community (along with immigrant communities from other parts of Asia) reached a tipping point that ensured demand could sustain relatively substantial retail precincts. These Asia-born communities comprised a mix of permanent and temporary immigrants, including those on study visas. They were concentrated in particular parts of the city: the temporary immigrants from Asia were in the Central Business District

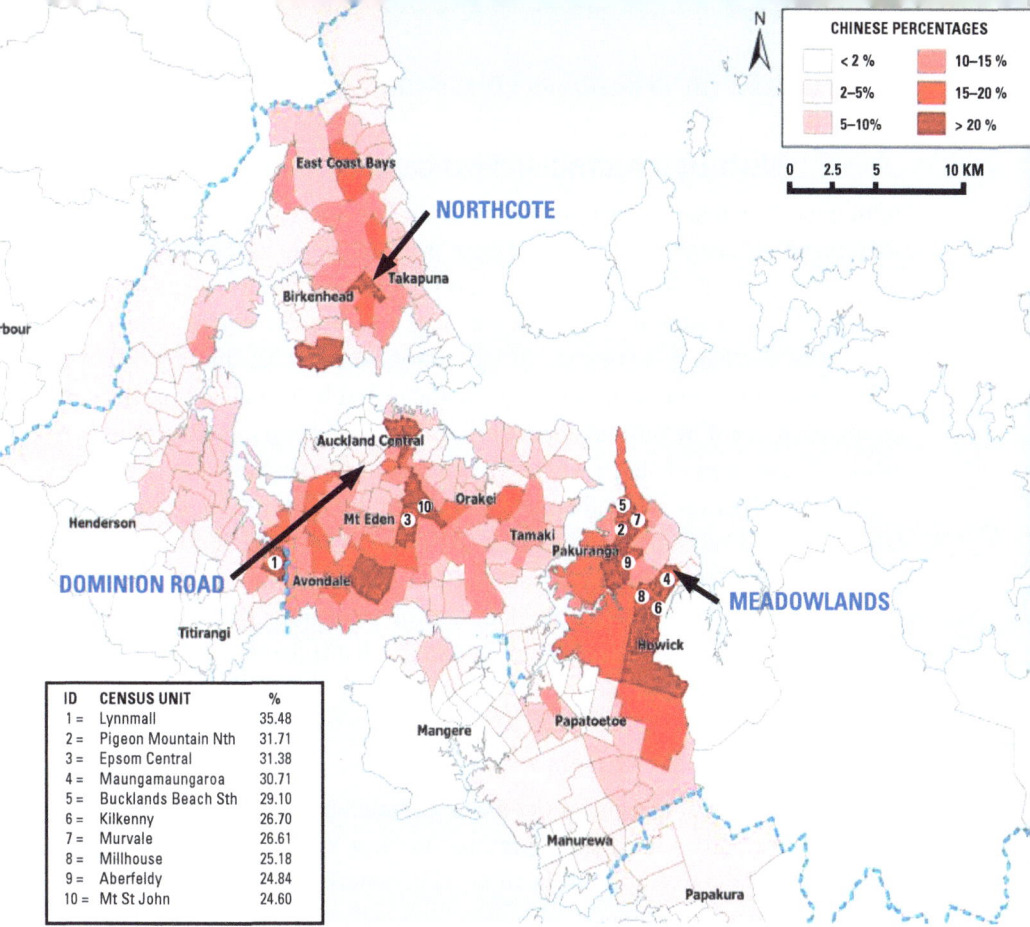

Map 1. Distribution of PRC-born Chinese in Auckland as a percentage of the total population and some key ethnic precincts. Map based on 2006 census data.
Source: Integration of Immigrants Programme

and inner suburbs, while Chinese ethno-burbs became established in the eastern suburbs, in a southeastern band on the city's periphery and in pockets on the North Shore, with the largest concentration in New Lynn. Retail businesses and then shopping centres were established to service these residential concentrations. By 2012 there were a number of types of Chinese/Asian ethnic precincts throughout the greater Auckland area. Some reflected the presence of a specific ethnic/immigrant group while others involved a range of Asian ethnic groups and an interesting array of business types. We will focus in this chapter on two case studies: Northcote, which resulted from the conversion of an existing shopping centre on the North Shore; and Meadowlands and Somerville, which were purpose-built to service the needs of a growing Chinese community in Southeast Auckland.

Ethnic precincts: Two case-studies

Ethnic precincts take a variety of forms, from the conversion of existing suburban retail centres (Northcote) to purpose-built precincts (Somerville/Meadowlands). This does not exhaust the possibilities, however, and the most important exception in our discussion of Chinese-dominated ethnic precincts in Auckland is the case of Dominion Road.[24] Dominion Road is an arterial route with strip retailing, characterised by significant blocks that are dominated by business operators from various parts of Asia. One example is a section of shops where 51 per cent of the businesses are run by Chinese, 16 per cent by Indian and 11 per cent by 'other' Asian groups. Dominion Road is not only emblematic of Auckland retailing but has also now become known as a site and destination that is characterised by its 'Asian-ness'.[25] We mention the development of Dominion Road here to stress that what follows is selective and does not exhaust the types of ethnic precinct now in Auckland.

NORTHCOTE, NORTH SHORE: A CONVERSION

The Northcote shopping centre was officially opened in June 1959 and was the first municipally owned shopping mall in New Zealand. It is located on the North Shore of Auckland in an area characterised by high levels of ethnic diversity and a relatively low household median income. In addition to 'a high percentage of migrant and refugee residents,'[26] there is also a significant proportion of Māori (9 per cent) and Pacific peoples (6 per cent) living in the suburb.[27] The median household income for the area is $54,000 per annum, compared with $69,100 for the remainder of the North Shore (North Shore City 2010). Immediately adjacent to the long-established shopping centre is a significant area of state housing (349 state houses in total),[28] one of only a few north of the harbour bridge. The Northcote Centre Plan describes the precinct in this way:

> *Northcote is a truly multicultural centre. The presence of a large number of HNZC*[29] *[Housing New Zealand Corporation] properties further contributes to a strong identity and a unique community in Northcote.*[30]

During the late 1980s and early 1990s, the area referred to in the media as 'Northcote central' developed a reputation for poor housing and anti-social behaviour, including gang activity. During this time about half of the children attending the nearby Onepoto Primary School were from sole-parent households and most of the parents with children at the school were unemployed.[31] The shopping centre was also in decline during the mid-1990s,[32] with around 15 per cent of the shops empty and rents modest or low for the North Shore. These circumstances were to provide an opportunity for new Asian business owners.

The number of Asian-owned shops began to increase during the 1990s and was boosted further after 2000 with the arrival of more China-born immigrants on the North Shore. The low rents provided a modest investment threshold for those wanting to establish a business. Inevitably, food was an important feature of these new Asian-owned businesses and over the first decade of the twenty-first century, several Asian supermarkets were established along with restaurants, meat, fish and vegetable shops. The local real estate agents began to employ Mandarin-speakers, and there were Asian-focused travel shops, Chinese dentists and doctors (and other Asian health professionals), shops selling Chinese health products, as well as video suppliers and hairdressers. These were supplemented by English language schools with a target audience of Asian students.

An initial survey in 2007 by Spoonley showed that three-quarters of the businesses in the centre were Asian-owned; most shopkeepers were China-born while some were Korean. Depending on the day of the week, half or more of the customers in these shops were Asian, predominantly from China, and many of the signs on shop fronts and in stores were in Chinese. In less than a decade, Northcote had been transformed into an ethnic Asian (mostly Chinese) precinct. Table 2 shows the results of a follow-up survey undertaken as part of the Integration of Immigrants Programme in 2010, by which time 87 per cent of the businesses were Chinese-owned and almost half sold food. Map 2 illustrates the ethnicity of business owners along Pearn Place and Pearn Crescent which form the focal point of small retail activity in the shopping centre.

Although the 2006 town-centre strategy and investment plan was silent on the Asian ethnic nature of the precinct,[34] the 2010 Northcote Town Centre Plan was not. In his foreword to the latter, then mayor of North Shore City[35] Andrew Williams noted that 'Northcote is distinctive as North Shore's multicultural centre with its strong Asian ... influence.'[36] While the 2006 version of the plan also made generalised comments about the value of cultural diversity, the later plan is much more specific in its approach to the high proportion of Asian-owned and -operated businesses in the centre. One of the precinct's two key functions, for example, is identified as 'serving a wider sub-regional catchment for Asian specialities'.[37] The predominance

Table 2. Retail businesses in the Northcote Shopping Centre by shop type and ethnicity of owner

79 Retail Businesses	Chinese	Other Asian	Other
Food	20	15	1
Chains (ASB, Countdown[33])	–	–	2
Retail (Two-dollar shops, clothing)	8	3	2
Medical (pharmacy, traditional Chinese medicine, doctors surgery, optician)	3	2	1
Services (travel, insurance, real estate)	8	3	2
Beauty and hair salons	3	2	2
Other	1	1	–
	43 (54%)	26 (33%)	10 (13%)

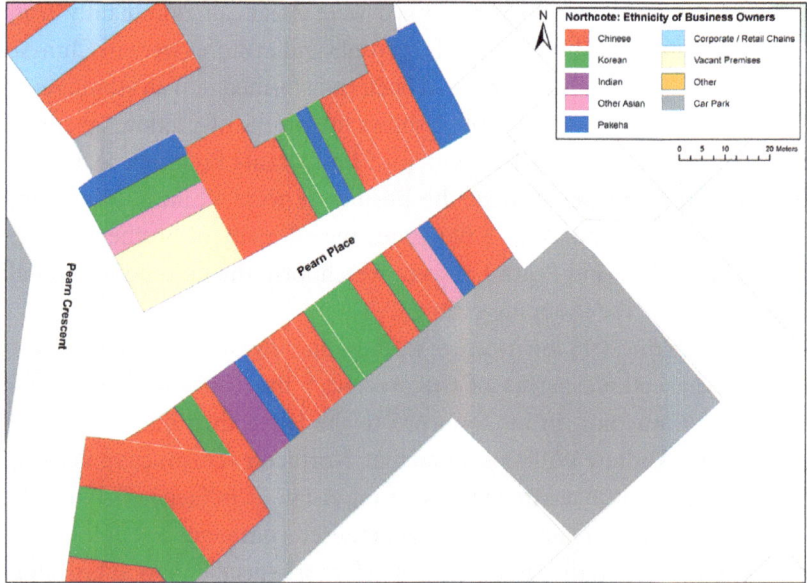

Map 2. Classification of businesses by ethnicity of owners along Pearn Place and Pearn Crescent, Integration of Immigrants Programme, 2010.
Source: Integration of Immigrants Programme, 2010.

of Chinese businesses is not mentioned in the plan, however, nor is there any acknowledgment that the needs of these businesses may differ from those owned by Pākehā or other ethnic groups.

Northcote has benefitted in various ways from the revival of the shopping centre, including a shift away from the previously dominant media image of Northcote as an area with multiple social problems. Part of this change has been demographic. Between 2001 and 2006, the number of Pākehā in the area dropped from 61 to 33 per cent and Māori from 22 to 11 per cent, while the number of Pacific peoples grew (33 per cent) as did the number of Asians (28 per cent).[38] Local groups began to improve the area. A graffiti removal service was founded, and a partnership between community organisations, the police and the Housing Corporation was formed to reduce the levels of violence and drug dealing and to improve the housing stock. Schemes to help the unemployed were also established.

The shopping centre began to gain a reputation for providing cheap and interesting products as well as offering a taste of Asia. It became the location for various Asian events, such as the celebration of Chinese New Year and the Moon Festival, occasions which are regularly attended by local dignitaries. The conversion from a run-down suburban shopping centre to one that offers Asian products, services and events is now complete. Elderly Chinese can be seen playing Chinese checkers at the purpose-built tables under the elm tree in Pearn Place or doing Tai Chi. People mingle and chat while the shops and the eating hall are always busy, with the majority of customers being Asian, mostly Chinese.

Somerville and Meadowlands, Manukau: Purpose-built ethnic precincts

Unlike Northcote, the Somerville and Meadowlands precincts were developed by Hong Kong immigrant Kit Wong with the specific purpose of serving the rapidly growing Chinese community in East Auckland. He chose to locate these ethnic precincts in the affluent post-war suburbs of Southeast Auckland, a part of the city that contains an interesting juxtaposition of affluence and poverty. The first major post-war development was the state housing area of Ōtara, which now has the largest concentration of Pasifika and Māori in the Auckland region and high levels of socio-economic disadvantage. Nearby were the affluent suburbs of Howick, Bucklands Beach and Pakuranga, home for significant numbers of Chinese immigrants over the last two decades.

Somerville and Meadowlands were green-field developments (i.e. the land had not previously been built on). From the 1990s Wong worked with others to develop a shopping precinct specifically designed to meet the needs of newly arrived Chinese. The premises are mainly single-storey buildings built in strips at right angles to the access road, so that shops in one strip face those in the next. There is nothing Chinese in the building design, but the 'Chinese-ness' of the precinct is immediately obvious in the signage, the products being sold and in the shopkeepers and customers. The shops are dominated by those selling food, either as restaurants or as grocery and fresh produce stores; interspersed among them are hairdressers, travel operators and video shops.

The centre was officially opened in 1997 by Prime Minister Jim Bolger and the Mayor of Manukau City, Sir Barry Curtis. Kit Wong managed the project for ten years before moving on to other ventures during the first decade of the new century. Meadowlands and Somerville have become an important part of the lives of Chinese and other immigrant communities living in this increasingly diverse part of Auckland. Data from the 2006 census show that some of the largest settlements of Chinese[40] are to be found in this part of the city in the suburbs of Bucklands Beach, Pakuranga and Howick. The percentages of ethnic Chinese in Census Area Units in Auckland show that seven out of the top ten are found in Southeast Auckland, ranging from 24.8 per cent in Aberfeldy to 31.2 per cent in Pigeon Mountain North. Table 3 shows that 73 per cent of the 76 premises operating in Meadowlands and Somerville in May 2010 were owned by ethnic Chinese, 23 per cent by Koreans and 4 per cent by those of other ethnicity. Map 3 illustrates the ethnicity of business owners in both precincts.

In terms of the mix of business types, there is little difference between these ethnic precincts and Northcote. All are dominated by Chinese businesses selling food. The main differences occur because Somerville and Meadowlands were built to meet the needs of Chinese communities, especially in terms of security, ease of access and delivering specific social benefits. In addition, the buildings are new and were deliberately marketed to arriving Chinese immigrants wanting to establish a business in Auckland – a purposefulness that is missing from the more organic development of the ethnic precinct at Northcote.

These two case-studies provide examples of the nature and development of Chinese ethnic precincts in contemporary Auckland. In most respects, they differ little from ethnic precincts elsewhere, in Australia or Canada for example.

Table 3. Retail businesses in the Meadowlands and Somerville Shopping Centres by shop type and ethnicity of owner

70 Retail Businesses	Chinese	Other Asian	Other
Food	25	7	–
Chains (ASB, Woolworths)	1	–	1
Retail (Two-dollar shops, clothing)	8	4	2
Medical (pharmacy, traditional Chinese medicine, doctors surgery, optician)	1	2	–
Services (travel, insurance, real estate)	13	2	–
Beauty and hair salons	3	1	–
Other	–	–	–
	51 (73%)	16 (23%)	3 (4%)

Source: Integration of Immigrants Programme, 2010.

Map 3. Classification of businesses by ethnicity of owners in the Somerville and Meadowlands shopping centres
Source: Integration of Immigrants Programme, 2010.

The recognition of ethnic precincts

Auckland's organisations, especially Auckland Council, are just beginning to explore the possibility that areas of immigrant business concentration may provide opportunities for new forms of consumption and economic activity. There is a considerable literature on the ways in which cities such as Sydney,[41] Vancouver, San Francisco, London[42] and Washington[43] have recognised immigrant business concentrations as sites of importance for the cities' economies and, increasingly, as destinations for tourists and local consumers. In the case of London, Sales et al. discuss how the institutionalisation of Chinatown occurred initially as a result of community associations making claims on the local authority.[44] In the same vein, Yeoh discusses how Singapore has begun to explore the possibility of heritage landscapes as a way of providing a 'sense of historical continuity' and an affirmation of the city's cosmopolitan nature, by recognising Chinatown, Little India and Kampong Glam (a Malay precinct).[45] After a period of urban renewal, during which many parts of these ethnic precincts were destroyed, there was a reversal of these policies and what remained of Chinatown in Singapore was recognised and preserved.[46]

By comparison, there are few places in Auckland that have been identified or branded as ethnic precincts.[47] Until the amalgamation of Auckland's eight legacy councils in 2010, there was a reluctance to recognise the co-location of minority ethnic or immigrant businesses and to consider the economic benefit that might accrue to the city. In considering the development of the Northcote Town Centre, for example, until quite recently there had been no reference to the fact that a majority of the businesses are Asian in ownership or activity; that it is the location of immigrant/ethnic festivals; or that the client or pedestrian mix is particular to that shopping centre.[48] While Manukau City Council adopted a logo and a branding message that did acknowledge cultural diversity, and Waitākere City Council established the Waitākere Ethnic Board in 2003, the policy recognition and support of post-1987 immigrants was generally left to particular agencies: the Auckland Regional Settlement Strategy and those responsible for its implementation; the Auckland Chamber of Commerce; and OMEGA.[49] Even though Auckland's immigrant population was nearing 40 per cent of its resident population by 2010, the city and its key institutions were either noticeably cautious about doing too much to acknowledge ethnic diversity or they declined to consider it at all.

Somewhere between these two positions was the Royal Commission on the governance of Auckland and the government's subsequent response to this document.[50] Diversity was seen as a positive influence on many levels, although it was unclear from either group exactly how this translated into economic action or post-arrival support for immigrant business development. On governance itself, the main concession to diversity from the Royal Commission was the recommendation that three Māori seats be established on the new super-city council. Pacific peoples and other ethnic or immigrant communities were recognised by proposed (and subsequently established) advisory panels. The possibility of specific Māori representation was a step too far for the National-led government and its key partner, ACT. The recommendation was overturned, much to the dismay of their other partner in government, the Māori Party.

Since the establishment of the new Auckland Council in November 2010, however, there have been indications of a shift towards acknowledging and supporting the development of Auckland's diverse ethnic economies. The Ethnic Peoples' Advisory Panel has made economic development generally, and the development of immigrant and refugee businesses in particular, key focuses during their first term.[51] The council's Economic Development Strategy[52] has the following cross-cutting themes sitting under its five strategic directions: creating a sustainable eco-economy; facilitating an iwi/Māori economic powerhouse; developing and enhancing an innovative rural and maritime economy; and supporting a diverse ethnic economy.

The possibility of branding areas in Auckland as Chinatowns has been raised several times during the last ten years but then quickly dismissed. In 2008, Mayor of Waitākere Bob Harvey argued that New Lynn ought to become a Chinatown. The area had the highest percentage of Chinese residents in Auckland (over 30 per cent in 2006) as well as a cluster of Chinese businesses. He suggested that the town centre might be enhanced by explicitly identifying it as a Chinatown with symbols such as traditional Chinese gates. On this occasion, the mayor was defeated by the opposition of some Chinese members of the community, as well as by local non-Chinese business owners and residents who did not welcome the idea that their centre might become even more Chinese than it already was.[53] In 2010 Spoonley noted in a radio interview that Auckland, despite the size of its Chinese population and the fact that a number of areas in the city had significant densities of Chinese businesses, still lacked an official Chinatown. A blog entitled 'A Chinatown state of mind'[54] was published in response to the comments, followed by a public campaign opposing the establishment of a Chinatown. Supporters of the 'no Chinatown' campaign felt that claiming its own space and future usurped the Chinese community's prerogative, and that local government involvement in the project would simply confirm their minority status and 'difference'.

More recently, in a report commissioned by Auckland Council on the Chinese ethnic precincts on Dominion Road,[55] we suggested that 'it would be interesting to explore with the current business owners ... whether there would be support for a themed or branded precinct that might be labelled a "Chinatown"'. Media responses to this proposal, and the public comments elicited in subsequent online forums, suggest that although some consider this ethnic theming an appropriate strategy for precincts in Auckland, the majority believe it to be at best unnecessary and at worst contrived and inauthentic. There were also comments that can only be described as racist.

Auckland's previous reluctance to recognise immigrant business activity and the presence of diversity more generally as an asset distinguishes it from a number of other immigrant destination cities. Vancouver made a decision in 1989 to consider cultural diversity a core requirement in governance and economic development. As elsewhere, ethnic precincts were seen as an important brand difference to the city, as consumer and tourist destinations, and as significant contributions to economic development. As Pang and Rath comment:

> *Urban cultural diversity is then a vital resource for the prosperity of cities and a potential catalyst for socio-economic development, particularly since business investors consider this diversity as one of the factors determining the location of businesses.*[56]

This recognition has led to the 'ethnic theming' of some areas and significant support for ethnic and immigrant business development. Cities often compete in terms of the ethnic and immigrant-related experiences they can offer, and ethnic diversity has itself become a commodity and a point of difference.[57] Collins notes that 'ethnic cultural tourism' involves tourist visits to ethnic precincts.[58] There is some evidence in Auckland that Chinese tour groups are channelled towards Chinese ethnic precincts, often to their dismay. There is, however, little doubt that such precincts have significant potential as part of a city's branding and tourism.[59] There are also examples, such as in Vancouver, where the planning and economic development processes are structured to specifically recognise and include immigrant communities.

... the public policy framework of city planning, regeneration, place-marketing and other functions may constrain, enable or encourage expressions of ethnic difference in the built environment (Shaw, Bagwell and Karmowska 2004, 1985).[60]

Shaw, Bagwell and Karmowska[61] note that more enlightened city governments shifted from a 'crude civic boosterism' in the 1990s to 'strategic niche management and competitive niche thinking', one key element of which was the spaces and activities that reflected one ethnic or immigrant community or another. It will be interesting to see to what extent this occurs in the context of the new Auckland Council.

Conclusion

In the last two decades, the diversification of immigration source countries and flows has significantly altered the demographic and cultural make-up of New Zealand, with Auckland as the gateway city being a particular beneficiary and site of these new dynamics. We have described one outcome – the development of Chinese-dominated ethnic precincts. We could have chosen those precincts that are dominated by Indian or Korean immigrants; we could have looked at precincts that are to be found in Wairau Park or Botany Downs; and we have only paid passing attention to Dominion Road, one of the well-known examples of an ethnic precinct that reflects the influence of immigrants from Asia. We finish by raising some of the questions that ethnic precincts pose for researchers, policy analysts and agencies such as Auckland Council.

In the considerable literature on ethnic precincts/enclaves,[62] there is a fundamental question as to whether these concentrations of businesses represent a choice or whether they are the outcome of thwarted labour market participation. The latter reflects the considerable data[63] which indicates that there are significant labour market barriers reducing the options for new and especially visible immigrants (combined with the discounting of credentials and experience from particular source countries). As others[64] note, the co-location of businesses utilises the familiar in terms of language, existing networks, cultural and linguistic behaviour, and trusted relationships. If barriers are encountered in the labour market, then the establishment of a small business with low thresholds in terms of capital and experience requirements becomes a viable option. However, this might not apply to all those establishing such businesses. The research reported here cannot answer the question of the extent to which the development of ethnic precincts reflects the forced options available to some, as opposed to the inclinations and desires of others who had always intended to establish a business. The evidence[65] does indicate important barriers and challenges for the immigrants that are the focus here, in both the labour market and in business establishment. Ethnic precincts appear to provide opportunities for those who are otherwise excluded; however, more work needs to be done before any authoritative answer can be provided.

The next question is whether ethnic precincts might be better described as enclaves; that is, are they places where immigrant business owners and their families and descendants become trapped? On the one hand, it can be argued that mobility is constrained after arrival because these locations provide 'early reception areas for recent immigrants'[66] and consequently restrict the opportunities for those immigrants to broaden their networks, experiences and economic options. In this way, ethnic precinct location becomes a permanent state. On the other hand, ethnic precincts offer a space replete with possibilities, as Zhou says of Chinatown in Los Angeles:

> *The area was indeed a place of refuge in its early years but it has evolved since then to become a large ethnic economy of considerable resilience and vigor. It is not only a residential area ... but a veritable enterprise zone.*[67]

This optimistic assessment is echoed elsewhere[68] although some are less convinced.[69] More than a decade has passed since Zhou made the comment above, but she, together with her colleague, Cho, remains confident that ethnic precincts (here referred to as ethnic enclaves as is common in North America) provide a base for socio-economic improvement:

> *... that an enclave economy rather than merely a concentration of ethnic businesses provides a material base for the ethnic community to function effectively ... that the vitality of the ethnic community and its ability to generate tangible and intangible benefits depends largely on the development of the enclave economy.*[70]

For Zhou and Cho, institutional completeness and 'high coethnic closure' does not lead to social isolation but is the base from which immigrant communities develop both community and economic success.[71] Again, this requires further work in the New Zealand context, although such research will be constrained because of the relatively recent arrival of the groups concerned combined with the newness of ethnic precincts. Whether the precincts will sustain and contribute to positive outcomes for immigrants, or will constrain subsequent social mobility or economic success because they are based on small-world networks, is difficult to establish given that most ethnic precincts are barely more than a decade old, at least in their current form.

Finally, there are questions about the institutional and political responsiveness to what has occurred. As Kloosterman and Rath[72] point out, it is important to focus attention on the dynamics that are internal to the community(ies) concerned, while recognising that they do not operate in a vacuum and that structural conditions and political context are equally important. We have claimed that there has, until recently, been limited understanding or recognition of the presence or importance of ethnic precincts by the local authorities or business organisations in Auckland. Although there are preliminary indications that the disinterest of previous Local Territorial Authorities might be replaced by more engagement, this is a transition period for Auckland Council, and significant questions remain. Will there be more substantive political recognition and resourcing? Will regulatory processes acknowledge the requirements of immigrant business activities? Will ethnic precincts become commodified as they have been elsewhere,[73] and transformed into tourist and consumer destinations? As Pang and Rath note:

> *Urban cultural diversity is then a vital resource for the prosperity of cities and a potential catalyst for socio-economic development, particularly since business investors consider this diversity as one of the factors determining the location of businesses.*[74]

Will Auckland's ethnic precincts be seen as a 'brand advantage' and part of the 'strategic niche management'[75] by council agencies such as Auckland Tourism, Events and Economic Development (ATEED), and indeed, by Auckland Council itself?

These and other policy and research questions that arise when considering the development of ethnic precincts in Auckland highlight the importance of understanding the processes that bring immigrants to New Zealand and Auckland, what keeps them here, and the dynamics that determine settlement outcomes. Auckland's ethnic precincts appear to be going from strength to strength and are important contributors to both

Chinese immigrant settlement and to the broader economy of the city. The next decades will provide a better indication of the role and importance of such developments as immigrant and resident communities, those who are active in ethnic precincts, and policy/regulatory organisations like the Auckland Council, all negotiate what it means to be a superdiverse city.

Endnotes

1. James Belich, *Making Peoples: A history of New Zealand*, Auckland: Allen Lane, 1996.
2. James Belich, *Paradise Reforged: A history of the New Zealanders*, Auckland: Allen Lane, 2001, 223–32.
3. Carina Meares, Elsie Ho, Robin Peace and Paul Spoonley, *Bamboo Networks: Chinese employers and employees in Auckland*, Albany: Massey University/ University of Waikato, 2010a.
4. See commentaries on media usage or the language deployed by New Zealand First: Andrew Butcher, '"Well, they're very good citizens": New Zealanders' perceptions of Asians in New Zealand', *Sites: A Journal of Social Anthropology and Cultural Studies* 5, 2, 2008, 5–30; Andrew Butcher and Paul Spoonley, 'Inv-Asian: Print media constructions of Asians and Asian immigration', in Paola Voci and Jacqueline Leckie (eds), *Localising Asia in Aotearoa*, Wellington: Dunmore Publishing, 2011, 98–115.
5. Richard Bedford and Elsie Ho, *Asians in New Zealand: Implications of a changing demography*, Wellington: Asia New Zealand Foundation, 2008.
6. Eric Fong, Wenhong Chen and Chiu Luk, 'A comparison of ethnic businesses in suburbs and city', *City & Community* 6, 2, 2007, 119–36.
7. See John Rex and Robert Moore, *Race, Community and Conflict: A study of Sparkbrook*, London: Oxford University Press, 1967, for material on housing classes in the United Kingdom; or Robert Miles, *Racism*, London: Routledge, 1989).
8. Wei Li, *Ethnoburb: The new ethnic community in urban America*, Honolulu: University of Hawai'i Press, 2009.
9. Rosemary A. Sales, Panos Hatziprokopiou, Xiujing Liang, Nicola Montagna, Alessio D'Angelo, Xia Lin and Flemming Christiansen, *Cityscapes of Diaspora: Images and realities of London's Chinatown*, London: Project Report, Arts and Humanities Research Council (AHRC) London, 2008, 6.
10. Sales et al, *Cityscapes of Diaspora*, 6.
11. Fong, Chen and Luk, 'A comparison of ethnic businesses in suburbs and city', 122.
12. Roger Waldinger, Robin Ward, Howard E. Aldrich and John H. Stanfield, *Ethnic Entrepreneurs: Immigrant business in industrial societies*, Newbury Park, London and New Delhi: Sage Publications, 1990.
13. Ching Lin Pang and Jan Rath, 'The force of regulation in the land of the free: The persistence of Chinatown, Washington DC as a symbolic ethnic enclave', in Martin

Ruef and Michael Lounsbury (eds), *The Sociology of Entrepreneurship: Research in the sociology of organisations*, Amsterdam: Elsevier, 2007, 202–03.
14 Robert Kloosterman and Jan Rath, 'Immigrant entrepreneurs in advanced economies: Mixed embeddedness further explored', *Journal of Ethnic and Migration Studies* 27, 2 , 2001, 189–201; Robert Kloosterman and Jan Rath, *Immigrant Entrepreneurs: Venturing abroad in the age of globalization*, Oxford: Berg, 2003.
15 Paul Spoonley and Carina Meares, 'Laissez-faire multiculturalism and relational embeddedness: Ethnic precincts in Auckland', *Cosmopolitan Civil Societies* 3, 1, 2011, 42–64.
16 Steven Vertovec, *Transnationalism*, London: Routledge, 2009, 37.
17 Meares, Ho, Peace and Spoonley, *Bamboo Networks*; Carina Meares, Elsie Ho, Robin Peace and Paul Spoonley, *Kimchi Networks: Korean employers and employees in Auckland*, Albany: Massey University/University of Waikato, 2010b.
18 Pang and Rath, 'The force of regulation in the land of the free', 205.
19 Belich, *Making Peoples*, 315.
20 Paul Spoonley and Richard Bedford, *Welcome to Our World? Immigration and the remaking of New Zealand*, Auckland: Dunmore Publishing, 2012, 38.
21 Ibid., 127–28.
22 Ibid., 132–36.
23 Melenaite Taumoefolau, 'Tongans', Te Ara – the Encyclopedia of New Zealand: www.TeAra.govt.nz/en/tongans; Misatauveve Melani Anae, 'Samoans', Te Ara – the Encyclopedia of New Zealand: www.TeAra.govt.nz/en/samoans
24 Trudie Cain, Carina Meares, Paul Spoonley and Robin Peace, *Half Way House: The Dominion Road ethnic precinct*, Auckland: Integration of Immigrants Programme, 2011.
25 Ibid.
26 North Shore City, *Northcote Town Centre Plan: A vision for the future*, Auckland: North Shore City, 2010, 20.
27 Parliamentary Library, *Northcote*, Wellington: Parliamentary Library, 2009.
28 This figure includes 44 new townhouses built in June 2010. North Shore City, *Northcote Town Centre Plan*.
29 The Housing New Zealand Corporation manages state-owned houses and tenancies.
30 North Shore City, *Northcote Town Centre Plan*, 30.
31 Simon Collins, 'Helping themselves', *New Zealand Herald*, 30 August 2008, B5.
32 North Shore City, *Northcote Town Centre Plan*, 18.
33 Formerly Woolworths.
34 North Shore City Council, *City Plan 2006–2016*, Auckland: North Shore City, 2006.
35 The eight legacy councils of the Auckland region were amalgamated into one large council in November 2010.
36 North Shore City, *Northcote Town Centre Plan*, 1.
37 Ibid., 13.

38 Simon Collins, 'Helping themselves', B5.
39 See www.auckland.gen.nz/sommerville/ and http://www.meadowlands.co.nz/
40 Those who identify as being of Chinese ethnicity.
41 Jock Collins and Kirrily Jordan, 'Ethnic precincts as ethnic tourism destinations in urban Australia', *Tourism, Culture and Communication*, 9, 2009, 79–92.
42 Sales et al., *Cityscapes of Diaspora*, 6.
43 Pang and Rath, 'The force of regulation in the land of the free'.
44 Sales et al., *Cityscapes of Diaspora*, 6.
45 Brenda Yeoh, *Proceedings of the Ethnic Neighbourhoods as Places of Leisure and Consumption Conference: Session on Singapore's Chinatown: Race definition, nation-building and heritage tourism in a cosmopolitan city*, 17–20 December 2008, Istanbul, 2008, 10.
46 Yeoh, *Proceedings of the Ethnic Neighbourhoods as Places of Leisure and Consumption Conference*.
47 There is a Chinatown in East Auckland, see www.nzchinatown.com/index.en.shtml
48 North Shore City, *Northcote Town Centre Plan*.
49 OMEGA matched skilled immigrants with mentors across a range of industries. It ceased to exist in December 2012.
50 The Royal Commission was charged with beginning the transition of Auckland's eight legacy councils into one single local authority.
51 Established under the Local Government Act 2010, the role of the panel is to communicate to council the views and preferences of the diverse ethnic communities of Auckland. The term of the current panel runs from March 2010 to November 2013. Four sub-committees have been set up by the Ethnic Peoples' Advisory Panel: economic; youth; communication and engagement; and social and community well-being (The Ethnic Peoples' Advisory Panel, 2011).
52 Auckland Council, *Draft Economic Development Strategy*, Auckland: Auckland Council, 2011.
53 Wayne Thompson, 'Mayor: Chinatown is money, not food', *New Zealand Herald*, 18 December 2008: www.nzherald.co.nz/nz/news/article.cfm?c_id=1&objectid=10548644
54 Tze Ming Mok, 'A Chinatown state of mind', (2010): www.publicaddress.net/default,2623.sm#post2623
55 Cain, Meares, Spoonley and Peace, *Half Way House*, 47.
56 Pang and Rath, 'The force of regulation in the land of the free', 207.
57 Kirrily Jordan, 'Multicultural place-making in Australia: Immigration, place and social value', unpublished PhD dissertation, University of Technology, Sydney, 2010, 65.
58 Cited in Jordan, 'Multicultural place-making in Australia', 67.
59 Collins and Jordan, 'Ethnic precincts as ethnic tourism destinations in urban Australia'.
60 Stephen Shaw, Susan Bagwell and Joanna Karmowska, 'Ethnoscapes as spectacle: Reimaging multicultural districts as new destinations for leisure and tourism consumption', *Urban Studies*, 41, 10, 2004, 1983–2000.

61　Ibid.
62　Min Zhou and Myungduk Cho, 'Noneconomic effects of ethnic entrepreneurship: A focused look at the Chinese and Korean enclave economies in Los Angeles', *Thunderbird International Business Review* 52, 2010, 83–96; Fong, Chen and Luk, 'A comparison of ethnic businesses in suburbs and city', 122; Pang and Rath, 'The force of regulation in the land of the free', 207.
63　Including for New Zealand, Carina Meares, Joanna Lewin, Trudie Cain, Paul Spoonley, Robin Peace and Elsie Ho, *Bakkie, Braai and Boerewors: South African employers and employees in Auckland and Hamilton*, Albany: Massey University/University of Waikato, 2011; Joanna Lewin, Carina Meares, Trudie Cain, Paul Spoonley, Robin Peace and Elsie Ho, *Namasté New Zealand: Indian employers and employees in Auckland*, Albany: Massey University/University of Waikato, 2011; Bronwyn Watson, Carina Meares, Paul Spoonley, Trudie Cain, Robin Peace and Elsie Ho, *Bangers 'n' Mash: British employers and employees in Auckland and Hamilton*, Albany: Massey University/University of Waikato, 2011.
64　Fong, Chen and Luk, 'A comparison of ethnic businesses in suburbs and city', 122; Sales et al, *Cityscapes of diaspora*, 6.
65　Meares, Ho, Peace, and Spoonley, *Bamboo Networks*; Meares, Ho, Peace and Spoonley, *Kimchi Networks*.
66　Min Zhou, *Chinatown: The socioeconomic potential of an urban enclave*, Philadelphia: Temple University Press, 1992, xiv.
67　Zhou, *Chinatown*, xiv.
68　Timothy P. Fong, *The First Suburban Chinatown: The remaking of Monterey Park, California*, Philadelphia: Temple University Press, 1994.
69　Peter Kwong, *The New Chinatown*, New York: Hill and Wang, 1996.
70　Zhou and Cho, 'Noneconomic effects of ethnic entrepreneurship', 93.
71　Ibid.
72　Kloosterman and Rath, *Immigrant Entrepreneurs*.
73　See Jock Collins and Kirrily Jordan, 'Ethnic precincts as ethnic tourism destinations in urban Australia', *Tourism, Culture and Communication*, 9 , 2009, 79–92, for a discussion of Australia and ethnic tourism.
74　Pang and Rath, 'The force of regulation in the land of the free', 207.
75　Shaw, Bagwell and Karmowska, 'Ethnoscapes as spectacle', 1986.

Bibliography

Anae, Misatauveve Melani, 'Samoans', Te Ara – the Encyclopedia of New Zealand: www.TeAra.govt.nz/en/samoans

Auckland Council, *Draft Economic Development Strategy*, Auckland: Auckland Council, 2011.

Aytar, Volkan and Jan Rath, *Selling Ethnic Neighborhoods: The rise of neighborhoods as places of leisure and consumption*, New York: Routledge, 2011.

Bedford, Richard and Elsie Ho, *Asians in New Zealand: Implications of a changing demography*, Wellington: Asia New Zealand Foundation, 2008.

Belich, James, *Making Peoples: A history of the New Zealanders from Polynesian settlement to the end of the nineteenth century*, Auckland: Allen Lane, 1996.

Belich, James, *Paradise Reforged: A history of the New Zealanders from the 1880s to the year 2000*, Auckland: Allen Lane, 2001, 223–32.

Butcher, Andrew, '"Well, they're very good citizens": New Zealanders' perceptions of Asians in New Zealand', *Sites: A Journal of Social Anthropology and Cultural Studies* 5, 2, 2008, 5–30.

Butcher, Andrew and Paul Spoonley, 'Inv-asian: Print media constructions of Asians and Asian immigration', in Paola Voci and Jacqueline Leckie (eds), *Localising Asia in Aotearoa*, Wellington: Dunmore Publishing, 2011, 98–115.

Cain, Trudie, Carina Meares, Paul Spoonley and Robin Peace, *Half Way House: The Dominion Road ethnic precinct*, Auckland: Integration of Immigrants Programme, 2011.

Collins, Jock and Kirrily Jordan, 'Ethnic precincts as ethnic tourism destinations in urban Australia', *Tourism, Culture and Communication*, 9, 2009, 79–92.

Collins, Simon, 'Helping themselves', *New Zealand Herald*, 30 August 2008, B5.

Fong, Timothy P., *The First Suburban Chinatown: The remaking of Monterey Park, California*, Philadelphia: Temple University Press, 1994.

Fong, Eric, Wenhong Chen, and Chiu Luk, 'A comparison of ethnic businesses in suburbs and city', *City & Community* 6, 2, 2007, 119–36.

Ip, Manying, 'Chinese immigrants and transnationals in New Zealand: A fortress opened', in Lawrence J.C. Ma and Carolyn Cartier (eds), *The Chinese Diaspora: Space, place, mobility and identity*, Lanham: Rowman and Littlefield, 2003, 339–58.

Jordan, Kirrily, 'Multicultural place-making in Australia: Immigration, place and social value', unpublished PhD dissertation, University of Technology, Sydney, 2010.

Kloosterman, Robert and Rath, Jan, 'Immigrant entrepreneurs in advanced economies: Mixed embeddedness further explored', *Journal of Ethnic and Migration Studies* 27, 2, 2001,189–201.

Kloosterman, Robert and Rath Jan, *Immigrant Entrepreneurs: Venturing abroad in the age of globalization*, Oxford: Berg, 2003.

Kwong, Peter, *The New Chinatown*, New York: Hill and Wang, 1996.

Lewin, Joanna, Carina Meares, Trudie Cain, Paul Spoonley, Robin Peace and Elsie Ho, *Namasté New Zealand: Indian employers and employees in Auckland*, Albany: Massey University/University of Waikato, 2011.

Li, Wei, *Ethnoburb: The new ethnic community in urban America*, Honolulu: University of Hawai'i Press, 2009.

Meares, Carina, Elsie Ho, Robin Peace and Paul Spoonley, *Bamboo Networks: Chinese employers and employees in Auckland*, Albany: Massey University/University of Waikato, 2010a.

Meares, Carina, Elsie Ho, Robin Peace and Paul Spoonley, *Kimchi Networks: Korean employers and employees in Auckland*, Albany: Massey University/University of Waikato, 2010b.

Meares, Carina, Joanna Lewin, Trudie Cain, Paul Spoonley, Robin Peace and Elsie Ho, *Bakkie, Braai and Boerewors: South African employers and employees in Auckland and Hamilton*, Albany: Massey University/University of Waikato, 2011.

Miles, Robert. *Racism*, London: Routledge, 1989.
Mok, Tze Ming, 2010, 'A Chinatown state of mind': www.publicaddress.net/default,2623.sm#post2623
North Shore City Council, *City Plan 2006–2016*, Auckland: North Shore City, 2006.
North Shore City, *Northcote Town Centre Plan: A vision for the future*, Auckland: North Shore City, 2010.
Pang, Ching Lin and Jan Rath, 'The force of regulation in the land of the free: The persistence of Chinatown, Washington DC as a symbolic ethnic enclave', in Martin Ruef and Michael Lounsbury (eds), *The Sociology of Entrepreneurship: Research in the sociology of organisations*, Amsterdam: Elsevier, 2007, 191–215.
Parliamentary Library, *Northcote*, Wellington: Parliamentary Library, 2009.
Rex, John and Robert Moore, *Race, Community and Conflict: A study of Sparkbrook*, London: Oxford University Press, 1967.
Sales, Rosemary A., Panos Hatziprokopiou, Xiujing Liang, Nicola Montagna, Alessio D'Angelo, Xia Lin and Flemming Christiansen, *Cityscapes of Diaspora: Images and realities of London's Chinatown*, London: Project Report, Arts and Humanities Research Council (AHRC), 2008.
Shaw, Stephen, Susan Bagwell and Joanna Karmowska, 'Ethnoscapes as spectacle: Reimaging multicultural districts as new destinations for leisure and tourism consumption', *Urban Studies*, 41, 10, 2004, 1983–2000.
Spoonley, Paul and Richard Bedford, *Welcome to Our World? Immigration and the remaking of New Zealand*, Auckland: Dunmore Publishing, 2012.
Spoonley, Paul and Andrew Butcher, 'Reporting superdiversity: The mass media and immigration in New Zealand', *Journal of Intercultural Studies* 30, 4, 2009, 355–72.
Spoonley, Paul and Carina Meares, 'Laissez-faire multiculturalism and relational embeddedness: Ethnic precincts in Auckland', *Cosmopolitan Civil Societies* 3, 1, 2011, 42–64.
Taumoefolau, Melenaite, 'Tongans', Te Ara – the Encyclopedia of New Zealand: www.TeAra.govt.nz/en/tongans
The Ethnic Peoples' Advisory Panel, *The Voice 1*, Auckland: Auckland Council, 2011.
Thompson, Wayne, 'Mayor: Chinatown is money, not food', *New Zealand Herald*, 18 December 2008: www.nzherald.co.nz/nz/news/article.cfm?c_id=1&objectid=10548644
Vertovec, Steven, *Transnationalism*, London: Routledge, 2009.
Waldinger, Roger, Robin Ward, Howard E. Aldrich and John H. Stanfield, *Ethnic Entrepreneurs: Immigrant business in industrial societies*, Newbury Park, London and New Delhi: Sage Publications, 1990.
Watson, Bronwyn, Carina Meares, Paul Spoonley, Trudie Cain, Robin Peace and Elsie Ho, *Bangers 'n' Mash: British employers and employees in Auckland and Hamilton*, Albany: Massey University/University of Waikato, 2011.
Yeoh, Brenda, *Proceedings of the Ethnic Neighbourhoods as Places of Leisure and Consumption Conference: Session on Singapore's Chinatown: Race definition, nation-building and heritage tourism in a cosmopolitan city, December 17–20, 2008*, Istanbul, 2008.

Zhou, Min, *Chinatown: The socioeconomic potential of an urban enclave*, Philadelphia: Temple University Press, 1992.
Zhou, Min and Myungduk Cho, 'Non-economic effects of ethnic entrepreneurship: A focused look at the Chinese and Korean enclave economies in Los Angeles', *Thunderbird International Business Review* 52, 2010, 83–96.

10. Valuing Multiculturalism
Business engagement with the challenge of multiculturalism

TIM BEAL, VAL LINDSAY AND KALA RETNA

The debate surrounding multiculturalism has become prominent in recent times. Opinions on the costs and benefits of multiculturalism are being voiced at a societal level around the globe, and academic literature contains a rich array of research and scholarly views on the topic. In this chapter, we first present a brief review of the literature and media sources on the issue of multiculturalism at a national economic and cultural-societal level. We then consider findings from the literature on the role of multiculturalism in business, as we consider this to be a major contributor to a country's economic improvement. We are particularly concerned with the question of how New Zealand businesses and government departments interact with multiculturalism in the context of their involvement in international markets. Specifically, we seek to understand the extent to which they both utilise the talents of immigrants from Asia in their endeavours to develop their business in Asian markets; our particular focus is China and India. We draw on established literature to help examine this question, and illustrate these findings with quotes from a range of participants involved in our empirical work. This provides a basis for understanding how the activities and perspectives observed in these organisations in New Zealand relate to the international perspectives of multiculturalism at an organisational level.

The empirical work presented in this chapter derives from a larger study involving an investigation into the internationalisation of 70 New Zealand firms into China and India, using a qualitative, interview-based approach.[1] We will not elaborate on the details of this study here, but instead will focus on the engagement of New Zealand firms with migrants in New Zealand from these countries. The chapter concludes with some reflections on the findings and offers conclusions on the overarching research context, namely valuing multiculturalism at a business and government level in New Zealand.

Critics of multiculturalism

The rapid growth of immigration that has accompanied the reduction of national boundaries within some of the world's largest trade blocs has led to the re-emergence of old concerns about the effects of immigrant workers on a country's own 'native' workforce.[2] According to some researchers, this has tended to lead to a backlash against multiculturalism.[3]

Many argue that multiculturalism is under attack. Scarcely a day goes past without news of clashes between religions, sects or ethnicities. Both fringe political parties and, increasingly, mainstream parties around the world (such as in the 2012 French presidential election debates) have condemned multiculturalism, calling for an end to immigration and the preservation of 'traditional values'. Critics of multiculturalism point to its role among the causes of a number of violent and socially divisive situations, such as the London bombings of 2005, the 2001 riots in British mill towns, the murder of film-maker Theo van Gogh in the Netherlands in 2004, and the Norway massacre of 2011. Many critics question whether these events are in part the result of too much tolerance of cultural diversity.[4]

In some societies, multiculturalism has been pronounced a 'failure', often by leaders of nations that once encouraged inflows of cheap immigrant labour. For example, German Chancellor Angela Merkel caused a stir in 2010 with a speech at Potsdam. According to Matthew Weaver of the *Guardian*:

> ... *[Merkel] courted growing anti-immigrant opinion in Germany by claiming the country's attempts to create a multicultural society have 'utterly failed'.*
>
> *Speaking to a meeting of young members of her Christian Democratic Union party, Merkel said the idea of people from different cultural backgrounds living happily 'side by side' did not work. She said the onus was on immigrants to do more to integrate into German society. 'This [multicultural] approach has failed, utterly failed,' Merkel told the meeting in Potsdam, west of Berlin, yesterday. Her remarks will stir a debate about immigration in a country which is home to around 4 million Muslims.*[5]

In Britain the BBC reported a similar sentiment from Prime Minister David Cameron:

David Cameron strode firmly into a debate where many politicians tread timidly ...

It is the first time he has spoken so directly as prime minister, but there are echoes of what has gone before. Tony Blair edged away from multiculturalism in the years after the 7/7 bombings in London, and his ministers moved to stop funding any community organisation that did not challenge extremism. And what of Gordon Brown's continual quest to strengthen 'Britishness'?[6]

Concerns about immigration and the effects of multiculturalism are also gaining momentum in the US, Canada and other parts of the European Union, where freedom of cross-border migration has facilitated increased immigration into many countries previously less accessible, and from a more diverse range of source countries. Typical among host-country concerns about multicultural immigration are the fiscal costs to the host country (including social welfare costs), and the potential accentuation of high unemployment levels.[7] Maria Aguirre suggests that sources of conflict concerning multicultural immigration at a national level arise from '... a misperception of the economic impact ... the impact on the receiving culture, and the difficulty found in harmonizing civil and political rights of minorities and majorities'.[8]

To a certain extent New Zealand is insulated from the deeper tensions of countries such as Germany and Britain, but, as some have pointed out, this should not encourage complacency. Kate McMillan noted that 'immigration and multiculturalism [have not] become the wedge issues they became in Australia, the United States and across Europe', not because of 'good management' but because of a 'less challenging set of circumstances'.[9]

Recently the sale of the Crafar farms – New Zealand's largest family-owned dairy business – to a Chinese conglomerate raised tensions throughout New Zealand society and brought the immigration and multiculturalism debate back into the forefront of political issues.[10] Apprehensions about Chinese immigration stretch back to the nineteenth century, but in contemporary New Zealand these have been supplemented by concerns about the effect on house prices, particularly in Auckland, and the impact on the social security and health systems. There has been resistance to Chinese involvement in forestry and mining, the transfer of manufacturing to China, and the effect of imports from China on local production. The sale of farmland to foreigners has been particularly contentious and, in our opinion, exceeded any rational calculation of costs and benefits, both actual and potential. Perhaps farmland is seen as the core attribute of the New Zealand myth, the place where the real Kiwi, a lonely individual, battles adversity to wrest a living from the land with few resources other than a supportive family, hard work, ingenuity and a little No 8 wire.[11] The sale of the Crafar farms was seen and portrayed as violating the New Zealand dream.[12]

Defence of multiculturalism

While multiculturalism has its critics, others offer perspectives in defence of the concept. Influential defenders of multiculturalism, such as Will Kymlicka, claim that the social and economic benefits of cultural diversity resulting from migration should be embraced.[13] Considerable research has been conducted into the economic effects of multicultural immigration, including its impacts on employment, income distribution and the welfare state of the host country. Contrary to the widely held view that immigration is detrimental to indigenous employment, research results consistently show no negative effects on employment and wages at the macro-economic level.[14]

At an organisational level much has been written about the human capital gains of multiculturalism, in particular the economic benefits of greater access to the wide-ranging and diverse talents of people from around the world. Jenny Hoobler posits, 'It is time for organisations to understand how to utilize all of the talent available to them.'[15]

Some defenders of multiculturalism conceptualise it as a 'counter-hegemony' movement and an enabler of intellectual and demographic diversity.[16] Extending this argument, Schubert suggests that a more constructive way of viewing the effects of multiculturalism is through the use of Pierre Bourdieu's concept of 'symbolic violence', which refers to 'the ways in which daily practices produce and foster domination, including those of the dominated themselves'.[17] Schubert claims multiculturalism must be supported in order to avoid societies and individuals succumbing to the negative effects of symbolic violence.

While supporting multiculturalism as an important concept, others propose new ways of looking at multiculturalism. For example, Modood suggests the idea of 'civic multiculturalism', which argues for the incorporation of democratic and civic values into the concept.[18] In a similar vein, Rodríguez-García advocates what he terms 'interculturalism', which 'reconciles cultural diversity with social cohesion'.[19]

In New Zealand multiculturalism receives support from the government through the work of a number of government agencies as well as specialist organisations, such as the Office of Ethnic Affairs and the Asia New Zealand Foundation (ANZF). The latter defines itself as 'a non-partisan and non-profit organisation dedicated to building New Zealanders' knowledge and understanding of Asia'.[20] Notwithstanding several public incidents exposing anti-immigration sentiments and intolerance of foreign cultures in New Zealand, particularly relating to Asia,[21] and on-going questions about New Zealand's multicultural position,[22] the country still enjoys good relations with its main Asian trading markets. As Mervin Singham, director of New Zealand's Office of Ethnic Affairs notes, the potential trade benefits for New Zealand from Asia's (notably China and India) impressive growth can be greatly enhanced if the country draws more on the talent and human capital of Asian immigrants living in New Zealand. He highlights that 'multiculturalism brings the globe within our borders', but cautions that New Zealand must put in place strategies to ensure that it gains from the opportunities offered by its multicultural society.[23]

A report resulting from the New Zealand government-initiated forum 'Seriously Asia' supports the need for more proactive engagement with multiculturalism in New Zealand, stating, 'We need to tap more effectively into the skills and networks of our Asian migrants. Asian communities, both new and old, bring Asia-relevant skills and connections to the regions.'[24] The challenge, from a business perspective, is to move from the representation of New Zealand as a country that values the cultural backgrounds of its citizens, to one that actually utilises those assets. In particular there is the use of the diaspora to project New Zealand into foreign markets.

Multiculturalism at a business level

Aguirre explains that culturally diverse immigration can contribute to a nation's economic efficiency by directly impacting on business practice. She identifies a number of ways in which this happens: business managers, through their migrant employees, gain cultural awareness and knowledge that is useful in export markets and for developing new culturally adapted goods and services for the domestic market; productivity is increased with lower absenteeism and turnover of workers; creativity is promoted through

Max Ma and Grace Gao of the Beijing office of the Christchurch-based company Commtest Instruments, 12 May 2010. Tim Beal

cultural diversity; and the flexibility of the firm is enhanced by virtue of the variety of talents, languages and thinking processes that comes from a multicultural workforce.[25]

In a study of US multinationals, Hoobler addresses the question of the extent to which multiculturalism is embraced by organisations, and the effectiveness of organisational diversity programmes. Following Foucault, Hoobler suggests that organisations traditionally internalise values of conformity and homogenisation[26] and states, 'the homogenisation of individuals is central to the philosophy of the modern organisation.'[27] She concludes that the multiculturalism efforts of modern US organisations are simply paying lip-service to the concept. This perspective is further explained by Lois Foster and David Stockley, who indicate that cultural pluralism threatens the power and class differences of modern organisations.[28]

In categorising immigrants and considering the extent of social embeddedness in their home and host countries, Xiaohua Lin identifies four types of immigrant that characterise four corresponding types of immigrant economic adaptation.[29] Three are particularly relevant to our study because they interact in some capacity with host country businesses:

namely, immigrant employees, returnee business people and transnational entrepreneurs. According to Lin, immigrant employees are employed in the mainstream economy of their host country, and tend to have quite strong social embeddedness. Returnee business people, sometimes referred to as 'returnee migrants'[30] or 'contemporary diasporic entrepreneurs',[31] are immigrants who have resettled in their home country but retain an affiliation with their former host country or countries. Although 'dually' embedded in both home and host country, they tend to be aligned more with the home country. Transnational entrepreneurs are immigrants engaged in business activities involving both host and home countries. They remain domiciled in the host country but committed to their home country, and usually establish business links across both countries.

Multiculturalism in New Zealand business

In this section, we explore these three immigrant types in more detail, drawing from the established literature and the interview data from our study of New Zealand firms. Specifically, we examine the ways in which businesses in New Zealand, in the context of their business engagement with China and India, interact with each of these immigrant types.

Immigrant employees

Henry Chung, Peter Enderwick and Jinda Naruemitmongkonsuk have examined the influence of immigrant employees within New Zealand's international service sector.[32] They show that firms utilised an immigrant employee's knowledge, social networks and contacts while conducting business in the employee's country of origin. This is termed the 'immigrant employee effect'.

In our study, we found that some managers doing business in China enjoyed the benefits of having an employee with experience in both China and New Zealand, as well as in the industry. Managers indicated that these employees can create a valuable resource for the business, for example by communicating with Chinese customers in the New Zealand office, as well as advising on operations in China:

> *[Our employee in NZ] is of Chinese descent, born there, has been ... schooled here and also went to university here, and he's been in multiple areas in the business. He's grounded in the industry and he's grounded*

in both China and New Zealand. He understands both cultures really well and, from our perspective, I guess we can learn a lot from that as well. And when it comes to an issue where we do need to pick up the phone, or ... where an understanding is important, particularly when it comes to language, he's the best person to have. He can speak Mandarin and Cantonese as well.[33]

The importance of having Chinese staff on the company's payroll has been of great value to one New Zealand company in the tourism industry: 'It's made an enormous difference to our business. It's been a big investment for us but it has been well worth it.'

In other cases, New Zealand managers with business connections in India have deliberately sought the talent and experience of Indian immigrants for employment in their firms:

... a lot of these guys are very well educated. A guy who is coming out of university there has gone through an extremely stringent competitive process ... So he's quite intellectual, he's got a lot of training, a lot of dexterity, a lot of capacity. We've got five Indians right now in [our branch in] Auckland. Every one [of them] has got a Masters in computer science or a Bachelors in engineering or computer science. So they're fairly well qualified and it's quite important to recognise that kind of skill set being available here, as well as the experience of these people. Quite a lot of the guys we have here worked in other countries – two of them have worked in the US, one in the UK and another one has just finished a project in the Middle East in Dubai.

The 'immigrant employee effect' is the impact of an immigrant's knowledge of their country of origin on the performance and strategy of the firm in which they are employed. Firms in service industries have a primary reliance on the provision of high-quality performance in order to succeed in their foreign markets. In addition, they require a good understanding of customers' preferences, cultures and local customs in these markets – aspects with which immigrant employees from these countries will be familiar. Research findings suggest that cultural understanding appears to be the primary contribution of immigrant employees.[34]

In the context of New Zealand and China, our study found that many New Zealand managers have deliberately sought Chinese nationals or New Zealanders with strong Chinese language and cultural fluency for employment in their New Zealand office, or to represent them in China. According to one manager from an electronics company:

> ... there were times when we deliberately aimed to employ Chinese-speaking people. Now whether that happened to have been a Kiwi who just spoke fluent Chinese, that would have been okay but, you know, we aim to hire people fluent in the language and the culture.

Immigrant employees also have a strong influence on creating and maintaining customer relationships, and their home-based social network links are important for trust and solidarity. They can also assist in adapting the firm's marketing strategy to local market (immigrant home-country) conditions.

A number of managers in our study recognised the talent available from the large number of Chinese graduates in New Zealand, and aimed to recruit and nurture appropriately skilled graduates. Having Chinese staff available in the New Zealand office as well as in China has helped some firms enormously by improving communications and overall customer service with Chinese customers. The manager of a software company noted:

> You can actually leverage off the skills of all these ... Chinese students ... we've got Chinese-speaking staff here in Auckland and in our London office, manning help desks and things like that. We're seriously considering recruiting for our Chinese office in Auckland and actually saying, 'Having finished your degree, do you want to go home to a job?' ... we are using the diaspora, which is here in New Zealand. And we intend to use it more ... We have quite a United Nations of staff.

Sometimes there is a multiplier effect, where the links of immigrant employees into their local ethnic community bolsters the performance of their employer. For instance, in the education sector, some New Zealand managers reported that local Indian communities in New Zealand helped with student recruitment into programmes at their institutions:

> ... we have a local Indian agency here and they're active in the Indian market. They've been active in recruiting a number of our students.

Chung indicates that the immigrant employee effect can help firms expedite their learning process about the foreign market. Immigrant employees can be hired to overcome differences between home and host countries, confirming the view that they contribute knowledge and reduce uncertainty.³⁵ One Chinese immigrant employee described her experiences and the benefits she was able to provide the New Zealand firm for which she worked:

> *There was a recruitment agent, and I was looking for a job after graduation. And at that point in time they were really looking for a Chinese person that had an education in New Zealand ... because ... the company knew it would be moving to China at some stage. And I just jumped up and they found me, and then we had a chat. And I thought at the time that it will be quite a good move for them as well, and for me to show ... not only my professional expertise but also ... my Chinese background. And that I can probably do something more than other New Zealanders can do. So it was a good opportunity for me, so then I decided to join [the company], and that was in 2005 ... I have started as a developer in the company, software development, and slowly moved on to help [the CEO] with the trade shows and with customer prospects – Chinese prospects here in China.*³⁶

Transnational entrepreneurs

Alejandro Portes, Guarnizo and Haller identify a transnational entrepreneur as a self-employed immigrant whose firm's success depends on their contacts and associates in another country, primarily their country of origin.³⁷

Transnational entrepreneurs rely on physical and virtual social networks between their host and home countries to create new opportunities, and often position others to act as intermediaries, usually in their home market. As such, transnational entrepreneurs are uniquely positioned to identify customers, distribution infrastructure providers and finance, for their own and others' businesses. Transnational entrepreneurs are generally seen as an elite, qualified, experienced and successful group.³⁸ This perception is exemplified by a number of the managers in our study.

Many business people of Indian descent living in New Zealand have networks in India that may be of direct value to New Zealand firms, such as the following consultant:

> *I'm a partner in this business, and I also have business interests back in India. And some of my childhood friends are now leading lawyers in India, and that's quite useful because they operate in the corporate world.*

They can act as conduits to introduce New Zealand managers to business people in India. They can take them through the legal minefield and all the regulation in India.

Many New Zealand managers that we interviewed saw innovation as key to gaining a competitive advantage in India. They indicated that Indian companies frequently seek innovation, as well as ways to improve their existing products and services and co-develop new offerings. The role of Indian business people in New Zealand in linking New Zealand managers with potential customers in India is seen to be extremely beneficial, as explained by this education consultant in India:

So you know, doing business in India gives India access to New Zealand innovation, but also gives New Zealand businesses access to India, to the Indian market. That's a role we can play – in connecting New Zealand firms with firms in India.

Our study found that, although not generally self-employed, researchers in the education sector otherwise display similar characteristics to transnational entrepreneurs. For example, some education sector participants in our study highlighted the research links that are often established between New Zealand and Indian universities. According to one education consultant in India:

There are research relationships that are active in India, but they're more often driven by the Indian diaspora members in New Zealand institutions, who can connect back into their own system, or what was their own system.

Returnee migrants

There is extensive literature on return migration, specifically concerning the issues and challenges returnees face before, during and after returning to their country of origin.[39] Some literature suggests that migration has multiple effects on returnee migrants, including return preparedness, re-employment, re-embedding and engagement with social networks.[40] Disorientation is not uncommon, and the nature of the confusion produced by conflicting identities is not merely a matter of cultural displacement – it is also very much embedded in the historical and evolving relationship between the countries involved.[41]

Several managers in our study expressed caution about the wisdom of employing a Chinese person in New Zealand if there was any intention to relocate that person to China as a company representative. They noted the difficulties these employees often face when returning to their home country, including dislocation from former networks and problems with realising expectations for themselves and their families. One design manager observed:

> [Our employee] spent three months here with us. She'd been working for a New Zealand company for a couple of years, she had a business degree, she had New Zealand experience, her English was flawless, and she was looking to go back to China. So we brought her in here for three months, and we liked her. She went to China and she panicked. She completely panicked. She was suddenly floundering, and within a month she resigned. She certainly had to go back to parental expectations and possibly she wasn't used to the level of, I guess, disregard that she faced, and she wasn't credible in the role.

This lack of credibility faced by returnee migrants in China can also be a result of the perception of New Zealand: although held in high esteem as a 'clean, green' country with beautiful scenery, New Zealand is not usually recognised in China as a place from which high-tech products and innovation emanate.[42]

> I think New Zealand companies should do much more promotion work ... In the [eyes] of ordinary Chinese people, New Zealand is a tourist destination. They are not business partners, because if you ask the Chinese people [what] country [they] want to do business with, they will choose America, Canada, Japan, Germany or even Australia, but for New Zealand they all said 'it's a beautiful country to spend holidays'.[43]

Some New Zealand managers in our study tried to ensure that their immigrant employees were well prepared for their role of representing the company in their country of origin. For example, a number employed Chinese graduates in their New Zealand operations before relocating them to China, to ensure that the employees developed company loyalty and a good understanding of the business to transfer to the market. One manager from an engineering consulting company said, 'If we can employ a key Chinese graduate, a Chinese national who has an aspiration to work in New Zealand for a period and then return to China, that's absolutely appropriate.' In another firm, a software company, an employee was appointed to run the office in China. She had been resident in New Zealand since she was 16 and travelled on a New Zealand passport.

Choosing the right people and providing them with the opportunity to use their talents in China has been a rewarding and successful strategy for some New Zealand managers:

He [a Chinese postgraduate] approached us and said he was looking to go back to China. His objective was to represent some New Zealand companies in China. We gave him a business card and he got us our first job in China.

The education sector tends to draw quite strongly on the Chinese diaspora. For example, many institutions in this sector employ Chinese graduates of New Zealand tertiary institutions to assist market expansion in China, as well as to bring Chinese graduates and New Zealand businesses together. Some of these former students remain in New Zealand to assist student and agent support services, while others return to China to assist in the market. A spokesperson for one educational institution noted:

We certainly have had our alumni becoming agents and working as agents on an on-going basis, or else introducing us to other agents or to other institutions. A lot of our marketing staff are our former students – we get first cut. They know the institution and they know at least one programme quite well, and, because they're often fairly recent graduates, they're more of the age group that can work with the students once they're here. Our marketing team really has two functions – servicing the agents, and also, either in the marketing division of student services or the administration area, to support Chinese students here. They are so valuable to us because [of] their knowledge of us and what we do ... they love New Zealand.

Some New Zealand firms undertaking business in India utilise the talents of the Indian diaspora in New Zealand. These include returnee Indian staff employed to manage branch or representative offices, who have had experience working for the company in New Zealand, as in this engineering company:

XXX is from India. He has worked in the company in New Zealand for two years, and [has] managed the installation in India during the last year. He has been our main person in this site. We're now doing a hand-over to a local Indian engineer, who will run our service office there.

Val Lindsay with Ashish Hemrajani of Bigtree Entertainment, Mumbai, which markets the cinema booking software of New Zealand company Vista Entertainment Solutions in India. Tim Beal

Potential for greater utilisation of diasporic links

These examples illustrate the effective engagement by New Zealand managers with multicultural immigrants in their businesses, and reflect mutual and varied benefits. By tapping into the New Zealand diaspora of various nationalities, New Zealand businesses gain access to valuable knowledge relating to the immigrants' countries of origin, as well as industry-related talent and networks of business counterparts in their home markets. The immigrant population gains access to employment, new cultural experiences, industry knowledge and, often, opportuntities to return to their country of origin as a representative of the New Zealand company for which they have worked. In addition, for transnational entrepreneurs, engagement with New Zealand firms provides further business opportunities.

While our study demonstrates relatively widespread utilisation of links with multicultural diaspora by New Zealand managers, many noted the considerable potential for wider and deeper engagement with diaspora by

New Zealand business. A number of managers acknowledged the valuable resource of people of Indian descent in New Zealand that is not being adequately tapped, while others highlighted the importance of the Chinese diaspora in assisting New Zealand's efforts to engage in China, particularly in the future. For example, they noted the opportunity to draw more heavily on Chinese people in New Zealand, particularly those who wish to return to China to work with New Zealand firms in the market. As the representative of one agritech company said:

> ... our best opportunity [in China] as a nation is all the Chinese who have come to immigrate to New Zealand. Once they have been in New Zealand for a while, and understand the way we do business, and our culture, and maybe see things as from a New Zealand perspective – they are the people who may be the best to go back – and certainly if they have the language.

Conclusion

The role and benefits of multiculturalism are widely debated. While a number of commentators suggest that multiculturalism has 'failed' because of its perceived connection with political and social unrest, others indicate that multiculturalism is essential for maintaining and enhancing world trade, political stability and cultural awareness, particularly among the younger generation.

Through examining the contemporary literature and relevant media reports on multiculturalism, we have noted the importance of national-level awareness and support for multiculturalism in achieving the economic and socio-cultural gains that have been reported. It is clear that an informed society, along with government-led initiatives that proactively manage the challenges and opportunities of multiculturalism, can lead to benefits on a societal level.

Multiculturalism presents New Zealand business with particular challenges, opportunities and responsibilities. A workforce of varied ethnicities, religions and cultures is more difficult to manage, but both the literature and our research suggest that it is possible to do this well, and in doing so to realise the benefits inherent in diversity. As a small, open economy seeking to engage globally, it is important that we endeavour to leverage domestic multiculturalism in order to interact knowledgeably and smartly with our overseas markets and embed ourselves into their economies, so that we grow as they grow. The more we can harness the resource of increasing multiculturalism, the better we will engage in the complex, demanding, but profitable markets that lie offshore.

Many firms in New Zealand are proactively engaging with multiculturalism through interaction with immigrant employees, transnational entrepreneurs and returnee migrants, and enjoying enhanced business opportunities as a result. Our findings suggest that the potential for more widespread engagement is substantial.

Endnotes

1. Lindsay, Val, Vivienne Shaw, Tim Beal, Malcolm Cone, Fergus McLean, Michel Rod and Nick Ashill, *Service Success in Asia*, Wellington: Victoria University of Wellington, 2011.
2. Maria S. Aguirre, 'Multiculturalism in a labour market with integrated economies', *Management Decision* 35, 7–8, 1997, 489–98.
3. Dan Rodríguez-García, 'Beyond assimilation and multiculturalism: A critical review of the debate on managing diversity', *Journal of International Migration and Integration / Revue de l'intégration et de la migration internationale* 11, 3, 2010, 251–71.
4. Ibid., 254.
5. Matthew Weaver, 'Angela Merkel: German multiculturalism has "utterly failed"', *Guardian*, 17 October 2010.
6. Laura Kuenssberg, 'Analysis [of Cameron's multiculturalism speech]', BBC, 5 February 2011.
7. Aguirre, 'Multiculturalism in a labour market with integrated economies', 35.
8. Ibid., 493.
9. Kate McMillan, 'The politics of immigration and multiculturalism in New Zealand', *Policy Network*, 16 November 2010.
10. Editorial, 'Apology to Chinese should be end of it', *New Zealand Herald*, 14 February 2002; John Hartevelt, 'Accusations of "weak-kneed leadership" on Crafar', *Dominion Post*, 27 January 2012.
11. No. 8 wire was reputedly widely used to repair imported products and machinery for which spare parts were unavailable. It has entered the New Zealand lexicon as a symbol of ingenuity and self-reliance.
12. Tim Beal and Yuanfei Kang, 'Barriers to New Zealand–China economic integration: A case of the dairy industry and beyond', *New Zealand Journal of Asian Studies* 15, 2, June 2013, 1–18.
13. Will Kymlicka, *Multicultural Citizenship: A liberal theory of minority rights*, Oxford: Oxford University Press, 1995. Cited in Sarah Song, 'Majority norms,

multiculturalism, and gender equality', *American Political Science Review*, 99, 4, 2005, iii–viiii.
14 See for example George J. Borjas, Richard B. Freeman and Lawrence F. Katz, 'On the labor markets effects of immigration and trade', in George J. Borjas and Richard B. Freeman (eds), *Immigration and the Work Force: economic consequences for the United States and source areas*, Chicago, IL: University of Chicago Press, 1992; Klaus F. Zimmermann, 'Tackling the European migration problem', *Journal of Economic Perspectives* 9, 2, 1995, 24–62. Cited in Aguirre, 'Multiculturalism in a labour market with integrated economies'.
15 Jenny M. Hoobler, 'Lip service to multiculturalism: Docile bodies of the modern organization', *Journal of Management Inquiry*, 14, 1, 2005, 49–56, 54.
16 Jung Min Choi and John W. Murphy, *The Politics and Philosophy of Political Correctness*, Westport, CT: Praeger, 1992. Cited in Daniel J. Schubert, 'Defending multiculturalism. From hegemony to symbolic violence', *The American Behavioral Scientist* 45, 7, 2002, 1088–102.
17 Schubert, 'Defending multiculturalism. From hegemony to symbolic violence', 1088.
18 Tariq Modood, *Multiculturalism*, Cambridge: Polity Press, 2007.
19 Rodríguez-García, 'Beyond assimilation and multiculturalism', 271.
20 www.asianz.org.nz
21 Martin Kay, 'Dikshit giggles: New Henry drama', 6 October 2010: www.stuff.co.nz
22 Mervin Singham, 'Multiculturalism in New Zealand – the need for a new paradigm', *Aotearoa Ethnic Network Journal* 1, 1, 2006, 33–37.
23 Ibid., 37.
24 *Our Future with Asia*, Wellington: Ministry of Foreign Affairs and Trade, 2007.
25 Aguirre, 'Multiculturalism in a labour market with integrated economies', 35.
26 Michael Foucault, *Discipline and Punish: The birth of the prison*, New York: Vintage Books, 1995.
27 Hoobler, 'Lip service to multiculturalism', 53.
28 Lois Foster and David Stockley, *Multiculturalism: The changing Australian paradigm*, Avon: Multilingual Matters, 1984. Cited in Hoobler, 'Lip service to multiculturalism', 54.
29 Xiaohua Lin, 'The diaspora solution to innovation capacity development: Immigrant entrepreneurs in the contemporary world,' *Thunderbird International Business Review* 52, 2, 2010, 124–36.
30 J. Edward Taylor and T.J. Wyatt, 'The shadow value of migrant remittances, income and inequality in a household-farm economy', *The Journal of Development Studies* 32, 6, 1996, 899.
31 Lin, 'The diaspora solution to innovation capacity development', 124.
32 Henry F.L. Chung, Peter Enderwick and Jinda Naruemitmongkonsuk, 'Immigrant employee effects in international strategy: An exploratory study of international service firms', *International Marketing Review* 27, 6, 2010, 652–75.
33 New Zealand logistics company. Unless otherwise mentioned, all the companies cited in this research are New Zealand-owned. For reasons of confidentiality the company name is not given, but the industry sector is specified.

34 Chung, Enderwick and Naruemitmongkonsuk, 'Immigrant employee effects in international strategy'.
35 Henry F.L. Chung, 'Contribution of immigrant employees to international marketing standardisation strategies selection: An exploratory study', *European Journal of Marketing* 42, 1/2, 2008, 16–22.
36 Software company – China representative office.
37 Alejandro Portes, Luis Eduardo Guarnizo and William J. Haller, 'Transnational entrepreneurs: An alternative form of immigrant economic adaptation', *American Sociological Review* 67, 2, 2002, 278–98.
38 Portes, Guarnizo and Haller, 'Transnational entrepreneurs'.
39 Jean-Pierre Cassarino, 'Theorising return migration: The conceptual approach to return migrants revisited', *International Journal of Multicultural Societies* 6, 2, 2004, 253–79; Oded Stark, *The Migration of Labor*, Cambridge: Basil Blackwell, 1991.
40 Erik Mobrand, 'Mobilization or repression of migrants in urban China? Hometown networks, leadership, and lessons from international and historical comparisons', *The Journal of Comparative Asian Development* 6, 2, 2007, 337–61.
41 Ruhi Khalid, 'Changes in perception of gender roles: Returned migrants', *Pakistan Journal of Social and Clinical Psychology* 9, 1–2, 2011, 16–20.
42 Fonterra's quality problems in 2013 clearly had an effect on Chinese perceptions of New Zealand dairy products but it is uncertain whether they had more than a marginal impact on the lack of high-tech image discussed here. Nevertheless, New Zealand's country image, and the regulatory structures that must underpin it, is a multi-faceted issue which requires further research and serious attention from government and business. See 'NZ businesses still suffering from botulism scare', *TV One News*, 15 September 2013: www.tvnz.co.nz/business-news/nz-businesses-still-suffering-botulism-scare-5584739; 'Commentary. New Zealand needs to start building trust in the long-term' *China Daily*, 5 August 2013: www.chinadaily.com.cn/xinhua/2013-08-05/content_9769307.html. Many Chinese in New Zealand took to social media in China to defend the reputation of their adopted country; 'Chinese Kiwis defend New Zealand on social media', *VicNews*, 15 August 2013: www.victoria.ac.nz/home/about/newspubs/news/newslatest#a203078
43 Returnee Chinese manager.

Bibliography

Aguirre, Maria, 'Multiculturalism in a labour market with integrated economies', *Management Decision* 35, no. 7–8, 1997, 489–98.

Beal, Tim and Yuanfei Kang, 'Barriers to New Zealand–China economic integration: A case of the dairy industry and beyond', *New Zealand Journal of Asian Studies* 15, no. 2, June 2013.

Borjas, G, R.B. Freeman and L.F. Katz, 'On the labor market effects of immigration and trade', in G. Borjas and R. Freeman (eds), *Immigration and the Work Force: Economic consequences for the United States and source areas*, Chicago, IL: The University of Chicago Press, 1992, 213–44.

Cassarino, J.P., 'Theorising return migration: The conceptual approach to return migrants revisited', *International Journal of Multicultural Societies* 6, no. 2, 2004, 253–80.

'Chinese Kiwis defend New Zealand on social media', *VicNews*, 15 August 2013: www.victoria.ac.nz/home/about/newspubs/news/newslatest#a203078

Choi, J.M. and J.W Murphy, *The Politics and Philosophy of Political Correctness*, Westport, CT: Praeger, 1992.

Chung, H.F.L., 'Contribution of immigrant employees to international marketing standardisation strategies selection: An exploratory study', *European Journal of Marketing* 42, no. 1/2, 2008, 16–22.

Chung, Henry F.L., Peter Enderwick and Jinda Naruemitmongkonsuk, 'Immigrant employee effects in international strategy', *International Marketing Review* 27, no. 6, 2010.

Editorial, 'Apology to Chinese should be end of it', *New Zealand Herald*, 14 February 2002.

'Commentary. New Zealand needs to start building trust in the long-term', *China Daily*, 5 August 2013: www.chinadaily.com.cn/xinhua/2013-08-05/content_9769307.html

Foster, L. and D. Stockley, *Multiculturalism: The changing Australian paradigm*, Avon, UK: Multilingual Matters, 1984.

Foucault, M., *Discipline and Punish: The birth of the prison*, New York: Vintage Books, 1995.

Hartevelt, John, 'Accusations of "weak-kneed leadership" on Crafar', *Dominion Post*, 27 January 2012.

Hoobler, J.M., 'Lip service to multiculturalism: Docile bodies of the modern organization', *Journal of Management Inquiry* 14, no. 1, 2005, 49–56.

Kay, Martin, 'Dikshit giggles: new Henry drama', 6 October 2010: www.stuff.co.nz/entertainment/tv-radio/4203109/Dikshit-giggles-New-Henry-drama

Khalid, Ruhi, 'Changes in perception of gender roles: Returned migrants', *Pakistan Journal of Social and Clinical Psychology* 9, no. 1–2, 2011.

Kuenssberg, Laura, 'Analysis [of Cameron's multiculturalism speech]', BBC, 5 February 2011.

Kymlicka, W., *Multicultural Citizenship: A liberal theory of minority rights*, Oxford: Oxford University Press, 1995.

Lin, Xiaohua, 'The diaspora solution to innovation capacity development: Immigrant entrepreneurs in the contemporary world', *Thunderbird International Business Review* 52, no. 2, 2010, 123–36.

McMillan, Kate, 'The politics of immigration and multiculturalism in New Zealand', *Policy Network*, 16 November 2010.

Ministry of Foreign Affairs and Trade, *Our Future with Asia*, Wellington, 2007.

Mobrand, E., 'Mobilization or repression of migrants in urban China? Hometown networks, leadership, and lessons from international and historical comparisons', *The Journal of Comparative Asian Development* 6, no. 2, 2007, 337–62.

Modood, Tariq, *Multiculturalism*, Cambridge: Polity Press, 2007.

'NZ businesses still suffering from botulism scare', *TV One News*, 15 September 2013: www.tvnz.co.nz/business-news/nz-businesses-still-suffering-botulism-scare-5584739

Portes, A., L.E. Guarnizo and W.J. Haller, 'Transnational entrepreneurs: An alternative form of immigrant economic adaptation', *American Sociological Review* 67, no. 2, 2002, 278–98.

Rodríguez-García, D., 'Beyond assimilation and multiculturalism: A critical review of the debate on managing diversity', *Journal of International Migration and Integration/Revue de l'intégration et de la migration internationale* 11, no. 3, 2010, 251–71.

Schubert, J.D., 'Defending multiculturalism: From hegemony to symbolic violence', *American Behavioral Scientist* 45, no. 7, 2002, 1088–102.

Singham, Mervin, 'Multiculturalism in New Zealand – the need for a new paradigm', *Aotearoa Ethnic Network Journal* 1, no. 1, June 2006.

Song, S., 'Majority norms, multiculturalism, and gender equality', *American Political Science Review* 99, no. 4, 2005, 473–89.

Stark, O., *The Migration of Labor*, Cambridge: Basil Blackwell, 1991.

Taylor, J.E. and T.J. Wyatt, 'The shadow value of migrant remittances, income and inequality in a household-farm economy', *Journal of Development Studies* 32, no. 6, 1996, 899–912.

Weaver, Matthew, 'Angela Merkel: German multiculturalism has "utterly failed"', *Guardian*, 17 October 2010.

Zimmermann, K.F., 'Tackling the European migration problem', *Journal of Economic Perspective* 9, no. 2, Spring 1995, 45–62.

12. Afterword
Multiculturalism, being Asian and belonging in Aotearoa New Zealand

JACQUELINE LECKIE

Lalita Hari knows all about multiculturalism.[1] She has an Indian name through her father, Nagar Hari, a second-generation migrant from Gujarat. His father, Hari Kara, sailed to New Zealand in 1920 from Jalalpore and after Hari visited his wife and family there, Nagar accompanied him to New Zealand in 1927.[2] The two worked in a family fruit and vegetable business in Otorohanga and Nagar was destined to marry a bride from Gujarat. Instead, while working around Lake Taupo, he fell in love with Meri. Her full name was Ahipene Hoete and she was of Ngāpuhi and Te Arawa descent. The couple had five children, Lalita one of them. She grew up with her Māori whānau but she did socialise with Indians who were living in the King Country. Her world was also firmly within Pākehā New Zealand, including studying at Auckland Girls' Grammar School during the 1960s, when she lived at the Māori girls' hostel. Lalita became a teacher and has taught students of many ethnicities during a career spanning 45 years. She is married to Graeme Kitto, who identifies as Pākehā but is fluent in te reo. So too is Lalita, who identifies as Māori, and as Māori-Indian.

This synopsis of Lalita's life is to reflect upon the key threads of this volume and to point to the complex future of New Zealand's multicultural population. Lalita's story reminds us that regardless of the intellectual and political debates about multiculturalism, it is a lived reality being constantly negotiated throughout people's lives and daily activities. This reality can also be perceived, distorted and reframed – as reiterated by several of our authors – perhaps most directly in Hilary Chung's exploration of multicultural and Asian New Zealand theatre.

Mary (Meri) Ahipene-Hoete and Nagar Hari, 4 January 1969 at the wedding of Luxmme and Peter Underwood, Methodist Church, Taumarunui. Lalita Hari

Bicultural encounters

Part One of this book interrogated the bicultural foundations of New Zealand. The subsequent chapters examined multiculturalism from an Asian perspective in New Zealand and explicitly or implicitly referenced the nation's complex roots and the unfolding of biculturalism.

Lalita's whakapapa and family history reveals the complexities of simplistic bicultural dualisms between Māori and Pākehā. Lalita's brother has both Indian and Māori names – Hari Mohan Nagar and Te Kapaiawaho (an eponymous ancestor from the Te Arawa region) but is known as Kapa Hari.[3] One of Lalita's sisters has two first names – Nuia and Lakhee. Meri was living with her whānau when she gave birth on New Year's Day and so named her daughter Nuia (New Year) Te Tau Hou. She informed Nagar of this via telegram (as he was working in a distant part of the North Island), who instead registered the baby with an Indian name, Lakhee.

The union of Hari and Meri is only one in a long complex history of encounters between Māori and Asians in Aotearoa, beginning at least half a century before the Treaty of Waitangi.[4] In an essay that places Manukau within the broader and longer history of Asian, Māori and Pacific communities, historian Lewis Mayo wrote, 'Asian and Pacific pasts of the Manukau harbour, like the history of its sands, run through and beyond the nation.'[5] During the late eighteenth century Māori had met lascars and sepoys from East India Company ships.[6] Some Asians lived with Māori during the early nineteenth century. These included a Bengali who deserted ship in the Bay of Islands in 1809, and a sailor from Surat who, along with five others, jumped ship in 1814.[7] He became known as Te Anu and was living with his Māori wife and son on Rakiura (Stewart island) in 1844.[8] As in Lalita's story, living with biculturalism has a long history among Asians in New Zealand.

Regardless of this reality, Asians were, as Chung stresses, mostly excluded from the bicultural framework. Did the substantial leap in new immigrants from Asia in recent decades intensify this exclusion? And if so, as Camille Nakhid and Heather Devere ask, how does that bear upon the accommodation of multicultural diversity and citizenship within the Treaty of Waitangi? The New Zealand Federation of Multicultural Councils sees the way forward through a Treaty-Based Multicultural New Zealand.[9]

Many Asias

Several authors in this book have examined biculturalism in relation to multiculturalism and immigration from Asia. In doing this, they have disrupted essentialised notions of the state and nation and unpacked the categories 'Asia' and 'Asians' to highlight the many 'Asias' – local and transnational – in New Zealand.[10] The label 'Asian' can operate as 'simplistic and racialised',[11] or in more subtle ways to become 'normative and sometimes pejorative', as Paul Spoonley, Carina Meares and Trudie Cain suggest in their chapter.[12] Geographer Richard Bedford regards Asia 'as a complete nonsense term', because 'It spans 60 per cent of the world's population and most would never call themselves Asian.'[13]

Lalita has lived with the complexities that come with the category Asian. She has an Indian father and an Indian name but does not call herself Asian. Her grandfather, who today would be categorised as an Asian, lived in an era in New Zealand when this term was hardly used. He was classified as a 'Race Alien'.[14] At other times he was possibly labelled Hindu or 'Hindoo' – along with fellow Indians, regardless of whether they followed religions such as Islam, Sikhism or Christianity. Since the late nineteenth century in New Zealand, Indians and Chinese were also discursively lumped together as Asiatics – the assumption being that they belonged to an Asian race.[15]

The categories 'Indian' and 'Chinese' are equally problematic and gloss over heterogeneous origins and identities. 'Indians' subsumes both the early settlers mainly from Gujarat and Punjab, and the later immigrants from the subcontinent and the Indian diaspora, including thousands who relocated after coups in Fiji beginning in 1987.[16] A similar pattern applies to the Chinese who comprise those of several generations in New Zealand[17] and the arrivals since the 1980s – or as Tze Ming Mok provocatively put it, the 'Old Generation' and the 'New Wave'.[18] Spoonley and Meares' chapter addressed the segmented communities within Auckland's large Chinese population, including those from Hong Kong and Taiwan who dominated arrivals during the 1990s, and the post-2000 migrants from China. Smaller Chinese communities from diasporic centres include those from Malaysia and Singapore. The geographical, national and historical diversity within the Indian and Chinese communities in New Zealand applies to other Asian ethnicities in New Zealand.[19] Culture, religion, language, caste, class, age, gender and sexual orientation, as well as different migration histories to New Zealand, further fragment these distinctions. Paola Voci and I also emphasised the diversity within the wider society and environment: 'Not only are there many Asias in New Zealand, but also their communities live within different New Zealands.'[20] Conversely, as Nakhid and Devere argue, although pan-ethnic labels may have originated as imposed racist categories, this can sometimes be reinterpreted to support group goals and contribute to belonging.

As Chung suggests, the Oryza Foundation has creatively asserted Asian belonging by privileging the extent that this 'Kiwi signifier' is the 'singular referent of identity'. Asian communities in New Zealand may share common experiences in New Zealand but this is not necessarily marked by the actors' ethnicity or performance.

It is perhaps with regard to New Zealand's Muslims that generalised assumptions of Asian identity are most questioned. Erich Kolig applied the phrase 'pragmatic brand of multiculturalism' to refer to 'a diffuse sense of tolerance' or indifference to cultural diversity – alongside the nation's legal compliance to safeguard multiculturalism.[21] Stephanie Dobson's chapter documented how the New Zealand brand of multiculturalism is played out through the impact of media stereotypes of Muslim – and especially Asian – women. She implicates the media in moulding shifting perceptions of belonging and identity. A participant of Indian origin revealed that being Muslim was far less significant during the 1970s than today – a shift from markers of race to religion – albeit stereotyped with extremism and terrorism.

Exclusion and belonging

The chapters on Muslims highlight how multiculturalism does not necessarily bring an acceptance of diversity. Other chapters by Spoonley, Nakhid, Devere and Chung reiterate how New Zealand's multiculturalism has been built upon a long history of discrimination against Asians. The effects of this dark side to our national history have profoundly affected belonging – legally, residentially, culturally, spiritually and psychologically. Chung emphasises that the legacy of exclusion continues to problematise New Zealand's sense of itself.

Historians have analysed the specific context, discourse and representations of anti-Asian exclusionism and xenophobia in New Zealand's past, such as the White New Zealand League at Pukekohe during the 1920s.[22] Both Māori and Pākehā stirred fears of miscegenation as a consequence of relationships between Indians or Chinese men and

Māori women. White New Zealanders also raised the spectre of economic competition from Asians. Fears of racial contamination may now appear to be buried in the past but a 'moral panic' against Asian immigrants, entwined with fears of economic competition, resurfaced during the 1990s.[23]

In 2010 former Governor-General Sir Anand Satyanand was the target of a high-profile debate over who 'belongs' to New Zealand. Broadcaster Paul Henry questioned Satyanand's nationality and identity as a Kiwi when he asked John Key, New Zealand's Prime Minister, who would be chosen as the next Governor-General. Henry doubted that Satyanand was 'even a New Zealander' and asked, 'Are you going to choose a New Zealander who looks and sounds like a New Zealander this time … are we going to go for someone who is more like a New Zealander this time?' TVNZ initially supported Henry's willingness 'to say the things we quietly think but are scared to say out loud'.[24] This endorsement was withdrawn, partly because of public outcry. When Satyanand was asked about his reaction to Henry's assertion, he replied, 'I'm reliably informed that I was born at Bethany Hospital, 37 Dryden Street, Grey Lynn in Auckland.'[25]

Satyanand's direct response resonates with Chung's account of the creative ways the production 'Native Alienz' challenged racial exclusion within the 'exclusive bi-racial parameters of New Zealand's national identity construction'. Not all New Zealand Asians who face discrimination have the confidence to proclaim their belonging as Kiwis. Dobson argued that media stereotypes can hamper Muslim women's 'sense of belonging as New Zealand citizens, significantly defining who is a Kiwi and who is not'. This exclusion was primarily from being Muslim, although ethnic and gender stereotyping were entangled in this.

Several authors here have stressed that exclusion and belonging must be taken seriously. Nakhid and Devere warned that the lack of a planned and consultative multicultural approach can lead to the isolation of ethnic communities, if they are uncertain as to their status in New Zealand society. Beal, Lindsay and Retna contended that platitudes and ignorance that hide or ignore complex difficulties may be perhaps more dangerous than racism. Their research highlights the effect that this can have on New Zealand's global economic partners. For example some individuals, especially those of Māori and Asian heritage, may face identity conflicts through racial stereotyping.[26]

Belonging

The creative and strategic reclaiming of 'Asian' is addressed throughout this book and relates to how New Zealand's diverse Asian communities locally and globally engage with multiculturalism. Voci and I have argued that 'locally defined contexts and historical experiences are equally or possibly even more relevant' than macro belongings to a motherland or to an ethnicity or diasporic community.[27] Yet Asian identities emanate from social and cultural locations that are not contained by, but intersect with and transcend the nation.[28] Several authors in this volume argue that for multiculturalism to go beyond mere pragmatism, or simply tolerance, it must embrace belonging. Lalita's family, like those of other migrants – whether recent or of several generations – offers glimpses into the realities of belonging. Her grandfather died in New Zealand on 24 September 1944, far away from his widow, Dai Kara and their children in India. He was buried in an unmarked grave in Otorohanga. Fifty-six years later, in 2000, his grandchildren installed a headstone to remember him and to mark the 25 years he lived and worked in New Zealand. His son, Nagar, had been expected to marry a woman from Gujarat but as retold here, Nagar's heart belonged to Meri, while his livelihood was embedded in rural New Zealand, where he lived close to Māori communities. Although he did not pass the Gujarati language on to his children, they do recall that when they lived in remote Kakahi their father tried to connect a shortwave radio to listen to broadcasts from India.

Belonging is not a simplistic decision to wholeheartedly commit to an adopted country, but a life spent mostly there may determine what Beal, Lindsay and Retna called 'social embeddedness'. Assumptions about national belonging are nebulous but the temporal, geographical, occupational or even the intimate belonging found in Lalita's family does not necessarily equate with national identity. Several authors in this book have also reiterated that belonging is not synonymous with citizenship, as although many Asians may consider themselves belonging to New Zealand they are not legally citizens.

Today's transnational migrants usually enjoy greater ease of movement between and communication with different centres. To some extent, Hari Kara did this in his journeys between Jalalpore and Otorohanga but obviously not on the scale or frequency possible with contemporary travel and technology. Beal, Lindsay and Retna's chapter investigated the complexities of belonging for transnational workers and entrepreneurs.

Their chapter highlighted the economic advantages of belonging through strategically utilising the resource of pragmatic multiculturalism. Returnee migrants may have resettled in their home country but can retain a significant affiliation with New Zealand. The reception afforded within New Zealand's multicultural framework (as well as economic advantages) is likely to have a bearing upon this sense of belonging.

Ethnic precincts can offer place and belonging to transnational and recent migrants. Spoonley, Meares and Cain's chapter outlined how ethnic precincts in Auckland are not just a geographical and economic space but embrace culture, community and family. Planned Chinatowns do not seem to be the New Zealand way.[29] The authors asked how ethnic precincts ease or hinder the acceptance of Asian immigrants within the local community. Acceptance does not necessarily mean that the wider community utilises these ethnic precincts, although familiarity with immigrants may facilitate the acceptance of new migrants.[30] The development of ethnic precincts may ease belonging for Asian migrants but the debate remains over whether this enriches or fragments multiculturalism.

The two chapters in this book by Henry Johnson and Hilary Chung addressed overt displays of belonging through celebration and performance, but critiqued how this represents multiculturalism. Johnson concluded that large, inclusive public Asian festivals such as Diwali and Chinese New Year reveal a 'paradox of belonging'. Individuals and communities may have privately celebrated a festival for decades in New Zealand but when they willingly participate in the new public celebration, they become part of a homogenous event, possibly more directed at creating a public sense of belonging and multiculturalism. This highlights the Asian presence in New Zealand but also collapses the cultural diversity among Asians. Yet, as Chung traced, multicultural counter-discursive theatre can disrupt superficial stereotypes of Asians and Asian performance 'in the symbolic space of the national narrative'.[31]

Faith perhaps offers the most fundamental anchor of belonging. However as chapters by Butcher and Weiland, Dobson and especially Kolig revealed, religion also tests the depth and commitment to multiculturalism. Will belonging among New Zealand Muslims continue to depend upon the freedom to practise faith and the usual public tolerance of aspects of cultural identity (such as dress or diet), or will this be tested if Muslims press for the greater cultural recognition Kolig traced in Europe?

Belonging in New Zealand's multicultural future

This collection has raised questions over the multicultural framework that best suits New Zealand's changing ethnic demographics as summed up in a press release of the 2013 census: 'New Zealand has more ethnicities than the world has countries.'[32] We have focused on Asian perspectives on multiculturalism – partly because this has been neglected within past debates on multiculturalism – and also because of the dramatic rise in New Zealand's Asian populations. Statistical evidence and projections provided by the authors are based on the 2006 census, but as this afterword was being written the initial results of the 2013 census were released.[33] Those identifying as Asian totalled 11.8 per cent (471,708) in 2013 – almost twice the figures of 2001. This compares to 14.9 per cent who identify as Māori, and 7.4 per cent as being of Pacific ethnicity in 2013. Indians now constitute the largest increase among Asian ethnicities with a total of 155,178 or an increase of 48.4 per cent since 2006, a shift from the past dominance of Chinese ethnicity within Asian categories. Chinese continued to constitute the largest Asian ethnic group with an increase of 16.2 per cent (171,411) while Filipinos more than doubled to 40,350 between 2006 and 2013. Of the Asians, 31.6 per cent were overseas-born in the 2013 census, with China and India being the key source areas from Asia. A further significant number of those who identify as Indian were born in Fiji.[34] The large increase in New Zealand's Indian population is also reflected in Hindi becoming the country's fourth most common language. Asian communities continue to be concentrated in Auckland but the latest census indicates that Asians comprise significant minorities in Wellington, Canterbury and Waikato. As noted earlier, Indian and Chinese settlement was part of New Zealand's regional histories. Also, as Lalita's story revealed, children with multiple ethnic heritages were born as a result of relationships between Asians and others.[35] I argue that compared to many parts of the world, there has been a quiet, even if sometimes troubled, acceptance of intermarriage between Asians and others in New Zealand. As families become more ethnically complex, so this has implications for how multiculturalism unfolds.

Demographics cannot illuminate the depth and nuances of cultural shifts within Asian communities and the dynamics with the wider society. The ongoing debate about the nation's constitutional framework and any adjustment of the bicultural framework to embrace multiculturalism continues. Chung reminded us that the insufficiently acknowledged discourse of race limits access to national belonging, partly because of the persistence of a monoculturalist outlook, despite the rhetoric of diversity and inclusion. Perhaps the way forward is in the texture that is woven inside the framework, as conveyed in Satyanand's message on Race Relations Day in 2007:

> *The question of our essential identity is one we are still posing of ourselves ... as it has been put 'kiwi [sic] culture is work in progress'. It may be many more years before we have a definitive answer. Perhaps we do not even need one. Suffice to say that in 2007, we are a blend of many people.*[36]

For Lalita there has been a continued renegotiation of identity, place and heritage of living in Māori, Asian and Pākehā worlds: 'You sort of can float from whichever cot you choose to and feel equally comfortable.' That comfort expresses belonging and living with multiculturalism.

Endnotes

1. Conversations with Lalita Hari by Jacqueline Leckie and Jade Aikman-Dodd, January 2010; Interview of Lalita by Aikman-Dodd, 21 January 2013. I am most grateful to Jade for research on Māori-Indians, made possible through a Summer Scholarship awarded by the Asian Migrations Research Theme, University of Otago. Many thanks to Lalita, Graeme Kitto and Kapa Hari for participating in the research project.
2. According to Auckland shipping lists (no. 23964) Hari arrived as a hawker, on the *Riverina*, 19 April 1920. Nagar arrived at Bluff between 1927 and 1929. He was born in 1914.
3. Interview, Kapa Hari by Aikman-Dodd, 2 February 2013.
4. See Jacqueline Leckie, *Indian Settlers: The story of a New Zealand South Asian community*, Dunedin: Otago University Press, 2007, 21–22; and passim for later on Māori-Indian accounts; also Edwina Pio, *Caste Away: Unfolding the Māori-Indian*, Ethnica New Zealand, 2012. On Māori -Chinese see Manying Ip, 'Maori-Chinese Encounters: Indigine–immigrant interaction in New Zealand', *Asian Studies Review* 27, 2003, 227–52; Manying Ip (ed.), *The Dragon and the Taniwha. Māori & Chinese in New Zealand*, Auckland: Auckland University Press, 2009; Manying Ip, Nigel Murphy, Beven Yee and Elsie Ho, *Being Māori-Chinese: Mixed identities = He Māori-he Hainamana he tuakiri aha? = Mao li yi hua ren*, Auckland: Auckland University Press, 2008.
5. Lewis Mayo, 'Prefects, chiefs and the history of sand: Systems of pre-eminence, and the Pacific and Asian pasts of the Manukau Harbour', in Paola Voci and Jacqueline

Leckie (eds), *Localizing Asia in Aotearoa*, Wellington: Dunmore Publishing, 2011, 45.

6   Anne Salmond, *Between Worlds: Early exchanges between Maori and Europeans 1773–1815*, Auckland: Penguin Books, 1997, 235, 290–92.

7   Leckie, *Indian Settlers*, 21–22; Peter Entwisle, *Taka: A vignette life of William Tucker 1784–1817: Convict, sealer, trader in human heads, Otago settler, New Zealand's first art dealer*, Dunedin: Port Daniel Press, 2005, 103–06.

8   Bishop Selwyn's notes, in *Census of People Living at Ruapuke and Stewart Island, Feb 1844*, Appendix J, in Basil Howard, *Rakiura: A history of Stewart Island, New Zealand*, Wellington: A.H. & A.W. Reed, for the Stewart Island Centennial Committee, 1940, 379.

9   Submission to New Zealand Government, 'New Zealand's constitution: A report on a conversation: He kōtuinga kōrero mō te kaupapa ture o Aotearoa', November 2013: www.ourconstitution.org.nz/store/doc/FR_Full_Report.pdf; New Zealand Federation of Multicultural Councils, 'Treaty-based multicultural New Zealand': www.nzfmc.org.nz/assets/Uploads/Documents/Multicultural-NZFMC-broch-A4-print.pdf

10 See also Henry Johnson and Brian Moloughney, 'Introduction: Asia and the making of multicultural New Zealand', in H. Johnson and B. Moloughney (eds), *Asia in the Making of New Zealand*, Auckland: Auckland University Press, 2006, 2–4.

11 Paul Spoonley and Richard Bedford, *Welcome to our World? Immigration and the reshaping of New Zealand*, Auckland: Dunmore Publishing, 2012, 96.

12 See also Andrew Butcher, '"Well, they're very good citizens": New Zealanders' perceptions of Asians in New Zealand', *Sites: A Journal of Social Anthropology and Cultural Studies*, 5, 2, 2008, 5–30; Andrew Butcher and Paul Spoonley, 'Inv-Asian: Print media constructions of Asians and Asian immigration', in Paola Voci and Jacqueline Leckie (eds), *Localizing Asia in Aotearoa*, Wellington: Dunmore Publishing, 2011, 98–115.

13 Cited in Greg Bruce, 'Our new society', *New Zealand Geographic*, 126, March–April 2014, 49.

14 A category used in the 1916, 1921 and 1926 censuses to refer to people not of European or Māori descent. See Jacqueline Leckie, 'From race aliens to an ethnic group: Indians in New Zealand', in M.C. Howard (ed.), *Ethnicity and Nation Building in the South Pacific*, Tokyo: United Nations University, 1989, 169–97.

15 Manying Ip and Jacqueline Leckie, '"Chinamen" and "Hindoos": Beyond stereotypes to Kiwi Asians', in Paola Voci and Jacqueline Leckie (eds), *Localizing Asia in Aotearoa*, Wellington, Dunmore Publishing, 2011, 77–106.

16 See Leckie, *Indian Settlers*; Jacqueline Leckie, 'A long diaspora: Indian settlement in Aotearoa New Zealand', in Sekhar Bandyopadhyay (ed.), *India in New Zealand: Local identities, global relations*, Dunedin: Otago University Press, 2010, 45–63; Jacqueline Leckie, 'Indians in the South Pacific: Recentred diasporas', in Jacob Edmond, Henry Johnson and Jacqueline Leckie (eds), *Recentring Asia: Histories, encounters, identities*, Leiden: Global Oriental/Brill, 2011, 54–84; W.H. McLeod,

Punjabis in New Zealand: A history of Punjabi migration 1890–1940, Amritsar: Guru Nanak Dev University, 1996.

17 See Manying Ip, *Dragons on the Long White Cloud: The making of Chinese New Zealanders*, Auckland: Tandem Press, 1996; Manying Ip (ed.), *Unfolding History, Evolving Identity: The Chinese in New Zealand*, Auckland: Auckland University Press, 2003.

18 Tze Ming Mok, 'Race you there', *Landfall 208*, 2004, 28–26.

19 See Richard Bedford and Elise Ho, *Asians in New Zealand: Implications of a changing demography*, Wellington: Asia NZ Foundation, 2008; Paul Spoonley and Richard Bedford, *Welcome to our World? Immigration and the reshaping of New Zealand*, Auckland, Dunmore Publishing, 2012, 95–122.

20 Paola Voci and Jacqueline Leckie, 'Beyond nations and ethnicities: Localizing Asia in New Zealand', in Paola Voci and Jacqueline Leckie (eds), *Localizing Asia in Aotearoa*, Wellington: Dunmore Publishing, 2011, 9.

21 Also Erich Kolig, *New Zealand's Muslims and Multiculturalism*, Leiden: Brill, 2010.

22 Jacqueline Leckie, 'In defence of race and empire: The White New Zealand League at Pukekohe', *New Zealand Journal of History* 19, 2, 1985, 103–29. Also Barbara Brookes, 'Gender, work and fears of a "hybrid race" in 1920s New Zealand', *Gender and History* 19, 3, 2007, 501–18; Manying, Ip and Nigel Murphy, *Aliens at my Table: Asians as New Zealanders see them*, Auckland: Penguin Books, 2005; Peter O'Connor, 'Keeping New Zealand white, 1908–1920' *New Zealand Journal of History* 2, 1, 1968, 41–65.

23 Butcher and Spoonley, 'Inv-Asian', 102.

24 Martin Kay, 'Henry apology for G-G race comments', 4 October 2010: www.stuff.co.nz/entertainment/tv/4194441/Henry-apology-for-G-G-race-comments

25 Anand Satyanand, interview by Jacqueline Leckie, 2 March 2011.

26 Actress Madeleine Sami, in the TV series *Here to Stay*, reported the slurs encountered from being of Māori and Indian ethnicity.

27 Voci and Leckie, 'Beyond nations and ethnicities', 9.

28 See Jacob Edmond, Henry Johnson and Jacqueline Leckie (eds), *Recentring Asia: Histories, encounters, identities*, Leiden: Global Oriental/Brill, 2011.

29 Mok, Tze Ming, 'A Chinatown state of mind', 22 October 2005: www.publicaddress.net/default,2623.sm#post2623

30 Spoonley and Bedford, *Welcome to our World?*, 228.

31 For an evaluation of documentaries on the Chinese in New Zealand with a more diasporic voice, see Paola Voci, '"Isn't it great? They all speak English!": Screen representations of Asia and Asians in New Zealand', in Paola Voci and Jacqueline Leckie (eds), *Localizing Asia in Aotearoa*, Wellington: Dunmore Publishing, 2011, 74–97.

32 Statistics New Zealand, 'New Zealand has more ethnicities than the world has countries': www.stats.govt.nz/Census/2013-census/data-tables/totals-by-topic-mr1.aspx

33 Statistics New Zealand, '2013 Census QuickStats about culture and identity', 2014: www.stats.govt.nz/Census/2013-census/profile-and-summary-reports/quickstats-culture-identity.aspx

34 The majority of the 52,755 recorded as born in Fiji are Fiji-Indians although the total figure includes indigenous Fijians and other ethnicities.
35 Today census totals in New Zealand for ethnicity include all people who stated each ethnic group, whether as their only ethnic group or as one of several. Where a person reported more than one ethnic group, they were counted in each applicable group.
36 Anand Satyanand, 'The Honourable Anand Satyanand Governor-General of New Zealand Race Relations Day 2007 Wellington', 21 March 2007: www.gg.govt.nz/node/614

Bibliography

Bagnall, A.G. (ed.), *Journal of a Ten Months' Residence in New Zealand [1820] by Richard A. Cruise Esq. Major in the 84th Regt. Foot*, Christchurch: The Pegasus Press, 1957.

Bedford, Richard and Elise Ho, *Asians in New Zealand: Implications of a changing demography*, Wellington: Asia NZ Foundation, 2008.

Brookes, Barbara, 'Gender, work and fears of a "hybrid race" in 1920s New Zealand', *Gender and History* 19, 3, 2007, 501–18.

Bruce, Greg, 'Our new society', *New Zealand Geographic*, 126, March–April 2014, 44–76.

Butcher, Andrew, '"Well, they're very good citizens": New Zealand's perceptions of Asians in New Zealand', in Jacqueline Leckie (ed.), *Sites: A Journal of Social Anthropology and Cultural Studies. Special Issue: Asia and Aotearoa in New Zealand*, 5, 2, 2008, 5–30.

Butcher, Andrew and Paul Spoonley, 'Inv-Asian: Print media constructions of Asians and Asian immigration', in Paola Voci and Jacqueline Leckie (eds), *Localising Asia in Aotearoa*, Wellington: Dunmore Publishing, 2011, 98–115.

Edmond, Jacob, Henry Johnson and Jacqueline Leckie (eds), *Recentring Asia: Histories, encounters, identities*, Leiden: Global Oriental/Brill, 2011.

Entwisle, Peter, *Taka: A vignette life of William Tucker 1784–1817: Convict, sealer, trader in human heads, Otago settler, New Zealand's first art dealer*, Dunedin: Port Daniel Press, 2005.

Here to Stay: Series two, 2009, [DVD] Auckland, Gibson Group.

Howard, Basil, *Rakiura: A history of Stewart Island, New Zealand*, Wellington: A.H. & A.W. Reed, for the Stewart Island Centennial Committee, 1940.

Ip, Manying, *Dragons on the Long White Cloud: The making of Chinese New Zealanders*, Auckland: Tandem Press, 1996.

Ip, Manying (ed.), *Unfolding history, Evolving Identity: The Chinese in New Zealand*, Auckland: Auckland University Press, 2003.

Ip, Manying. 'Maori–Chinese encounters: Indigine–immigrant interaction in New Zealand', *Asian Studies Review* 27, 2003, 227–52.

Ip, Manying (ed.), *The Dragon and the Taniwha. Māori & Chinese in New Zealand*, Auckland: Auckland University Press, 2009.

Ip, Manying and Jacqueline Leckie, '"Chinamen" and "Hindoos": Beyond stereotypes to Kiwi Asians', in Paola Voci and Jacqueline Leckie (eds), *Localizing Asia in Aotearoa*, Wellington: Dunmore Publishing 2011, 77–106.

Ip, Manying, Nigel Murphy, Beven Yee and Elsie Ho, *Being Māori-Chinese: Mixed identities = He Māori-he Hainamana he tuakiri aha? = Mao li yi hua ren*, Auckland: Auckland University Press, 2008.

Ip, Manying and Nigel Murphy, *Aliens at my table: Asians as New Zealanders see them*, Auckland: Penguin Books, 2005.

Johnson, Henry and Brian Moloughney (eds), *Asia in the Making of New Zealand*, Auckland: Auckland University Press, 2006.

Johnson, Henry and Brian Moloughney, 'Introduction: Asia and the making of multicultural New Zealand', in H. Johnson and B. Moloughney (eds), *Asia in the Making of New Zealand*, Auckland: Auckland University Press, 2006, 1–10.

Kay, Martin, 'Henry apology for G-G race comments': www.stuff.co.nz/entertainment/tv/4194441/Henry-apology-for-G-G-race-comments

Leckie, Jacqueline, 'In defence of race and empire: The White New Zealand League at Pukekohe, *New Zealand Journal of History* 19, 2, 1985, 103–29.

Leckie, Jacqueline, 'From race aliens to an ethnic group – Indians in New Zealand', in M.C. Howard (ed.), *Ethnicity and Nation Building in the South Pacific*, Tokyo: United Nations University, 1989, 169–97.

Leckie, Jacqueline, 'South Asians: Old and new migrations', in Stuart Greif (ed.), *Immigration and National Identity in New Zealand: One people, two peoples, many peoples?* Palmerston North: Dunmore Press, 1995, 133–60.

Leckie, Jacqueline, 'A long diaspora: Indian settlement in Aotearoa New Zealand', in Sekhar Bandyopadhyay (ed.), *India in New Zealand: Local identities, global relations*, Dunedin: Otago University Press, 2010, 45–63.

Leckie, Jacqueline, 'Indians in the South Pacific: Recentred diasporas', in Jacob Edmond, Henry Johnson and Jacqueline Leckie (eds), *Recentring Asia: Histories, encounters, identities*, Leiden: Global Oriental/Brill, 2011, 54–84.

Leckie, Jacqueline, *Indian Settlers. The story of a New Zealand South Asian community*, Dunedin, Otago University Press, 2007.

Mayo, Lewis, 'Prefects, chiefs and the history of sand: Systems of pre-eminence, and the Pacific and Asian pasts of the Manukau Harbour', in Paola Voci and Jacqueline Leckie (eds), *Localizing Asia in Aotearoa*, Wellington: Dunmore Publishing, 2011, 25–52.

McLeod, W.H., *Punjabis in New Zealand: A history of Punjabi migration 1890–1940*, Amritsar: Guru Nanak Dev University, 1986.

Mok, Tze Ming, 'Race you there', *Landfall 208*, 2004, 28–26.

Mok, Tze Ming, 'A Chinatown state of mind', 22 October 2005: www.publicaddress.net/default,2623.sm#post2623

New Zealand Government, 'New Zealand's constitution: A report on a conversation: He kōtuinga kōrero mō te kaupapa ture o Aotearoa', November 2013: www.ourconstitution.org.nz/store/doc/FR_Full_Report.pdf

New Zealand Federation of Multicultural Councils, 'Treaty-based multicultural New

Zealand': www.nzfmc.org.nz/assets/Uploads/Documents/Multicultural-NZFMC-broch-A4-print.pdf

O'Connor, Peter, 'Keeping New Zealand white, 1908–1920', *New Zealand Journal of History* 2, 1, 1968, 41–65.

Pio, Edwina, *Caste Away: Unfolding the Maori Indian*, Ethnica New Zealand, 2012: www.scribd.com/doc/56288814/Caste-Away

Salmond, Anne, *Between Worlds: Early exchanges between Maori and Europeans 1773–1815*, Auckland: Penguin Books, 1997.

Satyanand, Anand, 'The Honourable Anand Satyanand Governor-General of New Zealand Race Relations Day 2007 Wellington', 21 March 2007: www.gg.govt.nz/node/614

Spoonley, Paul and Richard Bedford, *Welcome to our World? Immigration and the reshaping of New Zealand*, Auckland: Dunmore Publishing, 2012.

Statistics New Zealand, '2013 Census QuickStats about culture and identity', 2014: www.stats.govt.nz/Census/2013-census/profile-and-summary-reports/quickstats-culture-identity.aspx

Statistics New Zealand, 'New Zealand has more ethnicities than the world has countries': www.stats.govt.nz/Census/2013-census/data-tables/totals-by-topic-mr1.aspx

Voci, Paola, '"Isn't it great? They all speak English!": Screen representations of Asia and Asians in New Zealand', in Paola Voci and Jacqueline Leckie (eds), *Localizing Asia in Aotearoa*, Wellington: Dunmore Publishing, 2011, 74–97.

Voci, Paola and Jacqueline Leckie, (eds), *Localizing Asia in Aotearoa*, Wellington: Dunmore Publishing, 2011.

Voci, Paola and Jacqueline Leckie, 'Beyond nations and ethnicities: Localizing Asia in New Zealand', in Paola Voci and Jacqueline Leckie (eds), *Localizing Asia in Aotearoa*, Wellington: Dunmore Publishing, 2011, 7–24.

Contributors

Tim Beal is a retired senior lecturer in the School of Marketing and International Business at Victoria University in Wellington. His most recent major research project was on Service Success in Asia, an investigation led by Val Lindsay on building a sustainable competitive advantage for New Zealand service firms in Asia, Spotlight on China, and Spotlight on India.

Andrew Butcher is director of research at the Asia New Zealand Foundation. He has held visiting fellowships at Victoria University of Wellington and the Institute of Southeast Asian Studies in Singapore and by invitation participated in the US State Department's International Visitor Leadership Programme.

Trudie Cain is a social researcher with the Research, Investigations and Monitoring Unit at Auckland Council. She was previously research manager for the Nga Tangata Oho Mairangi research programme (Massey University/University of Waikato), a project that examines population change in Aotearoa New Zealand. Her research interests include: gendered, sized and migrant identities; qualitative research methodologies and ethics; and the materiality of everyday lives.

Hilary Chung is a senior lecturer who teaches Asian cultural studies and comparative literature in the School of Cultures Languages and Linguistics at the University of Auckland. She has research interests in socialist realism, gender identity, the poetics of diaspora and exile and issues of multiculturalism. Her publications include *In the Party Spirit: Socialist realism and literary practice in the Soviet Union, East Germany and China* (1996), *Yang Lian: Unreal city: A Chinese poet in Auckland* (2006) and numerous articles and book chapters. Her two current projects are a comparative study of enactments of multiculturalism in Chinese diaspora theatre and a study of the representation of the Chinese migrant in European film.

Heather Devere is director of practice at the National Centre for Peace and Conflict Studies at the University of Otago. Her research interests include the politics of friendship, peace journalism, indigenous peace traditions; women and politics and conflict resolution.

Stephanie Dobson is a contributing lecturer in social anthropology and a researcher at the University of Otago. Her qualitative research and publications on Muslim women in New Zealand have focused on areas such as identity, faith, religious interpretation and multiculturalism, drawing on individual women's perspectives and lived experiences.

Gautam Ghosh is a lecturer in the Department of Anthropology and Archaeology at the University of Otago. He studied anthropology at the University of California Berkeley and the University of Chicago. His research has been funded by the Fulbright, Guggenheim, Rockefeller and MacArthur Foundations as well as the Davis Center of Princeton University. He has served on the editorial boards of *Anthropological Quarterly* and *SITES: A Journal of Social Anthropology and Cultural Studies*, as an executive for the Society for Urban, National, and Transnational/Global Anthropology, and an advisor for the Center for the Advanced Study of India.

Henry Johnson is professor of music at the University of Otago, New Zealand and holds a doctorate from the University of Oxford. He has edited or co-edited various journals, including *Yearbook for Traditional Music*, *Perfect Beat*, *Musicology Australia*, and *New Zealand Journal of Asian Studies*. His more recent books include *The Shakuhachi* (2014), *Recentring Asia* (2011; co-edited), *Cultural Transformations* (2010; co-edited), *The Shamisen* (2010), *Performing Japan* (2008; co-edited), and *The Koto* (2004). In New Zealand his research includes the music and performing arts of New Zealand's Asian diaspora.

Erich Kolig is an honorary fellow in religion at Otago University. He was a senior lecturer (reader) in social anthropology at Otago and visiting professor of cultural anthropology at Vienna University. He was also a research fellow at the University of Western Australia and a government anthropologist in Western Australia. Erich has done fieldwork in Afghanistan, Australia, Austria, Indonesia, New Zealand and Vanuatu. He has published several books (authored and edited) and many articles on Australian Aboriginal culture and religion; on indigenous politics in New Zealand, Vanuatu and Australia; on the historical exploration in New Zealand; on Muslims and Islam in New Zealand; radical Islam in Indonesia and several other topics.

Jacqueline Leckie is an associate professor and head of department in the Department of Anthropology and Archaeology at the University of Otago. Her research and publications relate to gender, ethnicity, migration, mental health, development and work within Asia Pacific. Her more recent books include *Indian Settlers: The story of a New Zealand South Asian community*; *To Labour with the State*; *Development in an Insecure and Gendered World* (edited); *Localizing Asia in Aotearoa* (co-edited) and *Recentring Asia: Histories, encounters, identities* (co-edited). She is president of the Pacific History Association and a co-director of the Asian Migrations Research Theme at the University of Otago.

Valerie Lindsay is professor and dean of the Faculty of Business at the University of Wollongong in Dubai (UOWD). Prior to joining UOWD, she held academic positions at Victoria University of Wellington, University of Auckland and at University of Warwick, specialising in international business and strategy. Her research interests lie in the area of international strategy, specifically, internationalisation and market entry, SMEs, services internationalisation and business in Asia. Her work has been published in leading journals, including *Management International Review*, *Organizational Dynamics*, *Industrial Marketing Management*, and *International Journal of Services Industry Marketing*, and she co-authored the book *Knowledge at Work*.

Carina Meares is a senior researcher in the Social and Economic Research team at Auckland Council's Research, Investigations and Monitoring Unit. Prior to that, she was research manager for the Integration of Immigrants Programme, a project run jointly by Waikato and Massey Universities. Her research interests include international migration, ethnicity, social cohesion, ethnic precincts, gender and qualitative research methodologies.

Camille Nakhid is an associate professor in the School of Social Sciences and Public Policy at Auckland University of Technology. Her research interests include work with ethnic communities, Pasifika and ethnic youth, and student achievement.

Kala Retna is a senior lecturer in the School of Management at Victoria University of Wellington. Her research has canvassed the cultural dynamics that confront learning models, such as the learning organisation concept. She teaches organisational behaviour at various levels including undergraduates. Kala also has extensive experience in professional development, facilitation and teaching in diverse cultural backgrounds.

Paul Spoonley is distinguished professor in sociology and pro-vice chancellor of the College of Humanities and Social Sciences at Massey University. He is the programme leader for the Nga Tangata Oho Mairangi project looking at the current and future demographic shape of New Zealand, funded by Ministry of Business, Innovation and Employment. He received a Fulbright Senior Scholar Award to the University of California Berkeley in 2010; has been a visiting research fellow at the Max Planck Institute of Religious and Ethnic Diversity in Germany; and is part of the Global Diversity project, which adds Auckland to the research on diversity and immigration in other global cities. He is a fellow of the Royal Society of New Zealand.

George Wieland is director of Mission Research and Training at Carey Baptist College, Auckland, where he also directs a programme in intercultural practice. His background includes secondary teaching in the UK, church and community work in Brazil and in the UK, and New Testament research and teaching at Aberdeen University and Auckland University. He holds honours degrees in history and theology and a PhD in the contextual study of the New Testament. He is the author of *The Significance of Salvation: A study of salvation language in the pastoral epistles* (Paternoster, 2006) and several book chapters and articles both on biblical interpretation and on migration, cultural diversity and the church.

Index

ACT Party, NZ 55, 253
Afghan war 164, 225
Afghani immigrants in NZ 141, 226
African immigration and immigrants, NZ 70, 139, 204, 205, 206
Agamben, Giorgio 23
agency 20, 23, 27, 29, 31n.22, 33n.44, 98, 109, 240, 241
Ahipene-Hoete, Mary (Meri) 285, 286, 287, 291
Akalaitis, JoAnne 96
Alexander, Cynthia 130
Ali, Yasmeen 177
Animal Welfare Commercial Slaughter Code 178–79, 188n.64
Appadurai, Arjun 27–28
Arab Spring 225
Asia, economic linkages with NZ 61–62, 68, 136, 176, 269
Asia New Zealand Foundation (ANZF) 98, 121, 122, 124, 125–26, 127, 129, 130, 132–33, 134, 135–36, 137, 269
Asian American Theatre Company 112
'Asian Century' 8, 24
Asian festivals, NZ 119–24, 132–38, 292; Northcote 249; traditional and contemporary components 125, 126, 127, 132, 134, 135, 137, 138, 143–46; see also Chinese New Year festivities; Diwali; Southeast Asian Night Market
Asian immigrants and descendants, NZ: alienation 101; Auckland 137, 142, 198, 200, 243–44, 249; belonging 291–92; and biculturalism 287; Christian Asians 193–95, 202–03, 204, 205, 206, 207, 208; drop in arrivals, 1990s 49, 68, 243; and economic relationships with Asian nations 61–62, 68, 136, 176, 269; English language proficiency requirement 68; ethnic precincts 239–40, 241, 244–45, 246–51, 253–54, 255, 257–58, 292; generalised assumptions of identity 75, 101, 288–89; impact of 1987 and later policy and legislation changes 10, 48, 50, 68, 120–21, 128, 238, 243; labels 'Asia' and 'Asian' 238, 288–89; Māori attitudes towards 40, 49, 53, 62, 72, 74–76, 94; and NZ national identity 105, 107, 108, 110; NZ-born 197, 218; Pacific peoples' attitudes towards 62; and perception of decline in Christian New Zealand 201–07, 208; population 10, 69, 74, 121, 139, 141, 174, 197–98, 243, 293; public opinion 43, 49, 62, 73, 77, 120, 187n.54, 198, 199–200, 237, 238, 243, 269, 289–90; religions 208; stereotypes 98, 101, 102, 104, 217, 290, 292; see also Oryza Foundation for Asian Performing Arts; and specific countries, e.g. Chinese immigrants and descendants, NZ
'Asian invasion' 11, 68, 77
assimilation 16, 67, 71, 93, 95, 96, 111, 165, 167, 169, 175, 196, 199
Association of Southeast Asian Nations (ASEAN) 129, 133
asylum seekers 54, 68, 78, 175
Auckland: Asian festivals 121, 122, 124–29, 132, 134, 138; Asian population 137, 142, 198, 200, 243–44, 249; Asian/Chinese precincts 238, 239, 244, 245, 246–51, 253–54, 255, 257–58, 292; attitudes to immigrants 73; Chapel Road 207–08; Chinatown proposals 253–54; Chinese population 133, 243, 245, 249, 250, 267; cultural diversity 22–23, 51, 98, 244, 246, 252–53, 254, 255;

ethnic/immigrant population 142, 252; Māori population 244, 246, 249; Pacific population 69, 76, 242, 244, 246, 249
Auckland Chamber of Commerce 252
Auckland Council: Economic Development Strategy 253; and ethnic precincts 238, 252, 254, 255, 257, 258; Māori representation 253
Auckland Regional Settlement Strategy 252
Auckland Tourism, Events and Economic Development (ATEED) 257
Australia 42, 50, 70, 71, 72; Christian population 204, 207; Christian population in NZ 205, 206; cultural diversity 51, 237; immigration control 54, 73, 175, 243; marginalisation of indigenous cultures 95; multiculturalism 27, 51, 94–95, 120, 123; Muslims 161, 166; nationalism 54
Awatere, Donna 45

backlash against multiculturalism 9, 266–67
Bangladeshi immigrants in NZ 141
Baptist Tabernacle, Auckland 193
belonging 33n.35, 39, 51, 55, 108, 124, 135, 200, 218, 231, 288, 289, 291–92; and exclusion 289–90; in NZ's multicultural future 293–94
biculturalism: and democracy 76; see also monoculturalism; multiculturalism
biculturalism, NZ 40, 119–20, 181, 182, 237; and Asians 287; and Christianity 207; and citizenship 45; and multiculturalism 10, 41–42, 51, 52–53, 56, 74, 75–76, 93, 104, 109–12, 120, 121, 173–74, 176, 238, 287, 293; and national identity 39, 93, 108, 110, 174; origin of term 70–71; privileging in cultural politics 52, 54, 56, 71–72, 94, 109; Treaty of Waitangi and immigration policy 61, 65, 70–72, 74, 76–80; see also Māori; monoculturalism; multiculturalism, NZ; Treaty of Waitangi
Bigtree Entertainment, Mumbai 278
Bill of Rights Act 1990 165, 173, 176–77, 179, 182
Bolger, Jim 8, 52, 250
Brash, Don 55, 71–72
Britain see United Kingdom
Buddhism, NZ 202, 203, 204, 207, 209n.2
business benefits of multiculturalism 269–71; NZ 271–80

Cambodian immigrants in NZ 129, 130, 140, 141
Cameron, David 8–9, 160, 266–67
Canada 42, 50, 54, 70, 72, 195, 204, 242, 250; multiculturalism 27, 51, 54, 94–95, 120, 123, 124, 237, 254, 267
Cantle Report 168, 169
Carey, Lord George 196
character of NZ 8
China: Christian church growth 207; economic linkages with NZ 176, 265, 267–68, 269, 271–73, 274, 276–77, 279, 282n.42; NZ firms in 265; protest restrictions, Chinese state visits to NZ 176, 187n.57
Chinatown: Auckland proposals 252–53, 292; London 252
Chinese Immigrants Act 1881 66, 241
Chinese Immigrants Amendment Act 1907 66, 242
Chinese immigrants and descendants, NZ 61, 73, 105–07, 121, 123, 133–34, 136; attitudes to 43, 62, 199, 267–68; Auckland 133, 243, 245, 249, 250, 267; Auckland precincts 238, 239, 244, 245, 246–51, 253–54, 255, 257–58, 292; Chinese employees 271–73, 274, 276–77, 279; Christian Chinese 193, 206; discrimination and controls, early settlers 62, 66, 68, 78, 241; ethnic categories 238,

288; historical interactions, Māori–
  Chinese 74, 108–10; language 52;
  Malaysian Chinese 10, 141, 238,
  243, 288; population 10, 70, 133,
  140, 141, 197–98, 243, 245, 293;
  restrictions on entry 66, 241–42;
  returnee migrants 276–77, 279
Chinese New Year festivities 121, 122,
  124–27, 132, 133–34, 135, 136,
  143–44, 165, 249, 292
Choudhary, Ashraf 163
Christchurch 137; Asian festivals 121,
  125, 126, 132, 134, 138
Christianity: equating 'Christian'
  with 'civilised' 42; and European
  identity 160; and migration 42,
  196; and multiculturalism 159;
  statistics 204
Christianity, NZ: Asians 193–95,
  202–03, 204, 205, 206, 207, 208;
  changes resulting from cultural
  diversity 207–08; Chinese 193, 206;
  cultural influence of 193–94; feared
  'death' or decline resulting from
  Asian immigration 201–07, 208;
  Indians 206; Koreans 193, 201–02,
  204, 206; Māori 204, 205; Pacific
  peoples 194, 204, 205, 206, 207;
  statistics 202–07, 208
Citizen 3 (Davina Goh) 103, 107
citizenship 23, 39; compliance
  requirements 54–55;
  conceptualisations of, in
  multicultural theatre 97–98; and
  'Europeanisation' 196; global 169;
  and multiculturalism 23; and
  nation 56; recognition of 40
Citizenship (Western Samoa) Act
  1982 242
Citizenship Amendment Act 2005 78–79
citizenship, NZ: and belonging 291;
  and biculturalism 45; British
  allegiance 54; compared to
  permanent residence 54; compliance
  requirements 54–55, 175; dual
  citizenship 54; exclusionary

views 45, 55; legal restrictions
  on immigrants 43–44, 54, 78–79;
  and multicultural diversity 39,
  40; recognition of 43–44, 45;
  Samoans 46; state-based 45; and
  Treaty of Waitangi 40
'civic multiculturalism' 268
Clark, Helen 127, 163
collective agency 25, 26–27; *see also* social
  cohesion
Collingwood, R.G. 23–25, 29, 30n.9,
  32n.33, 32n.35, 34n.36,
Collins, Judith 51
colonisation, NZ 40; homogeneity of
  early British settlers 39, 42–44, 46, 50,
  54, 62, 66, 70; impact on Māori 44,
  45; impact on Pacific peoples 47; and
  nationalism 40–44; privileging of
  colonial connections 46
Commtest Instruments 270
community theatre 97, 99
Conservative Party, NZ 55
constitution, NZ 45, 51, 62–63, 65,
  78–79, 293, 295n.9; *see also* Treaty of
  Waitangi
constitution, US 25

Cook Islands 242
Crafar farms sale 267–68
Creative New Zealand 98
criminal behaviour, distinction from
  cultural tradition 180–81
cultural associations, NZ 128–29, 135
'cultural closure' 170
cultural diversity: and immigration 54,
  62, 268, 269–70; and tolerance 22–
  23, 167–68, 266; urban 254, 255,
  257; *see also* ethnic minorities;
  multiculturalism
cultural diversity, NZ: Auckland 22–23,
  51, 98, 244, 246, 252–53, 254, 255;
  local authority failure to account
  for 241; projected increase by
  2026 198; recognition of 40, 55, 56,
  252–55; role of Pacific peoples 47–
  48; South Asians 134–35, 288;

see also ethnic minorities, NZ; multiculturalism, NZ
cultural freedom 120, 165, 167, 171–72, 177–79
cultural hegemony 99, 112, 170, 175; *see also* Western hegemony

Danish cartoon affair 160, 178, 179, 184n.15
De Bres, Joris 200
Death of a Princess (television docu-drama) 176, 184n.15
decolonisation politics 44–45
democracy: and biculturalism 76; tolerance and human rights 167–68; Western liberal democracy 16, 161, 165, 166, 167–68, 170, 172
diaspora, diasporic 101, 129, 131, 133, 134, 159, 164, 165, 269, 271, 273, 275, 277, 278–79, 288, 291
Diwali 121, 122, 127–29, 132, 134–35, 136, 137, 145, 165, 292
Dominion Road, Auckland 246, 254
Dunne, Peter 120
Durie, Eddie 63

economy, NZ: and attitudes to immigrants 73, 79; Chinese economic linkages with NZ 176, 265, 267–68, 269, 271–73, 274, 276–77, 279, 282n.42; and domestic multiculturalism 271–80; fears of economic competition from Asian immigrants 73, 290; and immigrant business concentrations 252–56, 258; immigrant labour 46, 52, 67, 69, 242; and immigration policy 46, 48, 52, 61–62, 67–68, 69; Indian economic linkages with NZ 265, 272, 274–75, 277–78; Māori socioeconomic status 52–53; Pacific peoples' socioeconomic status 52–53; relationships with Asian countries 61–62, 68, 136, 176, 269
education system, impact of immigrant communities 180–81, 238, 275, 277

employment: 'immigrant employee effect' 271, 272–73; immigrant employees 271; immigrant employees in NZ 46, 47, 52, 53, 67, 68, 69, 223, 240, 242, 243, 271–74, 276–77, 278, 279, 280; immigrant unemployment, NZ 53; impact of immigration on host country employment 73, 267, 268; and Māori urbanisation 44
ethnic diversity *see* cultural diversity
ethnic identity 123, 160, 170, 171, 290, 291; and cultural associations 128; and festivals 122, 124; generalised assumptions of Asian identity 75, 101, 288–89; media representation 219; and multicultural theatre 97, 101, 107–08; and regional conflict 226; tolerance of 292
ethnic minorities: and Christianity 201; relationship with majority group 74, 160, 167–68, 173, 175, 267; rights 167, 168, 195, 267; spatial concentrations 239; *see also* cultural diversity; immigration and immigrants; multiculturalism
ethnic minorities, NZ: 1.5 generation 51; acceptance of 173; danger of marginalisation 94; difficulty in demarcating 72; exclusionary views and practices 45, 55, 78, 105–06, 109–10, 198, 289–90; language and culture 53; media representation 219; multiple ethnic heritages 198, 285, 287, 293, 294; NZ-born 47, 51, 197, 202–03, 208, 218, 238; Office of Ethnic Affairs statement 115n.45; population 69–70, 77, 139–42; racism towards 79, 120, 173–74, 198; recognition of 51, 52, 55; rights 51, 53, 55, 56, 93, 167–68, 175–81; *see also* cultural diversity, NZ; immigration and immigrants, NZ; multiculturalism, NZ; and also under ethnicities, e.g. Chinese

immigrants and descendants, NZ Ethnic Peoples' Advisory Panel 253
ethnic precincts: Asian/Chinese precincts in Auckland 238, 239, 244, 245, 246–51, 253–54, 255, 257–58, 292; as base for socio-economic improvement 256–57; functions 239–41, 292; and immigrant diversity 239; influence on immigrant settlement outcomes 240–41, 256–58; and labour market barriers to immigrants 255–56; recognition by local authorities and business organisations 252–55, 257; restriction of further opportunities for immigrants to broaden networks 256; tourist visits 252, 254
ethnicity: analyses of 29–30n.3; as cultural capital 111–12; use of term in Office of Ethnic Affairs 115n.45
ethnoscape 27–28, 121–22, 129, 133, 137, 200
Eurasians, NZ 141
Europe: immigration control 175; multiculturalism 27, 159–60, 267; Muslims 159–61, 167; NZ immigrants from 48, 67, 70, 197, 205, 206
European Convention on Human Rights 172–73
exclusionary views and practices 45, 55, 78, 105–06, 109–10, 198, 289–90

Federation of Islamic Associations of NZ (FIANZ) 163
festivals: cultural, NZ 133, 173; as markers of cultural identity 124, 128; *see also* Asian festivals, NZ
Fiji-Indians 10, 141, 226, 227, 228, 288, 293
Fanon, Frantz 7, 25, 27, 29, 44
Fonterra 282n.42
fractals 28
France 171–72, 195
freedom: of expression 172–73, 176, 178; *see also* cultural freedom; human rights; religious freedom
Fukuyama, Francis 24, 32n.34, 160, 170, 183n.4, 185n.35

Gao, Grace 270
Garth, George 199
gender, and Muslims 172, 175, 177–78, 180–81, 227–30
genital 'mutilation', female 178
German immigrants in NZ 66, 198
Germany: declining church attendance 207; multiculturalism concerns 8, 266
ghetto theatre 97
Gilbert, Helen 95–97
Global Financial Crisis (GFC), 2008 53
globalisation: influence on NZ 119, 128; and migration 56, 128, 169; and NZ national identity 39–40, 42; resistance to 170
Goh, Davina, *Citizen 3* 103, 107
Green, Nancy 119

Habermas, Jürgen 24, 32n.34, 148n.18
halal slaughter method 179
Halliday, Denis 222
Hari, Kapa (Hari Mohan Nagar, Te Kapaiawaho) 287
Hari, Lalita 285, 287, 288, 291, 293, 294
Hari, Nagar 285, 286, 287, 291
Hari, Nuia/Lakhee 287
Harvey, Bob 253
hegemony *see* cultural hegemony; Western hegemony
Hemrajani, Ashish 278
Henry, Paul 290
Hinduism, NZ 202, 203, 204, 209n.2
Hobson, William 26, 71, 79
Hong Kong, immigrants in NZ 68, 197, 238, 243, 249, 288
Howard, John 51
Hughes, Darren 130
human rights 162, 165, 167, 169–70, 172–73, 178, 230; *see also* cultural freedom; freedom – of expression; religious freedom

Human Rights Act 1993 173
Human Rights Commission 124, 227
hybrid identities 51, 97, 107, 160, 170, 294; *see also* ethnic minorities, NZ – multiple ethnic heritages

identity *see* ethnic identity; hybrid identities; national identity; religious identity
imaginary 11, 22, 24, 29, 30, 32, 112, *see also* Taylor, Charles
Immigration Act 2009 68–69
Immigration Amendment Act 1961 67
Immigration Amendment Act 1991 67–68
immigration and immigrants: and globalisation 56, 128, 169; and national identity 169; and religion 195–97; types of economic adaptation 270–71; *see also* returnee migrants
immigration and immigrants, NZ: 1.5 generation 51; Africa 70, 139, 204, 205, 206; attitudes to immigrants 50, 72–74, 79–80, 198, 237, 243, 267–68, 269; Austria 66; Cambodia 129, 130, 140, 141; Europe 48, 67, 70, 197, 205, 206; Germany 66, 197, 198; Hong Kong 68, 197, 238, 243, 249, 288; Indonesia 129, 130, 131, 141; Japan 61, 133, 140, 141; Korea 61, 68, 75, 121, 133, 140, 141, 193, 197, 201–02, 204, 206, 243, 247, 250; Laos 141; Malaysia 121, 129, 130, 131, 141, 224, 243, 288; Middle East 48, 70, 78, 139, 141, 163, 204, 205, 206; Myanmar 129, 130, 131; and national identity 40, 41–42, 43, 73; North and South America 48, 70, 139, 204, 205, 206; Pacific 40, 44, 46–47, 49, 62, 67, 69, 70, 73, 78, 197, 242; Philippines 121, 129, 130, 131, 140, 141, 198, 204, 206, 293; racism 43–44, 46–47, 49, 50, 61, 62, 66–67, 76, 77, 78, 198; rate of immigration 72, 198; Singapore 68, 129, 130, 131, 238, 288; South Africa 73, 77; Sri Lanka 140; Taiwan 61, 68, 141, 197, 238, 243, 288; Thailand 129, 130, 131, 141; traditional and non-traditional flows 58; and Treaty of Waitangi 61, 65, 70–72, 74, 76–80; Viet Nam 129, 130, 131, 141; 'whites only' policy 62, 66, 69, 237, 242, 289, 290; *see also* Asian immigrants and descendants, NZ; Chinese immigrants and descendants, NZ; cultural diversity, NZ; ethnic minorities, NZ; Indian immigrants and descendants, NZ; multiculturalism, NZ; United Kingdom, immigrants in NZ
immigration policy, NZ: based on Treaty of Waitangi 61, 65, 70–72, 74, 76–80; economic factors 46, 48, 52, 61, 68, 69; framework from 1986 48, 51, 53, 54, 55, 56, 61–62, 67–68, 119, 120–21, 161, 175, 197–98, 237, 242–43; new settlers' request for consultation 50; pre-1986 43–44, 62, 66–70, 76, 241–42
Immigration Restriction Act 1899 66, 242
Immigration Restriction Amendment Act 1908 66, 242
Immigration Restriction Amendment Act 1920 43, 242
in-comers, NZ *see* immigration and immigrants, NZ
India: multicultural nation 134; NZ business connections 265, 272, 274–75, 277–78
Indian immigrants and descendants, NZ: attitudes to 43, 66, 73; ethnic precinct 246; festivals 134 (*see also* Diwali); Fijian Indians 10, 141, 226, 227, 228, 288, 293; impact of immigration policies 10, 61, 62, 66, 121, 197–98, 243; Indian Christians 206; Indian employees 272, 273, 277, 278,

279; and Māori 285-87, 288, 289-90, 291; Muslims 163, 223-24; nineteenth century 62, 66; origins and identities 288; population 10, 70, 140, 141, 197-98, 293; returnee migrants 277, 278; transnational entrepreneurs 274-75
Indian Ink Theatre Company 111
Indonesian immigrants in NZ 129, 130, 131
integration 67, 73, 76, 93, 122, 159, 160, 165, 167, 168-69, 171, 196, 266
Integration of Immigrants Programme 247, 248
'interculturalism' 269
interrogation as mode of inquiry 9-10
intervention in the development of multiculturalism, NZ 120, 121, 124, 125, 126, 127-28, 129, 132-33, 135-37, 138, 269
Intrusions (Misa Tupou) 102, 105-06
Iraq war 164, 221-22
Islam *see* Muslims
Islamic State (ISIS) 183n.10
Islamophobia 160, 161-62

Japanese immigrants in NZ 61, 133, 140, 141
Jewish animal slaughter methods 179, 188n.64

Kara, Hari 285, 291
Key, John 120, 164, 290
King, Jennifer 125
kinship relationships 77
Kirk, Norman 46, 67
kolbasti case 180
Korea, Christian church growth 207
Korean immigration and immigrants, NZ 61, 68, 75, 121, 133, 140, 141, 197, 243, 247, 250; Christian Koreans 193, 201-02, 204, 206

Labour governments, NZ: 1972-75 46, 67; 1984-89 48, 64; 1999-2008 72, 73, 163, 164

labour market participation *see* employment
Lantern Festival 122, 124-27, 133-34, 135, 136, 143-44, 165, 292
Laotian immigrants in NZ 141
Lesa, Falemai 46
Li, Ying, *The Loyal Customer* 102, 104-05
Liang, Renee, *Mask* 103, 106-07
Lo, Jacqueline 95-97
London, Chinatown 252
Long Shen Dao Reggae Band 126, 134
Loyal Customer, The (Ying Li) 102, 104-05

Ma, Max 270
Malaysian immigrants in NZ 129, 130, 131, 224; Chinese 10, 141, 238, 243, 288
Manukau City Council 252
Māori: accommodation of exceptionalism 182; and Asian immigrants 40, 49, 53, 62, 72, 74-76, 94; Auckland 244, 246, 249; Auckland Council representation and policy 253; Christians 204, 205; grievance settlement 39, 77; historical interactions with Asians 287; historical interactions with Chinese 74, 108-10, 289-90; impact of colonisation 44, 45; interactions with Indians 285-87, 288, 289-90, 291; kinship relationships 77; land and resources 43, 45, 63-64; language and culture 47, 52, 53, 62, 104; and multiculturalism 41-42, 52-53, 173-74; negative attitudes towards 55; and Pacific communities 47, 76; Pākehā gesture of incorporating into formal oratory 104; population 10, 70, 75, 139, 174, 198, 244, 293; renaissance 64, 71, 120, 242; resistance politics 41, 44-45, 46, 64, 242; rural-urban migration, 44; socioeconomic status 52-53, 56, 76; stereotypes 290; *see also*

biculturalism, NZ; Treaty of Waitangi
Māori Party 253
Māori sovereignty 41, 45; and NZ national identity 39, 45; Treaty of Waitangi 63, 65, 77
Mask (Renee Liang) 103, 106–07
maskophobia 187–88n.61
Massey, William 66
McNaughton, Kiel, *The Mooncake & The Kumara* 103, 108–09
Meadowlands/Somerville Chinese precincts 245, 246, 249–51
media: discourses 220–23; influence on racism and prejudice 218, 220–22, 224–26, 227–30; and public re-evaluation of Asian immigrants in NZ 49; representation of Iraq war 221–22; representation of Muslims 161–62, 217–20, 221, 222, 223–31, 289, 290; sources of reference about Islam 225–26
'melting pot' metaphor, cultural pluralism 95, 96
Merkel, Angela 8, 160, 266
Middle Eastern immigration and immigrants, NZ 48, 70, 78, 139, 163, 204, 205, 206
Midnight, State Highway 01 (Mukilan Thangamani) 102, 106, 107–08
migrant theatre 97
migration *see* immigration and immigrants
minaret prohibition, Switzerland 172
Ministry of Pacific Island Affairs, NZ 124
minority groups *see* ethnic minorities
mobility 20, 42, 72, 169, 170, 256–57
monoculturalism 97, 170, 171–72; homogeneity of early British settlers in NZ 42–44, 46, 50, 54, 62, 66, 70, 241; NZ 52, 62, 66, 69, 70, 94, 123, 173, 174, 237, 242–43, 294; *see also* biculturalism; multiculturalism
Mooncake & The Kumara, The (Mei-Lin Te-Puea Hansen, Kiel McNaughton) 103, 108–09

Morris, Paul 200
Mount Head (Hiroshi Nakatsuji) 102, 104
Multicultural Act, proposed 120, 123
Multicultural Services Centre (MSC) 123–24
multicultural theatre 95–98, 111–12; types of practice 97; *see also* Oryza Foundation for Asian Performing Arts
multiculturalism 71, 94–95, 121; Australia 27, 51, 94–95, 120, 123; backlash against 9, 266–267; at business level 269–71; Canada 27, 51, 54, 94–95, 120, 123, 124, 237, 254, 267; and citizenship 23; 'civic multiculturalism' 268; communitarian approach 181; criticisms of 8–9, 266–68, 279; defence of 268–69, 279; definitions 22, 122–23; Europe 27, 159–60, 267; German concerns 8, 266; liberalism 167–68, 171, 181–82; pragmatic 171; United Kingdom 8–9, 124, 267; United States 124, 267, 270; *see also* biculturalism; cultural diversity; ethnic minorities; monoculturalism
multiculturalism, NZ: accommodation of, and readiness to compromise 173–82; and biculturalism 10, 41–42, 51, 52–53, 56, 74, 75–76, 93, 104, 109–12, 120, 121, 173–74, 176, 238, 287, 293; in business 271–80; characteristics 123–24; cultural associations 128–29, 135; cultural representation and homogenisation 136–37, 138; difficulty in demarcating ethnic groups 72; government and public intervention to develop 120, 121, 124, 125, 126, 127–28, 129, 132–33, 135–37, 138, 269; grounded in Bill of Rights Act and Human Rights Act 165, 173;

historical trajectory 24; increase in awareness 123; lack of policy framework 51, 62, 112, 120, 123, 137, 181; liberalism 171, 182; and Muslims 165–68; pragmatic 34n.48, 159, 173, 289, 292; and term Pākehā 94; understandings of 9; and urbanisation 22–23; *see also* biculturalism, NZ; cultural diversity, NZ; ethnic minorities, NZ; immigration and immigrants, NZ

Muslims 159–60; adaptability 164; attitudes towards 196–97, 219–20; and cultural uniformity 175; *dhimma* system 181; identity 169, 171; integration into host country society 168–69, 175, 196, 266; Islam as a way of life 166–67; media representation 218–19, 221, 224–26; parallel society 168–69; radicalisation 9, 160, 167, 224–25, 226, 289; terrorism association 172, 195–96, 219–20, 225; in Western society 165, 167–69; women's activism and campaigning for human rights 230

Muslims, NZ 161–64, 209n.2; attitudes towards 78, 161–62, 219–20, 223–24, 227–30; identity 223; media representation 217–20, 223–31, 289, 290; multicultural accommodation and potential for conflict 165–68, 173–82, 292; NZ-born 202, 229; population 159; prayer rooms in universities 197; sharia jurisdiction 166; statistics 202, 203, 204; stereotypes 217, 218, 227, 228, 229, 231, 289; terrorism association 161, 162, 183n.10, 224, 227, 289; wearing of hijab, burqa and niqab 166, 172, 176–78, 218, 227–30

Myanmar immigrants in NZ 129, 130, 131

Nakatsuji, Hiroshi, *Mount Head* 102, 104
nation: boundaries 28; collective agency 26–27; conception and construction in NZ 39, 41, 45, 56; definitions 28, 39, 41, 56; and postcolonialism 41, 45; *see also* state

National Asian American Theatre Company 96

National governments, NZ: 1978–84 46; 2008– 120, 164, 253

national identity: Britain 95; impact of migration 169; multicultural 26–29, 42, 54–55, 111, 170–73; in multicultural theatre 96, 97; non-essentialising approach 27, 33n.43; United States 95

national identity, NZ: and belonging 291; and biculturalism 39, 93, 108, 110, 174; construction by Pākehā 41, 43, 108, 111; emergence 39; and globalisation 39–40, 42; impact of immigration 40, 41–42, 43, 73, 79, 108, 111; and Māori sovereignty 39, 45; and multiculturalism 40, 174–75, 294; need for official intervention to shape the way identity envisaged 111, 112; Office of Ethnic Affairs statement on ethnic people 115n.45; predicated on white-ness 42, 43, 107, 108; racial exclusion 43, 105, 107, 108, 110, 111, 112, 290; and sports teams 55

National Statement on Religious Diversity 200

nationalism: and attitudes to immigrants 79; and colonialism in NZ 40–44; and multiculturalism 8–10, 26–29, 32n.35, 33n.44, 170, 171; and postcolonialism 41

nationality: NZ, narrow, exclusive sense 40, 42, 54, 55; and states 40

nation-state 40, 44–45, 47; and multiculturalism 27; and popular sovereignty 26

Nelson 42
neo-liberalism 47, 48, 237, 240
New Plymouth 42
New York Shakespeare Festival 96

New Zealand Asian Studies
    Association 24
New Zealand Company 42
New Zealand Federation of Ethnic
    Councils (NZFEC) 123
New Zealand Federation of Multicultural
    Councils 123, 287
New Zealand First Party 49, 55, 68, 199,
    243
New Zealand Qualifications
    Authority 69
Ngā Tamatoa 44
Ngata, Sir Apirana 72
Niue 242
North America: Muslims 161; NZ
    immigrants from 48, 205, 206
Northcote ethnic precinct 245, 246–49,
    250, 252

Office of Ethnic Affairs, NZ 51, 72,
    115n.45, 124, 269
OMEGA 252
Orientalism 217, 229, 230, 231
Oryza Foundation for Asian Performing
    Arts 94, 98–99, 289, 292; 'Asian
    Tales: Native Alienz' 99, 100, 101–
    12; explanation of name 99–100;
    vision statement 98
Otorohanga 285, 291
'overstayers' 46, 77, 242

Pacific peoples in NZ 40, 44,
    46–47, 50, 62, 78, 197; and Asian
    immigrants 62; Auckland 69,
    76, 242, 244, 246, 249; and
    biculturalism 165; Christianity 194,
    204, 205, 206, 207; economic
    marginalisation 47; favourable
    treatment 165, 176; immigrant
    labour 46, 47, 52, 67, 69, 242; impact
    of NZ colonisation 47; language and
    culture 47, 165; and Māori 47, 76;
    NZ-born 47; population 69, 70, 139,
    174, 198, 293; public opinion of 47,
    49, 73, 77; racialisation of 'Pacific
    Islanders' 46–47; socioeconomic
    status 47, 52–53, 76; see also
    Samoans in NZ
Pākehā: definitions of term 93–94;
    gesture of incorporating Māori into
    formal oratory 104; hegemony of
    culture 99
Pakistani immigrants in NZ 141, 224
parallel societies 168–69
patriotism 169
Peters, Winston 49, 199
Philippines, immigrants in NZ 121, 129,
    130, 131, 140, 141, 198, 204, 206, 293
pluralism 13, 23, 76, 94, 96, 98, 99, 159,
    163, 166, 168, 170, 171, 181, 270
Poland 196
policy, NZ: core elements, suggested 51;
    lack of multicultural framework 51,
    62, 112, 120, 123, 137, 181; Treaty
    of Waitangi 45, 64–65; see also
    immigration policy, NZ
poll tax 66, 78
population, NZ 43, 69, 174; Asian 10,
    69, 74, 121, 139, 141, 174, 197–98,
    243, 293; 'British stock' 43, 49, 54;
    Chinese 10, 133, 140, 141, 197–98,
    243, 245, 293; ethnic groups 69–70,
    77, 130, 139–42; Indians 10, 293;
    Māori 10, 70, 75, 139, 174, 198,
    244, 293; Muslims 159; NZ-born
    descendants of immigrants 47, 51,
    197, 202–03, 208, 218, 238; Pacific
    peoples 69, 70, 139, 174, 198, 293;
    people born overseas 74, 293
postcolonialism: Britain 95;
    citizenship 40; and nation-building
    processes 41, 45, 54; and Treaty of
    Waitangi 45; see also colonialism
power: and biculturalism 71, 111;
    dominant society or groups 74, 77,
    219, 220; and globalisation 39; in
    interrogation 10; Māori and Chinese
    interactions, and power relations
    with Europeans 74; media 221, 225;
    Pākehā 31n.14; and tolerance 168;
    and vision 28–29
public opinion polls 49, 58n.30

race, and identity 107–08
racism: media influence 220–21; towards Muslims 31n.23, 160, 218–19
racism, NZ 56; in immigration policies 43–44, 46–47, 49, 50, 61, 66–67, 76, 77, 78; media influence 218, 220–22, 224–26, 227–30; towards Asians 43–44, 49, 66, 198, 199–200, 243, 269, 289–90; towards Chinese 43, 62, 66, 68, 78, 241–42; towards ethnic communities 79, 120, 173–74, 198, 269; towards Muslims 218, 223–24, 227–30; towards Pacific peoples 46–47
rakugo 104, 108, 115n.40
rationalism 171, 172
recognition 42, 51, 53, 55, 56, 93, 95, 97, 111, 123, 162, 165, 166, 168; of citizenship 40, 45, 175; of Maori rights 40, 45, 51, 52, 53, 55, 56, 57n.10, 70, 110
refugees 54, 68, 77, 78, 198, 246, 253
religion: and migration 195–97; *see also* Christianity
religion, NZ: central role 201, 208; expression of, as marker of social change 194; and immigration 194–95, 201, 207–08, 292; statistics 202–03; *see also* Christianity, NZ; Muslims, NZ
religious freedom 165, 166–67, 172, 177, 178–79, 292
religious identity 169, 170, 171, 172, 223, 225, 226, 289
returnee migrants 271, 275, 292; from NZ 276–77, 280
Royal Commission on Auckland Governance 252–53
Royal Society of New Zealand 24

Samoans, citizenship rights, NZ 46
Samoans in NZ: citizenship rights 46, 242; immigrant labour 242; language and culture 47
Sarkozy, Nicolas 160
Satyanand, Sir Anand 290, 294

Saudi Arabia 176, 228
Seriously Asia forum 269
Shakespeare, William: *Cymbeline* 96; *Othello* 96
sharia jurisdiction 161, 166, 178, 197, 225
Sikhs, Sikhism 173, 178, 187n.52, 188n.63, 201, 288
Singapore: Chinatown, Little India and Kampong Glam 252
Singaporean immigrants, NZ 68, 129, 130, 131, 238, 288
Singham, Mervin 72
social cohesion 24–26, 68, 69, 79, 168–69, 200–01, 269
Somalian Muslims 163
Somerville/Meadowland Chinese precincts 245, 246, 249–51
South African immigrants in NZ 73, 77
South American immigrants in NZ 48, 70, 139, 204, 205
South Asia, cultural diversity 134–35
Southeast Asian Night Market 129–31, 132–33, 135, 136, 146
sovereignty: popular 26; *see also* Māori sovereignty

Sponeck, Hans von 222
sports teams, and nationalism 55
Sri Lankan immigrants in NZ 140, 141
state: definition 39; and nationality 40; *see also* nation; nation-state
state, NZ: and biculturalism 39, 45, 56; and citizenship 45; and multiculturalism 56
State Owned Enterprises Act 1986 64
Switzerland 172

Taiwanese immigrants in NZ 61, 68, 141, 197, 238, 243, 288
Tamaki, Brian 199
tauiwi 94, 110, 113n.9
Taylor, Charles 29, 30n.12, 32n.35
Te Anu 287
Te Puni Kōkiri (Ministry of Maori Development) 65, 124
Te-Puea Hansen, Mei-lin, *The Mooncake*

& *The Kumara* 103, 108–09
terrorism 68, 199; association with Muslims 161, 162, 172, 183n.10, 195–96, 219–20, 224, 225, 227, 289; link to multiculturalism 8–9, 266, 267; 'War on Terror' 225
Terrorism Suppression Act 162
Thai immigrants in NZ 129, 130, 131, 141
Thangamani, Mukilan, *Midnight, State Highway 01* 102, 106, 107–08
Tibi, Bassam 160
tino rangatiratanga *see* Māori sovereignty
Tokelau Islands 242
tolerance 32n.30, 58n.30, 165, 167, 168, 266, 291; legally enforced 167–68, 170; NZ 22–23, 61, 69, 173, 181, 217, 228, 269, 289
Tonga 242
tourism, and ethnic precincts 252, 254
transnational entrepreneurs 271; NZ 274–75, 278, 280, 291–92
Treaty of Waitangi 46, 119, 174; articles 63; Asian peoples' relationships with 62, 74, 75, 110; citizenship rights deriving from 40; conflicts 63–64, 77; constitutional position 26, 45, 61, 62, 65, 70, 76, 237; contract between two peoples 13, 26, 33, 71, 237; good faith basis 63; and immigration policy 61, 65, 70–72, 74, 76–80; independent sovereignties of parties 63, 65; in legislation 64–65, 71; and multiculturalism 26, 54, 79–80; policy changes and adjustments of 1980s 45, 64–65, 237, 242; principles 64–65, 71, 76, 81n.24; and social cohesion 26, 76, 79–80; *see also* biculturalism, NZ; Māori
Treaty Tribes Coalition 65
'Trojan Horse' controversy 9
Tupou, Misa, *Intrusions* 102, 105–06

Undesirable Immigrants Exclusion Act 1919 66
United Future party 120

United Kingdom: colonialism 95; declining church attendance 207; demographic changes 195; multiculturalism 8–9, 124, 267; Muslims 160, 161, 172–73, 196–97, 203; NZ's historical connections 42–44, 46, 50, 54, 56, 237; postcolonial 95; religion 201, 204; terrorism 162
United Kingdom, immigrants in NZ 66–67, 69–70, 76, 78, 197, 198, 205, 206, 241, 242; attitudes towards British immigrants 73; homogeneity of early British settlers 42–44, 46, 50, 54, 62, 66, 70, 241
United Nations: human rights compacts and declarations 173; Oil-for-Food Programme 222
United States 42, 54, 70; Christian population 204; civil rights movement 44; constitution 25; Declaration of Independence 95; demographic changes 195; invasion of Iraq 164; 'melting pot' metaphor 95; multiculturalism 124, 267, 270; Muslims 196, 203; overseas-born population 72; terrorism 162, 195–96
urbanisation: and emigration from Britain 43; Māori 44; and mass 23; and multiculturalism 22–23
utopian 10, 25, 27, 182, 226

Vietnamese immigrants in NZ 129, 130, 131, 141
violence 16, 18, 32 n.30, 161, 163, 169, 185 n.34, 186 n.39, 199, 207, 223–27, 249, 266; domestic 175; in portrayals of Islam 19, 223–27, 229, 230; political 221; 'symbolic violence' 268; towards immigrants 79; towards women 19, 223–27, 230
vision 28–29
Vista Entertainment Solutions 278

Waitākere Ethnic Board 252
Waitangi Tribunal 65, 77
Walker, Ranginui 52, 71
Wellington 42, 137, 142; Asian festivals 121, 127–31, 132–33, 134, 135, 138
Western culture 29, 163, 164, 165, 166, 167, 171, 173, 175, 176, 178, 197, 201
Western hegemony, diminution of 171
Western liberal democracy 16, 161, 165, 166, 167–68, 170, 172
Whanganui 42
'white New Zealand' policy 62, 66, 69, 237, 242, 289, 290

Wilders, Geert 160
Williams, Andrew 247
Williams, Joe 77
Williams, Rowan 161, 197
Wong, Kit 249, 250
WOWMA (Women's Organisation of the Waikato Muslim Association) 217

Young Muslim Women's Association 227

Zaoui, Ahmed 78, 162
Zayed College for Girls 181